Counselling Individuals:
A Rational Emotive Behavioural Handbook

Third edition

This book is dedicated to

Albert Ellis, a true pioneer in the field of
Counselling and Psychotherapy

Counselling Individuals: A Rational Emotive Behavioural Handbook

Third edition

WINDY DRYDEN

Goldsmiths College, University of London

MICHAEL NEENAN

Centre for Stress Management, Blackheath, London

JOSEPH YANKURA

Private Practice, New York

Foreword by Albert Ellis
President, Albert Ellis Institute for Rational Emotive Behavior Therapy, New York

W

WHURR PUBLISHERS

LONDON

First published 1987 by Taylor & Francis Ltd
All rights acquired by Whurr Publishers Ltd 1990
Second edition published 1993 by Whurr Publishers Ltd.
Third edition published 1999 by Whurr Publishers Ltd.
19b Compton Terrace, London NI 2UN, England.

British Library Cataloguing in Publication Data

A catalogue record for this book
is available from the British Library.

ISBN 1 86156 056 7

Printed and bound in the UK by Athenaeum Press Ltd,
Gateshead, Tyne & Wear.

Contents

Foreword

Albert Ellis

I have read quite a number of books explaining what rational emotive behaviour therapy (REBT) is and how therapists and counsellors can effectively use it, and this book by Windy Dryden, Michael Neenan and Joseph Yankura is easily one of the very best. It is accurate, clear, comprehensive and well written. It includes excellent illustrations, case materials and verbatim transcripts of counselling sessions. It is up to date and it covers a number of different REBT styles; it also incorporates some useful techniques from other therapies which are often used with standard REBT procedures. All told, authors Dryden, Neenan and Yankura have done a fine job of describing the main theories and practices of RET, and have produced a book that is remarkably good for counsellors and therapists who have not extensively used it before; they have also made it quite useful for many of its seasoned practitioners.

The expanded ABCs of REBT

I originally pointed out in *Reason and Emotion in Psychotherapy* that rational-emotive counselling sees cognition, emotion and behaviour not as disparate aspects of human functioning but as integrated and interactive processes (Ellis, 1962). I have recently expanded this concept and shown how the ABCs of REBT inevitably interact with each other and how all of them include cognitive, emotive and behavioural elements (Ellis, 1994). In the original REBT, I showed how unfortunate activating events or adversities (As) in people's lives rarely directly cause them to feel and to behave in a disturbed manner and thereby create dysfunctional consequences (Cs). Instead, people largely (but not completely) disturb themselves with their self-defeating beliefs (Bs) about their As (Ellis, 1957, 1962; Ellis and Harper, 1997). In my revised ABCs of emotional disturbance, I show that even people's unfortunate activating events (As) are normally seen in the biased and influential light of their beliefs (Bs) and in the light of their reactions or consequences

(Cs). Also, their beliefs (Bs) and their consequences (Cs) are strongly influenced by the activating events (As) of their lives. Similarly, people's cognitions affect their feelings but the latter also significantly affect the former, and their behaviours largely follow from their thoughts and feelings, but these thoughts and feelings are also significantly affected by people's behaviours.

The ABCs of REBT, therefore, as explained in this book, are still at the core of REBT theory and practice; however, they include some complex interactions which affect people's relationships with themselves and with others, and which often have to be examined and dealt with in effective counselling.

REBT was always concerned with individuals and their cognitive-behavioural problems, as this book efficiently shows, but it also has specialised in interpersonal relationships, as indicated in my first book on REBT, *How to Live with a 'Neurotic'* (Ellis, 1957) and in many other REBT writings (Ellis, 1960; Ellis and Harper, 1961). The ABCs have been extended to show how one partner's emotional consequences (C_1) often serve as activating events (As) for the other partner, who then may upset herself in regard to these As and create her own disturbed consequences (C_1) about them. But then the other partner may easily make these Cs into his own activating events (A_2) and may upset himself at his own consequences (C_2) about them. The ABCs of interpersonal relationships, therefore, may again become quite complex (Ellis et al., 1989; Ellis, 1994).

Self-actualisation and counselling

Like most other therapies, REBT usually first focuses on clients' emotional and behavioural problems and tries to help them work on their presenting symptoms, to overcome them, and – as this book accurately shows – to attempt to make a profound philosophical change; through this clients can effect an *elegant* solution so that they rarely disturb themselves in the future and, when they do so, they are able fairly quickly to see what they are doing to upset themselves again and to work at un-upsetting themselves. However, REBT also assumes that once they are on the road to becoming less disturbable, clients also can use their innate self-actualising tendencies to create for themselves a more fulfilling and more enjoyable life than they would otherwise lead. REBT, therefore, with a good many clients, helps in reassessment of basic goals and values and an attempt to lead a more self-actualising existence (Dryden, 1991; Bernard, 1992; Ellis 1999). Ideally, it is not only therapeutic but also attempts to help people fulfil more of their growth potential.

Constructivism and REBT

As Windy Dryden, Michael Neenan and Joseph Yankura show in this book, REBT was first positivistic and therefore a bit on the overly rational side, even though it was always humanistic and existentialist (Ellis, 1962, 1973). I was apprised of the critical realism of Karl Popper (1962) and W. W. Bartley (1962) in 1976, however, by Michael Mahoney's book, *Scientist as Subject*

(1976) and have been non-positivistic ever since. Instead, REBT for the last two decades has to some extent followed, and even gone beyond, George Kelly's (1955) pioneering ideas about constructivism. Kelly believed that people do not merely react to situations and to their social learning, but that they creatively construct their individualised and often highly unique responses to the situations they encounter (Neimeyer, 1992). This is what REBT basically says when it points out that people take the activating events (As) of their lives and formulate beliefs (Bs) about them, which in turn significantly affect their consequences (Cs) that follow their As and Bs.

REBT, however, adds to Kelly's constructivist formulations the notion that people's belief systems (Bs) have two main parts when they are neurotic. First, they have preferential beliefs – 'I like *x* and I dislike *y*' – which are derived from: (1) their biological tendencies (e.g. to prefer sugar rather than salt in their coffee); (2) their learned goals and values (e.g. to wear certain styles of clothing), which they tend to [gullibly] accept from their parents, teachers and culture; and (3) the idiosyncratic tastes or habits which they tend to create or construct themselves (e.g. 'I like brandy and three spoonfuls of sugar in my coffee').

People's desires and preferences, as this book shows, rarely make them emotionally disturbed, because they include flexible *buts* and *neverthelesses*. For example: 'I very much prefer to succeed at work and at love *but* I never *have* to do so. Too bad if I fail, but the world won't come to an end.' 'I really dislike working hard to earn a living; *nevertheless* I'll be worse off if I don't, so I damned well better do it!'

People's absolutist *demands* and *commands*, says REBT, do often produce dysfunctions and disturbances because they are unrealistic, illogical and often impossible to achieve. Thus, they may imperatively believe, 'Because I very much prefer to succeed at work and love, I always *have to*, else I am a *rotten person!*' or 'Because I really dislike working hard to earn a living, I *must not* have to do so, and other people *should* always take care of me!' With these *demands* and *commands* they are in real trouble!

Like many other counselling methods, REBT holds that people may learn their absolutist shoulds and musts from their families and culture but even then they *choose* to accept and act on them. For they *could* see through the self-defeating *musts* of their families, *not* agree with them, and keep their socially imbibed *preferences* as only that – mere wishes and desires. But they very often have, says REBT, a powerful *innate* tendency to take almost any of their *strong* desires, no matter *how* they acquired or developed them, and *make them, construct them* into inflexible demands.

REBT, then, agrees with Kelly and other constructivists that humans have strong, innate tendencies to change their environment and themselves and to creatively go for self-improvement and self-fulfilment (Maslow, 1954; Kelly, 1955; Rogers, 1961). It is even more constructivist than most other therapies in that it hypothesises that, in addition to being inherently self-actualising, the vast majority of humans have a biological tendency to take their strong preferences, goals and values, and to *devise* and *construct* absolutist, inflexible *shoulds* and *musts* about them. Finally, by thinking about their thinking, and by thinking about thinking about their thinking, both of which are again their natural constructivist tendencies, they can reconstruct their self-defeating musturbatory constructions and use their human potentials to (1) un-upset themselves, (2) train themselves (after a while) to be much less upse*table*, and (3) use their cognitive, emotive and behavioural abilities to construct happier, more self-actualised lives. REBT, then, realistically acknowledges the three main sides of human constructiveness: first, people's innate tendancies to *construct* healthy, fulfilling goals, desires, purposes, meanings and ideals that enable them to survive and to lead creative, happy lives. Second, their strong human propensities to *de*construct their healthy preferences by raising them into unhealthy, self-defeating imperative demands, commands and 'necessities'. Third, their innate potential consciously to observe, think about and reassess their disturbed thoughts, feelings and behaviours, and to use a number of cognitive, emotive and behavioural methods to *re*construct and *re*actualise their lives. REBT helps clients (and other people) to see their constructive, deconstructive and reconstructive tendencies more clearly, and to work more constructively on themselves and their environment than they often do without using effective counselling methods.

Counselling Individuals: A Rational Emotive Behavioural Handbook, by Windy Dryden, Michael Neenan and Joseph Yankura, presents the REBT theory and practice of counselling so clearly and thoroughly that therapists who study it can truly understand and efficiently apply it, and so that many lay individuals can also appreciably benefit from its lucid and helpful pages. Good reading like this can nicely lead to good therapy!

Albert Ellis

References

BARTLEY, W. W., III (1962). The Retreat to Commitment. Peru, IL: Open Court.

BERNARD, M. E. (1992). Staying Rational in an Irrational World. New York: Carol Publishing.

DRYDEN, W. (1991). A Dialogue with Albert Ellis: Against Dogma. Milton Keynes, England: Open University.

ELLIS, A. (1957). How to Live with a 'Neurotic'. North Hollywood, CA: Wilshire. Revised edition, 1975.

ELLIS, A. (1960). The Art and Science of Love. New York: Lyle Stuart.

ELLIS, A. (1962). Reason and Emotion in Psychotherapy. Secaucus, NJ: Citadel.

ELLIS, A. (1973). Humanistic Psychotherapy: The Rational-Emotive Approach. New York: McGraw-Hill.

ELLIS, A. (1994). Reason and Emotion in Psychotherapy. Revised and updated edition. Secaucus, NJ: Carol Publishing.

ELLIS, A (1999). How to Make Yourself Happy and Remarkably Less Disturbable. San Luis Obispo, CA: Impact Publishers.

ELLIS, A. and HARPER, R. A. (1997). A Guide to Rational Living. North Hollywood, CA: Wilshire.

ELLIS, A. and HARPER, R. A. (1961). A Guide to Successful Marriage. North Hollywood, CA: Wilshire.

ELLIS, A. SICHEL, J., YEAGER, R., DiMATTIA, D. and DiGIUSEPPE, R (1989). Rational-Emotive Couples Therapy. New York: Pergamon.

KELLY, G. (1955). The Psychology, of Personal Constructs. New York: Norton.

MAHONEY, M. (1976) Scientist as Subject. Cambridge, MA: Ballinger.

MASLOW, A. H. (1954). Towards a Psychology of Being. New York: Van Nostrand Reinhold.

NEIMEYER, G. J. (1992) Back to the future with the psychology, of personal constructs. Contemporary Psychology 37, 994-997.

POPPER, K. R. (1962). Objective Knowledge. London: Oxford.

ROGERS, C. R. (1961). On Becoming a Person. Boston: Houghton Mifflin.

Preface

We are pleased to present this newly revised and expanded third edition. Like the first two editions, this book is primarily intended for those who work in a counselling role with individuals who are *not* severely psychologically disturbed. Here we adopt a pragmatic definition of counselling, by which we mean 'a mode of helping designed to encourage people to overcome their emotional and behavioural problems and thence to lead satisfying lives'. Since counselling (as defined here) is deemed to be most suitable for clients who are not severely disturbed, it is likely to be a relatively shorter-term intervention than psychotherapy, which is more appropriate for clients with more severe psychological problems. Thus, this book is designed for counsellors, from a broad range of professional groups, whose clients are likely to have non-severe problems of anxiety, shame, depression, guilt, unhealthy anger, hurt, unhealthy jealousy, unhealthy envy and self-discipline (e.g. procrastination).

The distinction we have made between counselling and psychotherapy raises issues that focus on the assessment of the severity of clients' psychological problems. Some counselling agencies ask all potential clients to attend for an 'intake' assessment interview to determine whether or not the 'applicant' is suitable for counselling (as defined here). In such cases, intake interviewers usually carry out detailed appraisals of: (a) the client's history of psychological disturbance, and (b) his or her current functioning. This assessment may indeed be carried out by counsellors themselves before offers of help are considered. If the present working definition of counselling is used as the criterion, then clients most likely to benefit from this mode of helping are those who have emotional and behavioural problems in the neurotic range of disturbance; who do not have a long history of poor psychological functioning; and who can demonstrate evidence of having experienced good interpersonal relationships in their lives. This book, then, is designed specifically for use with this clientele.

This book is definitely not designed for use with clients whose problems are in the psychotic range of disturbance, although it should not be forgotten that such individuals do have neurotic difficulties and counselling can be appropriate for such problems when the individuals are not actively psychotic.

This leaves clients who have severe personality problems, a long history of poor psychological functioning and impaired interpersonal relationships – the so-called 'personality disorders'. While this book can be used to inform therapeutic work with such individuals, it has not been written with this clientele in mind, and thus needs to be supplemented by such books as Albert Ellis's (1985a) *Overcoming Resistance: Rational-Emotive Therapy with Difficult Clients* and Michael Neenan and Windy Dryden's (1996a) *Dealing with Difficulties in Rational Emotive Behaviour Therapy.*

Not all counsellors carry out a detailed assessment-based intake interview before offering assistance to people seeking their help. Such helpers tend to assume that they can help a client unless evidence exists to the contrary, at which point they would seek to refer the client concerned to a more appropriate helping agent. For such counsellors we reiterate the above remarks concerning this book's proposed usage.

This book is best used as a supplement to training courses in rational emotive behavioural counselling (REBC) and should not be regarded as a training resource in its own right. The book is divided into two parts. Part One is devoted to outlining REBC. Here we discuss: (1) some of the major theoretical concepts that underpin REBC: (2) the role of cognition and action in rational emotive behavioural theory; (3) the rational emotive behavioural view of psychological disturbance and health. Part Two is devoted to the practice of REBC. Here we present: (a) a discussion of the indications and contraindications for individual counselling and the counsellor-client relationship; (b) strategies for inducting clients into REBC and assessing their major problems; (c) methods for promoting intellectual insight into rational concepts; (d) methods for promoting emotional insight into rational concepts; (e) a compendium of other REBC techniques; (f) the REBC sequence; (g) the REBC process; (h) a review of obstacles to client change and how to deal with them; (i) a discussion of the distinctive features of REBC as compared with other approaches to cognitive-behavioural counselling.

REBC is one of the major approaches to counselling based on cognitive-behavioural principles. Although rational emotive behavioural practitioners primarily use methods derived from REBC, they also use methods derived from these other approaches to cognitive-behavioural counselling (see Dryden and Golden, 1986). The present book outlines the major strategies and techniques that are most closely associated with REBC and does not seek to cover other cognitive-behavioural methods. In the final chapter we suggest several references that deal with these other methods.

Acknowledgements

We wish to thank the following:

The Albert Ellis Institute for Rational-Emotive Therapy, New York for granting us permission (a) to reproduce: the Biographical Information Form © 1968; the Personality Data Form © 1968; the RET Self-help Form © 1984; and the pamphlet entitled 'How to Maintain and Enhance Your Rational-Emotive Therapy Gains' © 1984 and (b) to use extracts in original and modified form from W.D.'s articles on Vivid RET first published in: *Rational Living*, 1983, 18(1), 7–12; *Journal of Rational-Emotive Therapy*, 1983, 1(1), 9–14 and *Journal of Rational-Emotive Therapy*, 1984, 2(1), 27–31.

Guilford Press for granting us permission to use and modify material published in a chapter entitled 'Rational-emotive therapy' by Windy Dryden and Albert Ellis in K. S. Dobson (Ed.), *Handbook of Cognitive-Behavioral Therapies*. New York: Guilford Press, 1987.

Harper & Row for granting us permission to use and modify material published in a chapter entitled 'Rational-emotive therapy' by Windy Dryden and Albert Ellis, in W. Dryden and W. L. Golden (Eds), *Cognitive-Behavioural Approaches to Psychotherapy*. London: Harper & Row, 1986.

Plenum Press for granting us permission to reproduce material (page 7, line 18 and page 9, line 6) from a chapter entitled 'What is rational-emotive therapy (RET)' by Albert Ellis and Michael Bernard, in A. Ellis and M. E. Bernard (Eds), *Clinical Applications of Rational-Emotive Therapy*. New York: Plenum Press, 1985.

PART I
Theory

Chapter 1
The Basic Theory of Rational Emotive Behavioural Counselling

Overview

In this opening chapter, we trace the historical development of rational emotive behavioural counselling (REBC) and outline some of its predominant philosophical and psychological influences. Then we cover the following major theoretical concepts of rational emotive behavioural counselling: rationality, hedonism and enlightened self-interest versus selfishness. We point out that rational emotive behavioural counselling has a decided humanistic emphasis and also highlight the role of activity in human happiness. We continue by outlining the rational emotive behavioural view that humans have two biologically based tendencies (i.e. relevant to their psychological problems): a tendency to think irrationally and a tendency to work towards changing such thinking. This leads on to a discussion of the two fundamental human disturbances put forward by REBC theory: ego disturbance and discomfort disturbance. We conclude the chapter by stating briefly the rational emotive behavioural position on *thought*, *emotion* and *action*, emphasising the interactional view it takes of these three processes.

The Historical Development of Rational Emotive Behavioural Counselling and Psychotherapy

Albert Ellis founded REBC in 1955 when he was a New York clinical psychologist, having begun his career in the helping professions in the early 1940s. As a result of research he was doing at that time for a massive work to be entitled *The Case for Sexual Liberty*, he gained a local reputation for being an authority on sexual and marital relationships. He was consulted by his friends on their sexual and relationship problems and discovered that he could be successful in helping them with these problems in a short period of time. He decided to pursue formal training in clinical psychology after discovering that there were no formal training possibilities then offered in sex and marital counselling. After getting a PhD degree in clinical psychology, he chose to be trained in psychoanalysis believing then that it was the deepest and most effective form of psychotherapy available. He decided on this course of action because his experiences as an informal sex-marital counsellor had taught him that disturbed relationships were really a product of disturbed persons, 'and that if people were truly to be helped to live happily with each other they first had better be shown how they could live peacefully with themselves' (Ellis, 1962, p. 3).

Ellis initially enjoyed working as a psychoanalyst partly because it allowed him to express both his helping and problem-solving interests. However, he became increasingly dissatisfied with psychoanalysis as an *effective* and *efficient* form of treatment. In the early 1950s, Ellis began to experiment with different forms of therapy, including psychoanalytically oriented psychotherapy and eclectic-analytic therapy. But although he became more effective with his clients, he remained dissatisfied about the efficiency of these methods. During this period of experimentation, he returned to his lifelong hobby of reading philosophy to help him with his search for an effective and efficient form of therapy. One of the major influences on his thought at that time was the work of the Greek and Roman Stoic philosophers (e.g. Epictetus and Marcus Aurelius). They emphasised the primacy of philosophic causation of psychological disturbances – a viewpoint that was not popular in America in the 1950s – and de-emphasised the part played by psychoanalytic and psychodynamic factors. In essence the Stoic viewpoint, which stated that people are disturbed not by things but by their view of things, became the foundation of REBC in particular, and this perspective (following Ellis' pioneering formulations) remains at the heart of present-day cognitive-behavioural approaches to psychotherapy.

Major philosophical influences

Apart from Stoicism, present-day REBC owes a philosophical debt to a number of other sources that have influenced its development. Immanuel Kant's writings on the power (and limitations) of cognition and ideation strongly impressed Ellis (Ellis, 1981a) and the work of Spinoza and Schopenhauer was also important in this respect. Philosophers of science, such as Popper (1959, 1963), Reichenbach (1953), and Russell (1965), were influential in helping Ellis see that all humans develop hypotheses about the nature of the world. Moreover, these philosophers stressed the importance of testing the validity of such hypotheses rather than assuming that they are necessarily correct; the practice of REBC is synonymous, in many respects, with the logico-empirical methods of science (Ellis, 1962, 1979a). REBC also stresses the flexibility and antidogmatism of the scientific method and holds that rigid absolutism is the very core of human disturbance (Ellis, 1983a, 1994).

Although the philosophy of REBC is at variance with devout religiosity, there is one respect in which Christian philosophy has been most influential. REBC's theory of human value (which will be discussed later) is similar to the

Christian viewpoint of condemning the sin but forgiving the sinner (Ellis, 1983a; Hauck, 1972; Powell, 1976). Due to its stand on self-acceptance and its bias against all forms of human rating, REBC allies itself with the philosophy of ethical humanism (Russell, 1930, 1965) which opposes the deification and devilification of humans. Since REBC considers that humans are at the centre of their universe (but not of *the* universe) and have the power of choice (but not of unlimited choice) with regard to their emotional realm, it has its roots in the existential philosophies of Heidegger (1949) and Tillich (1977). Indeed, REBC has a pronounced humanistic-existential outlook (Ellis, 1973).

Ellis was influenced, particularly in the 1960s, by the work of the general semanticists, (e.g. Korzybski, 1933). These theorists outlined the powerful effect that language has on thought and the fact that our emotional processes are heavily dependent on the way we, as humans, structure our thought by the language we employ.

Major psychological influences

In developing REBC, Ellis was similarly influenced by the work of a number of psychologists. He received a training analysis from an analyst of the Karen Horney school, and Horney's (1950) concept of the 'tyranny of the shoulds' was certainly an early, influence on his emphasis on the primacy of absolute, dogmatic evaluative thought in the development and maintenance of much psychological disturbance. The work of Adler was important to the development of REBC in several respects:

> Adler (1927) was the first great therapist to really emphasize inferiority feelings – while RET similarly stresses self-rating and the ego anxiety, to which it leads. Like Adler and his Individual Psychology, RET also emphasizes people's goals, purposes, values and meanings. RET also follows Adler in regard to the use of active-directive teaching, the stress placed on social interest, the use of a holistic and humanistic outlook, and the employment of a highly cognitive-persuasive form of psychological treatment. (Ellis, 1981b)

Although REBC was originally termed 'Rational Psychotherapy', it has always advocated the use of behavioural methods as well as cognitive and emotive techniques in the practice of counselling and therapy. Indeed, Ellis utilised some of the methods advocated by several of the earliest pioneers in behaviour therapy (Dunlap, 1932; Jones, 1924; Watson and Rayner, 1920), first in overcoming his own early fears of speaking in public and of approaching women, and second in the active–directive form of sex therapy which he practised in the early 1950s. This behavioural active–directive emphasis remains prominent in present-day rational emotive behavioural counselling and psychotherapy.

In response to critics, Albert Ellis changed the name of the therapy from Rational Therapy to Rational-Emotive Therapy in 1961 to stress that it did not neglect human emotions. In 1993 he changed its name again to Rational Emotive Behaviour Therapy to emphasise that it did not neglect the behavioural dimension of human experience. This latter change was prompted by critics' inaccurate but pervasive views of the therapeutic approach. These name changes do indicate, however, that REBC is a dynamic approach to counselling and is always seeking to actualise itself though the efforts of its founder and other leading REBC theorists and practitioners.

In its 44 years' existence, REBC has been practised in various therapeutic modalities (individual, group, marital and family), by many kinds of helping professionals (e.g. psychologists, psychiatrists, social workers) with a variety of client populations (e.g. adults, children, the elderly) suffering from a wide range of psychological disorders. Apart from their use in counselling and psychotherapy, rational emotive behavioural principles have been applied in educational, industrial, and commercial settings. A recent development has been the application of REBC to public education in the form of 9-hour intensive workshops. In this respect, it is playing a significant role in the field of preventive psychology. REBC is practised throughout the world and there are REBC institutes or centres in the USA, Israel, Italy, Germany, Holland, Australia, New Zealand, England and Mexico. It is thus a well-established form of cognitive-behavioural therapy.

Major Theoretical Concepts

Rational emotive behavioural counselling is based on a set of assumptions which stress the complexity and fluidity of human beings. Given this fundamental view of human nature, the REB approach to counselling rests on the following theoretical concepts.

Rationality

In our experience, when counsellors are first introduced to rational emotive behavioural counselling, they often become preoccupied with the term 'rational'. Their initial reaction to this term is usually negative because they think, erroneously, that it means 'unemotional' and conclude, again wrongly, that REB counsellors seek to help their clients by encouraging them to become unemotional. 'Rationality' *does* play a central role in rational emotive behavioural theory but it has a very specific meaning within this theory.

To understand the specific REBC meaning of 'rationality' it is first important to realise that within REBC theory humans are seen as having two basic goals – to stay alive and to be happy. While there are shared methods of pursuing the former basic goal (e.g. seeking adequate shelter from the elements, maintaining a proper diet, etc.) there are myriad different ways of pursuing the latter. Humans are remarkably idiosyncratic in what they find personally meaningful or fulfilling.

Given the above considerations, the term 'rational' means *that which helps people to achieve their basic goals and purposes*. Furthermore, in rational emotive behavioural theory, people are seen as having primary (but not exclusive) control over their major psychological processes (i.e. thoughts, emotions and actions). Given that we use these processes in the pursuit of our basic goals, it follows that our thoughts, feelings and actions are deemed to be 'rational' when they help us in the pursuit of these goals. Conversely, the term 'irrational' in REBC theory means *that which prevents people from achieving their basic goals and purposes*. Much REB counselling is spent helping clients to identify and change their 'irrational' (or self-defeating) thoughts, emotions and actions, given that such processes impede goal achievement.

There are no absolute criteria of 'rationality', in rational emotive behavioural theory. These criteria need to be seen as *relative* to the goals and purposes that the individual deems to be important. REB counsellors endeavour to help their clients remove the obstacles to goal attainment that clients themselves construct, and do not seek to impose an absolute standard of 'rationality' as some people, new to REBC, incorrectly think. Having said this, REBC theorists point to four major criteria when judging whether a belief is rational or irrational. These criteria are as follows:

● Is the belief flexible (rational) or inflexible (irrational)?
● Is the belief consistent with reality (rational) or inconsistent with reality (irrational)?
● Is the belief logical (rational) or illogical (irrational)?
● Does the belief lead to largely productive results for the individual and his or her social group (rational) or to largely unproductive results (irrational).

The subject of the concepts of rationality and irrationality will be taken up throughout this book.

Responsible hedonism

We have seen how rational emotive behavioural theory considers that humans are basically hedonistic – in the sense that they seek to stay alive and to achieve a reasonable degree of happiness. Again, counsellors new to rational emotive behavioural counselling wrongly consider that the rational emotive behavioural concept of responsible hedonism implies urging clients to pursue a life based on the 'pleasures of the flesh', rather than encouraging them to pursue their personally meaningful goals. Thus, people whose goal is to raise money for starving children in Ethiopia, and who involve themselves in activities directed towards this end, are acting 'hedonistically' in the sense that it is meaningful for them and that they are happy doing so. This responsibly, hedonistic decision – based on the principle of social interest (Adler, 1964) – is a far cry from the 'pleasures of the flesh' connotation of hedonism.

Rational emotive behavioural theory makes an important distinction between short-term and long-term hedonism. For example, it is important to us to write this book. It represents a personally meaningful project we have set for ourselves, i.e. to encourage counsellors to offer what we have found to be an effective, brief method of psychological counselling. As such, writing this book is an example of long-term hedonism, since it will take time for us to complete, and a longer time for it to have an effect on the counselling community. We might also enjoy watching television which, as it is immediately available to us, constitutes an example of short-term hedonism. Pursuing our short-term interest to the extent that it significantly interferes with our long-term hedonistic project is irrational according to the definition of 'rationality' provided above, since the book is personally more meaningful to us than is watching television. Pursuing our long-term hedonistic interests to the exclusion of our more immediately available interests may also be irrational in the sense that we might become stale; a condition that would probably affect our creativity. Therefore, counselling individuals involves not only encouraging them to become aware of their short- and long-term goals, but also helping them to achieve a healthy balance between the two. What represents a healthy balance for a given individual is ultimately best judged by that person, and not by his or her counsellor.

Enlightened self-interest versus selfishness

At this point, the reader may consider that rational emotive behavioural theory advocates selfishness. This is not so, if by selfishness is meant the exclusive pursuit of one's own goals while cynically disregarding the goals of others. Rather, rational emotive behavioural theory recommends that people act according to the principle of enlightened self-interest, which is deemed to be the healthy alternative to selfishness. By enlightened self-interest is meant putting oneself first most of the time, while putting others (particularly significant others) a close second. It thus includes an important dimension of what Adler (1964) calls 'social interest'. It is recognised that decisions concerning whose interests to serve at a given moment – self or others – are complex and depend on (1) the context, (2) the importance of one's own goals versus the importance that others attribute to their goals, and (3) the likely consequences of making such decisions.

Enlightened self-interest means that from a long-term perspective we shall give priority to pursuing our most important goals since, as Ellis (1979a) notes, it is likely that other people will do the same. Thus, if we do not give priority to our own goals it is unlikely that others will put our interests before theirs. In this respect, Ellis (1979a) notes that 'those people who spend their lives sacrificing themselves for others tend to get less than their share of happiness' (p. 55). However, if a given client genuinely considers that one of his basic goals is to put the interests of others before his own, and can provide good evidence that this stance will bring him happiness, then good REB counsellors will respect this decision and will not try to dissuade the client from pursuing this goal.

In summary, it can be seen from the above that in counselling individuals REBC counsellors strive to help their clients to be mindful of the balance between their own short- and long-term goals, and the balance between their own interests and the interests of others who live in their social world.

Philosophic and scientific emphases

As noted earlier, Ellis's formulation of REBC was heavily influenced by the work of a number of ancient and contemporary philosophers. Rational emotive behavioural theory recognises that all human beings are implicit philosophers, in the sense that we attempt to gain insight into and understanding of ourselves, other people, and the environment in which we exist. Typically, we utilise whatever understandings we achieve to impose a sense of order upon the world around us, and to develop guidelines which are used in the service of survival and goal-attainment. In essence, each of us formulates our own personal philosophy of life.

Our personal philosophies can be viewed as consisting of a constellation of self-generated hypotheses about the world and our place within it, and we are capable of applying our thinking skills to the process of testing and revising these hypotheses. In this sense, REBC agrees with George Kelly's (1955) view that human beings are also scientists. Often, however, we tend to be rather poor scientists, insofar as we may fail to test and reject hypotheses which lead us to think, feel, and act in self-defeating ways. With its philosophic and scientific emphases, REBC attempts to help clients to become 'better scientists' by showing them how they can identify, test and revise (as necessary, in order to function more effectively) the hypotheses which comprise their personal philosophies.

Humanistic emphasis

Rational emotive behavioural counselling does not pretend to be 'purely' objective, scientific, or technique-centred but takes a definite *humanistic-existential approach* to human problems and their basic solutions. It deals primarily with disturbed human evaluations, emotions and behaviours. As noted above, it is highly rational and scientific, but uses rationality and science in the service of humans in an attempt to enable them to live and be happy. It is hedonistic, but, as has been shown, espouses long-range instead of short-range hedonism; so that people may achieve the pleasures of the moment and those of the future, and may arrive at maximum freedom *and* discipline. It hypothesises that probably nothing superhuman exists and that devout belief in superhuman agencies tends to foster dependency and increase emotional disturbance. It assumes that no humans, whatever their antisocial or obnoxious behaviour, are neither damnable nor subhuman. It particularly emphasises the importance of *will* and *choice* in human affairs, even though it accepts the likelihood that some human behaviour is at least partially determined by biological, social and other forces (Bandura, 1986; Ellis, 1976). In addition, rational emotive behavioural theory emphasises the important role played by activity in human happiness. It acknowledges that humans have a better chance of being happy when they *actively* strive towards their goals, and that they are less likely to be successful in this regard if they are passive or half-hearted in their endeavours (Dryden, 1996). It also stresses the important role played by activity in the change process. Clients who translate their counselling-derived insights into action in their daily lives usually achieve better results from counselling than clients who do not take such action.

Two basic biologically based tendencies

Unlike most other theories of counselling which stress the impact of significant life events on the development of psychological disturbance, rational emotive behavioural theory hypothesises that the biological tendency of humans to think irrationally has a notable impact on such disturbance. Its view that irrational thinking is heavily determined by biological factors (always interacting with influential environmental conditions) rests on the seeming ease with which humans think crookedly, and the prevalence of such thinking even among people who have been rationally raised (Ellis, 1976). While Ellis has acknowledged that there are social influences operating here, he has also noted '. . . even if everybody had had the most rational upbringing, virtually all humans would often irrationally escalate their individual and social preferences into absolutistic demands on (a) themselves, (b) other people, and (c) the universe around them' (Ellis, 1984a, p. 20).

The following ten points constitute evidence in favour of the rational emotive behavioural hypothesis of the biological basis of human irrationality:

1. Virtually all humans, including intelligent and competent people, show evidence of major human irrationalities.
2. Virtually all the disturbance-creating irrationalities (absolutist 'shoulds' and 'musts') that are found in our society are also found in just about all social and cultural groups that have been studied historically and anthropologically.
3. Many of the irrational behaviours that we engage in, such as procrastination and lack of self-discipline, go counter to the teachings of parents, peers and the mass media.
4. Humans – even intelligent and competent people – often adopt other irrationalities after giving up former ones.
5. People who vigorously oppose various kinds of irrational behaviours often fall prey to these very irrationalities. Atheists and agnostics exhibit zealous and absolutist philosophies and even highly religious individuals act immorally.

6. Insight into irrational thought and behaviours helps only partially to change them. For example, people can acknowledge that drinking alcohol in large quantities is harmful, yet this knowledge does not necessarily help them abstain from heavy drinking.
7. Humans often return to irrational habits and behavioural patterns even though they have often worked hard to overcome them.
8. People often find it easier to learn self-defeating than self-enhancing behaviours. Thus, people very easily overeat but have great trouble following a sensible diet.
9. Psychotherapists, who presumably should be good role models of rationality, often act irrationally in their personal and professional lives.
10. People frequently delude themselves into believing that certain bad experiences (e.g. divorce, stress, and other misfortunes) will not happen to them.

However, rational emotive behavioural theory holds that humans have a second basic biological tendency, namely, to exercise the power of human choice and to work towards changing their irrational thinking. Thus, they have the ability to see that they make themselves disturbed by the irrational views they bring to situations, the ability to see that they can change their thinking and, most importantly, the ability to work actively and continually towards changing this thinking by the application of cognitive, emotive and behavioural methods. While rational emotive behavioural theory asserts that humans have a strong biological tendency to think irrationally (as well as rationally), it holds that they are by no means slaves to this tendency and can transcend (although not fully) its effects. In the final analysis the REBC image of the person is quite an optimistic one (Ellis, 1973; Ellis and Bernard, 1985).

Two fundamental human disturbances

According to rational emotive behavioural theory, humans can make absolute demands on self, other people and the world. However, if these demands are more closely investigated they can be seen to fall into two major categories of psychological disturbance: *ego disturbance* and *discomfort disturbance* (Ellis, 1979b, 1980a).

In ego disturbance, a person makes demands on self, others and the world, and if these demands are not met in the past, present or future, the person becomes disturbed by damning 'self'. As one of us has shown (Dryden, 1996), self-damnation involves the process of giving my 'self' a global negative rating, and 'devil-ifying' my 'self' as being bad or less worthy. The rational and healthy alternative to self-damnation is self-acceptance, which involves *both* refusing to give one's 'self' a single rating (because it is an impossible task, due to one's complexity and fluidity; and because it normally interferes with attaining one's basic goals and purposes) *and* acknowledging one's fallibility.

In discomfort disturbance, the person again makes demands on self, others and the world which are related to dogmatic commands that comfort and comfortable life conditions must exist. When these demands are not met in the past, present or future, the person becomes disturbed. Tolerating discomfort in order to aid goal attainment and long-range happiness is the healthy and rational alternative to demands for immediate gratification.

Thus, as will be shown later, self-acceptance and a high level of frustration tolerance are two of the main cornerstones of the rational emotive behavioural image of the psychologically healthy being (Ellis, 1979a).

Psychological interactionism: thoughts, emotions and actions

As discussed earlier in this chapter, REB counsellors are interested in helping their clients to stay alive and to pursue happiness. During the counselling process this involves the counsellor and client working as a team to identify and change aspects of the client's functioning that are irrational. Both client and counsellor seek to answer the question: 'How is the client stopping him or herself from pursuing his or her personally defined meaningful goals?' As counsellor and client investigate the factors concerned, the search normally involves close scrutiny of the *thoughts* that the client has about him or herself, others and the world in relation to the goal at hand; the relevant *emotions* he or she has about him or herself, others and the world; and his or her *actions* in the area of concern.

It is important to stress here that rational emotive behavioural theory states that a person's thoughts, emotions and actions cannot be treated separately from one another. Rather, they are seen as overlapping or interacting processes – an example of what psychologists call 'psychological interactionism'. For instance, let us take the case of one of our (WD's) clients, Helen, who has just moved to London. She wants to go out and make friends but does not do so because she is 'scared of meeting new people'. Her feelings of anxiety encourage her to brood on 'horrific' thoughts and images of rejection and loneliness and help to influence her tendency to withdraw from people. So she stays within the 'safe' but lonely confines of her bed-sitting room. Her thoughts (predictions of rejection and consequent attitude of self-loathing) help to create her anxiety and help to reinforce her inactivity – 'Why go out and expose myself to those outside risks?' Finally, her inactivity seems to encourage her negative thoughts about herself: 'I'm no good for being so gutless!' – and gives her ample opportunity for anxious brooding, even though withdrawal protects her from the greater anxiety of meeting new people.

REBC and rationalism

Almost from its inception, REBC has mistakenly been identified by a number of its critics as representing a form of philosophical rationalism. Classical rationalists subscribe to the view that human reason and intellect are the true source of knowledge; as such, they negate the role played by the senses, experience and everyday data-gathering in helping us to understand the world in which we live. Ellis, however, has made it clear (even in some of his earliest writings) that he does not subscribe to this anti-empirical perspective, and that REBC is not a rationalist system (Ellis, 1962, 1968b).

Despite Ellis's attempts to delineate the distinctions between REBC and rationalism, some cognitive-behavioural theorists with stature in the field have recently attempted to categorise the various cognitive therapies as to whether they fall into 'rationalist' or 'constructivist' camps. They have expressed the opinion that REBC can be clearly identified with the former orientation (Guidano, 1988; Mahoney, 1988).

Ellis (1990) has offered a rebuttal to this contention, and has suggested that REBC is actually more 'constructivistic' in its theory and practice than the forms of cognitive therapy espoused by his constructivist critics. As noted earlier, REBC does not posit absolutist and invariant criteria of rationality; rather, it adopts a relativistic stance and defines rationality in terms of thoughts, feelings and actions that aid the individual in the pursuit of valued goals and purposes. Also, as described in the preceding section, REBC clearly acknowledges that cognition (or thinking), emotion and behaviour interact and cannot be treated as distinct and separate entities. Hence, REBC holds the non-rationalist position that intellectual processes do not represent the sole vehicle to either psychological health or disturbance.

Nevertheless, REBC is noted within the fields of counselling and psychotherapy for the special place it accords cognition in human psychological processes. It especially emphasises the role played by evaluative cognitions (or beliefs, in REBC parlance) in producing either psychological health or disturbance, and embodies the constructivistic view that human beings create (and can modify) the beliefs to which they subscribe. In fact, one of rational emotive behavioural theory's unique contributions to the field of counselling lies in the distinction it makes between rational beliefs (evaluative cognitions that help people to achieve their basic goals and purposes) and irrational beliefs (evaluative cognitions that prevent people from achieving these goals). We shall elaborate upon this distinction in the following chapter; however, we should like the reader to keep in mind throughout the book that although rational emotive behavioural counselling does accord a special place to cognition in human functioning, it agrees with the interactionist position reviewed above and will employ cognitive, behavioural and emotive techniques in the service of helping clients to achieve beneficial therapeutic change.

Chapter 2
Cognition, Action and Emotion in Rational Emotive Behavioural Theory

Overview

In this chapter we consider in detail the different types of cognitions that are relevant to counselling, namely: beliefs, inferences, decisions, self-instructions, and problem-solving cognitions. We point out that while rational emotive behavioural theory emphasises that these cognitions interact and overlap, it also accords a central role to *beliefs* in psychological functioning. We also note that cognitions may occur in the form of words and images. Finally, we consider the role of action in rational emotive behavioural theory. In this respect, we note the purposive nature of actions, introduce the concepts of 'action tendencies' and 'response options' and comment on the issue of behavioural competence.

Although rational emotive behavioural theory has become most well known for its contribution to our understanding of one type of cognition (i.e. beliefs), REB counsellors also focus on other types of cognitions in the course of their practical work with clients. In the following section we distinguish among these different cognitions and, although for purposes of clarity we consider them separately, we wish to stress that in reality they interact and overlap.

Types of Cognition

Beliefs

One of rational emotive behavioural theory's unique contributions to the field of counselling lies in its distinction between rational beliefs and irrational beliefs.

Rational beliefs

In rational emotive behavioural theory, rational beliefs are *evaluative cognitions* of personal significance which are preferential (i.e. non-absolute) in nature. They are expressed in the form of desires, preferences, wishes, wants and 'likes' (and they can, of course, also take a negative form, e.g. 'I don't want X to occur').

Positive (non-absolute) *evaluative conclusions* result when individuals either get what they want or don't get what they don't want (e.g. 'It is *good* that . . .'). Similarly, negative (non-absolute) evaluative conclusions result when individuals either don't get what they want or do get what they don't want (e.g. 'It is *bad* that . . .').

Positive emotions of pleasure and satisfaction are experienced when individuals get what they want, whereas positive feelings of relief tend to occur when individuals don't get what they don't want. Likewise, negative emotions of displeasure and dissatisfaction (e.g. sadness, concern, remorse, healthy anger and disappointment) are experienced when people either don't get what they want, or do get what they don't want. These positive and negative emotions (the intensity of which is closely related to the strength of the individual's preference or desire) are regarded in rational emotive behavioural theory as healthy responses to negative events, and are unlikely to interfere significantly with a person's pursuit of established or new goals and purposes. This is one good reason why the term 'rational' in rational emotive behavioural counselling should not be equated with the term 'un-emotional'.

Rational beliefs also tend to be logically and empirically consistent. These two qualities can perhaps be best illustrated by examining an example of a rational belief: 'It is good to have an intimate, loving relationship with another person; therefore I *want* to have such a relationship.' This belief can be considered logically consistent, as it is quite reasonable to desire something regarded as being positive in nature. It is empirically consistent (i.e. verifiable and in congruence with consensual reality), as most human beings would agree that an intimate, loving relationship is 'good' in the sense that it can add an important dimension of pleasure to a person's life.

To summarise, rational beliefs are considered 'rational' in four respects: (1) they are non-absolute (or relative) in nature; (2) they tend not to impede attainment of a person's basic goals and purposes; (3) they are logical and (4) they are consistent with reality.

Irrational beliefs

Absolute (or dogmatic) *evaluative cognitions* of personal significance are termed irrational beliefs within rational emotive behavioural theory. Such beliefs are expressed in the form of 'musts', 'shoulds', 'have to's', 'ought to's', 'got to's', etc. (and they can, of course, also occur in the form of 'must not's', should not's', etc.).

Positive (absolute) *evaluative conclusions* result when individuals get what they believe they *must* have, or don't get what they believe they *must not* get (e.g. 'It is absolutely wonderful that . . .'). Negative (absolute) *evaluative conclusions* result when individuals either don't get what they believe they *must* have, or do get what they believe they *must not* get (e.g. 'It is absolutely terrible that . . .').

Rational emotive behavioural theory holds that positively toned emotions of mania are experienced when individuals either get what they believe they *must* have or don't get what they believe they *must not* get. Negative emotions such as depression, anxiety, guilt, unhealthy anger, etc. are experienced when individuals either don't get what they believe they *must* have, or do get what they believe they *must not* get. These negative emotions are regarded in REBC as unhealthy responses to negative events, and will tend to interfere significantly with a person's ability to make a constructive adjustment when their existing goals cannot be achieved.

Unlike rational beliefs, irrational beliefs tend to be illogical and are not consistent with reality. By way of illustration, consider the following irrational belief: 'Because I believe it is desirable to have an intimate, loving relationship with another person, I *must* have such a relationship'. This belief is illogical, as one does not *have to* achieve that which is deemed desirable. It is inconsistent with reality because if it were true that an individual *must* have an intimate, loving relationship, then that person would have to have such a relationship regardless of what he or she happened to believe. Also, with regard to the issue of empirical consistency, it would be difficult to find evidence to support the contention that an intimate, loving relationship with a partner is an absolute necessity for an adult human being.

Thus, irrational beliefs are 'irrational' in four respects: (1) they are absolute (or dogmatic) in nature, (2) they tend to impede goal attainment, (3) they are illogical, and (4) they are not consistent with reality.

Rational emotive behavioural theory makes four additional important points about beliefs:

1. People often *transform* their rational beliefs into irrational beliefs. For example, a person may begin by believing: 'I want very much to do well in my examination' and then transform this non-absolute belief into an absolute one thus: 'Since I want to get a good mark in my examination, therefore I absolutely have to do so'. It is important to note that this transformation process often occurs implicitly, and in counselling individuals it is helpful to check whether transformation has occurred whenever clients report rational beliefs. When clients stick rigorously to their rational beliefs (i.e. do not escalate their non-absolute beliefs into irrational beliefs) statements like '. . . but I don't have to', '. . . but there is no reason why I must', etc. are present, again often implicitly, e.g. 'I want very much to do well in my examination, (but I don't *have* to do so)'. It is for this reason that when REB counsellors help their clients to formulate their preferences, they encourage them to use their full preferences where their desire is stated and the demand is negated (e.g. 'I want to do well in the test, *but* I don't have to do so') rather than their partial preferences where the desire is stated, but the demand is not negated.

2. Rational beliefs seem to underlie constructive or functional actions (which facilitate the attainment of one's basic goals and purposes), whereas irrational beliefs tend to underpin unconstructive or dysfunctional actions

such as withdrawal, procrastination, alcoholism and substance abuse (which impede goal achievement) (Ellis, 1982a).

3. Beliefs (both rational and irrational) can be either general or specific. Taking the example of irrational beliefs: 'I must succeed at all important tasks' is an example of a general irrational belief, while: 'I must succeed at this particular task' is an example of a specific one. As Wessler and Wessler (1980) note, a specific belief may represent a special case of a general belief.

4. As one of us has noted elsewhere (Dryden, 1986), it is important to distinguish between a word and its meaning. This principle should be borne in mind when considering beliefs in rational emotive behavioural counselling. For example, take the word 'should'. The word 'should' *can* represent the presence of an irrational belief (e.g. 'You should not cheat me' – this really means here 'You *absolutely* should not cheat me'). However, the word 'should' has other meanings in the English language. For example, in a previous sentence, while referring to the important distinction between words and meanings, we wrote: 'This principle should be borne in mind when considering beliefs in REB counselling'. We hope, as readers of this book, you can see that we are not dogmatically insisting that you bear this point in mind; rather we are advising or recommending you to do so. Thus, not all 'shoulds', 'musts', etc. indicate the presence of irrational beliefs.

Inferences

Inferences (or interpretations) are cognitions that go beyond the information that is immediately available to a person. In order fully to understand what inferences are it is first necessary to introduce another type of cognition called a *description* (Wessler and Wessler, 1980).

Descriptions are cognitions that report the nature of any stimulus a person is aware of. They do not add anything that cannot be directly observed. For example, imagine that a man is standing facing a window with his hands in his pockets so that you can see only his back. If you were asked to describe his behaviour you might say: 'He is standing facing the window with his hands in his pockets'. This constitutes a description because you have not gone beyond the information that is immediately available to you. However, were you to say: 'He is looking out of the window', then that would not be a description in that you would be going beyond the data at hand, since his eyes may in fact be closed. It would be a hunch. If this hunch is not related to a personally significant incident, it is known as an *interpretation* in REBC theory, whereas if it is so related it is known as an *inference*. In counselling you thus deal with inferences far more frequently than you deal with interpretations.

So, inferences go beyond the data at hand. They are, in fact, hypotheses (or hunches) about the nature of reality. Since inferences are best viewed as hypotheses they need to be tested against the available data. This point is important since clients often make the error of confusing their 'hypotheses' with 'facts'. Inferences and interpretations, of course, can be accurate as well as inaccurate, e.g. in the above example the man *may* have been looking out of the window. Sometimes it is impossible to test the validity of one's inferences and interpretations. Again, take the example where the man is facing the window with his eyes closed. Imagine that you have made the interpretation that he is looking out of the window. In order to test the validity of your interpretation you would need to determine whether, in fact, he has his eyes open. Thus, you would have to approach him and look at his eyes. Just before you look at his eyes, however, they may be open but he decides to close them just before you look at them. Thus your previous interpretation would have been correct, but in the process of testing it, the situation changes and it *seems* as if your interpretation has been invalidated.

While we have used an interpretation in this example, the same point is relevant when inferences are the focus of clinical interest. While making inferences and interpretations, people are influenced by interpersonal and physical contexts. Thus, it is reasonable to expect that when a person has his hands in his pockets and is facing a window, then he is looking out of the window. Psychologists often say that a person's inference or interpretation (e.g. 'You are looking out of the window') represents the 'best bet' that can be made given the context and the available information (compare Gregory, 1966). In REB counselling (as in other forms of cognitive-behavioural counselling, compare Dryden and Golden, 1986), we often find that clients make the 'worst bet' in forming hypotheses about themselves, other people, and the world, in that their inferences can be viewed as distorted (particularly in a negative direction).

Inferences are partially, not fully, evaluative

Inferences are best seen as *partially evaluative* in nature in order to differentiate them from beliefs that are full cognitions. For example, during a counselling session a female client predicted that other people would laugh at her during a class presentation. Her inference, 'Other people will laugh at me', implies a negative evaluation. However, we do not know just from her stated inference whether her evaluation is an absolute negative one ('It would be terrible if they laughed at me'); a non-absolute negative one ('It would be unfortunate if . . .'); an absolute positive one ('It would be absolutely marvellous if . . .'); a non-absolute positive one ('It would be good if . . .'); or a neutral one (I don't care if . . .'). Thus, inferences are not fully evaluative because they do not tell us what a person's beliefs might be. As we shall see later in the book, the best way of identifying a person's evaluative beliefs is to examine carefully whether his or her emotions are unhealthy (e.g. depression, anxiety or guilt, etc.) or healthy (e.g. sadness, concern or remorse, etc.). Thus, inferences, no matter how distorted, are rarely on their own reliable guides to a person's emotions because they do not contain *explicit* reference to evaluative cognitions. Thus, in rational emotive behavioural theory *emo-*

tions are based largely on evaluative beliefs rather than on inferential thinking. Inferences can be grouped into various categories and we shall briefly review those that are most relevant to counselling.

Causal attributions

This category of inferences represents attempts to account for the 'causes' of one's own or another's emotions and actions. Causal attributions can be internal to the 'author' of the experience ('He didn't turn up on time because he didn't care enough'; 'I cry easily because I'm too sensitive'); external to the 'author' of the experience ('He didn't turn up on time because he was delayed by the traffic'; 'I cry easily, because my parents didn't love me as a child'), or a combination of internal and external factors ('He didn't turn up on time because someone called on him at the last moment and he was too unassertive to excuse himself'; 'I cry easily because my family members play on my oversensitivity').

One of the initial major tasks of REB counsellors is to help clients shift from making causal attributions about emotional and behavioural disturbance which are *exclusively* external in nature (e.g. 'I'm depressed because my lover has left me') to making causal attributions which are *largely* (but not exclusively) internal in nature (e.g. 'I'm depressed about my lover leaving me because that event has encouraged me to conclude that I am worthless'). It should be noted from the previous sentence that REB counsellors guard against encouraging clients from making causal attributions, which are exclusively internal in nature, about psychological disturbance. They do so because, according to REBC theory, external events do contribute to (but do not 'cause') such disturbance.

Predictions

Predictions vary along the important dimension of probability of occurrence. In general, high-probability events tend to have greater influence on people's responses than low-probability events. However, some clients will not, for example, take steps towards a valued goal if there exists the slightest chance that their efforts may prove unsuccessful. This is a very good sign that they are making dire evaluations (irrational beliefs) about the slight chance that they may fail ('It would be terrible if I were to fail').

In counselling, clients' predictions typically relate to others' responses to self (e.g. 'If I ask that woman to dance, then she will reject me'); changes in the physical environment (e.g. 'If I don't check one last time that I have turned off the oven, then it will explode during the night') or to one's own future reactions (e.g. 'If I go into that crowded supermarket, then I will faint'). Although most clients' predictions refer to events that would be evaluated negatively, some positively evaluated predictions feature in clients' problems (e.g. the compulsive gambler who predicts that he will win a fortune this time if he bets a week's wages on the favourite in the 3.30 race at Ascot).

Motives

Frequently, people try to infer why they and others act as they do, and discussions concerning these motives often occur in the counselling process. For example, in a recent counselling session, a young depressed student who regarded herself as unlovable inferred that the reason why a fellow student was being nice to her was that the other person wanted to borrow her notes. Testing such hypotheses, particularly those that relate to the motives of others, is fraught with difficulties. When it was suggested to the client that she could check this by asking the student concerned she replied: 'She would only deny wanting to borrow my notes and she would be lying.'

Rational emotive behavioural theory makes these additional important points about inferences:

1. As has been noted about beliefs, inferences can be either general or specific. Wessler and Wessler (1980) have argued that general inferences (e.g. 'All women will eventually leave me') tend to be more enduring than specific inferences ('Sarah will eventually leave me'). The latter may be specific examples of the former.

2. Clients may have particular inferential styles (i.e. consistent and recurring ways of forming inferences). Thus, some clients may consistently make causal attributions which are internal in nature. This may be particularly so with regard to their own behaviour. Thus, one particular client viewed 'intelligence' as accounting for much of the variance in people's behaviour. He consistently minimised the impact of environmental factors on behaviour. Clients who display an internal attributional style tend to use a small number of 'filters' in viewing the world. Clients often reveal the following typical filters through which they tend to view the world: 'caring', 'sanity', 'strength', 'intelligence', etc.

3. Inferences are often 'chained' together (Moore, 1983). The following represents a typical example of an inference chain that a client may reveal in counselling: 'If I speak up in class then I will say something stupid – If that happens then everybody will laugh at me – If that happens then I will blush severely – If I blush then people will play on that in the future – If they do that it will prove that they think I'm stupid.' As we shall see in Chapter 6, it is frequently helpful in counselling individuals to find the most relevant inference in the chain, i.e. the one which the client evaluates. This is often, but not always, the last reported inference in the chain.

Decisions

Wessler and Hankin-Wessler (1986) have stressed that decisions (or decisional cognitions) play an important role in the perpetuation of psychological disturbance and in determining whether or not people make changes in their lives. People can decide whether to inspect their distorted inferences and irrational beliefs and choose whether or not to change them. People can also decide to tolerate or avoid their own painful emotions and decide to change their behaviour or to continue to act in a dysfunctional manner. A very common form of decision that is often expressed by clients is 'I can't . . .'. It is important to realise that this statement may provide clues that the person is making negative inferences and holding irrational beliefs about events and his or her response options. In rational emotive behavioural counselling it is often important to deal with these cognitions before tackling decisions.

It is helpful to distinguish between short- and long-term goals when discussing clients' decisions. A common focus in rational emotive behavioural counselling is to encourage clients to tolerate uncomfortable emotions while they pursue their valued goals. Although a client may, for example, desire the long-term goal of gaining increasing social confidence, he or she may also have the short-term goal of avoiding discomfort. In order to gain the benefit of the former, the person has to *decide* to tolerate the latter. In our experience as rational emotive behavioural counsellors, it is not only important to help clients to challenge and change their negative inferences and irrational beliefs about the experience of discomfort, but also to help them to see the reasons why deciding to tolerate discomfort is so important in the change process.

Finally, as Greenwald (1973) has shown, it is important for clients to realise that the process of making decisions to change is not a singular event. Decisions to change cognitions or behaviours have often frequently to be reaffirmed if clients are to derive lasting benefits from counselling.

Self-instructions

One of the assumptions of rational emotive behavioural counselling is that people have both an experiencing and an observing part of themselves. Thus, people 'detach' their 'observing self from their 'experiencing self' when identifying and deciding whether or not to change the cognitions that underpin psychological disturbance. The 'observing self' can also give instructions to the 'experiencing self'. These are known as *self-instructions*. Here the work of Meichenbaum (1977, 1985) is particularly helpful. Meichenbaum has shown that people can help themselves by instructing themselves to tolerate and to cope with certain negative emotions, to act in productive ways, and to provide themselves with praise for doing well.

Coping with negative emotions

Imagine a person who is scared of having a panic attack. A counsellor might encourage this person to use the following self-instructions to cope with her anxious feelings: 'When anxiety comes, just pause; keep focusing on the present; label my anxiety on a 0–10 scale and watch it change; don't try to eliminate anxiety totally, just keep it manageable; take slow controlled breaths', etc.

Facilitating productive action

For a client who gets overwhelmed when confronted with many tasks, the counsellor might suggest the following self-instructions: 'Look at what I have to do; get my tasks into order of priority; focus on one thing at a time.'

Self-rewarding

When clients have succeeded in coping with their unhealthy negative emotions and/or are acting in a productive manner, they can instruct themselves in the following ways that are deemed to be self-rewarding: 'I handled my feelings pretty well; I did well that time, that's good; I'm really making progress on this.' When clients fail to cope with their unhealthy negative emotions and/or act unproductively, they often get discouraged. To counteract this tendency, counsellors need to help them to develop constructive self-instructions concerning their 'failures'. For example, they can use the following: 'OK, I had a panic attack. Look for what went wrong; I didn't manage it this time. Look for what can be learned from this experience.'

Clients can also use self-instructions to direct themselves to identify and challenge their distorted inferences and irrational beliefs. For example, a person might say 'OK, I'm anxious; look for and challenge my demands; seek out and correct my negative thoughts.'

Problem-solving cognitions

The ability to solve problems related to psychological disturbance has been broken down into several cognitively based skills (compare Platt, Prout and Metzger, 1986). People who do bring a problem-solving 'set' to their difficulties appear to use specific cognitions that are usually implicit or covert in nature. Very often clients lack these cognitions and have to be taught to use them during counselling. The following cognitively based skills are often associated with effective personal and interpersonal problem solving.

Problem defining

Clients often fail to solve personal and interpersonal problems because of the very way they define them (e.g. 'My anxiety, proves that I'm a nervous type and nothing can be done about it'). Helping clients to overcome problems involves encouraging them to redefine problems in a way that encourages problem solving (e.g. 'My anxiety is based on irrational beliefs that can be changed'). Redefining also involves the skill of *alternative thinking*, the capacity to generate and apply alternatives to personal and interpersonal problems (e.g. 'What other ways are there to view the situation?').

Consequential thinking

This involves the capacity to consider the consequences of one's actions. Impulsive clients, for example, often do not consider what impact their actions might have on themselves and other people, and can be trained to use outcome-oriented cognitions to good effect (e.g. 'What is likely, to happen if I do this?').

Means–ends thinking

While clients are developing alternative solutions to problems, they often need to consider the sequencing of planned remedial steps leading to their goals (e.g. 'What steps do I have to take before I can do 'X'?', 'What should I preferably do first?'). In addition, clients often need to anticipate obstacles and plan to overcome them if they are to achieve their ends (e.g. 'If 'Y' happens, what can I do to overcome it?').

Perspective-taking

This involves the ability to stand back and look at a situation from someone else's point of view, and the ability to put oneself into the position of others. This latter ability is particularly helpful when a client would judge others less harshly than she considers others would judge her. Clients often fail to solve their problems because they judge themselves, other people and situations from only one fixed, and often distorted, perspective. Teaching clients perspective-taking involves encouraging them to employ cognitions like: 'What would other people think if they were in my position?'; 'If other people did what I've just done would I judge them as I think they are judging me?'

Cognitive interactionism and the centrality of beliefs

Although the types of cognitions reviewed in this chapter have been discussed separately, in reality they overlap and interact with one another. However, rational emotive behavioural theory places beliefs (or fully evaluative cognitions) at the heart of this process of interacting cognitions. Thus, according to REBC theory, people's beliefs have a greater influencing effect on their other cognitions (i.e. inferences, decisions, self-instructions and problem-solving thinking), than these cognitions have on their beliefs.

One of us (WD) has conducted a series of experiments which provide empirical support for the hypothesis that beliefs can influence the form that inferences will take (Dryden, Ferguson and Clark, 1989; Dryden, Ferguson and Hylton, 1989; Dryden, Ferguson and McTeague, 1989). In one of these studies (which is essentially similar to the other two with respect to design and outcome), subjects were divided into two groups. Subjects in group 1 (the 'irrational belief' group) were asked to imagine that they truly believed: 'I absolutely must not see a spider, and it would be really terrible if I did'. Subjects in group 2 (the 'rational belief' group) were asked to imagine that they believed: 'I'd prefer not to see a spider, but there is no reason why I must not see one. It would be bad if I did, but not the end of the world'. Both groups were then asked to rate (while adhering to their assigned belief) the likelihood of there being a spider in the room; the size of the spider; the likelihood of their seeing the spider; the distance between themselves and the spider; the likelihood of the spider moving towards them; and the number of spiders in the room (i.e. inferences concerning probability, size, movement and number). The results of this experiment were as follows: relative to subjects in the 'rational belief' group (group 2), subjects holding an irrational belief (group 1) predicted a greater likelihood of there being a spider in the room; estimated a larger size of spider; thought it more likely that they would see the spider; predicted less distance between themselves and the spider; predicted it to be more likely that the spider would be moving towards them; and tended to predict larger numbers of spiders in the room. Thus, within the context of this role-playing task, the differing beliefs assigned to the two groups of subjects did appear to colour the sort of inferences that were made.

In an unpublished follow-up to the above study, two additional groups of subjects were provided with the inferences formerly made by the 'rational belief' group and the 'irrational belief' group, respectively. Both of these new groups were then asked to judge whether they held rational or irrational beliefs, assuming that they had just made their particular set of inferences about spiders. The results of this second experiment were far less clear-cut, suggesting that inferences, as such, are not reliable guides to the kinds of beliefs people hold about stimuli (in this case, spiders).

Words and images

REB counsellors share the view of other cognitive psychotherapists that cognitions can take the form of either words or images. However, given the central role accorded to beliefs in determining emotions in rational emotive behavioural theory, it is not the words and images themselves which have direct impact on emotions, but the evaluative meaning implicit in them. For example, one of us (WD) used to be very anxious when travelling on the London underground system at a time when he had mental images of throwing himself in front of a train. His anxiety could not be attributed to the images, because he still occasionally has these images, but without anxiety. Rather, the anxiety was largely determined by an irrational belief about the image ('It is terrible to have such images that I absolutely should not have'). His present feelings are those of discomfort rather than anxiety whenever he has the image, because he now rationally believes 'I don't like having this image, but there is no reason why I must not have it.' In addition, as discussed in the previous section, his beliefs also coloured his inferences, i.e. when his belief about the image was irrational he estimated that the likelihood that he would actually throw himself in front of a train was much greater than when his belief about the image was rational.

In Chapter 5 we shall consider REBC's ABC model of psychological disturbance and health. As we will show there, A stands for an activating event that the person focuses on in an emotional episode. This event can be actual or inferred, and when it is inferred, A can be said to be largely cognitive in nature. B stands for the evaluative beliefs that the person holds about the A in question. Beliefs are definitely cognitive because of their evaluative nature.

C stands for the consequences for the individual who holds a belief B about an activating event A. In the REBC literature two consequences are usually identified and discussed: emotional and behavioural consequences (to be discussed more fully in this chapter). However, consequences of Bs can also be cognitive in nature. For example, If I believe (at B): 'I must succeed at my job and I am a failure if I don't' and I bring this belief to an experience where I did poorly at work (at A), then I may feel depressed (emotional consequence) and I may quit my job (behavioural consequence). However, I may also think the following: 'I will never get another good job', 'Nobody will want to hire me', and 'My life is ruined'. In REBC theory these thoughts are known as cognitive consequences since they are powerfully influenced by my evaluative beliefs at B. We shall list the major cognitive consequences associated with different emotions later in this chapter.

It is instructive to note then that cognitions are ubiquitous in the ABC model. Cognitions can occur at A where the person is making inferences about what he is focusing on. Cognitions are at the heart of the belief experience, given their evaluative nature and cognitions (at C) often stem from the person's evaluative beliefs at B.

While cognitions are ubiquitous in the ABC model, remember the principle of psychological interactionism discussed in Chapter 1. This principle states that cognition, emotion and behaviour are overlapping interactive processes and rarely occur in a pure, separated form. Thus, if cognitions are ubiquitous in the ABC model, it also follows that behaviour and emotion are too.

The Role of Action in Rational Emotive Behavioural Theory

Rational emotive behavioural theory holds that people have the greatest chance of fulfilling themselves when they actively pursue their basic goals and purposes. Happiness is maximised when people actively absorb themselves in vocational and avocational pursuits, and when they engage in appropriate recreational activity (Ellis, 1979a). Conversely, when people are inactive they tend to sabotage their chances of happiness. Thus, action plays an important role in rational emotive behavioural theory.

Actions and beliefs

As has already been noted, people's actions are largely (but not exclusively) determined by their beliefs about themselves, others, and present and future situations. Productive actions tend to stem from rational beliefs, while unproductive actions tend to stem from irrational beliefs.

Actions can be purposive

REB counsellors tend to agree with their Adlerian colleagues that actions can be purposive, i.e. they seek to achieve something, such as the cessation of an emotional state (anxiety) or a response from the physical and interpersonal environment. An example of the latter might be a man who acts in a withdrawn and sulking manner when his wife refuses to have sex with him. Although he probably does hold the irrational belief 'It's terrible when I don't get what I want. Poor me!', his behaviour can also be seen as purposive in that his action is designed, albeit implicitly, to elicit a response from his wife – in this case remorse and, later, sex. It is important to note in this context that other people respond to our actions and behavioural expressions of emotion, rather than to the emotions themselves.

Action tendencies and response options

When people experience emotions they also have a tendency to act in a certain number of ways, depending upon the emotion that is experienced. Action tendencies are purposive; if actualised, they serve to help the person achieve a particular goal. In the emotional disorders such goals tend to be productive in the short term, but unproductive in the long term. Action tendencies can be seen as *general* categories of behaviour rather than as *specific* responses (withdrawal rather than walking out of church).

As an illustration, consider a person who is experiencing anxiety and has a pronounced tendency to withdraw from a threat. This action tendency, if actualised, tends to help the person to avoid discomfort, but it is unproductive in the long term as it tends to discourage the person from dealing constructively with the threat. Whether or not people actually respond according to an action tendency depends largely upon what alternative ways of responding exist, and the inferences and beliefs the person holds about these response options (response options are specific ways of responding that are available to the person in a given situation).

Imagine a woman who is anxious about going to church. Given her anxiety, she chooses from among her response options to sit near the exit so that she can leave easily if she gets anxious (action tendency = to withdraw). If she were to sit in the middle of a row near the front of the church, far from the exit, and become anxious in these circumstances, she might not choose the response option of leaving the church even though she still has the tendency to withdraw. This is because she infers that, were she to do so, other people might notice her and consider her to be 'strange', a prospect which she would evaluate in an absolute and negative manner (irrational belief = 'It would be terrible if other churchgoers were to think that I am strange'). Given that she has now excluded leaving the church as a viable response option, she is now left to experience her anxiety with no constructive ways of dealing with it. She is now caught in a dilemma since she believes both that 'It is terrible to be anxious in church', and 'It would be terrible to be noticed and considered strange.' It is little wonder that this woman did have a panic attack at her own wedding.

Among a person's response options are specific responses which serve to actualise given action tendencies and specific responses that run counter to given action tendencies. An important feature of rational emotive behavioural counselling is encouraging clients to act against their habitual self-defeating action tendencies – a strategy which aims to help them to tolerate discomfort and thence begin to cope better with the problematic situation.

Behavioural competence

Rational emotive behavioural theory recognises that people execute behaviours at varying levels of skill and REB counsellors try, when appropriate, to help their clients to become more skilful at executing acts that already exist in their behavioural repertoire, and to acquire behavioural responses that are absent from their repertoire (e.g. relaxation skills and assertive skills).

In addition, REB counsellors pay attention to the inferences and evaluations clients make about their level of competence. For example, at the inferential level, people can either underestimate or overestimate their level of skill, or give an improved level of skill a particular inferential meaning (e.g. 'If I become more assertive then I will lose my sensitivity towards people'). At the evaluative level people may rate *themselves* for having a certain level of skill (e.g. 'I'm not very socially skilled; that proves I'm no good' = irrational belief), or evaluate the effort that it may take to become more skilful ('It will take a lot of practice to learn more productive study skills; I wish it were easier but that doesn't mean that I can't tolerate the effort' = rational belief).

In conclusion, while it can be seen from this section that rational emotive behavioural theory accords action an important role in human functioning, it can also be seen that cognitions are deemed to play an influential part even in the realm of human action. However, this does not mean that REBC theory neglects emotions, as we shall now show.

Emotions in Rational and Emotive Behavioural Theory

Major Unhealthy Negative Emotions and their Healthy Counterparts

We shall now consider REBC's position regarding major unhealthy negative emotions for which clients seek counselling, and their healthy counterparts. In so doing we shall integrate into our analysis the cognitive and behavioural factors we have already discussed in this chapter.

Emotion	Healthy or unhealthy	Inference[1] in relation to personal domain[2]	Type of belief	Cognitive consequences	Action tendencies
Anxiety (ego or discomfort)	Unhealthy	• Threat or danger	Irrational	• Overestimates negative features of the threat • Underestimates ability to cope with the threat • Creates an even more negative threat in one's mind • Has more task-irrelevant thoughts than in concern	• To withdraw physically from the threat • To withdraw mentally from the threat • To ward off the threat (eg. by superstitious behaviour) • To tranquillise feelings • To seek reassurance
Concern	Healthy	• Threat or danger	Rational	• Views the threat realistically • Realistic appraisal of ability to cope with the threat • Does not create an even more negative threat in one's mind • Has more task-relevant thoughts than in anxiety	• To face up to the threat • To deal with the threat constructively
Depression (ego or discomfort)	Unhealthy	• Loss (with implications for future) • Failure	Irrational	• Sees only negative aspects of the loss or failure • Thinks of other losses and failures that one has experienced • Thinks one is unable to help self (helplessness) • Sees only pain and blackness in the future (hopelessness)	• To withdraw from reinforcements • To withdraw into oneself • To create an environment consistent with feelings • To attempt to terminate feelings of depression in self-destructive ways
Sadness	Healthy	• Loss (with implications for future) • Failure	Rational	• Able to see both negative and positive aspects of the loss or failure • Less likely to think of other losses and failures than when depressed • Able to help self • Able to look into the future with hope	• To express feelings about the loss or failure and talk about these to significant others • To seek out reinforcements after a period of mourning

Emotion		Rationality	Inferences/Cognitions	Action tendencies
Unhealthy anger	• Frustration • Self or other transgresses personal rule • Threat to self-esteem	Irrational	• Overestimates the extent to which the other person acted deliberately • Sees malicious intent in the motives of others • Self seen as definitely right; other(s) seen as definitely wrong • Unable to see the other person's point of view • Plots to exact revenge	• To attack the other physically • To attack the other verbally • To attack the other passive-aggressively • To displace the attack on to another person, animal or object • To withdraw aggressively • To recruit allies against the other
Healthy anger	• Frustration • Self or other transgresses personal rule • Threat to self-esteem	Rational	• Does not overestimate the extent to which the other person acted deliberately • Does not see malicious intent in the motives of the other • Does not see self as definitely right and the other as definitely wrong • Able to see the other's point of view • Does not plot to exact revenge	• To assert self with the other • To request, but not demand behavioural change from the other
Guilt	• Violation of moral code (sin of commission) • Failure to live up to moral code (sin of omission) • Hurts the feelings of a significant other	Irrational	• Assumes that one has definitely committed the sin • Assumes more personal responsibility than the situation warrants • Assigns far less responsibility to others than is warranted • Does not think of mitigating factors • Thinks that one will receive retribution	• To escape from the unhealthy pain of guilt in self-defeating ways • To beg forgiveness from the person wronged • To promise unrealistically that she will not 'sin' again • To punish self physically or by deprivation • To disclaim responsibility for wrong-doing
Remorse	• Violation of moral code (sin of commission) • Failure to live up to moral code (sin of omission) • Hurts the feelings of a significant other	Rational	• Considers behaviour in context and with understanding in making a final judgement concerning whether one has "sinned" • Assumes appropriate level of personal responsibility • Assigns appropriate level of responsibility to others • Takes into account mitigating factors • Does not think one will receive retribution	• To face up to the healthy pain that accompanies the realisation that one has sinned • To ask, but not beg, for forgiveness • To understand reasons for wrongdoing and act on one's understanding • To atone for the sin by taking a penalty • To make appropriate amends • No tendency to make excuses for one's behaviour or enact other defensive behaviour

Emotion	Type	Theme		Thinking	Behaviour
Shame	Unhealthy	• Something shameful has been revealed about self (or group with whom one identifies) by self or others • Others will look down on or shun self (or group with whom one identifies)	Irrational	• Overestimates the 'shamefulness' of the information revealed • Overestimates the likelihood that the judging group will notice or be interested in the information • Overestimates the degree of disapproval self (or reference group) will receive • Overestimates the length of time any disapproval will last	• To remove self from the 'gaze' of others • To isolate self from others • To save face by attacking other(s) who have 'shamed' self • To defend threatened self-esteem in self-defeating ways • To ignore attempts by others to restore social equilibrium
Disappoint-ment	Healthy	• Something shameful has been revealed about self (or group with whom one identifies) by self or others • Others will look down on or shun self (or group with whom one identifies)	Rational	• Sees information revealed in a compassionate self-accepting context • Is realistic about the likelihood that the judging group will notice or be interested in the information • Is realistic about the degree of disapproval self (or reference group) will receive • Is realistic about the length of time any disapproval will last	• To continue to participate actively in social interaction • To respond to attempts of others to restore social equilibrium
Hurt	Unhealthy	• Other treats self badly (self undeserving)	Irrational	• Overestimates the unfairness of the other person's behaviour • Other perceived as showing lack of care or indifference • Self seen as alone, uncared for or misunderstood • 'Tends to think of past 'hurts' • Thinks that the other has to put things right of own accord first	• To shut down communication channel with the other • To criticise the other without disclosing what one feels hurt about
Sorrow	Healthy	• Other treats self badly (self undeserving)	Rational	• Is realistic about the degree of unfairness of the other person's behaviour • Other perceived as acting badly rather than as uncaring or indifferent • Self not seen as alone, uncared for or misunderstood • Less likely to think of past 'hurts' than when hurt • Doesn't think that the other has to make the first move	• To communicate one's feelings to the other directly • To influence the other person to act in a fairer manner
Unhealthy jealousy	Unhealthy	• Threat to relationship with partner from other person	Irrational	• Tends to see threats to one's relationship when none really exists • Thinks the loss of one's relationship is imminent • Misconstrues one's partner's ordinary conversations as having romantic or sexual connotations • Constructs visual images of partner's infidelity	• To seek constant reassurance that one is loved • To monitor the actions and feelings of one's partner • To search for evidence that one's partner is involved with someone else

				• If partner admits to finding another attractive, thinks that the other is seen as more attractive than self and that one's partner will leave self for this other person	• To attempt to restrict the movements or activities of one's partner • To set tests which partner has to pass • To retaliate for partner's presumed infidelity • To sulk
Healthy jealousy	Healthy	• Threat to relationship with partner from another person	Rational	• Tends not to see threats to one's relationship when none exists • Does not think that the loss of one's relationship is imminent • Does not misconstrue ordinary conversations between partner and other men/women • Does not construct visual images of partner's infidelity • Accepts that partner will find others attractive but does not see this as a threat	• To allow partner to express love without seeking reassurance • To allow partner freedom without monitoring his/her feelings, actions and whereabouts • To allow him/her to show natural interest in members of the opposite sex without setting tests
Unhealthy envy	Unhealthy	• Another person possesses and enjoys something desirable that the person does not have	Irrational	• Tends to denigrate the value of the desired possession • Tries to convince self that one is happy with one's possessions (although one is not) • Thinks about how to acquire the desired possession regardless of its usefulness • Thinks about how to deprive the other person of the desired possession	• To disparage verbally the person who has the desired possession • To disparage verbally the desired possession • To take away the desired possession from the other (either so that one will have it or the other is deprived of it) • To spoil or destroy the desired possession so that the other person does not have it
Healthy envy	Healthy	• Another person possesses and enjoys something desirable that the person does not have	Rational	• Honestly admits to oneself that one desires the desired possession • Does not try to convince self that one is happy with one's possession when one is not • Thinks about how to obtain the desired possession because one desires it for healthy reasons • Can allow the person to have and enjoy the desired possession without denigrating the person or the possession	• To obtain the desired possession if it is truly what one wants

Figure 2.1: *A diagrammatic summary of healthy and unhealthy negative emotions*

Notes:

[1] Inference =Personally significant bunch that goes beyond observable reality and which gives meaning to it; may be accurate or inaccurate

[2] Personal domain = The objects – tangible and intangible – in *which* a person has an involvement (Beck, 1976). REBC theory distinguishes between ego and comfort aspects of the personal domain although these frequently interact.

Figure 2.1 presents a comprehensive diagrammatic summary of the major distinctions between healthy and unhealthy negative emotions. Looking at the columns from left to right, the first column provides the name of each emotion. You will note that there are eight pairs of unhealthy and healthy negative emotions, with the unhealthy negative emotion listed first. Please note that we have used the names of emotions that are employed in REBC theory.

However, please note that clients bring to therapy their own emotional terminology and may well not understand the REBC distinctions just by being introduced to the REBC emotional terminology. It is important to discover your client's emotional terminology, to explain the REBC version and to negotiate a shared language which reflects the distinctions between healthy and unhealthy negative emotions as they are made in REBC theory.

The second column from the left in Figure 2.1 shows whether the emotion listed in the first column is an unhealthy or a healthy negative emotion. The main way to distinguish between a healthy and an unhealthy negative emotion is to look at their effects. According to REBC theory, unhealthy negative emotions about negative As are unhealthy in the sense that they do not help people to change these negative As, if indeed they can be changed, nor do they encourage them to make a constructive adjustment if these As cannot be changed. Healthy negative emotions do encourage productive attempts to change negative As and do facilitate constructive adjustment to As that cannot be changed. Also, healthy negative emotions aid people in their pursuit of their basic goals and purposes, whereas unhealthy negative emotions impede people in this pursuit.

The third column gives the major inferences related to each healthy–unhealthy emotional pairing. To help you to understand inferences fully in the context of your client's emotional experiences, we need to introduce you to the concept of the 'personal domain'. This concept was first introduced in the mid-1970s by Aaron T. Beck (1976) and refers to the objects – both tangible and intangible – in which a person has an involvement. REBC theory distinguishes between ego and comfort-related aspects of the personal domain, although it does emphasise that these aspects frequently interact.

As we have seen, inferences are personally significant hunches about reality that give meaning to it. Inferences go beyond the data at hand and need to be tested out by the person concerned. They may be accurate or inaccurate.

If you consider the 'inference' column in Figure 2.1, you will note that within each pairing, a healthy negative emotion and its unhealthy counterpart share the same inference. This makes the REBC position on emotions very clear, i.e. inferences contribute to, but do not determine emotions. Put slightly differently, although inferences are important in determining the flavour of a negative emotion, they do not determine the health of that emotion. For this we need to turn to the next column which outlines the type of belief associated with each pair of healthy–unhealthy negative emotions. This is a central tenet of REBC theory and states that healthy negative emotions about negative As stem largely from rational beliefs, and unhealthy negative emotions about these As stem largely from irrational beliefs.

The fifth column from the left In Figure 2.1 outlines what we term cognitive consequences of holding different beliefs (and experiencing different emotions). Although the inferences listed in Column 3 give shape to the person's emotional experience (e.g. when the person faces a threat he or she will experience either anxiety or concern) the cognitive consequences listed in Column 5 detail the kinds of thinking that the person engages in once his or her beliefs at B have been activated. In other words, these different cognitions are the consequences of different emotions. As you will see if you inspect Column 5 carefully, the type of thinking that people engage in as a result of holding rational beliefs and experiencing healthy negative emotions is, in general, more functional than the type of thinking they engage in as a result of holding irrational beliefs and experiencing unhealthy negative emotions.

Finally, the sixth column (i.e. the one on the far right) outlines the ways in which people TEND to act when they experience different emotions. We term these 'action tendencies'. As we have stressed earlier in this chapter, it is far from inevitable that a person will act in accordance with a particular action tendency. Thus, when a person is anxious, he will experience a strong tendency to withdraw from the situation in which he is anxious. However, he can go against his action tendency and remain in the situation until his feelings of anxiety dissipate. Encouraging clients to act against their action tendencies is a core feature of REBC practice after you have helped your clients to dispute their irrational beliefs.

A mixture of emotions

Although Figure 2.1 lists unhealthy negative emotions (and their healthy counterparts) separately, it is not uncommon in counselling practice for clients to describe a mixture of emotions. For example, some clients report feeling simultaneously depressed and guilty. In practice it is often helpful to separate these emotions and deal with them one at a time. Also, clients sometimes report experiencing 'blended' emotions as in 'hurt anger' or 'jealous anger'. Since there are various types of anger, it is helpful to determine the nature of the emotional blend for assessment purposes, particularly when clients refer only to 'feeling angry', since the cognitions that underpin 'hurt anger' are somewhat different from those underlying 'jealous anger'.

'False' emotions

It is important to bear in mind that clients may report emotions that they do not, in fact, experience or emotions that are less important to their actual problems than other feelings that they do not disclose. Clients who report emotions that they do not experience sometimes do so because they think that they are supposed to have these emotions (DiGiuseppe, 1984). Clients who report emotions peripheral to their real concerns do so for similar reasons and, in addition, may feel ashamed about their real emotions, e.g. clients who report feeling depressed rather than their true feelings of unhealthy anger.

As Snyder and Smith (1982) have shown, some clients use emotions for impression-management purposes. For example, some clients present with 'false' feelings of depression based on self-devaluation in order to elicit pity from other people or to ward off attack from other people. In the latter instance, such clients are often anxious about being criticised and ward off criticism by seeming to put themselves down before they are put down by others (most people will not criticise those who are already criticising themselves; indeed, others are likely to boost the ego of those who are actively condemning themselves). It is difficult for counsellors to identify clients' 'false' emotions, at least initially. However, they should be alert to their existence, particularly when 'something does not seem to ring true' about clients' accounts of their emotional experiences.

Strength versus healthiness of negative emotions

Some counsellors who misinterpret rational emotive behavioural theory consider that strong negative emotions are reliable signs that these emotions are unhealthy. This is not necessarily the case. Thus one can experience mild anxiety (unhealthy emotion) and strong concern (healthy emotion). Strong healthy emotions occur when the person does not get what she strongly prefers, or gets what she strongly prefers not to get. Weak unhealthy emotions occur when the person demands weakly that she gets what she wants, or that she does not get what she does not want.

The clue to whether an emotion is healthy or unhealthy is whether or not the person demands that her desires are met. Thus, counsellors who try to help clients to reduce the strength of their healthy emotions make the unfortunate mistake of encouraging them to deny the strength of their desires.

Having covered REBC's perspective on cognition, behaviour and emotion, we shall now move on to say more about REBC's views on psychological disturbance and health.

Chapter 3
Psychological Disturbance
and Health

Overview

In this chapter we consider psychological disturbance and health from a rational emotive behavioural perspective. After outlining the rational emotive behavioural view of the nature of psychological disturbance and health, we focus on how humans acquire and perpetuate their own psychological disturbance. We conclude the chapter by considering the REBC theory of therapeutic change.

The Nature of Psychological Disturbance and Health

Psychological disturbance

Irrational beliefs and their derivatives

Rational emotive behavioural theory posits that at the heart of psychological disturbance lies the tendency of humans to make devout, absolutist evaluations (i.e. irrational beliefs) of the inferred events in their lives. As has been shown, these evaluations are couched in the form of dogmatic 'musts', 'shoulds', 'have to's', 'got to's', and 'oughts.' These absolutist beliefs represent a philosophy of religiosity which, according to rational emotive behavioural theory, is the central feature of human emotional and behavioural disturbance (compare Ellis, 1983a). As has been shown, these beliefs are deemed to be irrational in that they usually (but not invariably) impede and obstruct people in the pursuit of their basic goals and purposes. Absolute musts do not invariably lead to psychological disturbance because it is possible for a person to believe devoutly 'I must succeed at all important projects', have confidence that he or she will be successful in these respects, actually succeed in them, and thereby not experience psychological disturbance.

However, the person remains vulnerable because there is always the possibility that he or she may fail in the future. So, although on probabilistic grounds REBC theory argues that an absolutist philosophy will frequently lead to psychological disturbance, it does not claim that this is invariably so. Thus, even with respect to its view of the nature of human disturbance, rational emotive behavioural theory adopts an anti-absolutist position.

Rational emotive behavioural theory goes on to posit that if humans adhere to an absolutist and devout philosophy they will strongly tend to make a number of core irrational conclusions which are deemed to be derivatives of their 'musts.' These major derivatives are viewed as irrational because they too tend to sabotage a person's basic goals and purposes.

The first major derivative is known as *awfulising*. This occurs when an inferred event is rated as being more than 100 per cent bad – a truly exaggerated and magical conclusion which stems from the belief: 'This must not be as bad as it is.'

The second major derivative is known as *low frustration tolerance* (LFT). This means believing that one cannot experience virtually any happiness at all, under any conditions, if an event which 'must' not happen actually occurs, or threatens to occur.

The third major derivative, known as *damnation*, represents a tendency for people to rate themselves and other people as 'subhuman' or 'undeserving' if they or other people do something that they 'must' not do, or fail to do something which they 'must' do. 'Damnation' can also be applied to the world or life conditions which are rated as being 'rotten' for failing to give the person what he or she 'must' have.

While REBC holds that 'awfulising', 'LFT' and 'damnation' are secondary irrational processes, in that they stem from the philosophy of 'musts', these processes can sometimes be primary (Ellis, 1984a). Indeed, Wessler (1984) has argued that they are more likely to be primary and that 'musts' are derived from them. However, the philosophy of 'musts', on the one hand, and those of 'awfulising', 'LFT' and 'damnation' on the other, are, in all probability, interdependent processes and often seem to be different sides of the same 'cognitive coin.'

Other forms of distorted thinking stemming from irrational beliefs

Rational emotive behavioural theory notes that humans also make numerous kinds of illogicalities when they are disturbed (Ellis, 1985b). In this respect it agrees with cognitive therapists (Beck et al., 1979; Burns, 1980) that such cognitive distortions are a feature of psychological disturbance. However, rational emotive behavioural theory holds that such distortions almost always stem from the 'musts', although this hypothesis has yet to be fully empirically tested. Some of the most frequent distortions are:

1. *All-or-none thinking*: 'If I fail at any important task, as I *must* not, I'm a *total* failure and *completely* unlovable!'
2. *Jumping to conclusions and negative non sequiturs*: 'Since they have

seen me fail dismally, as I *absolutely should* not have done, they will view me as an incompetent worm.'

3. *Fortune telling*: 'Because they are laughing at me for failing, they know that I *absolutely should* have succeeded, and they will despise me forever.'

4. *Focusing on the negative*: 'Because I *can't stand* things going wrong, as they *must* not, I can't see any good that is happening in my life.'

5. *Disqualifying the positive*: 'When they compliment me on the good things I have done, they are only being kind to me and forgetting the foolish things that I *absolutely should* not have done.'

6. *Allness and neverness*: 'Because conditions of living *ought* to be good and actually are so bad and so intolerable, they'll *always* be this way, and I'll *never* have any happiness.'

7. *Minimisation*: 'My good shots in this game were lucky and unimportant. But my bad shots, which I *absolutely should* never have made, were as bad as could be and were totally unforgivable.'

8. *Emotional reasoning*: 'Because I have performed so poorly, as I *absolutely should* not have done, I feel like a total idiot, and my strong feeling proves that I *am* no damned good!'

9. *Labelling and overgeneralisation*: 'Because I *must* not fail at important work and have done so, I am a complete loser and failure!'

10. *Personalising*: 'Since I am acting far worse than I *absolutely should* act and they are laughing, I am sure they are only laughing at me; and that is *awful!*'

11. *Phoneyism*: 'When I don't do as well as I *ought* to do and they still praise and accept me, I am a real phoney and will soon fall on my face and show them how despicable I am!'

12. *Perfectionism*: 'I realise that I did fairly well, but I *absolutely should* have done perfectly well on a task like this, and am therefore really an incompetent!'

Although REB counsellors at times discover all the illogicalities just listed – and a number of others that are less frequently found with clients – they particularly focus on the unconditional shoulds, oughts and musts that seem to constitute the philosophic core of irrational beliefs that lead to emotional disturbance. For they hold that if they do not get to and help clients surrender these core beliefs, the clients will most probably keep holding them and create new irrational derivatives from them.

REB counsellors also particularly look for 'awfulising', for 'LFT' and for 'damnation'; and they show clients how these almost invariably stem from their 'musts' and can be surrendered if they give up their absolutist demands on themselves, on other people, and on the universe. At the same time, rational emotive behavioural counsellors usually encourage their clients to have strong and persistent desires, wishes and preferences, and to avoid feelings of detachment, withdrawal and lack of involvement.

More importantly, REBC holds that unrealistic and illogical beliefs do not in themselves create emotional disturbance. Why? Because it is quite possible for people unrealistically to believe, 'Because I frequently fail, I always do' and it is possible for them also to believe illogically, 'Because I have frequently failed, I always will.' But they can, in both these instances, rationally conclude, 'Too bad. Even though I always fail, there is no reason why I must succeed. I would prefer to but I never have to do well. So I'll manage to be as happy as I can be even with my constant failure.' They would then rarely be emotionally disturbed.

To reiterate, the essence of human emotional disturbance, according to rational emotive behavioural theory, consists of the absolutist *musts* and *must nots* that people think *about* their failure, *about* their rejections, *about* their poor treatment by others, and *about* life's frustrations and losses. Rational emotive behavioural counselling therefore differs from other forms of cognitive-behavioural counselling such as those inspired by Bandura (1969, 1977), Beck (1976), Goldfried and Davison (1976), Janis (1983), Lazarus (1981), Mahoney (1977), Maultsby (1984), and Meichenbaum (1977), in that it particularly stresses therapists looking for clients' dogmatic, unconditional *musts*, differentiating them from their preferences, and teaching them how to surrender the former and retain the latter (Ellis, 1984a).

Psychological health

If the philosophy of religiosity is at the core of much psychological disturbance, then what philosophy is characteristic of psychological health? Rational emotive behavioural theory argues that a philosophy of relativism or 'desiring' is a central feature of psychologically healthy humans. This philosophy acknowledges that humans have a large variety of desires, wishes, wants, preferences, etc., but if they refuse to transform these non-absolute values into grandiose dogmas and demands they will not become psychologically disturbed. They will, however, experience healthy negative emotions (e.g. sadness, remorse, disappointment, healthy anger) whenever their desires are not fulfilled. These emotions are considered to have constructive motivational properties in that they both help people to remove obstacles to goal attainment and aid them to make constructive adjustments when their desires cannot be met. This point will be developed further in Chapter 4.

Three major derivatives of the philosophy of desiring are postulated by rational emotive behavioural theory. They are deemed to be rational in that they tend to help people reach their goals, or formulate new goals if their old ones cannot be realised.

The first major derivative is known as *anti-awfulising*. Here, if people do not get what they want they acknowledge that it is bad. However, because they do not believe 'I have to get what I want' they contain their evaluation along a 0–100 per cent continuum of 'badness' and do not therefore rate this situation as 'awful' – a magical rating which is placed on a nonsensical 101 per cent – ∞ (infinity) continuum. In general, when people adhere to the desiring philosophy, the stronger the desire the greater their rating of badness will be when they do not get what they want.

The second major derivative is known as *high frustration tolerance* and is the rational alternative to 'low frustration tolerance.' Here the person acknowledges that an undesirable event has happened (or may happen); believes that the event should occur empirically if it does (i.e. does not demand that what exists must not exist); acknowledges that he or she can tolerate the event and that it is worth tolerating; fully accepts that he or she will not disintegrate nor forfeit the capacity to experience happiness if the undesirable event cannot be altered.

The third major derivative, known as *acceptance*, is the rational alternative to 'damnation.' Here, the person and others are accepted as fallible human beings who do not have to act other than they do and as too complex and fluid to be given any legitimate or global rating. In addition, life conditions are accepted as they exist. People who have the philosophy of acceptance fully acknowledge that the world is highly complex and exists according to laws which are often outside their personal control. It is important to emphasise here that acceptance does not imply resignation. A rational philosophy of acceptance means that the person acknowledges that whatever exists empirically should exist, but does not have to exist in any absolute sense forever. This prompts the person to make active attempts to change reality. The person who is resigned to a situation usually does not attempt to modify it.

Criteria of psychological health

Rational emotive behavioural theory puts forward 13 criteria of psychological health (Ellis and Bernard, 1985):

1. *Self-interest*: as has already been noted, emotionally healthy people tend to be primarily interested in themselves and to put their own interests at least a little above the interests of others. They sacrifice themselves to some degree for those for whom they care – but not overwhelmingly or completely.
2. *Social interest*: social interest is usually rational and self-helping because most people choose to live and enjoy themselves in a social group or community; and if they do not act morally, protect the rights of others, and abet social survival, it is unlikely that they will create the kind of a world in which they themselves can live comfortably and happily.
3. *Self-direction*: healthy people tend to assume responsibility for their own lives while simultaneously preferring to co-operate with others. They do not need or demand considerable support or succour from others.
4. *Tolerance*: rational individuals give both themselves and others the right to be wrong. Even when they intensely dislike their own and others' behaviour, they refrain from damning themselves or others, as persons, for unacceptable or obnoxious behaviour. People who are not plagued with debilitating emotional distress tend to go along with St Francis and

Reinhold Niebuhr by changing obnoxious conditions they can change, accepting those they cannot, and having the wisdom to know the difference between the two.

5. *Flexibility*: healthy and mature individuals tend to be flexible in their thinking, open to change, and unbigoted and pluralistic in their view of other people. They do not make rigid, invariant rules for themselves and others.

6. *Acceptance of uncertainty*: healthy men and women tend to acknowledge and accept the idea that we seem to live in a world of probability and chance where absolute certainties do not, and probably never will, exist. They realise that it is often fascinating and exciting, and definitely not horrible, to live in this kind of probabilistic and uncertain world. They enjoy a good degree of order but do not demand to know exactly what the future will bring, or what will happen to them.

7. *Commitment to creative pursuits*: most people tend to be healthier and happier when they are vitally absorbed in something outside themselves and preferably have at least one powerful creative interest, as well as some major human involvement, that they consider so important that they structure a good part of their daily existence around it.

8. *Scientific thinking*: non-disturbed individuals tend to be more objective, rational and scientific than more disturbed ones. They are able to feel deeply and act concertedly, but they tend to regulate their emotions and actions by reflecting on them and evaluating their consequences in terms of the extent to which they lead to the attainment of short- and long-term goals.

9. *Self-acceptance*: healthy people are usually glad to be alive and accept themselves just because they are alive and have some capacity to enjoy themselves. They refuse to measure their intrinsic worth by their extrinsic achievements, or by what others think of them. They frankly choose to accept themselves unconditionally; and they try completely to avoid rating their totality or their being. They attempt to enjoy rather than to prove themselves.

10. *Risk-taking*: emotionally healthy people tend to take a fair amount of risk and to try to do what they want to do, even when there is a good chance that they may fail. They tend to be adventurous, but not foolhardy.

11. *Long-range hedonism*: as was noted earlier, well adjusted people tend to seek both the pleasures of the moment and those of the future, and do not often court future pain for present gain. They are hedonistic, that is, happiness-seeking and pain-avoiding, but they assume that they will probably live for quite a few years and that they had therefore better think of both today and tomorrow, and not become obsessed with immediate gratification.

12. *Non-Utopianism*: healthy people accept the fact that Utopias are probably unachievable and that they are never likely to get everything they

want, or avoid all pain. They refuse to strive unrealistically for total joy, happiness, or perfection, or for lack of anxiety, depression, self-downing and hostility.

13. *Self-responsibility for own emotional disturbance*: healthy individuals tend to accept a great deal of responsibility for their own disturbance, rather than defensively blaming others or social conditions for their self-defeating thoughts, feelings and behaviours.

Acquisition and Perpetuation of Psychological Disturbance

Acquisition of psychological disturbance

Rational emotive behavioural theory does not put forward an elaborate view concerning the acquisition of psychological disturbance. This partly follows from the rational emotive behavioural hypothesis that humans have a distinct *biological* tendency to think and act irrationally (Ellis, 1976), but it also reflects the viewpoint that theories of acquisition do not necessarily suggest therapeutic interventions. Although rational emotive behavioural theory holds that humans' tendencies towards irrational thinking are biologically rooted, it also acknowledges that environmental variables do contribute to psychological disturbance and thus encourage people to make their biologically based demands (Ellis, 1976). Ellis (1984b) said 'parents and culture usually teach children *which* superstitions, taboos and prejudices to abide by, but they do not originate their basic tendency to superstitiousness, ritualism and bigotry' (p. 209).

Rational emotive behavioural theory also posits that humans vary in their disturbability. Some people emerge relatively unscathed psychologically from being raised by uncaring or overprotective parents, while others emerge emotionally damaged from more 'healthy' childrearing regimes (Werner and Smith, 1982). In this respect, rational emotive behavioural theory claims that 'individuals with serious aberrations are more innately predisposed to have rigid and crooked thinking than those with less aberrations, and that consequently they are likely to make less advances' (Ellis, 1984b, p. 223). Here Ellis is talking about severity of emotional and behavioural disorders. Thus, the rational emotive behavioural theory of acquisition can be summed up in the view that as humans we are not made disturbed simply by our experiences; rather we bring our ability to disturb ourselves to our experiences.

Perpetuation of psychological disturbance

Although rational emotive behavioural theory does not posit an elaborate view to explain the acquisition of psychological disturbance, it does deal more extensively with how such disturbance is perpetuated.

The three REBC insights

First, people tend to maintain their psychological problems by their own 'naïve' theories concerning the nature of these problems and to what they can be attributed. They lack what REBC calls *Insight 1:* that psychological disturbance is primarily determined by the absolutist irrational beliefs that people hold about negative life events. Rather they consider that their disturbances are 'caused' by these situations. Since people make incorrect hypotheses about the major determinants of their problems, they consequently attempt to change the events rather than their irrational beliefs. Secondly, people may have Insight 1 but lack *Insight 2:* that people remain disturbed by reindoctrinating themselves *in the present* with their irrational beliefs. Although they may see that their problems are determined by their beliefs, they may distract themselves, and thus perpetuate their problems, by searching for the historical antecedents of these beliefs, instead of directing themselves to change them as currently held. Thirdly, people may have Insights 1 or 2 but still sustain their disturbance because they lack *Insight 3:* only if people diligently work and practise in the present as well as in the future to think, feel and act against their irrational beliefs are they likely to change them, and make themselves significantly less disturbed. People who have all three insights see clearly that they had better persistently and strongly challenge their beliefs cognitively, emotively and behaviourally to break the perpetuation of disturbance cycle. Merely acknowledging that a belief is irrational is usually insufficient to effect change (Ellis, 1979c).

The philosophy of low frustration tolerance (LFT)

Rational emotive behavioural theory contends that the major reason why people perpetuate their psychological problems is because they adhere to a philosophy of low frustration tolerance (LFT) (Ellis, 1979b, 1980a). Such people believe that they must be comfortable, and thus do not work to effect change because such work inevitably involves experiencing discomfort. They are short-range hedonists in that they are motivated to avoid short-term discomfort even though accepting and working against their temporary uncomfortable feelings would probably help them to reach their long-range goals. Such people evaluate cognitive and behavioural therapeutic tasks as 'too painful', and even more painful than the psychological disturbance to which they have achieved some measure of habituation. They prefer to remain with their 'comfortable' discomfort rather than face the 'change-related' discomfort which they believe they must not experience. Maultsby (1975) has argued that people often back away from change because they are afraid that they will not feel right about it. He calls this the 'neurotic fear of feeling a phoney' and actively shows clients that these feelings of 'unnaturalness' are in fact the natural concomitants of relearning. Another prevalent form of LFT is 'anxiety about anxiety.' Here, individuals believe that they must not be anxious, and thus do not expose themselves to anxiety-provoking situations because they might become anxious if they did so – an experience they would evaluate as 'awful.' As such, they perpetuate their problems and restrict their lives to avoid experiencing anxiety.

Disturbances about disturbances

'Anxiety about anxiety' constitutes an example of the clinical fact that people often make themselves disturbed about their disturbances. Having created secondary (and sometimes tertiary) disturbances about their original disturbance, they become preoccupied with these 'problems about problems' and thus find it difficult to get back to solving the original problem. Humans are often very inventive in this respect. They can make themselves depressed about their depression, guilty about being angry, as well as anxious about their anxiety, and so on. Consequently, people often need to tackle their disturbances about their disturbances (sometimes known as meta-disturbances) before they can successfully solve their original problems (Ellis, 1979b, 1980a).

Defences

Rational emotive behavioural theory endorses the Freudian view of human defensiveness in explaining how people perpetuate their psychological problems (Freud, 1937). Thus, people maintain their problems by employing various defence mechanisms (e.g. rationalisation, avoidance) which are designed to help deny the existence of these problems, or to minimise their severity. The rational emotive behavioural view is that these defences are used to ward off self-damnation tendencies and that, under such circumstances, if these people were honestly to take responsibility for their problems, they would severely denigrate themselves for having them. In addition, these defence mechanisms are also employed to ward off discomfort anxiety; again, if such people admitted their problems they would rate them as 'too hard to bear' or 'too difficult to overcome.'

Payoffs

Rational emotive behavioural theory notes that people sometimes experience a form of perceived payoff for their psychological problems other than avoidance of discomfort (Ellis, 1979a). The existence of these payoffs serves to perpetuate the problems. Thus, a woman who claims to want to overcome her procrastination may avoid tackling the problem because she is afraid that should she become successful she might then be criticised by others as being 'too masculine', a situation she would evaluate as 'awful.' Her procrastination serves to protect her, she believes, from this 'terrible' state of affairs. It is important to note that rational emotive behavioural theory considers that people are affected by payoffs because they make inferences and evaluations about the consequences, or likely consequences, of their behaviour. They are not influenced directly by these consequences.

Self-fulfilling prophecies

Finally, the well documented 'self-fulfilling prophecy' phenomenon helps to explain why people perpetuate their psychological problems (Jones, 1977; Wachtel, 1977). Here, people act according to their evaluations and consequent predictions, and thus often elicit from themselves or from others responses which they then interpret in a manner that confirms their initial hypotheses. Thus, a socially anxious man may believe that other people would not want to get to know 'a worthless individual such as I truly am.' He then attends a social function and acts as if he were worthless, avoiding eye contact and keeping away from others. Unsurprisingly, such social behaviour does not invite approaches from others – a lack of response which he interprets and evaluates thus: 'You see, I was right. Other people don't want to know me. I really am no good.'

In conclusion, rational emotive behavioural theory holds that people 'naturally tend to perpetuate their problems and have a strong innate tendency to cling to self-defeating, habitual patterns and thereby resist basic change. Helping clients change then poses quite a challenge for REBC practitioners' (Dryden, 1984a, p. 244).

The Rational Emotive Behavioural Theory of Therapeutic Change

The rational emotive behavioural view of the person is basically an optimistic one. Although it posits that humans have a distinct biological tendency to think irrationally, it also holds that they have the capacity to choose to work towards changing this irrational thinking and its self-defeating effects.

There are various levels of change. Rational emotive behavioural theory holds that the most profound and long-lasting changes that humans can effect are ones that involve philosophic restructuring of irrational beliefs. Change at this level can be specific or general. Specific philosophical change means that individuals change their irrational absolute demands (musts, shoulds) about given situations to rational relative preferences. General philosophical change involves people adopting a non-devout attitude towards life events in general.

To effect a philosophical change at either the specific or general level, people had better:

1. Realise that, to a large degree, they create their own psychological disturbances and that although environmental conditions can contribute to their problems, they are in general of secondary consideration in the change process;
2. Fully recognise that they do have the ability significantly to change these disturbances;
3. Understand that emotional and behavioural disturbances stem largely from irrational, absolutist dogmatic beliefs;

4. Detect their irrational beliefs and discriminate them from their rational alternatives;
5. Dispute these irrational beliefs using the logico-empirical methods of science;
6. Work towards the internalisation of their new rational beliefs by employing cognitive, emotive and behavioural methods of change;
7. Continue this process of challenging irrational beliefs and using multimodal methods of change for the rest of their lives.

When people effect a philosophical change by modifying their irrational beliefs to rational beliefs, they are often able spontaneously to correct their distorted inferences of reality (over-generalisations, faulty attributions, etc.). However, they often had better challenge these distorted inferences more directly, as Ellis has always emphasised (e.g. Ellis, 1962), and as Beck (Beck et al., 1979) have also stressed.

Although rational emotive behavioural theory argues that irrational beliefs are the breeding ground for the development and maintenance of inferential distortions, it is possible for people to effect inferentially based changes without making a profound philosophical change. Thus, they may regard their inferences as hunches about reality rather than facts, may generate alternative hypotheses and may seek evidence and/or carry out experiments which test out each hypothesis. They may then accept the hypothesis that represents the 'best bet' of those available (Gregory, 1966).

Consider a man who thinks that his co-workers view him as a fool. To test this hypothesis he might first specify their negative reactions to him. These constitute the data from which he quickly draws the conclusion: 'They think I'm a fool.' He might then realise that what he has inferred to be negative responses to him might not be negative. If they seem to be negative, he might then carry out an experiment to test out the meaning he attributes to their responses. Thus, he might enlist the help of a colleague whom he trusts to carry out a 'secret ballot' of others' opinions of him. Or, he could test his hunch more explicitly by directly asking them for their view of him. As a result of these strategies this person may conclude that his co-workers find some of his actions foolish, rather than considering him to be a complete fool. His mood may lift because his inference of the situation has changed, but he may still believe: 'If others think I'm a fool that would be awful and prove that I really am worthless.' Thus, he has made an inferential change, but not a philosophical one. If this person were to attempt to make a philosophical change he would first assume that his inference was true, then address himself to his beliefs about this inference and hence challenge these if they were discovered to be irrational. Thus he might conclude, 'Even if I act foolishly, that makes me a person with foolish behaviour, not a foolish person. And even if they deem me a total idiot, this is simply their view with which I can choose to disagree.' Rational emotive behavioural counsellors hypothesise that people are more likely to make a profound philosophical change if they first assume that their inferences are true and then challenge their irrational beliefs, rather than if they first correct their inferential distortions and then challenge their underlying irrational beliefs. However, this hypothesis awaits full empirical enquiry.

People can also make direct changes in their situation. Thus, in the example quoted above, the man could leave his job or distract himself from the reactions of his colleagues by taking on extra work and devoting himself to this. Or he might carry out relaxation exercises whenever he comes in contact with his co-workers and thus distract himself once again from their perceived reactions. Additionally, the man might have a word with his supervisor, who might then instruct the other workers to change their behaviour towards the man.

When this model is used to consider behavioural change, it is apparent that a person can change his or her behaviour to effect inferential and/or philosophic change. Thus, again using the above example, a man whose co-workers view him as a fool might change his own behaviour towards them and thus elicit a different set of responses from them, which would lead him to reinterpret his previous inference (behaviour change to effect inferential change). However, if it could be determined that they did indeed consider him to be a fool then the man could actively seek them out and show himself that he could stand the situation, and that just because they think him a fool does not make him one, i.e. he learns to accept himself in the face of their views while exposing himself to their negative reactions (behaviour change to effect philosophic change).

Although rational emotive behavioural counsellors prefer to help their clients make profound philosophic changes in their beliefs, they do not dogmatically insist that their clients must make such changes. If it becomes apparent that clients are not able at any given time to change their irrational beliefs, then REB counsellors would endeavour to help them either to change the situation directly by avoiding the troublesome situation, or by behaving differently, or to change their distorted inferences about the situation. This book focuses on rational emotive behavioural methods of changing beliefs rather than inferences. For methods devoted to changing inferences, we recommend that the reader consult Beck et al. (1979) and Beck and Emery (1985).

In the next chapter, we build upon these theoretical underpinnings and consider a cognitively based analysis of the most common forms of psychological disturbance for which clients seek counselling.

PART II
Practice

Chapter 4
Counselling Individuals: Rationale and Key Elements

Overview

In this chapter, we begin by outlining the indications and contraindications for individual counselling. We then present an overview of the key elements involved in the practice of rational emotive behavioural counselling. Here we discuss counselling goals, aspects of the counselling relationship, the manner in which REBC affects counsellors' choice of interventions, and the personal qualities of effective rational emotive behavioural counsellors.

Considerations

Counselling and psychotherapy can be carried out in the context of individual, couples, family and group sessions. Although counsellors and therapists have all of these modalities from which to choose, research evidence suggests that most spend their working time engaged in individual treatment. Prochaska and Norcross (1983), for example, carried out a survey of the practices of 410 psychologists belonging to Division 29 (psychotherapy) of the American Psychological Association (APA). In addition, they have reported on a similar survey (Norcross and Prochaska, 1982) of a representative sample of psychologists who are members of APA Division 12 (clinical psychology). Both of these surveys revealed that members of both divisions spent most of their therapy time practising individual therapy (65.3 per cent Division 29 members; 63.5 per cent Division 12 members). Likewise, a survey of 993 British psychologists belonging to the Clinical Division of The British Psychological Society (BPS) indicated that those who practised individual therapy (99 per cent of the sample) allotted 74 per cent of their treatment time to that format (Norcross, Dryden and Brust, 1992). Although there are no available data on the distribution of working time of therapists and counsellors of

48

different theoretical orientations, there is little reason to believe that a different pattern would be found among rational emotive behavioural counsellors.

One of us has argued (Dryden, 1984b) that there are various sources of influence that impinge upon the counsellor and client as they seek to determine in which modality to work. First, counsellors are influenced by the settings in which they work. Such settings may impose practical limitations on the practice of counselling in modalities other than individual counselling. Alternatively, different settings may have different norms of practice which favour one particular modality over others. Counsellors who work in private practice usually find that the exigencies of this mode of work mean that individual counselling constitutes the major part of their workload. Secondly, counsellors are influenced by the ways in which they account for their clients' disturbances. Since the rational emotive behavioural model of disturbance emphasises the role played by the individual's belief system upon his or her psychological problems, this may influence practitioners to work more frequently in the modality of individual counselling than in other modalities. Thirdly, clients' preferences are very salient here and these often exert a considerable influence on the choice of therapeutic modality.

In this regard, Ellis (in Dryden, 1984b, p. 15) has argued 'I am usually able to go along with the basic desire of any clients who want individual, marital, family or group psychotherapy. It is only in relatively few cases that I talk them into taking a form of therapy they are at first loath to try.' Information is needed concerning the impact of clients' precounselling modality preferences on the working practices of REB counsellors. Given that we do not have any data concerning how REB counsellors distribute their working time among the various counselling modalities, what factors determine such decisions, and who is largely responsible for making these decisions, much of our thinking on the issue of when and when not to undertake individual counselling is determined by clinical experience. Based upon this experience, we present the following lists of indications and contraindications for individual counselling.

Indications for individual counselling

1. Individual rational emotive behavioural counselling, by its nature, provides clients with a situation of complete confidentiality. It is indicated, therefore, when it is important for clients to be able to disclose themselves in privacy without fear that others may use such information to their detriment. Some clients are particularly anxious concerning how others, for example in a group counselling context, would react to their disclosures, and such anxiety precludes their productive participation in that modality. Similarly, clients who otherwise would not disclose 'secret' material are best suited to individual rational emotive behavioural counselling. As in other situations, transfer to other modalities may be indicated later when such clients are more able and/or willing to disclose themselves to others.

2. Individual counselling, by its dyadic nature, provides an opportunity for a closer relationship to develop between counsellor and client than may exist when other clients are present. This factor may be particularly important for some clients who have not developed close relationships with significant people in their lives and for whom group counselling, for example, may initially prove too threatening.

3. Individual rational emotive behavioural counselling can be conducted to best match the client's pace of learning. Thus, it is particularly suited for clients who, due to their present state of mind, or speed of learning, require their counsellor's full undivided attention. This is especially important for clients who are quite confused and who would only be distracted by the complexity of interactions that can take place in other therapeutic modalities.

4. Likewise, clients who feel hopeless and suicidal may benefit more from individual sessions in which they have the counsellor's full attention, as such sessions can allow the counsellor more readily to focus interventions upon helping the client to emerge from the suicidal crisis. It is noted, however, that counsellors have a responsibility to protect the welfare of suicidal clients who appear to be at risk of doing harm to themselves. In some circumstances this responsibility may preclude individual outpatient counselling, as when it appears advisable to recommend psychiatric hospitalisation.

5. Individual counselling is particularly indicated when clients' major problems involve their relationship with themselves rather than their relationship with other people.

6. Individual counselling may be indicated for clients who wish to differentiate themselves from others, for example, those who have decided to leave a relationship and wish to deal with individual problems that this may involve. Here, however, some conjoint sessions with the partner may also be helpful, particularly in matters of conciliation (Gurman and Kniskern, 1978).

7. It can be helpful for counsellors to vary their therapeutic style with clients in order to minimise the risk of perpetuating the client's problems by providing an inappropriate interactive style. Individual rational emotive behavioural counselling provides counsellors with an opportunity to vary their interactive styles with clients free from the concern that such variation may adversely affect other clients who may be present.

8. Individual counselling is particularly indicated for clients who have profound difficulties sharing therapeutic time with other clients.

9. Individual counselling may also be indicated for negative reasons. Thus, clients may be seen in individual counselling who may not benefit from working in other modalities. Therefore, clients who may monopolise a counselling group, be too withdrawn within it to benefit from the experience, or who are thought too vulnerable to benefit from family counselling, are often seen individually in rational emotive behavioural counselling.

Contraindications for individual counselling

1. Individual counselling is contraindicated for clients who are likely to become overly dependent on the counsellor, particularly when such dependency becomes so intense as to lead to client deterioration. Such clients may be more appropriately helped in group counselling where such intense dependency is less likely to develop due to the fact that the counsellor has to relate to several other people.

2. Individual rational emotive behavioural counselling, which does not in general advocate close interpersonal relationships between counsellors and clients, can still be a close interpersonal encounter for the client and as such is less likely to be indicated for clients who may find such a degree of intimacy, or the prospect of such intimacy unduly threatening.

3. Individual counselling may be contraindicated for clients who find this modality too comfortable. Based on the idea that personal change is often best facilitated in situations where there is an optimal level of arousal, individual counselling may not provide enough challenge for such clients. Ravid (1969) found that it may be unproductive to offer individual therapy to clients who have had much previous individual therapy, but who still require further therapeutic help.

4. Individual counselling may not be appropriate for clients for whom other modalities are deemed to be more therapeutic. For example, clients who are particularly shy, retiring and afraid to take risks are more likely to benefit from group counselling (if they can be induced to join) than from the less risky situation of individual counselling. Secondly, partners who can productively use the conjoint situation of couples counselling often benefit more from this modality than from working in individual rational emotive behavioural counselling. This is particularly true when they have largely overcome their disturbed feelings about their unproductive relationship and are dealing with issues devoted to enhancement of relationship satisfaction, a situation which particularly warrants their joint participation.

Other issues

Once counsellors and clients have decided to work in a particular modality, it is important to stress that this decision is not irrevocable. Clients may move from modality to modality, and thus individual counselling, in this context, can best be viewed as part of a comprehensive treatment strategy. This can occur for both positive and negative reasons. Productive movement to and from individual counselling occurs when clients have made therapeutic gains in one modality, but may benefit further from being transferred to a different one. Negative movement in and out of individual counselling occurs when the clients do not improve in a given therapeutic modality.

   Although we have provided some indications and contraindications for the practice of individual counselling, we conclude by stressing that the state of the art concerning this issue is far from being well developed and would advise REB counsellors thus: work with clients in the modality which seems to be most productive for them, but regard such decisions as tentative and to a large degree experimental. Perhaps the best way of determining whether a client will benefit or not from individual counselling is to work with them in that modality and to monitor their response to it. We shall next consider key elements involved in the practice of rational emotive behavioural counselling.

Key Elements in the Practice of Rational Emotive Behavioural Counselling

As described in Part 1, REBC presents a clear and coherent theory as to the manner in which human beings acquire and perpetuate their own psychological disturbance. Although this theory does not dictate rigid and absolutistic 'rules' for the implementation of rational emotive behavioural counselling, it does suggest particular emphases and guidelines which may contribute to more effective practice. The sections that follow will outline the goals of rational emotive behavioural counselling, important features of the relationship between counsellor and client, issues pertaining to therapeutic style, and the relationship between REBC theory and counsellors' decisions concerning choice of therapeutic interventions. The chapter concludes with consideration of some of the personal qualities that may characterise effective rational emotive behavioural counsellors.

The goals of rational emotive behavioural counselling

Rational emotive behavioural counsellors seek to help their clients minimise the frequency with which they experience emotional disturbance and engage in self-defeating patterns of behaviour. As REBC theory holds that irrational beliefs are a major determinant of such psychological problems, counsellors set themselves the task of teaching clients how to detect and dispute the irrational beliefs to which they subscribe. Clients are further assisted to replace their irrational beliefs with more rational ones, which can help them to work more effectively toward their valued goals. This, in turn, may contribute to their experiencing more happiness and satisfaction in life.

Typically, clients first enter counselling because they are seeking relief from 'symptoms' which are distressing in a more or less immediate sense. Thus, a depressed client may seek relief from the emotional pain that his or her depression entails, while an obese client may seek relief from the distress associated with overeating and being unattractively overweight. Rational emotive behavioural counsellors will attempt to help clients to overcome the emotional and behavioural disturbances which are of most immediate relevance to them, using the techniques and interventions that REBC provides.

It is noted, however, that rational emotive behavioural counsellors maintain a therapeutic goal with more far-reaching implications than mere symptom relief: they are interested in helping their clients to attain a beneficial and enduring modification in their basic personal philosophies. Such profound philosophic change means that clients become less prone to placing rigid irrational demands upon themselves, other people, and circumstances as they exist in the world, with the result that they are able greatly to reduce their general tendencies to make themselves disturbed. When clients work at effecting the type of profound philosophic change which REBC advocates, they are better able to approach the 13 criteria for psychological health that were presented in Chapter 3 (see pp.39–41).

Rational emotive behavioural counsellors recognise, however, that not all clients will be interested in expending the amount of time and effort which is very often required for attaining a profound philosophic change. They may be quite satisfied when they experience improvement in a circumscribed problem area, and may wish to terminate treatment at that point. Thus, while rational emotive behavioural counsellors may encourage their clients to work at attaining a broad philosophic restructuring, they are flexible in terms of adjusting their goals to meet their clients' goals.

It is also noted that REB counsellors demonstrate flexibility when dealing with clients who are unable or unwilling to work at identifying and disputing the irrational beliefs that negatively affect specific areas of their functioning. Here, counsellors will modify their therapeutic goals and may choose to use strategies and techniques which, although less likely to result in philosophic change, may still offer some degree of relief from distressing symptoms. Hence, they may help certain clients to make changes in their inferences, modify the negative events in their lives, or work directly at changing their behaviour in some fashion, so that they experience self-defeating consequences less often. It is recognised, however, that these clients may well remain vulnerable to significant future upsets because they have not addressed the ideological core of their psychological problems.

The counselling relationship

REBC not only recommends that counsellors be flexible in their choice of therapeutic goals and strategies; it also encourages them to exercise flexibility with regard to the parameters of the counselling relationship. Thus, rational emotive behavioural counsellors are able to consider such variables as their own personality characteristics, their clients' personality characteristics, and clients' preferences concerning counsellor behaviour in making decisions as to the therapeutic conditions and styles most likely to facilitate effective counselling for given individuals. Nevertheless, REB counsellors tend to favour particular types of conditions and styles, as REBC theory suggests that these will generally prove to be therapeutically beneficial for clients.

Therapeutic conditions

As noted in Chapter 3, REBC posits that self-acceptance is one of the hall-marks of the psychologically healthy individual. While rational emotive behavioural counsellors will often attempt directly to teach clients how to become more self-accepting, they will also employ less direct interventions to help clients approach this aspect of psychological health. Hence, throughout the course of treatment – regardless of how poorly clients might behave – counsellors strive to provide them with unconditional acceptance. By doing so they hope to encourage clients to accept *themselves* as fallible human beings who engage in both good and bad acts, but who are never *essentially* bad or good. Counsellors will, however, comment on aspects of a client's behaviour which appear to be self-defeating or negatively affect other individuals, including the counsellor (Ellis, 1973). Such feedback is given in order to assist clients in modifying patterns of behaviour that tend to garner negative consequences, and is provided in an atmosphere that encourages clients to examine critically and rate their acts while refraining from globally rating their 'self.'

REB counsellors strive to be as open as therapeutically feasible, and do not hesitate to give highly personal information about themselves, should their clients ask for it, except when they judge that clients would use such information either against themselves or the counsellor (Dryden, 1991b). In addition, rational emotive behavioural counsellors generally do not engage in self-disclosure on a gratuitous basis; they attempt to employ it for therapeutic purposes. Thus, a counsellor may disclose to a client that he or she once had a problem similar to the one that the client is working on, and then describe the manner in which he or she used REBC to overcome it. This intervention can serve several useful purposes:

1. It provides clients with a model of how they can work at overcoming their own problems.
2. It can increase the counsellor's credibility as an expert problem-solver.
3. It conveys to clients that their counsellor is not ashamed of having had personal problems, and that they need not feel ashamed of themselves.

This last function may be particularly important, as it highlights the fact that counsellor self-disclosure may serve as a vehicle for modelling self-acceptance to clients. Clients who are able to accept themselves with their psychological disturbance may well experience greater success in using REBC to counter it.

Ellis (1977a, 1987) has noted that human beings may tend to make themselves more vulnerable to emotional disturbance when they take themselves and their problems, other people, and the world too seriously. As such, REB counsellors will often strive to inject various sorts of humorous interventions into their sessions with clients. Usually, this humour is directed at helping clients to see the absurd and illogical aspects of their irrational beliefs.

Humour is never used, however, to poke fun at clients themselves, and rational emotive behavioural counsellors take steps to make certain that clients do not perceive its use in this way. In addition, it is noted that REBC opposes therapists indulging themselves unethically (by overusing or otherwise misusing any type of intervention) in order to enjoy counselling sessions at their clients' expense (Ellis, 1983b).

Rational emotive behavioural counsellors are advised to remain alert to the likelihood that counsellors and clients may ascribe widely different meanings to the same words and phrases within counselling (Dryden, 1986). REBC theory, for example, defines various 'feeling words' (such as anxiety, concern, depression and sadness) in very specific ways (see Chapter 4). Clients new to REBC, however, will be unfamiliar with these definitions, hence they may often describe their affective experiences in an idiosyncratic fashion. It is desirable for REB counsellors to make inquiries that serve to clarify the manner in which clients use words to describe their feelings, and to teach clients REBC's definitions of the various healthy and unhealthy emotions. In a similar vein, counsellors can check with clients to be sure that the latter are correctly grasping the many other terms and concepts typically presented during a course of rational emotive behavioural counselling. Treatment will generally proceed more smoothly (and a particular source of client resistance can be avoided) when counsellor and client are 'speaking the same language'.

REB counsellors show their clients a special kind of empathy. They not only offer them affective empathy (i.e. communicating that they understand how their clients feel) but also offer them philosophic empathy, i.e. showing them that they understand the philosophies that underlie these feelings.

Thus, with certain modifications, they agree with Rogers' (1957) views concerning counsellor empathy, genuineness and unconditional positive regard. However, rational emotive behavioural counsellors are very wary of showing the vast majority of their clients undue warmth. Rational emotive behavioural theory holds that if rational emotive behavioural counsellors get really close to their clients and given them considerable warmth, attention, caring and support, as well as unconditional acceptance, then these counsellors run two major risks (Ellis, 1977c, 1982b). The first is that counsellors may unwittingly reinforce their clients' dire needs for love and approval – two irrational ideas that are at the core of much human disturbance. When this happens, clients appear to improve because their counsellors are indeed giving them what they believe they must have. They begin to 'feel better' but do not necessarily 'get better' (Ellis, 1972). Their 'improvement' is illusory because their irrational philosophies are being reinforced. Since they seem to improve, their counsellors have restricted opportunities to identify these ideas, show them how they relate to their problems and help them challenge and change them. Consequently, while such clients are helped by their counsellors, they are not shown how they can help themselves, and are thus vulnerable to future upset.

The second major risk concerns the fact that counsellors may unwittingly reinforce their clients' philosophy of low frustration tolerance (LFT) – a major form of discomfort disturbance. Clients with LFT problems 'almost always try to seek interminable help from others instead of coping with life's difficulties themselves. Any kind of therapy that does not specifically persuade them to stop their puerile whining, and to accept responsibility for their own happiness, tends to confirm their belief that others *must* help them. Close relationship therapy is frequently the worst offender in this respect and thereby does considerable harm' (Ellis, 1977c, p. 15).

However, since rational emotive behavioural theory is relative in nature and is against the formulation of absolute, dogmatic therapeutic rules, it does recognise that under certain conditions (e.g. where a client is extremely depressed, accompanied by powerful suicidal ideation) distinct counsellor warmth may be positively indicated for a restricted period of time (Ellis, 1985c).

Therapeutic style

REBC can accurately be viewed as a psychoeducational approach to counselling. Ellis, in fact, has sometimes conceptualised the role of the effective REB counsellor as that of an authoritative (but not authoritarian) and encouraging teacher who strives to teach his or her clients how to be their own counsellor once formal counselling sessions have ended (Ellis, 1979c, 1984b). Given this view of the counsellor's role, and given the fact that it is often quite difficult for clients to relinquish their strongly held irrational beliefs, it is not surprising that Ellis (1979d) recommends that counsellors adopt an active–directive stance with most clients, and a particularly forceful version of that style with some very disturbed and resistant clients.

Not all rational emotive behavioural counsellors, however, concur with this view. Garcia (1977) and Young (1977), for instance, recommend a more passive, gentle approach under specific, or most, conditions with clients. Eschenroeder (1979, p. 5) notes that it is important to ask in rational emotive behavioural counselling 'which therapeutic style is most effective with which kind of client?' In the same vein, recent proponents of eclectic forms of counselling argue that counsellors would be wise to vary their style of therapeutic interaction to meet the special requirements of individual clients (Lazarus, 1981; Beutler, 1983). While this is a scantily researched area in rational emotive behavioural counselling, it may be best for REB counsellors to avoid an overly friendly, emotionally charged style of interaction with 'histrionic' clients; an overly intellectual style with 'obsessive-compulsive' clients; an overly directive style with clients whose sense of autonomy is easily threatened (Beutler, 1983); and an overly active style with clients who easily retreat into passivity. This line of reasoning fits well with the notion of flexibility, which rational emotive behavioural counsellors advocate as a desirable therapeutic quality. Varying one's therapeutic style in rational emotive behavioural counselling does not mean departing from the theoretical principles on which the content of this approach to counselling is based. As

Eschenroeder (1979, p. 3) points out, in rational emotive behavioural counselling 'there is no one-to-one relationship between theory and practice'. Finally, the nature of the relationship between counsellor and client often changes during the course of rational emotive behavioural counselling, particularly with respect to the activity of the counsellor. At the outset the client usually does not have much insight into rational concepts and, as such, the counsellor is usually quite active in helping the client to understand these concepts. Once the client has understood the concepts and has begun to put them into practice, the counsellor is usually less active and strives to remind the client of what he or she already knows, while encouraging continual work to translate this knowledge into practice. At this later stage, the counsellor is usually less active than at the beginning of the counselling process.

Relationship between theory and choice of techniques

Since REBC theory ascribes a place of central importance to irrational beliefs in producing and maintaining psychological disturbance, it follows logically that rational emotive behavioural counsellors devote much of their therapeutic attention to helping clients surrender their disturbance-provoking dogmatic shoulds, musts and oughts. Their choice of strategies and techniques for accomplishing this end, however, is guided by a number of important rational emotive behavioural principles.

Role of force and energy in therapeutic change

Rational emotive behavioural theory posits that the human tendency to think irrationally has a biological basis. This perspective can assist REB counsellors in being mindful of the ease with which their clients create irrational beliefs, as well as the tenacity with which they often cling to them; it also suggests that counsellors may have to employ considerable force and energy within sessions in order to accomplish effective disputing. Ellis (1979d) advocates the use of force and energy as a therapeutic tool for effecting cognitive restructuring, and engages in a number of verbal behaviours in his own sessions with clients that can be considered characteristic of the manner in which he translates these terms into actual clinical practice. These behaviours include his (judicious) use of profanity, his repetition of rational messages, his persistence in disputing particular irrational beliefs that his clients hold, and his directive and confrontational stance (Yankura and Dryden, 1990). Over the course of therapy, counsellors can communicate to clients the rationale and means for using force and energy to dispute their irrational beliefs, such that they become more effective at conducting disputation on an independent basis.

Multi-modal emphasis

As noted in Chapter 1, REBC theory adheres to the principle of psychological interactionism in so far as it acknowledges that cognition, emotion and behaviour are overlapping and interacting processes. As these three dimensions of human functioning influence each other to a significant degree, it makes sense for rational emotive behavioural counsellors to utilise as many channels of intervention as practical in the service of helping clients to modify their self-defeating belief systems. Thus, they will not restrict themselves to using only cognitive disputing (as REBC's critics sometimes inaccurately charge) and will employ a variety of cognitive, emotive-evocative, imaginal and behavioural techniques in order to approach the above goal. In this sense they agree with Lazarus' (1981) multi-modal approach to therapy, which holds that the effectiveness of treatment can be increased significantly by attacking problem areas on a number of therapeutic fronts. In addition, REB counsellors are generally not averse to referring clients for medication when it appears that psychopharmacological intervention will increase their capacity to benefit from the counselling process.

Selective eclecticism

With its multi-modal emphasis, REBC encourages counsellors to utilise a wide range of therapeutic techniques and strategies, including some that have been originated within other, divergent schools of therapy. Rational emotive behavioural counsellors do not subscribe to the theories of psychological disturbance which underpin these alternative approaches to therapy, however, and borrow techniques from them in order to assist clients in the process of identifying, challenging and replacing their irrational beliefs.

REBC theory provides counsellors with guidelines that they can use when choosing therapeutic interventions. As pointed out in the earlier discussion of counsellor warmth, REBC de-emphasises the use of interventions that may unintentionally serve to reinforce clients' irrational ideologies. Catharsis and abreaction techniques can also be considered to fall into this category, as they may actually help clients to practise and subscribe ever more strongly to their anger-producing philosophies (Ellis, 1982c).

In addition, rational emotive behavioural counsellors will generally avoid using techniques that might serve to sidetrack clients from focusing their efforts on modifying their irrational belief systems. Relaxation techniques, for instance, may help clients to attain some degree of relief from their emotional upsets; if clients utilise them to the point of excluding direct cognitive change methods, however, they may never address their self-defeating personal philosophies. In such an instance they will probably derive limited benefits from counselling, as their disturbance-producing irrational beliefs remain largely unchallenged. REB counsellors, then, attempt to practise a theoretically consistent approach to eclecticism (Dryden, 1987).

Utilisation of homework assignments

Counsellors and clients typically meet for a single one-hour session per week. If this single hour comprises all of the time devoted to achieving therapeutic goals, counselling will probably proceed in a very gradual fashion. In order to increase the efficiency and effectiveness of treatment, counsellors from a number of different therapeutic schools (particularly those practising behavioural and cognitive-behavioural approaches) will encourage their clients to undertake extra-therapy activities between sessions.

Such activities, usually referred to as homework assignments, are viewed as particularly important within REBC. Given the difficulty that human beings typically experience as they attempt to adopt more rational personal philosophies, REBC theory holds that it is desirable for counselling clients to commit themselves to considerable work and practice in the service of this end. When clients in counselling devote effort to identifying and disputing their irrational beliefs on an independent basis, they will probably fare better (in terms of avoiding or dealing with new upsets) after their counselling has ended. Ellis (1983d) and Persons, Burns and Perloff (1988), in fact, have reported empirical data which suggest that clients who undertake homework assignments within cognitively oriented approaches to therapy achieve better outcomes than those who do not. Thus, rational emotive behavioural counsellors place considerable value on homework assignments due to their recognition that irrational beliefs are difficult to modify, and that it is desirable for clients to become able to function independently without interminable assistance from a mental health professional.

In order to increase the probability that homework assignments will be enacted between sessions, REB counsellors attempt to convey a rationale for carrying them out and will work collaboratively with clients to negotiate their design. At the earlier stages of treatment, counsellors will generally take a more active and directive role with respect to promoting and designing homework assignments; as counselling proceeds, however, this responsibility is ideally transferred to the client. Throughout therapy, counsellors will assist clients in conducting troubleshooting when difficulty is experienced in implementing particular homework assignments.

Personal qualities of effective rational emotive behavioural counsellors

Unfortunately, no research studies have been carried out to determine the personal qualities of effective rational emotive behavioural counsellors. Rational emotive behavioural theory, however, does put forward several hypotheses concerning this topic (Ellis, 1978), but it is important to regard these as both tentative and awaiting empirical study.

1. Since rational emotive behavioural counselling is fairly structured, its effective practitioners are usually comfortable with structure, but flexible enough to work in a less structured manner when the situation arises.
2. Rational emotive behavioural counsellors tend to be intellectually, cognitively, or philosophically inclined and become attracted to this approach to counselling because the approach provides them with opportunities fully to express this tendency.

3. Since rational emotive behavioural counselling is often conducted in a strong active–directive manner, its effective practitioners are usually comfortable operating in this mode. Neverthless, they have the flexibility to modify their interpersonal style with clients so that they provide the optimum conditions to facilitate client change.
4. Rational emotive behavioural counselling emphasises that it is important for clients to put their counselling-derived insights into practice in their everyday lives. As a result, effective rational emotive behavioural practitioners are usually comfortable with behavioural instruction and teaching, and with providing the active prompting that clients often require if they are to follow through on 'homework' assignments.
5. Effective rational emotive behavioural counsellors tend to have little fear of failure themselves. Their personal worth is not invested in their clients' improvement. They do not need their clients' love and/or approval and are thus not afraid of taking calculated risks if therapeutic impasses occur. They tend to accept both themselves and their clients as fallible human beings and are therefore tolerant of their own mistakes and of the irresponsible acts of their clients. They tend to have, or persistently work towards acquiring, a philosophy of high frustration tolerance, and do not get discouraged when clients improve at a slower rate than they desire.
6. Thus, effective rational emotive behavioural practitioners tend to score highly on most of the criteria of positive mental health outlined in Chapter 3, and serve as healthy role models for their clients.
7. Rational emotive behavioural counselling strives to be scientific, empirical, anti-absolutist and undevout in its approach to helping people overcome the obstacles to their goals (Ellis, 1978). Thus, its effective practitioners tend to show similar traits and are definitely not mystical, anti-intellectual or magical in their beliefs.
8. Rational emotive behavioural counselling advocates the use of techniques in a number of different modalities: cognitive, imagery, emotive, behavioural and interpersonal. Its effective practitioners are thus comfortable with a multi-modal approach to treatment and tend not to be people who like to stick rigidly to any one modality.

Finally, Ellis notes that some practitioners of rational emotive behavioural counselling often modify its preferred practice according to their own natural personality characteristics (Ellis, 1978). Thus, for example, some helpers practise rational emotive behavioural counselling in a slow-moving passive manner, do little disputing, and focus counselling on the relationship between them and their clients. Whether such modification of the preferred practice of rational emotive behavioural counselling is effective is a question awaiting systematic empirical enquiry.

    In the following three chapters we outline the practice of rational emotive behavioural counselling according to the following sequence: induction and assessment - promoting intellectual insight - promoting emotional insight -

termination. For the sake of clarity, we shall assume in these chapters that the client is seeking counselling help for one major psychological problem. We illustrate the application of REBC to an actual client problem by presenting the rational emotive behavioural counselling sequence in Chapter 9.

Chapter 5
Beginning Rational Emotive Behavioural Counselling

Overview

In this chapter, we deal with the beginnings of the rational emotive behavioural counselling process. We have assumed that counsellors will, at some point during the beginning phase of rational emotive behavioural counselling, assess clients' suitability for this type of counselling and have deemed it to be a suitable mode of helping for them. First, we discuss how clients can be inducted into REBC counselling. Then, we cover the basic elements and sequence of rational emotive behavioural assessment of clients' emotional and behavioural problems. We conclude the chapter by outlining some assessment methods that are particularly vivid in nature.

Inducting Clients into REB Counselling

When clients seek help from rational emotive behavioural counsellors they vary concerning how much they already know about the type of therapeutic process they are likely to encounter. Some may approach the counsellor because they know he or she is a practitioner of REBC, while others may know nothing about this method of counselling. In any event, many rational emotive behavioural counsellors consider that it is beneficial to explore clients' expectations for counselling at the outset of the process. Duckro, Beal and George (1979) have argued that it is important to distinguish between preferences and anticipations when expectations are assessed. Clients' preferences for counselling concern what kind of experience they want, while anticipations concern what service they think they will receive. Clients who have realistic anticipations for the rational emotive behavioural counselling process and have a preference for this process, in general require far less induction into rational emotive behavioural counselling than clients who have unrealistic anticipations of the process and/or preferences for a different type of therapeutic experience.

Induction procedures, in general, involve showing clients that rational emotive behavioural counselling is an active–directive, structured approach which is oriented to discussions about clients' present and future problems, and which requires clients to play an active role in the change process. Induction can take a number of different forms. First, counsellors may develop and use a number of pre-counselling role induction procedures where a typical course of rational emotive behavioural counselling is outlined and productive client behaviours are demonstrated (Macaskill and Macaskill, 1983). Secondly, counsellors may give a short lecture at the outset of counselling concerning the nature and process of rational emotive behavioural counselling. Thirdly, counsellors may employ induction-related explanations in initial counselling sessions using client problem material to illustrate how these problems may be tackled and to outline the respective roles of client and counsellor in rational emotive behavioural counselling.

Albert Ellis, in his therapeutic practice, tends not to initiate any special induction procedures before he focuses on one of his client's major psychological problems. He is prepared to correct any misconceptions about rational emotive behavioural counselling when it becomes clear, through problem-focused dialogue, that his client holds these. His clientele tend to be relatively psychologically sophisticated and thus may not require elaborate induction into rational emotive behavioural counselling. Howard Young (1984a), on the other hand, found through his work with lower-class clients of Huntington, West Virginia, USA, that specific induction procedures facilitated later problem-focused counselling. His clientele would often demand services outside the scope of rational emotive behavioural counselling and he developed a specific sequence for teaching clients the ground rules of counselling to obviate misunderstanding and future disappointment.

Young's sequence was as follows:

1. *Use a biographical data sheet* on which clients can state (among other things) the problems that bring them to counselling. This provides counsellors with a good idea concerning what given clients view as appropriate problems for counselling intervention.

2. *Ask the client what he or she expects from counselling.* This direct approach sometimes reveals startling misconceptions. For example, some of Young's clients gave answers ranging from 'a prescription for nerve pills' to 'the removal of warts.' The replies that clients give to this question often provide clear indications concerning how much induction-orien-ted education they will require before assessment is initiated. While Young (1984a) does not distinguish between anticipation- and preference-based expectations, it is often helpful to assess both at this phase of induction.

3. *Offer an example.* When it was clear that the client did require education about the counselling process, Young would offer a concrete example, often derived from work with another client and usually tailored to what

believed his client's own problem might be. Young (1984a, p. 41) provides the following as an illustration: 'Yesterday, a woman came in to see me because she felt depressed – as if life no longer mattered. It seems all her children are grown, her husband works all the time, and she no longer feels needed. I'm helping her figure out how to cope with the situation.'

4. *Advise the client that counselling is primarily a thinking endeavour.* Young found that teaching his lower-class clients that counselling could help them to 'look at problems in another light' helped to counteract their tendency to want to forget or ignore their problems. At this point, we find it helpful to add that thinking about things differently can often help one not only to feel differently but also to deal with life more constructively, i.e. we emphasise that rational emotive behavioural counselling is not just about thinking, but also about feeling and acting.

5. *Use a client-understood analogy.* At this point, Young would offer an analogy with which his clients could identify to reinforce other explanations about what takes place in counselling. We often tell our clients that going to see a rational emotive behavioural counsellor is like going to see a golf professional, as in the following dialogue:

Counsellor: Imagine that many, years ago your uncle taught you how to play golf, but taught you badly. Also imagine that you practised diligently the wrong strokes and only realised later that this way of playing was not helping you to lower your scores. If you wanted to improve your game whom would you consult?
Client: A golf coach.
Counsellor: What kind of help would you hope to get from him or her?
Client: Well, I would hope he would be able to diagnose my errors, point them out to me and show me how to put these right.
Counsellor: Right. And after he had shown you the correct strokes would that be sufficient for you to improve?
Client: No.
Counsellor: What more would be needed?
Client: I'd have to practise to learn the correct strokes.
Counsellor: Right, in order for them to become second nature you would have to practise. Now coming to see me is like going to see that golf pro. My skills are in helping you to diagnose where you've been going wrong psychologically and how to put this right. But just like a golf pro, I can't practise for you. Your major task is putting into practice in your daily life what you learn in counselling. Now, that process won't go smoothly, just as it won't in golf, and I'll be on hand to help you through the problems of practising. In doing so, you'll begin to learn how to diagnose and correct any future psychological problems you may have. But just like in golf where no one player consistently plays perfect golf, you won't become perfectly free from these problems, but you'll be able to deal with them.

It should be stressed that analogies are best tailored to the clients' interests. In this respect, it is often helpful to ask questions on biographical data forms about clients' hobbies and interests so that such specially tailored explanatory analogies can best be grasped by the client.

6. *Help the client understand what counselling cannot provide.* Young used to tell his clients that it is unlikely that counselling will cure all their problems so that they can live happily ever after. He also pointed out that 'sometimes therapy makes it easier to bear the problem that cannot be solved. Sometimes I explain it in terms of therapy helping one choose the lesser of two evils and learning to live with the results. It is important that therapy be explained to lower-class clients in this way, as in many cases the solution to their problems involves choosing between negative alternatives' (Young, 1984a, p. 41).

Rational emotive behavioural counsellors generally make the distinction between practical problems (e.g. poor housing, financial problems, etc.) and psychological problems (e.g. depression, anxiety, procrastination), and stress that rational emotive behavioural counselling aims to help people with their psychological problems. While it may encourage people to take productive steps to improve their housing conditions and financial situation by helping them overcome their psychological problems about such practical problems, it cannot directly alleviate the latter.

Finally, when working with individuals it is helpful to stress that rational emotive behavioural counselling cannot directly change other people who are not involved in the counselling process. However, it can help the client try to influence or persuade others to change, if that is deemed to be productive. For example, one client came for help with changing her boss, who was sexually harassing her. She was first helped to overcome her destructive anger towards him and then assisted in reviewing the relative merits of her behavioural options, most of which centred on influencing the boss to change. None of the options she tried worked in the desired manner and she decided to leave her job, very pleased with the help she received. The important point here is that early on in counselling she was helped to distinguish between what she could change (her behaviour) and what she could not change (his behaviour).

The principle here is that, as rational emotive behavioural counsellors working with individuals, you can help clients change only what is in their power to change - *their* thoughts, feelings and actions. If bad events remain unchanged in their lives, clients do have a choice concerning how to view these events. Under such conditions counsellors can help the client to be sorry and disappointed about such events (i.e. by thinking rationally about them and experiencing healthy negative emotions) rather than be miserable about them (by thinking irrationally about them and experiencing unhealthy negative emotions).

In conclusion, as a final point about induction, we have often found it helpful to encourage clients to commit themselves to a 'trial' of rational emotive behavioural counselling of about five sessions so that they can learn first-hand whether or not this approach to counselling will be helpful to them. In our experience, clients who agree to this arrangement will often become so engaged in the counselling process that they continue in treatment beyond their five-session trial.

Assessment in Rational Emotive Behavioural Counselling

As has been mentioned, some REB counsellors like to have their clients fill in a form which provides basic biographical information as well as information concerning their presenting problems. In Figure 5.1 the biographical information form routinely employed by counsellors at the Albert Ellis Institute for REBT in New York is presented as a representative example of such forms.

In addition, counsellors at the Institute routinely ask clients to fill out a Personality Data Form (Figure 5.2) which provides the counsellor with information concerning the irrational beliefs that are likely to underpin the client's problems. However, the use of this form is designed to supplement rather than to replace a thorough assessment of the client's problems.

Most REB counsellors like to structure the therapeutic process at the outset in order to emphasise that therapy will be problem-focused. For example, such questions as, 'What are you bothered most about?' and 'What is your major problem at this time?' are employed to encourage clients to adopt a problem-solving focus. Indeed, Albert Ellis routinely reads aloud the information provided by the client on Item 23 of the biographical information form and asks him or her to start talking about what is most bothersome among this list of problems.

Before proceeding to the assessment stage of counselling, the REBC practitioner often seeks an agreement with the client concerning the first problem to tackle. When this has been achieved, the therapist proceeds to help the client to understand his or her problems according to rational emotive behavioural counselling's ABC framework, where 'A' stands for an activating event or inferences about the activating event; 'B' stands for beliefs about the actual or inferred event; and 'C' stands for the emotional, behavioural and cognitive consequences of holding the belief at 'B'.

Assessment: basic elements

Because REB counselling is strongly cognitive, emotive and behavioural, it not only assesses clients' irrational beliefs, but also their unhealthy feelings and self-defeating behaviours. The usual rational emotive behavioural assessment process almost always includes the following:

1. Clients are helped to acknowledge and describe their unhealthy negative feelings – anxiety, depression, unhealthy anger and shame, and these are clearly differentiated from their healthy negative feelings – concern,

Date _____   Name _____
    mo.   day   yr.   (last)   (first)   (middle)

Consultation Center

Albert Ellis Institute for Rational Emotive Behavior Therapy
45 East 65th Street • New York, N. Y. 10021

Biographical Information Form

Instructions To assist us in helping you, please fill out this form as frankly as you can. You will save much time and effort by giving us full information. You can be sure that, like everything you say at the Institute, the facts on this form will be held in the strictest confidence and that no outsider will be permitted to see your case record without your written permission. PLEASE TYPE OR PRINT YOUR ANSWERS.

1. Date of birth:_____   Age: _____ Sex: M_____ F_____
              mo.   day   yr.

2. Address: _____   _____
              street   city   state   zip

3. Home phone: _____   Business phone: _____

4. Permanent address **(If different from above)** _____

_____

5. Who referred you to the Institute? **(check one)**

    _____ (1) self _____ (2) school or teacher _____ (3) psychologist or psychiatrist _____ (4) social agency

    _____ (5) hospital or clinic _____ (6) family doctor _____ (7) friend _____ (8) relative _____ (9) other

    (explain) _____ _____ _____

    Has this party been here? _____ Yes _____ No

6. Present marital status:

    _____ (1) never married _____(2) married now for first time _____(3) married now for second (or more) time

    _____ (4) separated _____ (5) divorced and not remarried _____ (6) widowed and not remarried

    Number of years married to present spouse _____ Ages of male children _____ Ages of female children _____

7. Years of formal education completed (circle number of years).

    1 2 3 4 5 6 7 8 9 10 11 12 13 14 15 16 17 18 19 20 more than 20

8. How religious are you? **(circle number on scale that best approximates your degree of religious belief):**

    very   average   atheist
    1 2 3 4 5 6 7 8 9

9. Mother's age: _____ If deceased, how old were you when she died? _____

10. Father's age: _____ If deceased, how old were you when he died? _____

11. If your mother and father separated, how old were you at the time? _____

12. If your mother and father divorced, how old were you at the time? _____

13. Total number of times mother divorced _____ Number of times father divorced _____

14. Number of living brothers _____ Number of living sisters _____

Figure 5.1: *Biographical information form.* (Reproduced with the permission of the Albert Ellis Institute for Rational Emotive Behavior Therapy (Albert Ellis Institute, 1968).)

15. Ages of living brothers _____   Ages of living sisters _____

16. I was child number _____ in a family of _____ children

17. Were you adopted? _____Yes _____No

18. What kind of treatment have you previously had for emotional problems?

    _____hours of individual therapy, spread over _____ years, ending _____ years ago,

19. Hours of group therapy _____ Months of psychiatric hospitalization _____

20. Are you undergoing treatment anywhere else now? _____Yes _____No

21. Number of times during past year you have taken antidepressants _____

22. Type of psychotherapy you have mainly had **(briefly describe method of treatment—e.g., dream analysis, free association, drugs, hypnosis, etc.)** _____

    _____

23. Briefly list (PRINT) your present main complaints, symptoms, and problems: _____

    _____

    _____

24. Briefly list any additional **past** complaints, symptoms, and problems: _____

    _____

    _____

25. Under what conditions are your problems worse? _____

    _____

    _____

26. Under what conditions are they improved? _____

    _____

    _____

27. List the things you like to do most, the kinds of things and persons that give you pleasure: _____

    _____

    _____

28. List your main assets and good points: _____

    _____

    _____

Figure 5.1: (continued)

29. List your main bad points: _____

30. List your main social difficulties: _____

31. List your main love and sex difficulties: _____

32. List your main school or work difficulties: _____

33. List your main life goals: _____

34. List the things about yourself you would most like to change: _____

35. List your chief physical ailments, diseases, complaints, or handicaps: ___

36. What occupation(s) have you mainly been trained for? _____

Present occupation _____ ____ Full time ____ Part time

37. Spouse's occupation _____ Full time ____ Part time

38. Mother's occupation _____ Father's occupation _____

39. Mother's religion _____ Father's religion _____

40. If your mother and father did not raise you when you were young, who did? _____

Figure 5.1: (continued)

41. Briefly describe the type of person your mother (or stepmother or person who substituted for your mother) was when you were a child and how you got along with her: _____

_____

_____

_____

42. Briefly describe the type of person your father (or stepfather or father substitute) was when you were a child and how you got along with him:_____

_____

_____

_____

43. If there were unusually disturbing features in your relationship to any of your brothers, briefly describe:

_____

_____

_____

44. If there were unusually disturbing features in your relationship to any of your sisters. briefly describe:

_____

_____

_____

45. Number of close male relatives who have been seriously emotionally disturbed: _____ Number that have been hospitalized for psychiatric treatment, or have attempted suicide: _____ Number of close female relatives who have been seriously emotionally disturbed: _____ Number that have been hospitalized for psychiatric treatment. or have attempted suicide: _____

46. Additional information that you think might be helpful

_____

_____

_____

_____

_____

_____

_____

_____

_____

_____

_____

_____

Figure 5.1: (continued)

Consultation Center
Albert Ellis Institute for REBT
45 East 65th Street, New York, NY 10021

Personality Data Form – Part 2

Instructions: Read each of the following items and circle after each one the word STRONGLY, MODERATELY, or WEAKLY to indicate how much you believe in the statement described in the item. Thus, if you strongly believe that it is awful to make a mistake when other people are watching, circle the word STRONGLY in item 1; and if you weakly believe that it is intolerable to be disapproved by others, circle the word WEAKLY in item 2. DO NOT SKIP ANY ITEMS. Be as honest as you can possibly be.

1. I believe that it is awful to make a mistake when other people are watching	STRONGLY	MODERATELY	WEAKLY
2. I believe that it is intolerable to be disapproved of by others	STRONGLY	MODERATELY	WEAKLY
3. I believe that it is awful for people to know certain undesirable things about one's family or one's background	STRONGLY	MODERATELY	WEAKLY
4. I believe that it is shameful to be looked down upon by people for having less than they have	STRONGLY	MODERATELY	WEAKLY
5. I believe that it is horrible to be the center of attention of others who may be highly critical	STRONGLY	MODERATELY	WEAKLY
6. I believe that it is terribly painful when one is criticized by a person one respects	STRONGLY	MODERATELY	WEAKLY
7. I believe that it is awful to have people disapprove of the way one looks or dresses	STRONGLY	MODERATELY	WEAKLY
8. I believe that it is very embarrassing if people discover what one really is like	STRONGLY	MODERATELY	WEAKLY
9. I believe that it is awful to be alone	STRONGLY	MODERATELY	WEAKLY

Figure 5.2 Personality data form (Ellis, 1968). (Reproduced with the permission of the Albert Ellis Institute for Rational Emotive Behavior Therapy. © Albert Ellis Institute, 1968b).

10. I believe that it is horrible if one does not have the love or approval of certain special people who are important to one   STRONGLY   MODERATELY   WEAKLY

11. I believe that one must have others on whom one can always depend for help   STRONGLY   MODERATELY   WEAKLY

Frustration

12. I believe that it is intolerable to have things go along slowly and not be settled quickly   STRONGLY   MODERATELY   WEAKLY

13. I believe that it's too hard to get down to work at things it often would be better for one to do   STRONGLY   MODERATELY   WEAKLY

14. I believe that it is terrible that life is so full of inconveniences and frustrations   STRONGLY   MODERATELY   WEAKLY

15. I believe that people who keep one waiting frequently are pretty worthless and deserve to be boycotted   STRONGLY   MODERATELY   WEAKLY

16. I believe that it is terrible if one lacks desirable traits that other people possess   STRONGLY   MODERATELY   WEAKLY

17. I believe that it is intolerable when other people do not do one's bidding or do not give one what one wants   STRONGLY   MODERATELY   WEAKLY

18. I believe that some people are unbearably stupid or nasty and that one must get them to change   STRONGLY   MODERATELY   WEAKLY

19. I believe that it is too hard for one to accept serious responsibility   STRONGLY   MODERATELY   WEAKLY

20. I believe that it is dreadful that one cannot get what one wants without making a real effort to get it   STRONGLY   MODERATELY   WEAKLY

21. I believe that things are too rough in this world and that therefore it is legitimate for one to feel sorry for oneself   STRONGLY   MODERATELY   WEAKLY

22. I believe that it is too hard to persist at many of the things one starts, especially when the going gets rough   STRONGLY   MODERATELY   WEAKLY

23. I believe it is terrible that life is so unexciting and boring   STRONGLY   MODERATELY   WEAKLY

24. I believe it is awful for one to have to discipline oneself   STRONGLY   MODERATELY   WEAKLY

Figure 5.2 (continued)

Injustice

25. I believe that people who do wrong things should suffer strong revenge for their acts — STRONGLY / MODERATELY / WEAKLY

26. I believe that wrong doers and Immoral people should be severely condemned — STRONGLY / MODERATELY / WEAKLY

27. I believe that people who commit unjust acts are bastards and that they should be severely punished — STRONGLY / MODERATELY / WEAKLY

Achievement

28. I believe that it is horrible for one to perform poorly — STRONGLY / MODERATELY / WEAKLY

29. I believe that it is awful if one fails at important things — STRONGLY / MODERATELY / WEAKLY

30. I believe that it is terrible for one to make a mistake when one has to make important decisions — STRONGLY / MODERATELY / WEAKLY

31. I believe that it is terrifying for one to take risks or to try new things — STRONGLY / MODERATELY / WEAKLY

Worth

32. I believe that some of one's thoughts or actions are unforgivable — STRONGLY / MODERATELY / WEAKLY

33. I believe that if one keeps failing at things one is a pretty worthless person — STRONGLY / MODERATELY / WEAKLY

34. I believe that killing oneself is preferable to a miserable life of failure — STRONGLY / MODERATELY / WEAKLY

35. I believe that things are so ghastly that one cannot help feel like crying much of the time — STRONGLY / MODERATELY / WEAKLY

36. I believe that it is frightfully hard for one to stand up for oneself and not give in too easily to others — STRONGLY / MODERATELY / WEAKLY

37. I believe that when one has shown poor personality traits for a long time, it is hopeless for one to change — STRONGLY / MODERATELY / WEAKLY

38. I believe that if one does not usually see things clearly and act well on them, one is hopelessly stupid — STRONGLY / MODERATELY / WEAKLY

39. I believe that it is awful to have no good meaning or purpose in life — STRONGLY / MODERATELY / WEAKLY

Figure 5.2 (continued)

Control

	STRONGLY	MODERATELY	WEAKLY
40. I believe that one cannot enjoy oneself today because of one's poor early life	STRONGLY	MODERATELY	WEAKLY
41. I believe that if one kept failing at important things in the past, one must inevitably keep failing in the future	STRONGLY	MODERATELY	WEAKLY
42. I believe that once one's parents train one to act and feel in certain ways, there is little one can do to act or feel better	STRONGLY	MODERATELY	WEAKLY
43. I believe that strong emotions like anxiety and rage are caused by external conditions and events and that one has little or no control over them	STRONGLY	MODERATELY	WEAKLY

Certainty

44. I believe it would be terrible if there were no higher being or purpose on which to rely	STRONGLY	MODERATELY	WEAKLY
45. I believe that if one does not keep doing certain things over and over again something bad will happen if one stops	STRONGLY	MODERATELY	WEAKLY
46. I believe that things must be in good order for one to be comfortable	STRONGLY	MODERATELY	WEAKLY

Catastrophizing

47. I believe that it is awful if one's future is not guaranteed	STRONGLY	MODERATELY	WEAKLY
48. I believe that it is frightening that there are no guarantees that accidents and serious illnesses will not occur	STRONGLY	MODERATELY	WEAKLY
49. I believe that it is terrifying for one to go to new places or meet a new group of people	STRONGLY	MODERATELY	WEAKLY
50. I believe that it is ghastly for one to be faced with the possibility of dying	STRONGLY	MODERATELY	WEAKLY

Figure 5.2 (continued)

sadness, healthy anger and disappointment. In doing so, REB counsellors frequently teach clients the rational emotive behavioural language of emotions and help them to distinguish between healthy and unhealthy negative emotions by helping them to identify and distinguish between rational and irrational beliefs.

2. Clients are helped to acknowledge and delineate their self-defeating behaviours (e.g. compulsions, addictions, phobias and procrastination) rather than to overemphasise idiosyncratic but non-deleterious behaviours (e.g. unusual devotion to socialising, sex, study or work).

3. They are asked to point out specific activating events in their lives that tend to occur just prior to their experienced disturbed feelings and behaviours.

4. Their rational beliefs that accompany their activating events, and that lead to constructive emotive and behavioural consequences, are assessed and discussed.

5. Their irrational beliefs that accompany their activating events and that lead to disturbed emotive and behavioural consequences are assessed and discussed.

6. Their irrational beliefs that involve absolutistic musts and grandiose demands on themselves, others, and the universe are particularly determined.

7. Their second-level irrational beliefs that tend to be derived from their absolutistic shoulds and musts - e.g. their 'awfulising', their 'low frustration tolerance', and their 'damning' of themselves and others - are also revealed.

8. Their irrational beliefs that lead to their disturbance about their disturbance - e.g. their anxiety about their anxiety and their depression about being depressed - are particularly revealed and discussed.

As these specialised components of REBC assessment are instituted, specific treatment plans are made, normally in close collaboration with clients, to work first on the most important and self-sabotaging emotional and behavioural symptoms that they present, and later on related and possibly less important symptoms. Rational emotive behavioural counsellors, however, always try to maintain an exceptionally open-minded, sceptical and experimental attitude towards clients and their problems, so that what at first seems to be their crucial and most debilitating ideas, feelings and actions may later be seen in a different light and the emphasis may be changed to working on other equally or more pernicious irrationalities that might not be evident during the early sessions.

REB counsellors, in general, spend little time gathering background information on their clients, although they may ask them to fill out forms designed to assess which irrational ideas they spontaneously endorse at the outset of counselling (Figure 5.2). Rather, they are likely to ask clients for a description of their major problem(s). As clients describe their problems,

REB counsellors intervene fairly early to break these down into their ABC components.

Assessment: basic sequence

REBC has an ABC model that it uses to assess clients' problems. To recap, A stands for an activating event (actual or inferred), B stands for the beliefs (rational or irrational) held by individuals about A, and C stands for emotional, behavioural and cognitive consequences of holding the beliefs at B.

In REBC, A and C are normally assessed before B, and are usually assessed in the order that the client reports. When A is assessed, REB counsellors usually encourage clients to provide a representative concrete example of the events, actual or inferred, that they are disturbed about. Clients are encouraged to be as specific as they can about A but not to go into unnecessary detail about the event. Clients sometimes jump from event to event or give unnecessary historical material relating to the event at hand. When this happens the counsellor should preferably interrupt them tactfully and bring them back to the original A, or the A which they now see as most relevant (known as the critical A).

C refers to the emotional, behavioural and cognitive consequences of the rational and irrational beliefs that are operative at B. Careful assessment of emotional Cs is advocated in REBC, since they serve as a major indicator of what type of evaluations are to be found at B. In this regard, it is important to reiterate that 'healthy' negative emotions are different from 'unhealthy' negative emotions (as discussed in Chapter 4). To review: emotions such as sadness, remorse, healthy anger and concern are termed healthy in REBC, in that they are deemed to stem from rational, preferential beliefs at B and encourage people to attempt to change, for the better, obnoxious situations at A. The 'unhealthy' versions of the above emotional states are depression, guilt, unhealthy anger and anxiety. These are deemed to stem from irrational, *mustur*batory beliefs at B, and tend to interfere with people's constructive attempts to change undesirable situations.

When emotional Cs are being assessed, it is important to bear in mind the following points. First, clients do not necessarily use affective terminology in the same way as REB counsellors do (as shown in Chapter 3). It is often helpful to inform them about the nature of the unique discriminations made between 'healthy' and 'unhealthy' negative emotional states, so that counsellor and client can come to use a shared emotional 'language.'

Secondly, emotional Cs are often chained together. For example, unhealthy anger is frequently chained to anxiety in that one can experience such anger to cover up feelings of inadequacy. And one can feel depressed after a threat to one's self-esteem – the 'anxiety–depression' chain (Wessler, 1981).

Thirdly, rational emotive behavioural counsellors are advised to realise that clients do not always want to change every 'unhealthy' negative emotion as defined by rational emotive behavioural theory; i.e. they may not see a particular 'unhealthy' emotion such as anger as being truly self-defeating. Thus, a good deal of flexibility and clinical acumen is called for in the assessment of emotional Cs to be targeted for change.

Fourthly, clients sometimes find it difficult to admit to themselves and/or to their counsellors that they experience certain emotions. This may be due to their belief that they are not supposed to have such feelings and/or that they are worthless for having them. In other words, such clients have second-order problems about their original feelings. If counsellors suspect that this is the case, they can ask the clients how they would feel if they did experience the emotion in question, thus switching their assessment strategy to the second-order problem.

Fifthly, clients often become emotional in counselling sessions and when this happens, counsellors have a good opportunity to assess the beliefs that underpin these expressions of affect as they occur. Thus, counsellors may ask clients a question such as the following: 'I see that you're feeling upset. What are you telling yourself *right now* to bring on that upset?'

Sixthly, as mentioned in Chapter 3, emotions can sometimes be blended rather than pure. Thus, clients talk about feeling 'hurt anger' or a 'guilty depression.' In such cases counsellors can either treat the blended emotion (e.g. 'hurt anger') as C, or separate it into its component parts – hurt and anger – and deal with each accordingly.

Finally, as we also mentioned in Chapter 3, clients' 'emotional problems' at C can be 'false', i.e. not germane to their real problems. It is difficult to determine this immediately in the assessment process and counsellors are urged to keep this in mind as a possibility and to ask themselves whether such emotions may mask serious problems. For example, one particular client complained of feeling depressed about her marriage. Assessment proceeded in the normal way, but the client was not really involved in the process. She was then asked, 'If you didn't feel depressed what would you feel?' She was taken aback and got quite scared in the session. It transpired that what she called 'depression' was really a numbness that served to protect her from feelings of anxiety about coping on her own.

Although we have chosen to highlight the assessment of emotional Cs, similar points can be made about the assessment of behavioural Cs. As noted earlier, withdrawal, procrastination, alcoholism and substance abuse are generally regarded as dysfunctional behaviours and related to irrational beliefs at B (Ellis, 1982a). Counsellors can thus regard such behaviours as Cs in their own right and thence proceed to an assessment of irrational beliefs at B that underpin them. Another strategy that is often helpful is to remember that such behaviour can be purposive (see Chapter 2) and may serve to protect clients from an emotional experience (such as anxiety) or encourage clients to obtain an emotional experience (e.g. pleasant sensations associated with being 'stoned'). Taking the example of procrastination, which often serves to protect clients from an emotional experience: it is fruitful to view such behaviour as the actualisation of an action tendency (see Chapter 2). The client might be taught about action tendencies and the feelings and beliefs that occasion them, and be asked to reflect on what possible feelings and beliefs might have promoted such behaviour. Also, the client might be shown that such behaviour is only one of a number of response options available to her in the given situation that she describes. Enquiries might then be directed towards possible emotional Cs that might be experienced if a more productive response option were chosen. Thus, the counsellor might say, 'If you decided to sit down to work on that essay rather than deciding to procrastinate, what might you have felt?.'

As a prelude to assessing B, some rational emotive behavioural counsellors like to employ a procedure known as *inference chaining* (Dryden, 1991a; Moore, 1983) in order to identify the particular aspect of A that serves to trigger clients' irrational beliefs, given that C is self-defeating. In conducting inference chaining, Moore (1983) advises that counsellors employ 'then what?' and 'why?' questions as a means of prompting clients to verbalise their inferences about problematic As. The following example illustrates how such questions were used to identify the specific inference that triggered a given client's irrational beliefs:

Client: So . . . I get very scared when I think about going to the supermarket.
Counsellor: What do you think you are scared of?
Client: I'm afraid I might start feeling faint while waiting in line to pay for my purchases. [Inference 1]
Counsellor: And if that happens, then what?
Client: Well . . . I'd panic!
Counsellor: Why?
Client: Because I might pass out. [Inference 2]
Counsellor: And if you did, then what?
Client: People would gather round me and think that I'm strange. [Inference 3]
Counsellor: And if they did?
Client: Oh, God! I just couldn't stand to have that happen!

In this example, 'then what?' questions are utilised to elicit further inferences in the chain. 'Why' questions are employed to prompt continued reporting of inferences when the client's reference to an emotional consequence ('. . . I'd panic!') threatens to derail the assessment process.

In our experience, clients sometimes appear to experience difficulty in responding to 'then what?' questions with further inferences. This potential difficulty can often be avoided or overcome by utilising assessment questions that are anchored to some variant of the client's target emotion (C):

Client: . . . I might pass out.
Counsellor: If you did, then what?
Client: Um . . . I'm not sure.
Counsellor: Well, what would be anxiety-provoking in your mind about that?
Client: Oh! People would gather round me and think that I'm strange.

It is noted that inference chaining may sometimes yield unexpected data of clinical importance, in terms of revealing additional Cs that were not clearly evident in a client's initial presentation of a problem. This type of outcome is illustrated below:

Counsellor: So, what was your major feeling here?
Client: I guess I was angry.
Counsellor: Angry about what? [The counsellor has obtained a particular C and is probing for A.]
Client: I was angry that my boyfriend didn't send me a birthday card. [Initial description of A]
Counsellor: And what was anger-provoking in your mind about that? [Probing to see if this is the most relevant aspect of A]
Client: Well . . . he promised me he would remember. He broke his promise! [Inference 1]
Counsellor: Okay – and what was anger-provoking about the fact that he broke his promise? [Probing for relevance of Inference 1]
Client: I felt that he didn't care enough about me. [Inference 2]
Counsellor: For the moment, let's assume that's true. What would be disturbing about that? [Probing for relevance of Inference 2]
Client: He might leave me. [Inference 3]
Counsellor: And if he did, then what? [Probing for relevance of Inference 3]
Client: I'd be all alone. [Inference 4]
Counsellor: And if you were alone? Then what? [Probing for relevance of Inference 4]
Client: Oh, that would be absolutely awful! I couldn't make it on my own!

In this example, the counsellor and client began the exchange with a focus upon the client's feeling of unhealthy anger. Inference chaining, however, revealed an aspect of A ('I'd be all alone') likely to be related to some other emotional C (in this case, probably anxiety). The counsellor is thus presented with two potential foci in terms of treatment, and has to make a decision as to whether to deal with the client's feeling of anger toward her boyfriend, or her anxiety connected to the prospect of being alone. This decision can be facilitated by obtaining feedback from the client as to the inference that is most relevant in the chain:

Counsellor: Okay, let's back up a minute. What would be most disturbing for you: the birthday card incident, the fact that your boyfriend doesn't care, being abandoned by your boyfriend, or being alone?
Client: Definitely being alone.

The above example also shows that, for the purposes of getting to B, the counsellor does not question the accuracy of the client's inferences, but treats them as if they are correct for the time being. In other dialogues clients may be encouraged to assume the worst about their inferences, so that again B can properly be assessed. Thus, with a client who is afraid to fly in an aeroplane because she assumes it might crash, the counsellor would not initially discuss with the client the relatively low probability of such an event ever occurring. Instead, the counsellor would encourage the client to assume (for the moment) that this event *will* occur. This leaves the way open for the client to express irrational beliefs about this eventuality, or to express further inferences that might be more relevant to her anxiety. In one particular case, the client was scared not about flying but about surviving a crash as a paraplegic!

After the counsellor has assessed adequately the unhealthy C and the A, he can then begin to assess B. This is frequently done by asking such questions as: 'What were you telling yourself to make yourself angry?'; 'What did that experience mean to you?'; or even 'What *must* were you telling yourself about the possibility of failure?' The important point here is for counsellors to employ a variety of questions to elicit clients' irrational beliefs rather than repeating questions that have not yielded statements of irrational beliefs.

In Chapter 3, we mentioned that irrational beliefs occur in the form of a premiss, e.g. 'I *must* pass my exam' and a derivative, e.g. 'I'm no good if I fail my exam.' The premiss of irrational beliefs occurs in the form of absolute 'musts', 'shoulds', 'have-to's', etc., whereas irrational derivatives may represent examples of 'awfulising', 'low frustration tolerance' or 'damnation.' When assessing irrational beliefs, we find it helpful, if possible, to assess both the premiss and associated derivatives. While Ellis seems to prefer to target 'musts' as a priority for assessing irrational beliefs, he sometimes switches to an assessment of irrational derivatives when 'must assessment' is not productive.

When irrational beliefs are assessed, clients are helped to see the link between these irrational beliefs and their self-defeating consequences at C. Some rational emotive behavioural counsellors like to give a short lecture at this point on the role of the 'musts' in emotional disturbance, and how they can be distinguished from 'preferences'. Ellis, for example, often uses the following teaching dialogue:

Ellis: Imagine that you prefer to have a minimum of £11 in your pocket at all times and you discover you have only £10. How will you feel?

Client: Frustrated.

Ellis: Right. Or you'd feel concerned or sad, but you wouldn't kill yourself. Right?

Client: Right.

Ellis: OK. Now this time imagine that you absolutely *have* to have a minimum of £11 in your pocket at all times. You must have it, it is a necessity. You *must*, you *must*, you *must*, have a minimum of £11, and again you look and you find you have only £10. How will you feel?

Client: Very anxious.

Ellis: Right – or depressed. Right. Now remember it's the same £11 but a different belief. OK, now this time you still have that same belief. You *have* to have a minimum of £11 at all times, you *must*. It's absolutely *essential*. But this time you look in your pocket and find that you've got £12. How will you feel?

Client:	Relieved, content.
Ellis:	Right. But with that same belief - you have to have a minimum of £11 at all times - something will soon occur to you to scare you shitless. What do you think that would be?
Client:	What if I lose £2?
Ellis:	Right. What if I lose £2, what if I spend £2, what if I get robbed? That's right. Now the moral of this model - which applies to all humans, rich or poor, black or white, male or female, young or old, in the past or in the future, assuming that humans are still human - is: People make themselves miserable if they don't get what they think they must, but they are also panicked when they do - because of the must. For even if they have what they think they must, they could always lose it.
Client:	So I have no chance to be happy when I don't have what I think I must - and little chance of remaining unanxious when I do have it?
Ellis:	Right! Your *must*urbation will get you nowhere - except depressed or panicked!

We have stressed that an important goal of the assessment stage is to help clients distinguish between their primary problems (e.g. depression, anxiety, withdrawal, addiction) and their secondary problems, that is, their problems about their primary problems (e.g. depression about depression, anxiety about anxiety, shame about withdrawal, and guilt about addiction).[1] Rational emotive behavioural counsellors often assess secondary problems before primary problems because these often require prior therapeutic attention - since, for example, clients frequently find it difficult to focus on their original problem of anxiety when, for example, they are blaming themselves severely for being anxious. Secondary problems are assessed in the same manner as primary problems. If such second-order problems are identified it is important for the counsellor to help the client to understand why such problems are assessed and targeted for change *before* the client's primary problems. For example, a client may be shown that if she is guilty about her anger, she will be less successful at working on and overcoming her anger problem while she is guilty about it. However, there are occasions when clients will not accept this rationale despite the counsellor's explanations. A guiding rule under these conditions is for the counsellor to work at a level that the client will accept.

Three other points relevant to the assessment stage of REBC bear mention. First, counsellors are advised to be alert to problems in *both* major areas of disturbance, i.e. ego and discomfort disturbance. In particular, ego and discomfort disturbance often interact and careful assessment is required to disentangle one from the other. Secondly, REB counsellors pay particular attention to other ways that humans perpetuate their psychological problems and attempt to assess these carefully in counselling. Thus, humans often seek to defend themselves from threats to their ego and sense of comfort. Counsellors are often aware that much dysfunctional behaviour is defensive, and help their clients to identify the irrational beliefs that underlie such defensive dysfunctional behaviour. In addition, psychological problems are

---

[1] Secondary problems are sometimes referred to as meta-problems and primary problems as original problems.

sometimes perpetuated because the person defines their consequences as payoffs. These payoffs also require careful assessment if productive therapeutic strategies are to be implemented. Finally, during the assessment process, counsellors are also concerned with correcting any misconceptions that clients may have about the therapeutic enterprise. As in induction procedures, counsellors endeavour to show their clients that REB counselling is a form of help that is problem-focused and educational in nature, and that counsellors will often adopt an active and directive approach. Counsellors also encourage clients to see that their initial task is to learn to focus on the cognitive determinants of their problems and, in particular, to learn to search for absolute musts and their derivatives when they are disturbed at C.

Vivid Assessment Methods

Effective rational emotive behavioural counselling depends initially on the counsellor gaining a clear understanding of the client's problems in cognitive, emotional and behavioural terms, and the contexts in which the client's problems occur. To a great extent the counsellor is dependent on the client's oral reports to help him gain such an understanding. It is in this area that many obstacles to progress may appear. Some clients have great difficulty identifying and/or accurately labelling their emotional experiences. Other clients are in touch with and able to report their emotions, but find it hard to relate these to activating events, either external or internal. Yet a further group of clients is easily able to report problematic activating events and emotional experiences, but has difficulty seeing how these may relate to mediating cognitions. Vivid methods, i.e. those that are rich, stimulating and arousing, can be used in a variety of ways to overcome such obstacles to a valid and reliable assessment of client problems.

Vividness in portraying activating events

With some clients, traditional assessment procedures through oral dialogue do not always yield the desired information. When this occurs, rational emotive behavioural counsellors often use imagery. They ask clients to conjure up evocative images of activating events. Such evocative imagery often stimulates the client's memory concerning his or her emotional reactions, or indeed in some instances leads to the re-experiencing of these reactions in the session. While focusing on such images, the client can also begin to gain access to cognitive processes below the level of awareness, which cannot be easily reached through oral dialogue.

One particularly effective use of imagery in the assessment of client problems is that of bringing future events into the present. This is illustrated by the following exchange with a client who was terrified that her mother might die, which led her to be extremely unassertive with the mother.

Counsellor: So you feel you just can't speak up to her. Because if you did, what might happen?

Client: Well, she might have a fit.

Counsellor: And what might happen if she did?

Client: She might have a heart attack and die.

Counsellor: Well, we know that she is a fit woman, but let's go along with your fear for the moment. Okay,?

Client: Okay.

Counsellor: What if she did die?

Client: I just can't think . . . I . . . I'm sorry.

Counsellor: That's okay. I know this is difficult, but I really think it would be help-ful if we could get to the bottom of things. Okay? (Client nods). Look, Marjorie, I want you to imagine that your mother has just died this morning. Can you imagine that? (Client nods and begins to shake). What are you experiencing?

Client: When you said my mother was dead I began to feel all alone like there was no one to care for me, no one I could turn to.

Counsellor: And if there is no one who cares for you, no one you can turn to?

Client: Oh God! I know I couldn't cope on my own.

Instructing clients vividly to imagine something that has been warded off often leads to anxiety itself. It is important to process this anxiety as it is sometimes related to the client's central problem. Issues like fear of loss of control, phrenophobia (fear of going mad) and extreme discomfort anxiety are often revealed when this anxiety is fully assessed. However, some clients do find it difficult to imagine events spontaneously and require counsellor assistance.

Although imagery is now routinely used in cognitive-behavioural coun-selling (e.g. Lazarus, 1984), there has been little written on how counsellors can stimulate clients' imagery processes. We have used a number of vivid methods to try to help clients utilise their potential for imagining events.

Vivid, connotative counsellor language

One effective way of helping clients to use their imagery potential is for the counsellor to use rich, colourful and evocative language while aiding clients to set the scene. Unless the counsellor has gained prior diagnostic informa-tion, he or she is sometimes uncertain about which stimuli in the activating event are particularly related to the client's problem. Thus, it is best to give clients many alternatives. For example, with a socially anxious client one of us (WD) proceeded thus after attempting to get him to use his own potential for imagery, without success:

Counsellor: So at the moment we are unclear about what you are anxious about. What I'd like to suggest is that we use your imagination to help us. I will help you set the scene based on what we have already discussed. However, since we have yet to discover detailed factors, some of the things I say might not be relevant. Will you bear with me and let me know when what I say touches a nerve in you?

Client:	Okay.
Counsellor:	Fine. Just close your eyes and imagine you are about to walk into the dance. You walk in and some of the guys there glance at you. You can see the smirks on their mocking faces and one of them blows you a kiss. (Here the counsellor is testing out a hypothesis based on previously gained information.) You start to *seethe* inside and . . .
Client:	Okay, when you said I was starting to seethe, that struck a chord. I thought I can't let them get away with that, but if I let go I'll just go berserk. I started feeling anxious.
Counsellor:	And if you went berserk?
Client:	I couldn't show my face in there again.
Counsellor:	What would happen then?
Client:	I don't know I . . . It's funny – the way I see it I would never go out again.

Here, words like 'smirks', 'mocking', 'blows' and 'seethe' were deliberately used in an attempt to stimulate the client's imagination. It is also important for the counsellor to vary his or her tone so that this matches the language employed.

Photographs

We have at times asked clients to bring to interviews photographs of significant others or significant places. These are kept on hand to be used at relevant moments in the assessment process. We have found the use of photographs particularly helpful when the client is discussing an event in the past that is still bothering him or her. Thus, for example, one client who spoke without feeling about being rejected by his father, who died seven years previously, broke down in tears when asked to look at a picture of him and his father standing apart from one another. Feelings of hurt and anger, with their associated cognitions, were expressed, which enabled counsellor and client to move on to the disputing stage.

Other mementoes

In a similar vein, we have sometimes asked clients to bring in mementoes to counselling sessions. These may include pictures they have drawn, paintings that have meaning for them and poems written either by themselves or by other people. The important point is that these mementoes are to be related to issues that the client is working on in counselling. A roadblock to assessment was successfully overcome with one client when she was asked to bring in a memento that reminded her of her mother. She brought in a bottle of perfume that her mother was accustomed to wearing. When she was asked to smell the perfume at a point in counselling when the assessment process, through oral dialogue, was again breaking down, the client was helped to identify feelings of jealousy toward her mother, which she experienced whenever her mother left her to go out socialising. Moreover, the client was ashamed of such feelings. This issue was centrally related to her presenting problem of depression.

Another client was depressed about losing her boyfriend. It proved difficult to help her to identify any related mediating cognitions through traditional assessment procedures. Several tentative guesses on the counsellor's part also failed to pinpoint relevant cognitive processes. She was then asked to bring to her next session anything that reminded her of her ex-boyfriend. She brought in a record of a popular song that had become known to them as 'our song.' When the song was played at an appropriate point in the interview, the client began to sob and expressed feelings of abandonment, hurt and fear for the future. Again, a vivid method had unearthed important assessment material where traditional methods had failed.

It should be noted from the above examples that quite often such dramatic methods lead to the expression of strong affective reactions in the session. This is often an important part of the process because such affective reactions are gateways to the identification of maladaptive cognitive processes that are difficult to identify through more traditional methods of assessment.

The empty chair technique

Rational emotive behavioural counselling embodies theoretically consistent eclecticism, whereby techniques are borrowed from other counselling approaches for purposes consistent with rational emotive behavioural theory. Thus, we have sometimes used the empty chair technique, popularised by gestalt therapists. For example, traditional assessment methods did not reveal important clinical material with a client who suffered from tension headaches after visiting her mother. She was thus encouraged to imagine that her mother was sitting in an empty chair that was placed before her and then invited to disclose her feelings to her mother. An example follows:

Client:	I feel numb when I'm in your presence . . .
Counsellor:	Now sit in the empty chair and talk as your mother to yourself.
Client (as Mother):	You're such a child. You've got no backbone. Never have.
Counsellor:	Now reply to her from your chair.
Client:	Damn it. You're always criticising me. I hate you.

This technique demonstrates that the client felt angry with her mother. This discovery led to a discussion about her being scared to express negative feelings towards her mother in case her mother disowned her completely.

The 'Interpersonal nightmare technique'

This technique may be best used with clients who are able to identify only sketchily an anticipated 'dreaded' event involving other people, but are neither able to specify in any detail the nature of the event, nor how they would react if the event were to occur. First the client is given a homework assignment to imagine the 'dreaded' event. He or she is told to write a brief segment of a play about it, specifying the exact words that the participants would use. The client is encouraged to give full rein to imagination while focusing on what he or she fears might happen. One example will suffice. The following scenario was developed by a 55-year-old woman with alcohol problems who was terrified of making errors at the office where she worked as a typist.

Scene: Boss's office where he sits behind a very large desk. He has found out that one of the typists has inadvertently filed a letter wrongly, and sends for her. She comes in and is made to stand in front of the boss.

Boss: Have you anything to say in this matter?

Typist (me): Only that I apologise and will be more careful in the future.

Boss: What do you mean by saying you will be more careful in the future – what makes you think you have a future? (At this point he starts banging on the desk.) I have never yet met anyone less competent or less suited to the job than you are. You mark my words, I will make life so uncomfortable for you that you will leave. When I took over this job I intended to have the people I wanted working for me and you are not on that list. I have already got rid of two typists, and I shall see that you are the third. Now get out of my office you stupid, blundering fool and remember I shall always be watching you and you will never know when I shall be behind you.

The scene was reviewed with the client, and she was asked to describe the tone in which she thought her boss would make these statements and to identify which words the boss would emphasise. Arrangements were then made for a local actor who was the same age as the boss to enact the scene realistically on cassette. In the next session the client was instructed to visualise the room in which the encounter might take place. She briefly described the room, paying particular attention to where her boss would be sitting and where she would be standing. She was then played the cassette, which evoked strong feelings of fear of being physically harmed and humiliated. Again, important data had been collected which traditional assessment procedures had failed to uncover.

Rational-emotive behavioural problem-solving

Knaus and Wessler (1976) described a method which they called rational-emotive problem-solving (REPS). This method involves the counsellor creating conditions in the counselling session that approximate to those the client encounters in his or her everyday life and which give rise to emotional problems. Knaus and Wessler contend that this method may be used in either a planned or impromptu fashion, and is particularly valuable when clients experience difficulty in identifying emotional experiences and related cognitive processes through oral dialogue with their counsellors. One of us (WD) employed this method with a male client who reported difficulty in acting assertively in his life, and claimed not to be able to identify the emotions and thoughts that inhibited the expression of assertive responses. During the session, WD began to search around for his pouch of pipe tobacco. Finding it empty, he interrupted the client and asked him if he would drive to town and purchase his favourite tobacco, adding that if he hurried he could return for the last five minutes of the interview. He immediately got up, took the money, and walked out of the office towards his car! WD rushed after him, brought him back into the office, and his reactions to this simulated experience were processed.

It is clear that this technique must be used with therapeutic judgement and that its use may threaten or even destroy the therapeutic alliance between client and counsellor. However, since rational emotive behavioural counsellors value risk-taking they are often prepared to use such techniques when more traditional and less risky methods have failed to bring about therapeutic improvement. It is further important, as Beck et al. (1979) have stressed, for the counsellor to ask the client for the latter's honest reactions to this procedure, to ascertain whether it may have future therapeutic value for the client. When a client indicates that he or she has found the rational emotive behavioural problem-solving method unhelpful, the counsellor is advised then to explain the rationale for attempting such a procedure, and disclose that he or she intended no harm but was attempting to be helpful. Normally, clients respect such disclosures and in fact the counsellor, in doing so, provides a useful model for the client: namely that it is possible to acknowledge errors non-defensively without damning oneself. However, with this method, it is apparent that counsellors cannot realistically disclose their rationale in advance of initiating the method, since this would detract from its potential therapeutic value.

Paradoxical counsellor actions

This method is often best used when clients, through their actions, communicate messages to the counsellor about themselves based on irrational beliefs. For example, WD once saw a female client who experienced a lot of rheumatic pain but had an attitude of low frustration tolerance toward it. Her behaviour in sessions indicated the attitude: 'I am a poor soul, feel sorry for me.' This prompted WD to adopt an overly sympathetic and diligent stance towards her. Thus, at the beginning of every, session he treated her as if she could hardly walk and escorted her by arm to her chair and made frequent enquiries about her comfort. This eventually prompted her to make statements like: 'Don't treat me like a child', 'I can cope', 'It's not as bad as all that', etc. WD then helped her to identify some of her implicit irrational messages. Whenever she began to lapse back into her self-pitying attitude, WD began to behave in an overly solicitous manner again, which provided a timely reminder for her to attend to the behavioural components of her philosophy of low frustration tolerance, and then to the philosophy itself.

Using the counsellor–client relationship

Wessler (1984) has written that it is important for the rational emotive behavioural counsellor to enquire about the nature of the client's reactions to him or her, that is, to examine some of the client's here-and-now beliefs. Little has been written in the rational emotive behavioural literature about this approach, and thus relatively little is known about its potential as a framework for identifying irrational beliefs. Wessler (1984) also advocates that counsellors give clients frank feedback about the clients' impact on them, and explore whether clients have a similar impact on other people. Such generalisations must of course be made with caution, but such discussion is often a stimulus for clients to become more sensitive to their impact on other people, and often leads them to ask other people about their interpersonal impact (Anchin and Kiesler, 1982).

The advantage of using the counsellor–client relationship in this way is that it provides both parties with an opportunity to process the client's beliefs in an immediate and often vivid fashion. For example, one particular client who complained of loneliness had the habit of putting his feet up on his counsellor's coffee table. The counsellor did not mention this at first, but later on, when he felt irritated about the client's behaviour, he disclosed these feelings and wondered if other people had similar reactions to him. The counsellor suggested that he get some feedback from other people. The client did so and reported that other people reported the same reactions as the counsellor. This led to a discussion concerning his implicit beliefs that underpinned such soundly aversive behaviour and the following irrational belief was identified: 'I must be able to do what I want in social affairs without being criticised.' This belief helped to explain why this client had no friends.

Dreams

Although Albert Ellis once wrote a regular column for Penthouse magazine, providing interpretations of readers' dreams inspired by REBC theory, rational emotive behavioural counsellors are not generally noted for using dream material. However, there is no good reason why dream material cannot be used in rational emotive behavioural counselling as long as it does not predominate in the therapeutic process and the counsellor has a definite purpose in mind in using it.

Freeman (1981, pp. 228-9) has outlined a number of further guidelines for the use of dreams for assessment purposes:

1. The dream needs to be understood in thematic rather than symbolic terms.
2. The thematic content of the dream is idiosyncratic to the dreamer and must be viewed within the context of the dreamer's life.
3. The specific language and imagery are important to the meaning.
4. The affective responses to the dreams can be seen as similar to the dreamer's affective responses in waking situations.
5. The particular length of the dream is of less import than the content.
6. The dream is a product of, and the responsibility of, the dreamer.
7. Dreams can be used when the patient appears stuck in counselling.

WD inadvertently stumbled on the usefulness of dream material for assessment purposes when working with a 28-year-old depressed student who would frequently reiterate: 'I'm depressed and I don't know why.' WD had virtually exhausted all the assessment methods he knew, including those described in this chapter, to help her identify depressogenic thoughts in situations where she experienced depression, but without success. In a desperate last attempt, he asked her if she could remember any of her dreams, not expecting in the least that this line of inquiry would prove fruitful. To his surprise she said yes, she did have a recurring dream. In this dream she saw herself walking alone along a river bank, and when she peered into the river, she saw a reflection of herself as a very old woman. This image filled her with extreme sadness and depression. On further discussion she said that she believed that this dream meant that she had no prospect of finding any happiness in her life, either in love relationships or in her career, and that she was doomed to spend her years alone, ending up as a sad, pathetic old woman. This account of the dream and subsequent discussion of its meaning enabled WD to help her identify a number of irrational beliefs which provided the focus for subsequent cognitive restructuring.

Daydreams may also provide important material for assessment purposes. For some people, particular daydreams occur in response to and as compensation for a negative activating event. Thus, one client reported having the daydream of establishing a multinational corporation after failing to sell insurance to prospective customers. The use of such daydreams by clients may not necessarily be dysfunctional, but may impede them, as in the above example, from getting to the core of their problems. Often, daydreams are an expression of our hopes and aspirations, and we have found it valuable to ask clients not only about the content of such material but also what would stop them from actualising their goals. Much important assessment material is gathered in this manner, in particular concerning ideas of low frustration tolerance.

In vivo counselling sessions

Sacco (1981) has outlined the value of conducting counselling sessions in real-life settings in which clients experience emotional difficulties. We have found moving outside the interview room to such settings particularly useful in gaining assessment material when traditional methods have failed to provide such data. For example, WD once saw a male student who complained of avoiding social situations. He did so in case others would see his hands tremble. Traditional assessment methods yielded no further useful data. To overcome this treatment impasse, WD suggested to him that they needed to collect more data and they eventually conducted a counselling session in a coffee shop, where he was asked to go and get two cups of coffee. He refused because he feared that his hands might tremble, but WD firmly persisted with his request. The client was able to identify a stream of negative cognitions on his way from the table to the service counter. He returned without the coffees but with valuable information, which was processed later in WD's office. It is important for counsellors to explain their rationale for conducting *in vivo* sessions in advance in order to gain client cooperation. In addition, obtaining clients' reactions to these sessions is often helpful particularly if *in vivo* sessions are planned for use later in the therapeutic process.

Some cautions about the use of vivid methods in rational emotive behavioural counselling

In this chapter we have introduced the concept of using vivid methods in rational emotive behavioural counselling and will elaborate on the concept in the chapters on 'Promoting intellectual insight' and 'Promoting emotional rational insight'. However, we wish at this stage to outline some cautions about using such methods in rational emotive behavioural counselling:

1. It is important for counsellors to determine the impact on clients of introducing vivid methods into the therapeutic process. Thus, using the guidelines of Beck et al. (1979) it is perhaps wise for the counsellor to ask the client at various points to give frank feedback concerning the methods and activities used. While the counsellor may not always agree not to use such techniques just because a client has a negative reaction to them, clients' negative reactions to particular procedures should be obtained and understood.

2. It is important in the use of vivid and dramatic techniques not to overload the client. One vivid and dramatic method carefully introduced into the counselling session at an appropriate time is much more likely to be effective than several dramatic methods employed indiscriminately in a session.

3. It is also important that rational emotive behavioural counsellors be clear about the rationale for using vivid methods, and not see their use as a goal in itself. The important thing to remember is that vivid methods are to be used as a vehicle for facilitating assessment and promoting client attitude change, and not to make the therapeutic process more stimulating for the

counsellor. It is also extremely important to ascertain what the client has learned from the vivid methods the counsellor has employed. The client will not magically come to the conclusion the counsellor wants him or her to. It is also important that counsellors do not promote 'false' change in their clients. Change is 'false' when the client feels better as a result of some of these vivid methods but does not get better. Ellis (1972) has written an important article on such a distinction. Thus, counsellors should invariably ask questions like: 'What have you learned from doing this vivid method?' and 'How can you strengthen this learning experience for yourself outside counselling?'

4. Dramatic and vivid methods are not suitable for all clients. They are particularly helpful for those clients who use intellectualisation as a defence and/or who use verbal dialogue to tie rational emotive behavioural counsellors in knots. Although there are no data at the moment to support the following hypothesis, we would speculate that it is inadvisable to use dramatic and vivid methods with clients who have overly dramatic and histrionic personalities. It is perhaps more appropriate to assist such clients to reflect in a calm and undramatic manner on their experiences than to overstimulate an already highly stimulated personality.

With these words of caution, we leave the issue of assessment and consider the issue of promoting intellectual rational insight in the following chapter.

Chapter 6
Promoting Intellectual Rational Insight

Overview

In this chapter, we deal with issues concerning the promotion of intellectual rational insight. First, we distinguish between two forms of rational insight: intellectual and emotional. Then we cover standard and vivid methods of disputing irrational beliefs (premisses and derivatives) which are designed to help clients achieve intellectual insight. For each disputing method we include some indications for its use and contraindications against its use. We conclude the chapter by discussing various homework aids that clients can use to facilitate the process of achieving intellectual rational insight.

Rational Insight: Intellectual and Emotional

Once the client can see clearly and agree that his or her emotional or behavioural problem of C is based on an irrational belief of B, and that in order to get over this problem the client needs to change the irrational belief, then the therapeutic stage is set for the counsellor to help the client to change this belief. The counsellor tries to effect this change by disputing the client's belief, i.e. asking for evidence to support or refute it. The major goal of the disputing process at this stage of counselling is to help the client understand and acknowledge that there is no evidence that exists to support the irrational belief but that there *is* evidence to support its rational equivalent. When the client can acknowledge this – i.e. see that it is true – then it is assumed that she has achieved intellectual rational insight, which is defined here as 'weak and occasional conviction that an irrational belief is false and a rational belief is true'. Here the rational belief is lightly and occasionally held. Intellectual rational insight, in general, does not lead to significant emotional and behavioural change. In this chapter we describe rational emotive behavioural techniques designed to help clients achieve intellectual rational insight.

Intellectual rational insight is distinguished from emotional rational insight, which is defined here as 'strong and frequent conviction that an irrational belief is false and a rational belief is true'. Here the rational belief is strongly and frequently held. Emotional rational insight does often lead to significant emotional and behavioural change. In the next chapter we consider rational emotive behavioural techniques designed to help clients move from intellectual to emotional rational insight. At this point, it should be noted that intellectual rational insight very frequently precedes emotional rational insight. It is extremely rare for a client to relinquish an irrational belief and immediately believe in its rational alternative with such conviction that he or she will be able to act on it straight away.

Disputing Irrational Beliefs

When disputing irrational beliefs, rational emotive behavioural counsellors often attempt to engage their clients in a Socratic dialogue. This involves asking clients questions about the validity of their irrational beliefs, helping them to see why their wrong answers are incorrect, and then asking again for evidence supporting the validity of the same irrational belief. This process is continued until the client can acknowledge that there exists no evidence in favour of the irrational belief, but that evidence does exist in favour of the rational belief. In other words, the process continues until the client achieves intellectual rational insight.

Debating and discriminating

Disputing involves two major activities: debating and discriminating (Phadke, 1982). Debating consists of the counsellor asking a variety of questions designed to help the client examine the validity of his or her irrational belief. Questions that are frequently employed include: 'Where is the evidence that . . .?'; 'Where is the law of the universe that . . .?'; 'Where is the proof that . . .?'; 'How does it follow that . . .?' Discriminating involves the counsellor helping the client to distinguish clearly between a rational belief (want, preference, desire, etc.) and an irrational belief (must, absolute should, have-to, etc.). These two activities are frequently used in concert as the counsellor strives to teach the client the differences between rational and irrational beliefs, and that there exists no evidence in favour of irrational beliefs. An example of this process follows:

Counsellor: So you can see that your anxiety is based on your belief that you must achieve, in the academic arena anyway, whatever you set your sights on?

Client: Yes.

Counsellor: So if you want to get over your anxiety, what would it be advisable for you to change?

Client: That belief.

Counsellor: Right. So now I'm going to ask you some questions to help you assess the validity of that belief. Why *must* you achieve whatever you set your sights on? (Debating intervention).

Client: Because it's important to me to do so.

Counsellor: No, that's why it's desirable. Note that I didn't ask you the question why is it desirable for you to achieve your academic goals but why do you absolutely have to do so. Can you see the difference between your belief 'I want to achieve my academic goals' and your belief 'I must achieve my academic goals'? (Discriminating intervention).

Client:- Not really.

Counsellor: Well, the belief 'I want to achieve my academic goals' is relative. It allows for the possibility that you won't achieve them. That belief, if fully stated, is really: 'I want to achieve my goals, but there is no law in the universe which states that I absolutely have to.' Whereas the belief 'I absolutely have to achieve my goals', is an absolute one. If that belief were true there would be no way for you to fail. That's the difference. Do you see that?

Client: Yes, I do.

Counsellor: Fine, but I want to be sure that I've made myself clear. Can you put into your own words the differences between the two beliefs?

Client: Well, my belief 'I want to achieve my goals' is an expression of what's important to me, but doesn't mean that I necessarily will achieve them. The belief 'I must achieve my goals' means that no matter what, I will achieve them.

Counsellor: That's right. Now let me ask you again. Where's the evidence that you *must* achieve what it's important for you to achieve? (Debating intervention).

Client: There isn't any.

Counsellor: That's it, and if you really work on convincing yourself that there is no evidence that you must achieve your goals, and stick rigorously with your rational belief that you really want to achieve them but don't have to, then you'll still be concerned about failing, but not anxious about it. And that concern will motivate you to try your best, whereas if you do as some of my clients do, jump to 'It doesn't matter if I pass or fail' then (a) you'll be lying to yourself because you really do care, and (b) you won't be motivated to try to do your best, since it won't matter to you.

Client: So desire is helpful and the *must* will lead to anxiety, which will interfere with me achieving my goals.

Counsellor: Yes, and indifference?

Client: That won't help me either.

Note from this exchange that when it is clear that a client does not understand the difference between his rational and irrational beliefs, the counsellor gives a brief explanation to clarify the difference between the two beliefs. Rational emotive behavioural counsellors routinely employ Socratic disputing and didactic explanation where appropriate. In this exchange the counsellor does not persist in using a strategy (i.e. Socratic disputing) which does not appear to help the client. When the counsellor uses a didactic explanation to clarify a rational concept, note that his explanation is brief and concise and that he requests feedback from the client that the latter understands the difference between a rational belief and an irrational belief by asking the client to state his understanding of this point in his own words.

Note also that the counsellor helps the client to see the links between B and C. He stresses that the client's irrational belief leads to anxiety and that his rational belief will lead to concern – a healthy negative emotion which is more likely to encourage the client to reach his goals than the unhealthy negative emotion of anxiety. This is an important point. When disputing clients' irrational beliefs it is often desirable to help them understand that rational alternatives to these irrational beliefs will lead to less debilitating negative emotions, and will often encourage clients to persist in goal-directed activities and to make a constructive adjustment when these goals can no longer be achieved. On this latter point it is likely that the client would feel depressed if he did not achieve his academic goals and clung to his irrational belief, whereas if he adhered to his rational belief in a rigorous manner he would feel sad and disappointed about his future. Sadness and disappointment would very likely promote his constructive adjustment to a situation where he could not achieve his goals, whereas depression would impede such adjustment.

The final point to note from this interchange is that the counsellor helps the client to discriminate between his rational belief based on desire and a belief based on indifference. Clients often consider that the only alternative to an irrational belief is one that is based on indifference, e.g. 'I don't care if I don't reach my academic goals.' Here the counsellor attempts to forewarn the client about this possibility, which the client appears to understand.

As has been noted already, an irrational belief has a premiss and one or more derivatives. Disputing can therefore be targeted at the premiss form of the irrational belief or at the derivative form or, of course, at both forms. We personally find it effective to dispute *both* the premiss *and* the derivative forms of clients' irrational beliefs.

Indications: Disputing can be used with all clients until incoming information suggests otherwise. Terms like 'irrational' and 'rational' can be off-putting for some clients because of their connotations of mental instability and lack of emotion respectively. In these cases, it is better to use terms like self-defeating or unhelpful v. self-enhancing or helpful. Sometimes REBC disputing and discriminating as exemplified in the textbooks can be as dry as dust and therefore hardly likely to fire the client's imagination; in these cases, it would be advisable to use the client's idiolect to frame the questions, e.g. 'Which of these two beliefs is more likely to "do your head in" and why?'

Contraindications: Disputing as a process of debating and discriminating should be used sparingly with clients who show little if any skill, interest or sophistication in thinking about their thinking. Such clients are best served with forceful coping statements like 'Tough shit' (an attitude based on acceptance of grim reality and resilience), which should be contrasted with their initial statements of despair or indifference, e.g. 'Who gives a shit?' (an attitude designed to make existing problems worse). For those few clients who might find even this approach too taxing, therapists are advised to try rational indoctrination (Grieger and Boyd, 1980) whereby clients are encouraged to repeat rational ideas frequently until they 'sink in' and the clients begins to act on them.

Disputing irrational premisses

Disputing irrational premisses involves challenging the validity, of clients' irrational beliefs expressed in the form of 'musts', 'absolute shoulds', 'oughts', 'have-to's', etc. As above, the purpose of disputing 'musts', etc. is to show clients that there is no evidence in support of such absolute beliefs. Thus, if there was a law of the universe that stated, for example, that I must achieve my goals in life, I would have to achieve them *no matter what*. Thus, absolute musts go against reality, and in this context it is often useful to help clients understand that when they believe in such dogmatic attitudes they are demanding that what exists absolutely *must not exist*. Indeed, the *empirical* form of the word 'must' indicates that if I do not achieve my goals then conditions exist so that I must not achieve them, i.e. what does not exist must not exist.

Another helpful strategy in disputing absolute musts, etc. is to help clients understand that the evidence that they provide in support of absolute musts constitutes, in reality, evidence in favour of their rational beliefs. For example, in a disputing sequence with a female client, the following items were listed as evidence in support of her irrational belief, 'I must be loved by my husband': (a) I would feel better if he did love me; (b) we would get on better if he loved me; and (c) his love means more to me than most other things in life. In response to the question 'Why do you want very much your husband's love?', she listed the same reasons. This helped her to see that she had not yet provided any support in favour of the irrational form of her belief.

When disputing clients' irrational beliefs expressed in the form of 'musts' it is important to ascertain first that the must is indeed irrational, in the sense of being unconditional. As noted above, not all musts are irrational and some musts are in fact conditional, as in the phrase 'If I want to pass my examination I must learn the material.' Here, passing the examination is conditional on learning the material. It is thus an error to dispute conditional musts.

The same point can be made when considering the word 'should', in that not all 'shoulds' are dogmatic and unconditional, and thus irrational in nature. In particular, when disputing irrational beliefs expressed in the form of 'shoulds', it is important for the counsellor to help the client discriminate between 'preferably should' (rational belief) and 'absolutely should.' We recommend that when disputing irrational 'shoulds' the counsellor use the qualifier 'absolutely.' If the qualifier is not used the client may think that the counsellor is asking for evidence in support of the preferential form of the word 'should', and not the absolute form of the word. In such cases therapeutic impasses frequently ensue. As with other terms employed in rational emotive behavioural counselling, it is important for the counsellor and client to share a commonly agreed meaning framework in the course of the therapeutic work (Dryden, 1986).

Finally, it is important for the counsellor to discover which form of the irrational premiss the client best understands as reflecting a statement of absolutism. Thus, with some clients, disputing 'have-tos' is more effective in this respect than disputing 'musts', etc., because for these clients the term 'have-to' best captures the meaning of absolutism and personal dogma.

Indications: Use with clients who agree (though usually not without some struggle) that explicit or implicit unconditional demands lie at the core of their emotional disturbance and therefore need removal through disputation. It is important that REB counsellors do not attempt to force clients to see their viewpoint or bludgeon them into submission.

Contraindications: Do not use with clients who are not persuaded by the theory of *must*urbatory thinking, who do not believe there are any essential differences between demands and preferences, wishes and needs, and who want only to focus on their version of disturbance-producing ideas, e.g. the depression-inducing 'I wish my wife would love me instead of ignoring me.' Here the client can be shown that wishing alone is ineffective and that he needs to embark on a course of action to try to regain his wife's attention. This therapeutic approach is known as general REBC because it is perceived to be synonymous with cognitive-behaviour therapy (CBT) and therefore falls short of philosophic restructuring.

Disputing irrational derivatives

As shown in Chapter 3, there are three major derivatives from irrational premisses: 'awfulising', 'low frustration tolerance' and 'damning'.

Disputing 'awfulising'

In rational emotive behavioural theory, the term 'awful', when it stems from an irrational belief, means '101 per cent bad' or 'worse than it absolutely must be.' In this sense it is not a synonym of the term 'very bad', although it is often judged to be so in everyday language. Thus, it is important for rational emotive behavioural counsellors to help clients discriminate between such phrases as 'very bad' and the word 'awful.' When this is done, clients are shown that whatever they evaluate as 'awful' could, in reality, be worse; and that the concept of 101 per cent badness is a magical one that does not exist except by definition. A good way of reinforcing this is to ask clients to rate what is evaluated as 'awful' on a 0–100 scale of badness, as in the following example:

Counsellor: So you're saying that being rejected by Harry is awful, right?
Client: Right.
Counsellor: So on a scale from 0 to 100 of badness, how bad would being rejected by Harry be?

Client:	100 per cent.
Counsellor:	So if you are going to rate that as 100 per cent then how would you rate being rejected by Harry *and* losing a leg?
Client:	(laughs). I hadn't thought of it like that. I guess that would be 100 per cent.
Counsellor:	OK. Now where would you rate being rejected by Harry, losing a leg and having a very large rates bill that you couldn't pay?
Client:	That would be 100 per cent too . . . Oh, now I see what you're getting at. Looking at it like that, being rejected by Harry wouldn't be that bad.
Counsellor:	Right, but it still would be very bad. Now can you see the differences between very bad and awful?
Client:	Yes, I see that now.
Counsellor:	Right, awful doesn't really exist unless we invent it, because we can keep adding bad things to the list, and if we do that when shall we ever get to 100 per cent badness?
Client:	Never, I guess, because things could always be worse.
Counsellor:	That's exactly it. Now, awful really stems from the belief 'It mustn't be as bad as it is.' Now, granted that being rejected by Harry is bad, why *must* that not be as bad as it is? . . .

Ellis (personal communication) has argued that the method whereby clients are encouraged to rate events as 'bad' rather than 'awful' should be used with caution. This is because a person could rate a situation as 40 per cent bad and still believe that it *must not* be as bad as it is, and thus make him or herself disturbed. Thus, when using this method it is important *also* to dispute any remaining irrational premises, as in the example presented.

In addition, when clients are encouraged to rate events as bad rather than awful, counsellors should be careful to stress the distinction between these two terms (e.g. 'Right, so if you continue to show yourself that it was *bad* that it happened, *but not awful*, then you will get over your depression').

An interesting way of disputing 'awfulising' beliefs has been described by Young (1984a) in his work with lower-class clients in West Virginia.

> I usually accomplish this by using a sheet of paper on which I put two columns. One column I label 'Pain in the neck – HASSLES' and the other column I label 'End of the world – HORRORS.' Next I encourage the client to tell me exactly what is wrong in his problem. Then, after we list all the disadvantages and inconveniences involved, I will ask the client in which column the problem belongs – the hassle column or the horror column. Clients always see the point and admit that their problems belong in the hassle column. I ask them how they would feel if they could see their problem as a hassle instead of a horror. Clients usually admit that they would feel much less upset. I then inform them that their job is constantly to tell themselves the truth – that the problem is a pain-in-the-neck, nothing more and nothing less. (Young, 1984a, p. 47)

Note in this example that Young does not deal overtly with the philosophical issue that nothing merits inclusion in the 'end of the world' 'horror' or 'awful' column. Young probably did not do this because his clientele would not grasp this point. This raises another important principle in rational emotive behavioural counselling: *Work at a level that your client can understand.* Our own preference in this regard is to assume that clients will be able to grasp the full meaning of rational concepts until evidence is obtained that suggests otherwise.

Indications: Use with clients who can demonstrate their understanding of awfulising by answering such questions as 'What is the difference between a catastrophe like famine and awfulising about it?' 'Why is death not considered an awful experience in REBC?' As indicated above, clients who lack a philosophical bent can be asked more homespun questions like 'What is the difference between a nightmare and a nuisance?' As with disputing the other derivatives in this section, some clients might find this a more powerful intervention than challenging their irrational premisses.

Contraindications: Do not use with clients who insist that events in their lives are 'awful', e.g. the death of a child. Here the therapist should allow sufficient time for the client to explore his or her anguished feelings as well as agreeing with the client's viewpoint. The goal of therapy is the client learning how to cope with this 'awful' experience, possibly with the help of a local support group.

Disputing 'low frustration tolerance'

The purpose of disputing 'low frustration tolerance' beliefs is to help clients see that this term, when it stems from an irrational premiss, means 'I will never experience happiness again' and is thus rarely true. Indeed, we find it helpful to encourage clients to see that even when they believe and tell themselves 'I can't stand it' they are, in fact, 'standing it', albeit not very well. The discussion can then shift to helping clients explore ways of tolerating it better. Another way of demonstrating to clients that they can stand what they believe they cannot is to ask them if there are circumstances under which they could stand 'it', as is shown in the following interchange:

Counsellor: So you're saying that you can't stand that feeling of jelly legs when you go out and that's why you don't go out. Is that right?

Client: Yes, that's right.

Counsellor: Now, as we've seen, as long as you believe that you can't stand that feeling you won't go out. But let's see if that belief is true. Let's suppose that your sister has been kidnapped by terrorists and the only way the terrorists will release her is if you delivered the ransom money on your jelly legs, or else they would kill her. Now under these conditions, should we arrange for her funeral or would you go?

Client: I'd go and deliver the money.

Counsellor: But how could you if you couldn't stand having these feelings of jelly legs?

Client: Well, I'd do it even though I couldn't stand it.

Counsellor: But if you couldn't stand it you'd collapse in the attempt – that's what you've been saying about the feeling isn't it?

Client: Well, I wouldn't focus on it in that instance.
Counsellor: You mean you could stand it enough not to dwell on it?
Client: I suppose so.
Counsellor: Now, if you'd go out on jelly legs to save your sister will you do it for the sake of your recovery, even though it's damned uncomfortable?
Client: I see your point.
Counsellor: Now, as you do this, really work on convincing yourself that you can stand these uncomfortable feelings even though you'll never like them. And don't forget to remind yourself that you're choosing to stand them for a reason – your mental health!

Here, as elsewhere, rational emotive behavioural counsellors can use the methods of general semantics to show clients that when they say 'I can't stand it' they really mean, as in the above example 'I haven't learned to stand it yet' and 'I am having great difficulty standing it at the moment, but that doesn't mean that I never will.'

Indications: Use with clients who have low frustration tolerance (LFT) beliefs with regard to their presenting problems and/or the hard work of initiating and maintaining therapeutic change. REBC practitioners need to be careful that 'I-can't-stand-it-itis' is not used indiscriminately, e.g. a client with chronic fatigue syndrome (CFS) is challenged on her putative LFT beliefs because she fears the pain involved when she exerts herself.

Contraindications: Where it would be clinically counterproductive or downright offensive for the therapist to suggest to clients that they have underlying LFT beliefs, Muran and DiGiuseppe suggest that clients who have experienced traumatic or highly stressful events endure greater frustration than the average person. Therefore, to imply that these clients have LFT because they are not willing to face their problems is inaccurate and invalidating. A variation on LFT would be frustration intolerance which acknowledges 'the high degree of frustration they [clients] have endured while focusing on the belief that their task is "too difficult" to tolerate' (1994, p. 167).

Disputing 'damning' beliefs

When applied to people, the process of damning implies that a person can be given a global rating, that this is negative and that the person is damnable, i.e. subhuman. The purpose of disputing damning beliefs, which again tend to be derivatives from irrational premises, is to show the client that a person is too complex to be given a single rating; a person's traits, behaviours or thoughts are part of the person, but never equal to the person; and the essence of the person is fallibility (i.e. being capable of good and bad), rather than goodness or badness. Below, we provide examples to demonstrate each principle in action. Although they each refer to irrational beliefs about the self, similar points apply to irrational beliefs the client may hold about others and about life conditions.

1. The 'self' is too complex

Counsellor: OK, so you say that you're worthless for cheating on your wife, is that right?

Client: Yes, that's what I believe.

Counsellor: OK, but let's test that out. Are you saying that you are worthless, or what you've done is worthless?

Client: I'm saying that I'm worthless, not just what I did.

Counsellor: OK, but let's see if that is true or false. You know when you say 'I'm worthless' you are giving you, your personhood or your essence, a single rating. Can you see that?

Client: Yes.

Counsellor: But let's see if you warrant that. You're 35. How many thoughts have you had from the day you were born till now?

Client: Countless, I guess.

Counsellor: Add to that all your actions and throw in all your traits for good measure. From that time till now how many aspects to you are there?

Client: Millions, I guess.

Counsellor: At least now when you say that Y-O-U ARE WORTHLESS you can see that you're implying that you are about as complex as a single cell amoeba, and that this cell is worthless. Now, is that true from what we've just been discussing?

Client: No, of course it's not.

Counsellor: So do you, in all your complexity, merit a single rating?

Client: No, but I did do a pretty worthless thing and it was serious.

Counsellor: Agreed, but what has greater validity, the belief, 'I'm worthless in all my essence' or the belief, 'I am too complex to be rated, but I did do something lousy which I regret.'

Client: The second.

Counsellor: Right and if you really worked on believing that, would you still feel suicidal as you do now?

Client: No I wouldn't. I see what you mean.

Indications: Use with all clients until clinical evidence suggests otherwise, or the initial assessment indicates a poor outcome for this intervention.

Contraindications: Do not use with clients who find the concept itself too complex to grasp, too far-fetched or 'its just normal to rate yourself'. These clients can be shown how to become better problem-solvers in order to rate themselves less frequently. Also, do not use with clients who have persistent identity disturbance and therefore their sense of self is difficult to pin down, e.g. borderline personality disorder.

2. I equal what I do (think, feel)

This example is taken from Young's (1984a) work with a lower-class client who is convinced that you are what you do.

Counsellor: Maybe I can show you a better way to think about yourself. (I pointed at her hand). Is that your hand?

Client:	(laughing) Yes!
Counsellor:	Is it important to you?
Client:	Yes.
Counsellor:	Tell me why. Suppose you didn't have that hand?
Client:	It would handicap me. There would be lots of things I couldn't do. It would be pretty bad for me.
Counsellor:	So your hand's important! Now let me ask you this: Is that hand part of you or is it you? Now really think for me. Does that important hand equal you? Could you describe yourself simply as a hand?
Client:	No.
Counsellor:	Why not? You gave the right answer. Now tell me why it is the right answer.
Client:	Because my hand is only part of me.
Counsellor:	Do you have any other part, such as your eyes, ears, nose, or big toe that is your whole self? Is there any part of your body, inside or out, that you could say is you?
Client:	No, I guess I'm made up of a lot of parts.

Indications: Use with clients who need immediate and tangible examples of this concept rather than philosophical discussions about it.

Contraindications: Do not use with clients who cannot be dissuaded that the part does equal the whole, e.g. 'If I lost my leg, I'd be nothing.' Other kinds of arguments would need to be used. e.g. 'If you're nothing with one leg, what would you be with both legs gone?'

3. The essence of the self is fallibility

In order to make the point that the essence of a person is fallibility, WD will sometimes draw three big circles on a sheet of paper and show this to the client. He says that these three circles represent three people: A, B and C. First he takes circle A and sticks as many small gold stars within the circle as he can. Next he sticks as many black dots as he can within circle B. Finally he sticks a mixture of gold stars and black dots in circle C. He explains to the client that the gold stars represent good deeds, thoughts, feelings and traits; and the black dots represent bad deeds, thoughts, feelings and traits.

He then asks his client what we generally call someone who has only the equivalent of gold stars; who has only the equivalent of black dots; and who has a mixture of the two. The client usually gives such replies as: perfect, a saint, an angel; bad, the devil, evil; and human, normal, ordinary, respectively. WD then asks the client two more questions: whether he or she really knows anyone like the people represented by circles A and B, to which the answer is almost always no; and which circle best represents her, to which the answer is invariably C. In this manner clients can see that the essence of human beings is a mixture of good and bad (or fallibility) and that they also belong in the category: 'fallible human being.'

A final note on language. As with irrational premises, clients use different words to damn themselves and others. For example, Young (1984b) has shown that clients can be 'bad me' thinkers, 'less me' thinkers or 'damn me' thinkers. As elsewhere, it is recommended that the counsellor use the client's language in disputing sequences unless there are sound reasons to do otherwise.

Indications: Use or try with all clients, as this is a fundamental tenet of REBC and a bedrock of emotional stability (there are many different ways to teach the concept of human fallibility).

Contraindications: Do not use with clients who rigidly believe the essence of the self is infallibility or perfectionism. With these clients, the emphasis is on the pursuit of excellence in their lives which might involve setbacks, but these setbacks are part of the striving for greatness and not the 'curse' of fallibility.

Dissonance-inducing interventions

According to cognitive dissonance theory (e.g. Festinger, 1957), when a person is confronted with information that conflicts with one of his importantly held beliefs, a state of cognitive dissonance, a form of psychological tension, is induced. In order to reduce dissonance that person *may* change his belief. We stress the word *may* in the above sentence because in order to reduce dissonance the person may change other features of the dissonant situation, e.g. he may cast doubt on the validity of the conflicting information or on the credibility of the source of the new information. Thus, although rational emotive behavioural counsellors employ dissonance-inducing interventions to promote intellectual rational insight, they do so with caution.

One dissonance-inducing intervention that is commonly used in rational emotive behavioural counselling attempts to show clients that they have already engaged in adaptive behaviour which is inconsistent with their maladaptive belief. Thus, clients who believe that they are 'failures' are asked to provide evidence of their successes; those who believe that they are unlovable are asked for evidence that they have been loved. Since clients frequently append 'but that doesn't count' to their evidence we have often found it helpful to say something like: 'Of course I realise that any evidence that you give you will immediately dismiss in some way, but let's hear it anyway', before letting the client answer. We do this to reduce in advance the potency of their attempts to maintain their irrational belief by denying the importance of their evidence. The success of this type of dissonance-inducing intervention often depends on the wealth of evidence the client provides, and then it is important to keep asking for more and more evidence until a portfolio of evidence which conflicts with the client's irrational belief has been assembled.

Another dissonance-inducing intervention concerns the counsellor demonstrating that the client's irrational belief is incongruent with one of the client's cherished ideas, as in the following example:

Counsellor: So you're furious with Bill because he upset your friend and you believe he absolutely should not have done that. Is that right?

Client: Yes, indeed.

Counsellor: I remember you said on your biographical form that one of your pet hates is totalitarianism. Have I remembered correctly?

Client: That's right, but what's that got to do with it?

Counsellor: I'm coming to that, bear with me for a moment. Why are you against state control?

Client: Because it restricts the individual's freedom.

Counsellor: His or her freedom to act?

Client: Yes.

Counsellor: So even if the individual acts really badly he or she, in your opinion, should preferably have that choice?

Client: Yes. Of course there have to be laws and consequences for the individual, but basically yes.

Counsellor: So I guess you're saying all people have the right to act badly except Bill, because aren't you demanding, in a totalitarian way, that he absolutely should not have acted badly towards your friend?

Client: (Laughs loudly) OK, Doc, you've got me. I give in.

Counsellor: Now what would a non-totalitarian attitude towards Bill sound like?

Indications: Use with clients who are able to acknowledge their ideational conflicts and implement a rational resolution of them. REB counsellors should be alert to the possible emergence of secondary emotional problems, as in the above extract, the client might see her dissonant self exposed as hypocrisy and thereby experience shame about this, which then has to be addressed.

Contraindications: Do not use with clients who might say, 'I think this way one minute, and then another way the next minute. So what?' The therapist might suggest that such rapid cognitive shifts are precisely the reason why the client is in therapy. This could turn into a dissonance-inducing intervention! Also, do not use with clients who do not see or respond to any conflicts in their ideas.

A final dissonance-inducing strategy that is often quite powerful concerns showing the client that her attitude towards herself conflicts with her attitude towards her best friend, e.g.:

Counsellor: So you say that you're a bad person for having those evil thoughts. Is that right?

Client: Yes.

Counsellor: Well let's test that out. Now, we'll agree for the moment that those thoughts of stabbing your child are evil. But how are you evil for having evil thoughts?

Client: Well, it's obvious isn't it?

Counsellor: Is it? Aren't you saying that because part of you is evil that you are thoroughly evil?

Client: Yes.

Counsellor: Well, does that follow?

Client:	Well . . .
Counsellor:	Let's put it another way. Who's your best friend?
Client:	Cathy.
Counsellor:	Well, let's suppose that Cathy came to you and said: 'Sue, I'm evil because I've had thoughts of stabbing my child.' Would you say to her 'Get out of my sight you evil person?'
Client:	No, I wouldn't.
Counsellor:	Would you think it?
Client:	No.
Counsellor:	Why not?
Client:	Because she isn't evil.
Counsellor:	Even though she's had evil thoughts?
Client:	I see what you mean.
Counsellor:	Now do you think there should be one rule for Cathy and a different one for you? Does that make sense?
Client:	No, I guess not.
Counsellor:	So why not work at applying your attitude towards Cathy to you?

Here, as elsewhere, rational emotive behavioural counsellors should guard against clients giving themselves second-order problems as a consequence of the counsellors' interventions. Thus, some clients may conclude from the last example 'Oh, I am treating my friend more compassionately than myself as I must not. That really proves how worthless I am.' Questions like: 'How do you feel about the fact that you seem to be harsher on yourself than you are on your best friend' should preferably be asked after the intervention to determine the existence of such second-order problems.

Indications: This technique can be used generally, although therapists should first ascertain that the client actually does have friends and likes them without automatically assuming it.

Contraindications: Do not use with clients who do not have friends, as the therapist's unthinking intervention could reinforce their sense of isolation and depression; or with perfectionists, as they may be charitable to others who fail because they perceive them as inferior, but harshly condemn themselves for any failure on their own part.

Goals and rational beliefs

As we have already noted, an important part of the disputing process involves helping clients to discriminate between irrational and rational beliefs. As these distinctions are clarified it is advisable for counsellors to encourage clients to see that rational beliefs are related to more functional healthy emotions, which are still often negative in nature. For example, imagine that a client is anxious about performing well in her driving test, because she is demanding that she must pass the test. In the process of helping this client to dispute this belief, the counsellor will show her that her rational belief is 'I very much want to pass the test, but I don't have to', and that if she subscribed only to this belief she would feel concerned, but not anxious about driving well. However, if the client's goal is to be calm and not concerned about the prospect of failing the test, she will resist adopting the new rational beliefs. Thus, rational emotive behavioural counsellors often discuss clients' emotional and behavioural goals during the process of disputing their irrational beliefs to ensure that their goals can be achieved by adopting healthy beliefs. In the example we have provided, the counsellor would attempt to show the client that concern is a healthy negative emotion, based on a rational belief that will motivate her to do well, whereas calmness, which can be achieved only by the client lying to herself by telling herself 'It doesn't matter if I do well or not', hardly provides her with the motivational base to do as well as she can. Thus, while rational emotive behavioural counsellors often elicit their clients' emotional and behavioural goals, they do not accept uncritically clients' stated goals, and are particularly sceptical of the functionality of goals which signify attitudes of indifference.

The above example also highlights another feature of the disputing process; namely, that counsellors attempt to help clients to understand the logical consequences of holding rational and irrational beliefs. Here, the counsellor might say, 'As long as you believe that you must do well you will be anxious, and this anxiety may interfere with your driving performance. However, if you work at believing that while it is important to you to do well, you don't have to, you'll be concerned, and thus be in a better frame of mind to do well.' This part of the disputing process, which can be done Socratically as well as didactically, as above, is often referred to as 'pragmatic disputing' in that it draws the client's attention to the pragmatic consequences of holding rational and irrational beliefs.

Indications: Use with clients who are able both to formulate clear and specific goals for change and adopt rational beliefs as the best means of realising these goals. REB counsellors should remember that some clients will need to think about their goals and, therefore, it is not a task that has to be completed in the first session.

Contraindications: Do not use with clients who see therapy in terms of process rather than outcome, e.g. 'I want to explore myself in therapy. How will rational beliefs help me if I've no idea where I'm going.' These clients can eventually be persuaded to focus on outcomes, such as 'What is it that you don't want to achieve?' or, if such approaches eventually prove unsuccessful, they can be referred to non-REB counsellors.

Comprehensive cognitive disputing

Earlier, we noted that we prefer to target both the premiss and the derivative forms of clients' irrational beliefs during the disputing process. In our experience, this thoroughgoing approach helps to increase the likelihood that clients will achieve the types of attitude change that contribute to psychological health.

In a seminal article, DiGiuseppe (1991) presents a model for conducting thoroughgoing disputing within rational emotive behavioural counselling. He describes four categories of variables which he views as having particular relevance to the disputing process, and advocates manipulation of these variables within counselling sessions as a means for ensuring that disputing will be accomplished in a complete and comprehensive manner. These variables include: (1) the *type* of disputing argument utilised by the counsellor; (2) the particular *style* by which the counsellor presents the disputing argument to the client; (3) the *level of abstraction* of the irrational beliefs targeted for disputing; and (4) the particular irrational belief *processes* targeted for disputing.

With respect to the *type* of disputing argument the counsellor employs, the reader will recall that Chapter 2 described irrational beliefs as illogical, anti-empirical and dysfunctional in nature, and as representing significant impediments to goal attainment. Hence, irrational beliefs can be disputed with logical, empirical and pragmatic arguments. With reference to Kuhn's (1970) work on the factors that influence scientists to reject old theories (or paradigms) in favour of new, alternative ones, DiGiuseppe (1991) argues that clients will be more likely to surrender their irrational beliefs and replace them with more rational ones when the former are attacked with all three types of disputing arguments. He further emphasises that it is desirable for counsellors to help their clients to construct new 'theories' about themselves and the world by working with them to formulate new, alternative rational beliefs of relevance to their particular problem areas. This recommendation is based upon the hypothesis that clients may be prone to cling to their old irrational beliefs despite technically correct efforts at disputing these beliefs – if an alternative rational philosophy is not made available to them.

With regard to the manner in which disputing arguments are presented to clients, DiGiuseppe (1991) describes four particular disputing styles: didactic, Socratic, humorous and metaphorical. To this list we would add a further category: self-disclosing style. DiGiuseppe (1991) hypothesises that clients are influenced as much by the manner of presentation of disputing arguments as they are by the arguments themselves. As such, it appears advisable for counsellors to experiment judiciously with these various disputing styles in order to identify the ones that work best with particular clients.

DiGiuseppe (1991) identifies the level of abstraction of the irrational beliefs targeted for change as another variable germane to comprehensive cognitive disputing. Clients may subscribe to irrational beliefs in a very general form (e.g. 'I *must* have what I want when I want it') and in increasingly specific forms as well (e.g. 'My friends and family *must* give me what I want'; 'My wife *must* give me what I want'). Disputing that is directed only at the most abstract form of a given irrational belief may fail to help clients deal more effectively with *specific* problematic activating events (which may trigger more concrete, specific forms of the irrational belief), whereas disputing targeted at only a specific form of the irrational belief may be of limited usefulness because it fails to convey general principles that could help clients to deal with a wide variety of difficult situations. By moving up and down the 'ladder of abstraction', counsellors can help to increase the probability that clients will be able to generalise their application of REBC from one problematic activating event to others.

We have presented a model in this text wherein irrational beliefs are viewed as being comprised of a premise and one or more derivatives. With respect to irrational belief processes, DiGiuseppe (1991) presents the premiss form of an irrational belief as embodying the core process of demandingness, with awfulising, low frustration tolerance and damning representing belief processes that tend to stem from this core process. Counsellors are advised not to assume that their disputing efforts aimed at one irrational belief process will generalise to other irrational belief processes that a particular client may endorse, and to work at identifying and disputing all irrational belief processes that may be relevant to the client's emotional problems.

We concur with DiGiuseppe's (1991) recommendations concerning comprehensive cognitive disputing, as it is likely that this approach currently represents the most efficient and effective means for helping clients to surrender their irrational beliefs in favour of more rational ones. In addition, by manipulating the variables relevant to the disputing process, counsellors can refine their disputing skills significantly. In Chapter 9, 'The rational emotive behavioural counselling process', we present a model for REBC that integrates the various components of disputing with key elements of assessment, homework utilisation and the working-through process.

Indications: Use with clients who would not feel overwhelmed by this all-embracing verbal disputing process and can provide feedback on the reasons for its thoroughgoingness.

Contraindications: Do not use with clients who would benefit from constricted cognitive disputing as their time, attention and intellect are limited, e.g. a client is able to tackle only a derivative belief ('I'm useless') in a specific context with the largely didactic help of the therapist.

Vivid Disputing Methods

In this section, we outline various vivid methods of disputing clients' irrational beliefs which many rational emotive behavioural counsellors have employed with good results. As with the other vivid methods described in this book, these tend to be used after the more traditional disputing methods, outlined in the previous section, have proved unsuccessful. Vivid techniques do need to be employed selectively and we refer the reader to the previous chapter for cautions about the use of such methods in rational emotive behavioural counselling.

Biographical information

Before initiating the vivid disputing process we often find it helpful to gather certain information about the client, such as his or her interests, hobbies and work situations. We have found this information often helps us adapt our interventions, using phrases that will be meaningful to our clients given their idiosyncratic life situations. Thus, if a client is passionately interested in boxing, a message utilising a boxing analogy may well have greater impact than a golfing analogy.

We also find it helpful to discover who our clients admire. We do this because later we may wish to ask clients how they think these admired individuals might solve similar problems. This may prompt clients to identify with a model to imitate. Lazarus (1984) has employed a similar method with children. For example, one of us (WD) asked a male client to imagine that his admired grandfather experienced public speaking anxiety and inquired how he would have overcome it. This helped him to identify a rational belief which he subsequently used to overcome his own public speaking anxiety problem. This approach is best used if the client can also acknowledge that the admired individual is fallible and thus prone to human irrationality. In addition, it is important that the client sees the feasibility of imitating the model.

We find it invaluable to ask clients about their previous experience of attitude change. We try to discern the salient features of such change for possible replication in our in-session disputing strategies. For example, one anxious female client indicated that she had changed her mind about foxhunting after reading a number of personal accounts offering arguments against foxhunting. As part of a disputing plan, this client was directed to autobiographies of people who had overcome anxiety. Another client claimed she had in the past received help from speaking to people who had experienced problems similar to her own. Arrangements were made for this client to speak to some ex-clients who had experienced but overcome comparable problems.

Indications: Use as part of the induction, assessment and planning for treatment process in REBC.

Contraindications: Do not use with clients who are severely depressed (the information can be gleaned later); with paranoid clients who may feel threatened by the therapist's inquisitiveness; with clients who are slow to develop trust in the therapist, e.g.'I'm not sure about you yet to tell you these things.'

We now propose to outline a number of ways in which rational emotive behavioural counsellors can employ vivid disputing techniques. The importance of tailoring interventions to meet the specific, idiosyncratic requirements of clients should be borne in mind throughout.

In the previous chapter we outlined a number of ways of vividly portraying activating events to help clients identify their emotional reactions and the cognitive determinants of these reactions. We outlined various visual, auditory and olfactory methods. These same methods can be used as context material in the disputing process. For example, one client brought along a drawing of herself and her mother. She portrayed her mother as a very large, menacing figure and herself as a small figure crouching in fear in front of her mother. The client was asked to draw another picture where she and her mother were of the same height, standing face to face looking each other in the eye. When she brought in this drawing, an inquiry was made as to how her attitude toward her mother differed in the two pictures. This not only provided her with a demonstration that it was possible for her to evaluate her mother differently, but also led to a fruitful discussion in which some of the irrational beliefs inherent in her first drawing were disputed, while having her focus on the second.

Imagery methods

One very effective imagery method that can be used in the disputing of irrational beliefs is that of time projection (Lazarus, 1984). When a client makes grossly exaggerated negative evaluations of an event, she often stops thinking about it and therefore cannot see beyond its 'dreaded' implications. The purpose of time projection is to enable clients to see vividly that time and the world continue after the 'dreaded event' has occurred. Thus, for example, a Malaysian student whose tuition fees were paid for by his village concluded that it would be terrible if he failed his exams because he couldn't bear to face his fellow villagers. He was helped to imagine his return to his village while experiencing shame and as time was gradually advanced forward via imagery, he began to see that it was likely that his fellow villagers would eventually come to adopt a compassionate viewpoint toward him, and even if they did not, he could always live happily in another part of the country, or in another part of the world.

Indications: Use with clients who are able to create mental images and thereby switch from irrational to rational views of their problems. Specifically, time projection can be used with clients who have experienced or who expect to experience unpleasant events in their lives, e.g. loss of a job or relationship.

Contraindications: Do not use with clients who have no interest in, or capacity for, working in an imagery modality (though imagery improving exercises [Lazarus, 1984] can be suggested). Time projection is best avoided with depressed clients as this exercise may actually strengthen their view of a hopeless future, and themselves helpless to do anything about it.

The Rational Emotive Behavioural Counsellor as raconteur

Rational emotive behavioural counsellors often capitalise on the therapeutic value of relating various stories, parables, maxims and aphorisms to clients. Each one, of course, is designed to teach a rational concept. For example, Wessler and Wessler (1980, p. 126) relate the story of Nathan Leopold to illustrate the concepts of human complexity and the futility of evaluating oneself and others.

> Nathan Leopold . . . along with Richard Loeb committed the 'Crime of the Century,' in the 1920s by kidnapping and killing a young boy. Years later, Leopold was pardoned as a changed person, became a social worker, married, and spent much of the rest of his life doing good works. After telling or reminding the client of Leopold's story, we ask, 'Now was Nathan Leopold a good man or a bad man?'. Again we get a variety of answers. The one we are looking for is 'He was neither. He was a man who did both good and bad things.' Leopold is an extreme case (which makes him a good example) and leads to a discussion of human fallibility.

Indications: Use with clients who can understand the rational message contained within the stories and who are able to relate it back to their own problems; in the example of Leopold, it is worth asking the client before telling the story whether he believes 'there is some good even in the worst of us' in order to gauge his possible reaction to the story. I (MN) believe this story should be used with caution as the therapist may appear as a 'do-gooder' or 'liberal hand-wringer' on law and order, and thereby with some clients do possibly irreparable harm to the therapeutic relationship.

Contraindications: Do not use with concrete thinkers who can focus only on the specifics of their own problems; if the answer is 'no' to the above question, or if the client believes in capital punishment, then the Leopold story should be abandoned. The story of 'The Wise Rabbi' may also be used to good effect with some clients. This tale is particularly helpful for conveying the fatuous nature of an awfulising philosophy, as it humorously illustrates the concept that circumstances can almost always be worse than they actually are:

> Many years ago a religious Jewish couple were having difficulties arising from living in a one-room apartment with two screaming children. They both believed that their situation was awful, and they were making themselves disturbed as a result. They decided to seek help from their local rabbi, a wise old man respected for his sage advice. On listening to the couple's story he advised them to invite both sets of parents to live with them, and instructed them to return in a month's time to report on progress. The couple were perplexed by this advice, but since they thought highly of the rabbi they carried out his advice to the letter.
>
> One month later they returned to the rabbi even more distressed than before. 'We're getting to the end of our tether, rabbi. Things have gone from bad to worse. Both sets of parents are arguing and the children are screaming even louder

than before.' The rabbi listened carefully, and then pronounced the following words: 'I want you to go home and collect up all your geese and chickens from the yard and have them live with you, your children, and your respective parents – and come and see me again in a month's time.'

If the couple were perplexed before, they were dumbfounded now. But again, being dutiful, they followed the rabbi's advice to the letter.

One month later they returned at their wits' end. 'We're at breaking point, rabbi,' they said. 'The animals are creating pandemonium, our parents have almost come to blows, and the children's screams can be heard at the other end of town. We're desperate, rabbi. Please, please, PLEASE help us!'

The rabbi again listened patiently, and then said, 'I want you to go home, put the geese and chickens back into the yard, send both sets of parents home, and come and see me in a month's time.'

One month later, the couple returned. This time they looked cheerful and happy. 'Things are so much better, rabbi. You have no idea. It's so peaceful. The kids are still screaming but that's bearable now. You've helped us so much, rabbi – thank you!'

Often, it is important that the counsellor modify the content of such stories to fit the client's idiosyncratic situation. Telling identical stories to two different clients may well have two different effects. One client may be deeply affected by the story, while for another the story may prove meaningless. It is important that rational emotive behavioural counsellors become acquainted with a wide variety of these stories and be prepared to modify them from client to client without introducing unwarranted distortions. In addition, it is recommended that counsellors check with clients to ensure that the intended meaning of the story has been understood.

Indications: Use with clients whose main problems revolve around how 'awful things are in my life'. As the story is intended to be comical, it is important for the therapist to ascertain that the client has a sense of humour. The wise rabbi, depending on the context of the client's problems, will need to be changed to 'wise friend' or 'wise grandmother' as necessary.

Contraindications: Do not use with concrete thinkers, those who have a short attention span (the wise rabbi story is not to be rushed as its effect lies in the build-up of the details), humourless clients or those too disturbed by their 'awful' problems.

Active–visual methods

Active–visual methods combine therapist or client activity with a vivid visual presentation. Young (1984b) has outlined one such method, which he uses to help clients see the impossibility of assigning a global rating to themselves. He asks a client to describe some of his behaviours, attributes, talents, interests, etc. With every answer the client gives, Young writes the attribute on a white sticky label, and invites the client to attach it to him or herself. This continues until the client is covered with white sticky labels and can begin to see the impossibility of assigning one global rating to such a complex being. Wessler and Wessler (1980) outline similar active–visual methods to communicate a similar point. For example, they ask their clients to assign a comprehensive rating to a basket of fruit on a desk. Clients are encouraged actively to explore the components of the fruit basket while attempting to assign a global rating to it. They soon come to realise that they can rate components of the basket but not its essence.

Indications: Use with all clients who require, or whose understanding will be enhanced by, a visual representation of rational ideas.

Contraindications: Do not use with clients who are literal-minded, e.g. 'A bowl of fruit is a bowl of fruit - there's nothing more to be said about it.' Or with clients who might feel, as with the above examples, ridiculed by being covered with labels or insulted by being compared to a bowl of fruit.

Visual models

We have designed a number of visual models, each of which demonstrates a rational message. For example, one of us (WD) employs a model called the 'LFT Splash.' In the model a young man is seated at the top of a roller coaster, with a young woman standing at the bottom. Clients are told that the young man does not move because he is telling himself that he can't stand the splash. Clients are asked to think what the young man would have to tell himself in order to reach the woman. This model is particularly useful in introducing to clients the idea of tolerating acute time-limited discomfort which, if tolerated, would help them achieve their goals.

In the earlier section of this chapter on disputing clients' 'damning' beliefs, a counsellor/client dialogue was presented in order to illustrate the manner in which clients can be taught the concept that the 'self' is too complex to warrant a single, global rating. This concept can also be presented to clients with a visual model that we term the 'Big I/Little i' diagram. Created by Arnold Lazarus (1977), this model was used to good effect by WD in his work with his client 'Sarah', whose counselling experience forms the basis for the book, *Daring To Be Myself: A Case-Study in Rational-Emotive Therapy* (Dryden and Yankura, 1992). The following excerpt from this book shows how the model was utilised within Sarah's sixth counselling session, during a discussion of her guilt feelings about the occasional angry outbursts she would direct toward her husband, Art:

Dr Dryden: You just went from 'I've done something unpleasant' to 'I'm not a very pleasant person.' Can you see the sort of jump that you're making?

Sarah: (in a small voice) No, not really.

Dr Dryden: Well - have I ever spoken with you about the difference between the 'Big I' and the 'Little i'?

Sarah: No.

Dr Dryden: Okay - let me just write this out for you. I'm writing a big block 'I' here, and I'm making lots and lots of little 'i's' inside it. Now, I'm going to circle one of the little 'i's.' Take a look at this: the big 'I' represents you in your wholeness, your totality - right? But as you can see, you're made up of lots and lots of little 'i's.' You have lots of behaviours, lots of thoughts, lots of feelings. Now, how many little 'i's do you think you're made up of?

Sarah: I suppose thousands, if you put it like that.

Dr Dryden: That's right! Now, the one circled is what you've just said to Art, which wasn't very pleasant, right? How does that one unpleasant . . .

Sarah: It doesn't make me a *whole* nasty person!

Dr Dryden: That's right!

Sarah: Mm.

Dr Dryden: Now, if you were to regard what you said as unpleasant and undesirable, but didn't jump to 'I am an unpleasant person', what sort of difference do you think that would make?

Sarah: There's a big difference between saying there's a *little* part of me that can be nasty and snappy, and saying that all of me is! The way you've put it now - and thinking about what you've said in the past - I'm not *always* like that. Far from it!

It is noteworthy that when Sarah was interviewed by JY for the above-mentioned book approximately eight years after the last of her sessions with WD, she described the 'Big I/Little i' diagram as being one of the most memorable and helpful features of her counselling.

Indications: Use as with active–visual methods.

Contraindications: Do not use with literal-minded clients, clients who have a poor imagination, or are too disturbed to benefit from such models (though they can be introduced later when the disturbance has moderated).

Flamboyant counsellor actions

A common disputing strategy that rational emotive behavioural counsellors use in verbal dialogue when clients conclude they are stupid for acting stupidly, is to ask some variant of the question 'How are you a stupid person for acting stupidly?' Alternatively, instead of asking such questions, the counsellor could suddenly leap to the floor and start barking like a dog for about 30 seconds and then resume his or her seat, then ask the client to evaluate this action. Clients usually say that the action is stupid. The counsellor can then ask whether that stupid action makes him or her a stupid person. Such flamboyant actions often enable clients to discriminate more easily between global self-ratings and ratings of behaviours or attributes.

Indications: Use with clients who have already indicated that they appreciate fun, spontaneity, unpredictability, etc. in therapy.

Contraindications: Do not use with clients who want a formal or serious approach or with clients who come to therapy to see an expert and instead believe they have an 'idiot who thinks he's a dog'.

Counsellor self-disclosure

In Chapter 4, it was noted that rational emotive behavioural counsellors strive to be as open as therapeutically feasible with their clients. Some clients find self-disclosure by the counsellor an extremely persuasive method; for others, however, it is contraindicated. One way of attempting to ascertain a client's possible reactions to counsellor self-disclosure is to include an appropriate item in a precounselling questionnaire. It may well be wise for counsellors to avoid using self-disclosure with clients who respond negatively to the item. In any case, the counsellor should ascertain the client's reaction to any self-disclosing statements that he or she might make. The research literature on this topic indicates that it is inadvisable for counsellors to disclose personal information about themselves too early in the therapeutic process (Dies, 1973).

When counsellors do disclose information about themselves it is our experience that the most effective forms of self-disclosure are those in which they portray themselves as coping rather than mastery models. Thus, for example, it is better for the counsellor to say to the client: 'I used to have a similar problem, but this is how I overcame it', rather than to say: 'I have never had this problem, because I believe . . .' Occasionally, WD will tell clients with shame-based anxieties how he overcame his anxiety about stammering in public. He tells them that he used to believe: 'It would be terrible if I stammered in public and it would prove I was worthless if I did.' He then discloses how he changed his belief to 'I don't like stammering in public but if I do I do, too bad! I can accept myself with my stammer even if others put me down.' At the end of a session in which he has disclosed his experience in overcoming this personal problem, WD will generally ask clients how they reacted to his disclosure, what they learned from it, and whether or not they would have preferred to have had this information. The clients' feedback is used to gauge the likely future benefit of additional self-disclosure.

Indications: Use with clients who believe that 'I can be helped only by someone who has gone through what I've been through' (e.g. substance abusers) and with clients who are pleased to see that they are being counselled by a human being rather than a supreme one. Some clients may not know how to talk about themselves intimately and therefore therapist self-disclosure acts as a way of 'opening up' such clients. Use generally as part of the process of building rapport with clients.

Contraindications: Do not use with clients who would use such information against the therapist, e.g. 'I'm here to talk about my problems not listen to yours. If I'd known what you were going to be like, I wouldn't have bothered coming.' Counsellor self-disclosure should also not be used with clients who expect their therapist to understand their problems without having experienced these themselves. Also, some clients believe that their problems are unique and therefore they may feel affronted that their therapist is claiming similar experiences, thereby making the clients' problems more commonplace.

Rational humorous songs

Ellis (1977a) has written about the use of his now famous rational songs in counselling. For example, the counsellor can hand a client a song sheet and sing, preferably in an outrageous voice, a rational song that has been carefully selected to communicate the rational alternatives to the client's target irrational belief. Since Ellis tends to favour songs that were written many years ago, it may be more productive for the counsellor to rewrite the words to more up-to-date and popular songs for clients not familiar with some of the 'old favourites.'

The following is a rational humorous song written by WD to the tune of 'God save the Queen':

> God save my precious spleen
> Send me a life serene
> God save my spleen
> Protect me from things odious
> Give me a life melodious
> And if things get too onerous
> I'll whine, bawl and scream

Once clients can identify their own irrational belief in the lyrics, they can then be helped to rewrite the words of the song to reflect a rational philosophy.

Indications: Use with clients who enjoy humour in therapy and see the therapeutic purpose of singing humorous songs in order for the rational lyrics to 'sink into my head like advertising jingles'.

Contraindications: Do not use with clients who would be appalled at coming to therapy for a 'singalong'; with clients who see therapy as a serious endeavour, not a light-hearted one, or who would feel embarrassed or very uncomfortable at the prospect of singing in front of and/or with the therapist.

Rational prescriptions

One of us (JY) will occasionally make a great show of writing the client a 'rational prescription' at session's end, as illustrated in the following dialogue:

Counsellor: Okay – we spent a good part of today's session discussing how you *can stand* feeling anxious while you're out driving in your car, even though you don't *like* feeling that way: We've run out of time now so we'll have to stop, but before we do, I just want to give you a prescription that will help you as you try to apply this concept. (Scribbles on a small notepad, tears off the sheet with a flourish, and hands it to the client.)

Client: (reading sheet) It says, 'TOUGH SHIT!'
Counsellor: That's right – and if you apply a 'tough shit' philosophy when you begin feeling anxious – meaning, 'I don't like it but I can stand it' – you'll be better able to resist the urge to flee homeward when you're out driving!
Client: (laughs) A 'tough shit' philosophy! I like that – and I can think of about a hundred other situations that I can use it for! (Client folds the 'prescription' and places it in her bag.)

It is noted that a good number of clients have actually reported that they stowed their 'rational prescriptions' in a safe place (such as a wallet or handbag) for use at times when they experienced a significant emotional disturbance. It is possible that these little slips of paper serve to augment clients' independent efforts at disputing their irrational beliefs in their everyday lives, as they may prompt recall of the counsellor's 'rational voice'. Ideally, as counselling proceeds, clients make progress in internalising a rational philosophy, so that such external props are no longer required.

Indications: Use with clients who find it difficult to formulate their own coping statements and do not object to the therapist's directiveness in supplying one.

Contraindications: Some clients may have unpleasant or hostile associations with medical doctors writing prescriptions in order to get rid of or not listen to them also, do not use with clients who show signs of becoming dependent upon a regular supply of rational prescriptions from the therapist instead of devising their own rational coping statement.

Reduction to absurdity

Here the counsellor assumes temporarily that the client's irrational belief is true and carries it to its logical extreme, thus illuminating its absurdity. For example, Richard Wessler, once director of training at the then-named Institute for RET in New York, related the following episode when he was working with a client who irrationally demanded a guarantee that bad things would not happen in his life. Wessler suddenly jumped up and hid under his desk, inviting his client to join him there. His puzzled client enquired why and was told by Wessler that this was the only way to guarantee that the ceiling would not fall on them. The client refused to join Wessler, having understood the point of his intervention. Note how Wessler, in this example, combined a reduction to absurdity intervention with a flamboyant counsellor action to illustrate an appropriate rational concept.

Indications: Use with clients who can distinguish between the absurdity of their ideas and not damning themselves as absurd for holding these ideas.

Contraindications: Do not use with clients who believe that they or their problems are being ridiculed and/or cannot see the logical conclusions of their irrational beliefs.

We urge readers to be creative and devise novel vivid disputing methods, which should preferably be tailored to help individual clients. It has been our experience that effective rational emotive behavioural counsellors are creative in this respect and tend to avoid the slavish replication of vivid techniques devised by others.

Homework Aids in Promoting Intellectual Rational Insight

While we have focused thus far on counsellors' in-session interventions, which aim to promote clients' intellectual rational insight, an important part of this process is carried out by clients between sessions. These are frequently embodied in 'homework' assignments negotiated between client and counsellor.

Listening to audiotapes of sessions

It sometimes happens that clients become confused during the disputing process in counselling sessions. This may occur, for example, when clients become emotionally distracted in the sessions, and/or counsellors work too quickly for the clients' level of understanding. In such cases, clients can often facilitate their acquisition of rational concepts by reviewing audiotapes of their sessions. This has the advantage that clients can replay segments of the tape as many times as they find valuable to clarify their understanding of what transpired between them and their counsellors. When this technique is suggested, counsellors should preferably encourage clients to write down any issues they wish to discuss in their following counselling session, and in particular to make a note of any doubts they may have about the invalidity and self-defeating nature of their irrational beliefs.

Some clients do not find listening to tapes of their therapy sessions very useful. These are often clients who blame themselves for their lack of understanding as demonstrated in the session, or for the sound of their voice. Although it is sometimes helpful to suggest that such clients use the tapes as stimuli to dispute their irrational beliefs about these two features, counsellors should preferably not insist that clients listen to these tapes, when doing so is not helpful for them.

Indications: Use with all clients who do not object to their sessions being taped and have accepted, usually tentatively at first, that inter-session listening to these tapes can facilitate their therapeutic progress.

Contraindications: Do not use with clients who refuse to be audiotaped because 'I can't relax or be myself with that bloody thing on!' or, as mentioned above, with clients who might make themselves more disturbed by listening to the tapes and do not wish to persist in overcoming this, e.g. the depression-inducing belief 'I just can't believe how pathetic I am when I listen to myself endlessly moaning. I don't want to listen to my garbage any more – it's bad enough saying it in the sessions.'

Structured disputing

There exist a number of forms that structure the disputing process for clients to use between counselling sessions. A good example is *DIBS* (disputing irrational beliefs) and Ellis (1979c, pp. 79-80) has outlined its form thus:

Question 1:   What irrational belief do I want to dispute and surrender?
Answer: I must be as effective and sexually fulfilled as most other women.
Question 2:   Can I rationally support this belief?
Answer: ....
Question 3:   What evidence exists of the truth of this belief?
Answer: ....
Question 4:   What evidence exists of the falseness of my belief that I must be as orgasmic as other women are?
Answer: ....
Question 5:   What are the worst possible things that could actually happen to me if I never achieved the orgasm that I think I must achieve?
Answer: ....
Question 6:   What good things could happen, or could I make happen, if I never achieved the heights of orgasm that I think I must achieve?
Answer: ....

As a homework exercise DIBS is best used after a general Socratic and/or didactic disputing sequence has been successfully completed, and after the counsellor has demonstrated the use of DIBS in the session, taking the irrational belief that has been successfully disputed as an example.

Apart from DIBS, there exist a number of structured disputing exercises that can be suggested for use as cognitive homework assignments. Two examples of these appear in Figures 6.1 and 6.2. The major purpose of these forms is to help clients to identify, challenge and change their irrational beliefs, and they appear to have a number of shared components. They encourage clients to identify activating events (or inferences about these events); unhealthy negative feelings and/or self-defeating actions that occur in the context of these events; and their mediating irrational beliefs. Furthermore, these forms invite clients to question their irrational beliefs and provide spaces for them to identify rational alternatives to that irrational belief. They also help clients to formulate likely emotional and/or behavioural effects of these new rational beliefs. It is recommended that rational emotive behavioural counsellors demonstrate the use of these forms in counselling sessions before asking clients to use them in their daily lives.

Indications: Use with clients who have shown some ability at verbal disputing using logical, empirical and pragmatic arguments and at using the forms

10 Steps to Dealing with
Emotional and Behavioural Problems
Using an ABCDE form

Step 1   Describe the problem/situation- *put it in the box below:*

Problem/Situation:

Step 2   **Complete C**

i)   *Choose **one** unhealthy negative emotion from the list below that best captures how you felt in the above situation and put it in the 'major unhealthy negative emotion' box below:*

- Anxiety
- Depression
- Unhealthy Anger
- Guilt
- Shame
- Hurt
- Unhealthy Jealousy
- Unhealthy Envy

ii)   *Write down the major self-defeating behaviour associated with your unhealthy negative emotion in the 'major self defeating behaviour' box below. This could include what you "felt like" doing even though you didn't do it (this is known as an action tendency).*

iii)   *Use one form for each emotion if you experienced more than one emotion for each event.*

iv)   *If your problem only concerns self-defeating behaviour leave the 'major unhealthy negative emotion' box blank.*

C = CONSEQUENCE

Major unhealthy negative emotion:	Major self-defeating behaviour (or action tendency):

Step 3   **Complete A**

i)   *Describe the aspect of the situation that you were most disturbed about in the 'activating event' box below.*

ii)   *It is very important at this point that you assume temporarily that A is true. Note that:*

- *A can be internal to you or external to you.*
- *A can refer to an event in the past, present or future.*
- *A can be an inference.*

A = ACTIVATING EVENT

Activating event:

Figure 6.1

Step 4   Write down your irrational beliefs (iBs) about A

i)   *Work from the top to the bottom of the four boxes under irrational beliefs (iBs).*

ii)   *Leave any box blank that does not apply.*

iii)   *Look for:*

- DOGMATIC DEMANDS - musts, absolute shoulds, oughts
- AWFULISING - it's awful, terrible, horrible, more than 100% bad
- LOW FRUSTRATION TOLERANCE - I can't stand it, I can't bear it
- SELF/OTHER DOWNING - I'm bad, worthless/you're bad, worthless.

Irrational Beliefs (iBs)	Disputing (D1)
DOGMATIC DEMAND:	Why this isn't true:
	Why this isn't logical:
	Why this isn't helpful:
AWFULISING:	Why this isn't true:
	Why this isn't logical:
	Why this isn't helpful:
LOW FRUSTRATION TOLERANCE (LFT):	Why this isn't true:
	Why this isn't logical:
	Why this isn't helpful:
SELF/OTHER DOWNING:	Why this isn't true:
	Why this isn't logical:
	Why this isn't helpful:

Step 5   Complete D1 - Disputing

i)   *Work from the top to the bottom of the four boxes under disputing (D1) above.*

ii)   *For each irrational belief give the appropriate explanations:*

- Explain why your irrational belief (iB) isn't true/isn't realistic/isn't consistent with reality.
- Explain why your irrational belief (iB) isn't logical/doesn't logically follow from your rational belief.
- Explain why your irrational belief (iB) isn't helpful to you.

Figure 6.1 (continued)

Step 6   Complete rational beliefs (rBs)

i)   *Work from the top to the bottom of the four boxes under rational beliefs (rBs).*

ii)   *Leave blank any boxes which do not apply.*

iii)   *Strive for:*

- NON-DOGMATIC PREFERENCES - prefer, want, desire
- ANTI-AWFULISING - it's bad, unfortunate
- HIGH FRUSTRATION TOLERANCE - I can stand it, I can bear it
- SELF/OTHER ACCEPTANCE - I am/you are a fallible human being

It is important that you <u>assert the rational belief</u> *and* <u>negate the irrational belief</u> in each section e.g. I would *prefer* to pass my exam, *but I don't have to do so.*

Rational beliefs (rBs)	Disputing (D2)
NON-DOGMATIC PREFERENCE:	Why this is true:
	Why this is logical:
	Why this is helpful:
ANTI-AWFULISING:	Why this is true:
	Why this is logical:
	Why this is helpful:
HIGH FRUSTRATION TOLERANCE (HFT):	Why this is true:
	Why this is logical:
	Why this is helpful:
SELF/OTHER ACCEPTANCE:	Why this is true:
	Why this is logical:
	Why this is helpful:

Step 7   Complete D2 - Disputing

i)   *Work from the top to the bottom of the four boxes under disputing (D2) above.*

ii)   *For each rational belief give the appropriate explanations:*

- Explain why your rational belief (rB) is true/is realistic/is consistent with reality.
- Explain why your rational belief (rB) is logical/logically follows from your rational belief.
- Explain why your rational belief is helpful to you.

Figure 6.1 (continued)

Step 8   Complete E

i)   *Provide a healthy negative emotion from the list below and put it in the 'new healthy negative emotion' box - ensuring that it is a constructive alternative to the unhealthy negative emotion you placed under C:*

- Concern   (unhealthy = Anxiety)
- Sadness   (unhealthy = Depression)
- Healthy Anger   (unhealthy = Unhealthy Anger)
- Remorse   (unhealthy = Guilt)
- Disappointment   (unhealthy = Shame)
- Sorrow   (unhealthy = Hurt)
- Healthy Jealousy   (unhealthy = Unhealthy Jealousy)
- Healthy Envy   (unhealthy = Unhealthy Envy)

ii)   *Write down your constructive negative behaviour associated with the healthy new emotion and put it in the 'new constructive behaviour' box below. Again this could include your action tendency (i.e. what you felt like doing).*

iii) *If your problem was only associated with self-defeating behaviour just complete the 'new constructive behaviour' box below.*

E = New Effect

New healthy negative emotion:	New constructive behaviour (or action tendency):

Step 9   Reconsider A

i)   *While holding your new rational beliefs go back to A (the 'activating event' box on the first page) and correct any distorted inferences that you find there and complete the 'What I now think happened at A' box below.*

iii) *Ask yourself the following:*

- Is this what really happened?
- Is there a more accurate inference I could have made?
- What would a team of objective observers say happened at A?

Revised A

What I now think happened at A:

Step 10   Homework

i)   *Discuss a suitable homework assignment with your therapist to strengthen your conviction in your rational beliefs.*

ii)   *Complete the box below with your agreed homework assignment.*

Homework

My homework is:

Figure 6.1 (continued)

REBT SELF-HELP FORM

Albert Ellis Institute for Rational Emotive Behavior Therapy

45 East 65th Street, New York, NY 10021

(212) 535-0822

(A) ACTIVATING EVENTS, thoughts. or feelings that happened just before I felt emotionally disturbed or acted self-defeatingly: _____

(C) CONSEQUENCE or CONDITION–disturbed feeling or self-defeating behavior–that I produced and would like to change: _____

(B) BELIEFS–Irrational BELIEFS (IBs) leading to my CONSEQUENCE (emotional disturbance or self-defeating behavior). Circle all that apply to these ACTIVATING EVENTS (A).	(D) DISPUTES for each circled IRRATIONAL BELIEF. Examples: *"Why MUST I do very well?"* *"Were is it written* that I am a BAD PERSON?" *"Were is the evidence* that I MUST be approved or accepted?"	(E) EFFECTIVE RATIONAL BELIEFS (RBs) to replace my IRRATIONAL BELIEFS (IBs). Examples: *'I'd PREFER to do very well but I don't HAVE TO." 'I am a PERSON WHO acted badly, not a BAD PERSON." "There is no evidence that I HAVE TO be approved, though I would LIKE to be."*
1. I MUST do well or very well!		
2. I am a BAD OR WORTHLESS PERSON when I act weakly or stupidly.		

Figure 6.2 REBT self-help form (Sichel and Ellis, 1984). (Reproduced with the permission of the Albert Ellis Institute for Rational Emotive Behavior Therapy, New York, USA (© Albert Ellis Institute, 1984.)

3. I MUST be approved or accepted by people I find important!

4. I am a BAD, UNLOVABLE PERSON if I get rejected.

5. People MUST treat me fairly and give me what I NEED!

6. People who act immorally are undeserving, ROTTEN PEOPLE!

7. People MUST live up to my expectations or it is TERRIBLE!

8. My life MUST have few major hassles or troubles.

9. I CAN'T STAND really bad things or very difficult people!

Figure 6.2 (continued)

(OVER)

10. It's AWFUL or HORRIBLE when major things don't go my way

11. I CAN'T STAND IT when life is really unfair!

12. I NEED to be loved by someone who matters to me a lot!

13. I NEED a good deal of immediate gratification and HAVE TO feel miserable when I don't get it!

Additional Irrational Beliefs:

14.

15.

(OVER)

Figure 6.2 (continued)

16.

17.

18.

(F) FEELINGS and BEHAVIORS I experienced after arriving at my EFFECTIVE RATIONAL BELIEFS:

I WILL WORK HARD TO REPEAT MY EFFECTIVE RATIONAL BELIEFS FORCEFULLY TO MYSELF ON MANY OCCASIONS SO THAT I CAN MAKE MYSELF LESS DISTURBED NOW AND ACT LESS SELF-DEFEATINGLY IN THE FUTURE.

Figure 6.2 (continued)

in the session. Therapists need to be alert that clients are writing their own rational responses rather than copying the examples contained in some of the forms.

Contraindications: Do not use with clients who have little, if any, formal disputing ability and, instead, are relying on simple coping statements on flash cards and/or are functionally illiterate. Some clients might see the forms as too complex or time-consuming to fill in, possibly reflecting their low frustration tolerance, and therefore valuable therapy time might be wasted trying to persuade these clients to fill in the forms.

Rational self-help material

Rational emotive behavioural counsellors frequently suggest that clients read or listen to self-help materials between sessions in order to build upon and reinforce the rational intellectual insight that clients gain within sessions. Since there is a wide range of such aids available, counsellors are recommended to monitor clients' reactions to these so that they can suggest material that is most appropriate to the client's level of understanding of rational concepts. Frequently suggested books include Ellis and Harper's (1975) *A New Guide to Rational Living*, Ellis and Becker's (1982) *A Guide to Personal Happiness*, and Dryden and Gordon's (1990) *Think Your Way To Happiness*. When using these books, counsellors, in the first instance, are advised to assign chapters that reinforce the message that beliefs determine emotions and actions, and thereafter recommend particular chapters relevant to the client's problem(s). It is helpful to encourage clients to note points for future discussion in counselling sessions, particularly those that they do not understand and those with which they disagree. If clients find the three books mentioned difficult to understand, they can be asked to read less complex material such as Young's (1974) *A Rational Counseling Primer* or Kranzler's (1974) *You Can Change How You Feel*.

In addition, REBC-oriented books are available that are devoted to particular client problems, such as depression, anger, anxiety, procrastination, etc., and in this regard Windy Dryden and Paul Hauck's books in the Sheldon Press *Overcoming Common Problems* series are particularly popular with British clients.

In addition to reading material, there exist numerous audiotapes on general and specific applications of rational emotive behavioural theory that clients can use for the same purposes as the books we have mentioned. Again, counsellors are advised to elicit clients' reactions to such material, paying particular attention to doubts and disagreements, which can then be discussed in regular sessions.

Indications: Use with clients who see the benefits of using self-help material to deepen understanding of their problems and the possible solutions to

them. Some clients may find this material to be the main vehicle of constructive change. REB counsellors should always ask for feedback at the next session to ensure that the material has been read or listened to.

Contraindications: Do not use with clients who have little interest in reading books and pamphlets or who have little patience for listening to tapes.
With these clients, action-oriented tasks are more likely to be effective
(unless the client steadfastly refuses to do any homework assignments).

While the achievement of *intellectual* rational insight is an important
stage for clients in the counselling process, as noted earlier, it is rarely sufficient for meaningful psychological change to occur. For such change to take
place, clients need to achieve *emotional* rational insight, and the next chapter is devoted to its promotion.

Chapter 7
Promoting Emotional Rational Insight

Overview

In this chapter, we deal with issues concerning the promotion of emotional rational insight. First, we note that helping clients to achieve this type of insight is difficult and list a number of reasons why this is so. Then, we highlight standard and vivid techniques that are used during this stage of rational emotive behavioural counselling. Thus, we describe cognitive, imagery and behavioural techniques, most of which have a decidedly emotive quality. As before, we conclude with some indications for, and contraindications against, the use of these techniques. Finally, we outline a number of vivid cues that counsellors can use to encourage clients to initiate the process of promoting emotional rational insight.

Promoting Emotional Rational Insight is Difficult

When clients have achieved intellectual but not emotional insight into rational concepts, they typically make such statements as, 'Yes, I see that what you say makes sense, but I don't believe it yet', or 'I understand it up here in my head, but not down here in my gut.' It is important to explain to clients that gaining intellectual rational insight is an important step in the change process, but one that is usually insufficient to bring about meaningful emotional and behavioural change. Rational emotive behavioural counsellors further explain that, in order to achieve significant attitude change that affects feelings and actions, i.e. emotional rational insight, clients will usually have to employ repeatedly and persistently a variety of cognitive, emotive and behavioural techniques.

As rational emotive behavioural practitioners note (e.g. Grieger, 1985), helping clients to move from intellectual to emotional rational insight is often a difficult painstaking process for a number of reasons. First, as Ellis (1976) in particular has argued, humans have a distinct biologically based tendency towards irrational thinking and often have a hard time working against this tendency.

Second, even those rational emotive behavioural counsellors who adopt a social learning perspective, rather than a biological perspective on human irrationality, acknowledge that changing irrational beliefs is a difficult process. Such theorists (e.g. Grieger, 1985) note that once clients have learned to think irrationally and to act in accordance with their irrational beliefs, they become habituated to these ideas and 'changing anything so well learned, therefore, requires repeated energetic efforts, even for those who are willing and committed to change' (Grieger, 1985, p. 144).

Third, many clients have a philosophy of low frustration tolerance (LFT) and believe that they should not have to work so hard to effect meaningful psychological change and, as Grieger (1985, p. 145) notes, 'left to their own devices, they drift, goof and act on their acknowledged irrational, self-defeating beliefs even though they know better.' Attacking clients' LFT beliefs is a prominent feature of promoting emotional rational insight.

Fourth, and related to the above, clients often become habituated to their problems and become used to the 'comfortable discomfort' that these problems bring. They fear that change may bring more acute discomfort and therefore will not risk changing. Rational emotive behavioural counsellors need to help clients understand that they may indeed feel more uncomfortable in the short term, but if they work at tolerating such discomfort, the long-term rewards will usually outweigh the short-term rewards of avoiding discomfort.

Fifth, as Fransella (1985) has shown, clients often give their psychological problems a central position in their sense of identity (e.g. a person who stammers sees himself as 'a stammerer') and they cannot imagine how they, would lead their lives if they did not, for example, stammer. Here, rational emotive behavioural counsellors may choose to employ general semantic methods, such as helping clients to use more precise and accurate language (e.g. changing 'I am a stammerer' to 'I am a person who stammers under certain conditions and not under other conditions'). In addition, they would help such clients construct a view of what life might be like if they did not stammer as often.

In a related vein, one of us (JY) has noted that clients with a strong self-created 'need' for other people's approval may be quite tuned in to what they think significant others want and prefer, but are out of touch with their own wants and preferences. Such individuals often have a difficult time envisioning a future existence in which they have given up their primary agenda of 'people pleasing', as this agenda historically provided them with a set of goals and behavioural guidelines (albeit dysfunctional ones) for structuring their daily lives. These clients can benefit from counselling interventions designed to help them develop their awareness of their own personal likes and dislikes. Once identified, these likes and dislikes can then be translated into new life goals for which to strive.

Sixth, clients may experience sources of secondary gain as a result of having their problems. Thus, a woman who wishes to lose weight in order to be more attractive to men might find, if she is successful, that she has to be assertive in declining to sleep with men, which she would find difficult. An advantage of being fat for this woman, then, is that she does not place herself in situations where she might act promiscuously, for which she would evaluate very negatively. It is clear, then, that rational emotive behavioural counsellors need to focus particular attention on assessing potential obstacles to the change process and deal with these as they become relevant during this stage of counselling. This issue will be discussed more fully in Chapter 11.

Seventh, as Grieger, among others, has noted, clients often make unrealistic predictions of what their lives might be like if they adhered to a rational philosophy of life: these include a 'fear of losing one's identity or becoming a phony . . . ; fears of becoming emotionally dulled or machine-like by thinking rationally; and fears of becoming mediocre and losing one's specialness by giving up perfectionistic ideas' (Grieger, 1985, p. 144). One of WD's clients recently announced that she didn't think much of life according to REBC philosophy because it meant never falling in love! It is important that rational emotive behavioural counsellors be aware that clients may well misinterpret rational emotive behavioural philosophy and be ready to correct such misconceptions. We advise rational emotive behavioural counsellors to ask clients directly about how they would construe their lives if they indeed achieved what they hoped to gain from counselling, rather than waiting for clients to disclose such constructions. In such exploration, counsellors should pay particular attention to misinterpretations of REBC philosophy and deal with them accordingly.

Finally, clients may find it difficult to put their intellectual rational insights into consistent practice because the balance of their outside relationships would be disturbed if they did. For example, asserting oneself with one's spouse may lead to marital problems; getting over one's depression may be a trigger for one's partner to become depressed, etc. Rational emotive behavioural counsellors need to be sensitive to the fact that clients in individual counselling have a wide variety of interpersonal relationships in their daily lives which may exert a positive or negative influence on their attempts to achieve their counselling goals. Rational emotive behavioural counsellors may indeed suggest to clients that they involve their significant others in counselling, particularly if these others may wittingly or unwittingly sabotage clients' attempts to change. Since this book is concerned with counselling individuals, we refer the reader to Ellis and Dryden (1997) for a discussion of the practice of REBC in its other modalities. In the final analysis, however, if significant others do react negatively to clients' attempts to change and do not want to become involved in counselling, then rational emotive behavioural counsellors encourage their clients to view this situation as another troublesome A in the ABC framework, to be coped with using rational thinking.

Techniques to Promote Emotional Rational Insight

The remainder of this chapter will focus on methods and techniques that clients can use to achieve emotional rational insight. In addition to using repeatedly and persistently the disputing methods outlined in the previous chapter, clients are encouraged to use a variety of cognitive, behavioural and emotive assignments in the service of achieving emotional and behavioural changes. We shall focus especially on methods and techniques that are most frequently used in rational emotive behavioural counselling, and those which are particularly vivid. In this latter respect, Ellis (1958, p. 45, italics added) from REBC's inception strongly recommended that clients undertake 'some kind of activity which itself will act as a *forceful* counter-propagandist agency against the nonsense they believe.' Ellis continues to stress that for clients who will agree to do them, *dramatic*, *forceful* and *implosive* activities remain the best forms of promoting emotional insight. This is due to the fact that since clients, according to Ellis, have a pronounced tendency to think irrationally, they need to counter this tendency forcefully and repeatedly.

Cognitive techniques

Clients are encouraged to use cognitive techniques to convince themselves outside counselling sessions that rational philosophies, which they can acknowledge as correct in counselling, are indeed correct and functional for them. The emphasis here is particularly on clients weakening their adherence to irrational beliefs and strengthening their adherence to rational beliefs. We have found that techniques that encourage clients to provide evidence in favour of rational beliefs are particularly helpful at this stage of rational emotive behavioural counselling, and these will be discussed first.

Building your rational portfolio

Here, as noted above, counsellors encourage clients to focus on evidence in favour of rational beliefs. Thus, a client who can see that there is no evidence in support of her irrational belief 'I *must* control my emotions in public' is asked to explain in detail why it would be better but not essential if she could control her emotions in public. The role of the counsellor in this process is to encourage the client to find a variety of different reasons in support of the rational belief and to suggest others when the client has exhausted her own supply. We call this technique 'Building your rational portfolio.'

Indications: Use with clients who are able to accumulate and articulate the evidence underpinning their newly emerging rational beliefs.

Contraindications: Do not use with clients who continually struggle to formulate and support a rational response – a few coping statements may be all that can be expected in such cases.

Devil's advocate disputing

Once a client has sufficiently built up her portfolio in the above manner and shows some skill at disputing her irrational beliefs, the counsellor can adopt the role of a devil's advocate and attack the client's rational thinking. The client's role is to point out flaws in the reasoning of the devil's advocate and destroy his arguments, thus strengthening further his or her rational belief:

Counsellor: (as devil's advocate)   But how can you possibly say that you don't need a man in your life? Look at all your friends, they do and they're normal. Aren't you abnormal for trying to deny your needs?

Client: Just because my friends believe they need a man in their life doesn't mean that I have to believe the same. Most of them are anxious when they don't have a man and anxious when they do in case he leaves them. I don't want that for myself. Also I'm not denying my need, I'm trying to challenge it and if I am abnormal in this regard I'm abnormally healthy, not sick as you seem to imply.

In devil's advocate disputing the counsellor looks for issues that the client does not deal with and feeds this back into the discussion. Thus, in the above example, if the client did not deal with the issue of abnormality the counsellor in his role of devil's advocate would have raised this issue again.

When beginning devil's advocate disputing, the counsellor should preferably raise one issue at a time until the client shows some skill at this procedure. The example provided above is with a client who has previously demonstrated a high level of skill at this form of disputing. Thus, the counsellor, in the example, can raise two or three issues at once.

Another major counsellor goal in devil's advocate disputing is to find vulnerable points in the client's rational thinking so that these can be dealt with. Here the counsellor presents irrational beliefs to the client to which she experiences difficulty in responding. When this occurs it is best to stop the procedure and discuss the new irrational belief in a more traditional manner.

Devil's advocate disputing is one example of what Kassinove and DiGiuseppe (1975) call rational role reversal, where the counsellor adopts an irrational role and the client adopts a rational role. Although we have focused on devil's advocate disputing where the counsellor attacks the client's thinking, rational role reversal can take different forms. For example, the counsellor plays the irrational part of the client and supplies the client with irrational messages. The client's task is to respond rationally to these irrational messages. In another version the counsellor plays a naïve client with an emotional problem that is usually similar to the client's, and presents an irrational belief identical to the one targeted for change. The client is encouraged to adopt the role of the rational emotive behavioural counsellor and help the 'client' to dispute his or her irrational belief.

It should be reiterated that all versions of rational role reversal are best used when the client has demonstrated a fair measure of skill at disputing his or her own irrational beliefs using more traditional methods, as described in the previous chapter. As noted above, they can also all be used to identify weaknesses in the client's rational arguments in response to irrational beliefs articulated in 'reversed role' by counsellors.

Indications: Use with clients who have already shown some ability or flair in disputing and are now ready to move on to this more difficult phase in the disputing process.

Contraindications: Do not use with clients who lack the cognitive sophistication to undertake this technique, who would become confused if the therapist attacked their rational beliefs or who need a lot of therapist support, not confrontation, in their attempts to absorb rational ideas.

The courtroom evidence technique

In the courtroom evidence technique, the client is asked to play the roles of prosecuting attorney and defence attorney, providing evidence for and against the client's rational belief in one 'trial', and doing the same with the client's irrational belief in another 'trial'. The goal, of course, is to provide more compelling evidence in favour of the rational belief and to contradict the 'evidence' in favour of the irrational belief. At the end of this procedure the client is asked to play the role of judge and sum up all the evidence presented and provide a verdict, which hopefully is: 'I thus conclude that the rational belief is valid and the irrational belief is invalid.' If the client concludes otherwise the counsellor is provided with useful information concerning the client's doubts and reservations about the relevant rational belief. These are then discussed once the 'trial' has been concluded. After these have been discussed the counsellor calls for an appeal against the previous verdict and the procedure is repeated.

Indications: As with devil's advocate disputing.

Contraindications: Do not use with clients who show no prior skill at disputing.

Rational essays

Another technique that can be used under the heading of strengthening rational beliefs is to suggest that the client write an essay on a theme suggested by a rational belief, e.g. 'Why I cannot legitimately give myself a global rating.' Here is an extract from an essay written by one of WD's clients on this theme:

I have many different roles in my life. But let me take one, 'mother', to show how complex this role is. Breaking this role down into its component parts, I find there are many different aspects of mothering. But let me take one, 'disciplining.' Even this has different components including 'setting limits', 'working with my husband', 'voice tone', etc. Let me take one: voice tone. Even this has different components including firmness, gentleness, harshness, etc. Yesterday, in the space of an hour I used what I consider to be a good voice tone (firmness) with my child, and a bad voice tone (harshness). Can I say I have a good voice tone? Hardly. How stupid it is then for me to say 'I'm a good or bad disciplinarian with my child.' If that is stupid how even more stupid for me to say, 'I'm a good or bad mother.' Looking at it this way how can I possibly say that I'm a good or bad person? Obviously I can't. As Dr Dryden suggested, I will undertake to use the sentence 'I am a person who . . .' whenever I can. But if I don't and I do rate myself, I won't rate *myself* badly for rating myself.

Indications: Use with clients who have already indicated they enjoy writing or that writing helps to make things clear in their mind, or who have no objection to undertaking such an assignment.

Contraindications: Do not use with clients who are illiterate, who have no interest in writing essays (e.g. 'I have no idea what to say'), or who prefer action assignments instead of armchair ones.

Rational proselytising (Bard, 1973)

Here, clients are encouraged to teach rational emotive behavioural principles to their friends and relatives. In teaching others to live more rationally it is hypothesised that clients will become more convinced of rational emotive behavioural philosophy, and in our experience this often happens. In the process of teaching these principles to significant others, clients learn to counter their objections and thus learn to think 'on their feet' when confronted with their own irrational beliefs. In addition, when clients report being unable to counter objections from significant others, these are discussed further in regular counselling sessions. This technique, however, is best used with caution and clients should be warned against playing the role of unwanted counsellor to friends and relations.

Indications: Use with clients who have demonstrated a good understanding of REBC principles and would use discretion in teaching these to others in order not to become an 'REBC bore'.

Contraindications: Do not use with clients who seem to misunderstand REBC and therefore would disseminate a warped version of it, or with those clients who do have a good grasp of REBC but who have the potential for turning it into zealotry or act as an unwanted 'agony aunt' trying to solve everyone's problems.

Tape-recorded disputing

In this technique, clients are encouraged to put a disputing sequence on tape and instructed to play both the rational and irrational parts of themselves. They are further encouraged to try to make the rational part more persuasive and more forceful in responding to the irrational part. Clients then play excerpts of these tapes to their counsellors, who check whether their clients have indeed successfully disputed their irrational beliefs and listen carefully to the tone of the dialogue. When clients do not dispute their irrational beliefs forcefully and persuasively this may be attributed to two factors. First, this may indicate their difficulties in responding to certain elements of their irrational philosophy, in which case their doubts and lack of intellectual insight should be targets for discussion in sessions. Second, it may indicate that clients find it difficult to be forceful in adopting the rational role. When clients experience such difficulty, counsellors should model appropriate ways of disputing forcefully and encourage clients to practise responding to their irrational beliefs in similar ways.

Indications: Use with clients who can gain greater insight into their disputing attempts by listening to themselves on tape.

Contraindications: Do not use with clients who feel enduringly embarrassed or awkward about listening to themselves on tape and who would become preoccupied with these feelings rather than focusing on their disputing efforts, or who would refuse to do it and/or see no reason for its use.

Passionate rational self-statements

Clients who are intellectually unable to do cognitive self-disputing in the traditional sense can be encouraged to use passionate rational self-statements instead. Here, clients and counsellors work together to develop appropriate rational self-statements that clients can use in their daily lives. Clients are then encouraged to repeat these statements in a very forceful manner instead of in their normal voice tone. Another variation of this technique is to encourage clients to say rational self-statements to their reflection in a mirror, using a passionate tone and dramatic gestures to reinforce the rational message.

Indications: Use with clients who have found no benefit from, or are unable to undertake, formal REBC disputing or who desire plain-speaking messages rather than 'therapy speak' as an aid to change.

Contraindications: Do not use with clients who require an intellectual framework in order to understand the potential efficacy of their new rational beliefs and would deprecate the use of simple and 'lightweight' exclamatory utterances like 'Get on with it!' (for procrastination).

Encouraging clients to go against their dysfunctional action tendencies

In Chapter 2, we introduced the concepts of action tendencies and response options. In Chapter 3 we argued that different emotions lead to different action tendencies and that, given a certain tendency to act, a person will choose certain response options and avoid others. We also argued that unhealthy negative emotions lead to dysfunctional action tendencies, which in turn influence individuals to choose responses that tend to be self-defeating. It follows that if clients are to be encouraged to act rationally, then counsellors need to encourage them to go against dysfunctional action tendencies. Also, as is argued in the next section, behavioural change is often the best way of encouraging clients to change their irrational beliefs. In order to encourage such behavioural change, rational emotive behavioural counsellors often have first to help clients to dispute the irrational beliefs that are implicit in their dysfunctional action tendencies.

For example, one of WD's clients experienced anxiety about asking girls to dance at a discotheque. His irrational belief in this situation was, 'I would be worthless if they refused to dance with me.' This client was helped to dispute this belief and to achieve intellectual rational insight. However, he still would not ask any girls to dance and work toward emotional rational insight due to his tendency to avoid anxiety (dysfunctional action tendency). Implicit in this action tendency was another irrational belief, 'I must be comfortable when I ask girls to dance.' Thus, in order to help this client to achieve emotional rational insight it was necessary first to help him to challenge this latter belief and change it to 'I prefer being comfortable when I ask girls to dance, but I can still do so even though I feel uncomfortable.' Then, he was encouraged to push himself to act on this latter belief and choose a different option from his response repertoire, i.e. ask girls to dance rather than avoid the situation. He did this repeatedly and achieved emotional rational insight on both the aforementioned beliefs.

When action tendencies encourage clients to avoid situations rather than to confront them constructively, activities that help them to reverse this trend have been called 'stay in there' activities by Grieger and Boyd (1980).

Another example: one of JY's clients wanted to overcome her car-driving phobia. She would, however, make herself anxious about the possibility of breaking down in some remote spot where assistance would not be readily available. In order to avoid this possibility, and the distressing anxiety she experienced whenever she thought about its occurrence, she would almost never venture more than a few blocks away from home in her car. After her irrational ideas had been elicited and disputed in traditional oral dialogue, she was encouraged to drive a lengthy distance in order to visit an old friend whom she had not seen for some time. She did indeed make herself anxious while travelling in her car to this friend's neighbourhood but, as agreed in session, disputed her belief that 'I *can't stand* feeling this way' and resisted her urge to flee homeward. She reached her destination and later returned home without mishap, and was thus able to re-evaluate her overestimation of the probability of having a breakdown while out driving. More importantly, she proved to herself that she could 'stay in there' and tolerate her anxious feelings, even though they were quite uncomfortable for her.

Indications: Use with any clients who need to acquire high frustration tolerance and/or an anti-awfulising outlook as part of their goals for change.

Contraindications: Do not use with clients who have been insufficiently prepared through in-session cognitive rehearsal to handle the situation, or with clients who are still emotionally disturbed about the situation and therefore will not enter or stay in it for long.

The same methods can be used when action tendencies encourage clients to act in self-defeating ways other than avoidance. However, whatever action tendencies are involved in clients' problems, the following principle can be recommended: whenever clients find it difficult to choose appropriate options from their repertoire, and in fact choose to act in accordance with their irrational action tendencies, look for and dispute their low frustration tolerance (LFT) ideas, since clients often have these in such situations.

Behavioural techniques

As shown above, one of the best ways of encouraging clients to achieve emotional rational insight is to have them change their self-defeating behaviour in relevant situations. We wish to reiterate this point, since many people wrongly believe that rational emotive behavioural counsellors employ cognitive techniques only to help clients change irrational beliefs. However, behaviour change should ideally be enacted while clients are simultaneously working cognitively to change their irrational beliefs. Thus, in the example we introduced in the previous section, the client asked girls to dance while convincing himself, 'I can do this even though I feel uncomfortable and I'm not a worm if I'm rejected.' With this point in mind we shall discuss in this section certain behavioural techniques that rational emotive behavioural counsellors particularly favour.

Ellis (1983c) has criticised some popular behavioural techniques on the grounds that they do not necessarily encourage clients to achieve emotional rational insight as efficiently as possible. In particular, he criticises those methods that encourage clients to confront dreaded events in a gradual manner. He argues that 'gradualism' may indeed reinforce some clients' low frustration tolerance ideas, e.g. 'I do need to go slowly; you see, even my counsellor believes I can't stand feeling anxious.' Whenever possible, then, rational emotive behavioural counsellors encourage their clients to act in dramatic and vivid ways because they believe significant attitude change is more likely to follow the successful completion of such tasks. In addition, dramatic behavioural assignments are recommended to help clients overcome their LFT beliefs. Here the focus is oriented toward clients changing their irrational beliefs concerning their internal experiences of anxiety or frustration, so that they are able to see that they can tolerate these feelings.

Shame-attacking exercises

Here clients are encouraged to act in a manner which they regard as 'shameful' while disputing their shame-creating beliefs. Clients are encouraged to act in ways that will encourage other people in the environment to pay attention to them and criticise them negatively, without breaking the law, bringing harm to themselves or the other people, or unduly alarming others. Clients are encouraged in particular to engage simultaneously in vigorous disputing such as, 'They may think I'm an idiot but I choose to accept myself even though I may be acting stupidly.' Examples of shame-attacking exercises that some of our clients have undertaken include: asking for directions to a street along which one is already walking; asking for a bar of chocolate in a hardware store; and wearing clothes back to front. One of the difficulties with shame-attacking exercises for clients is actually eliciting the aversive responses from others that clients predict will occur. For example, if a client is anxious about a shopkeeper laughing at him for acting stupidly, then the client may have to carry out shame-attacking exercises several times before he encounters such a shopkeeper. However, this actual encounter is important if the client is going to have the experience of disputing his shame-inducing belief in the context of the feared event. Otherwise the client may make an inferentially based change, i.e. he may come to learn 'it is unlikely that shopkeepers will laugh at me when I act stupidly.' While this change is not to be decried, it is less preferable than evaluative belief change, e.g. 'If shopkeepers laugh at me, I can still accept myself.'

Indications: Use with clients who fear criticism, disapproval or ridicule from others and therefore lead lives of excessive self-restraint because, for example, 'I'm afraid to upset others'.

Contraindications: Do not use with clients who might feel overwhelmed or highly anxious about carrying out this exercise and are not convinced by the therapist's rationale of the potential benefits to be gained, with clients who want to feel 'more comfortable' in social situations and are not striving for self-acceptance, or with any client who thinks it is a pointless exercise.

Risk-taking exercises

In risk-taking exercises clients are encouraged to do something they regard as being 'too risky.' These exercises are particularly helpful in encouraging clients to dispute discomfort-related irrational beliefs relating to certainty. For example, a client may be encouraged to take the risk of acting in an unpredictable manner, not knowing how others will respond, while disputing his belief 'I can stand the uncertainty of not knowing what will happen.'

Indications: Use with any clients who are prepared to venture into the unknown as part of building up their tolerance for new, uncertain or uncomfortable situations.

Contraindications: Do not use with any clients whose idea of risk-taking might put themselves or others in jeopardy or with clients whose view of therapy is that it should be protective, nurturing and virtually risk-free (these kind of clients might not be suitable for REBC).

Step-out-of-character exercises

Wessler (1984) has modified this exercise from Kelly (1955). Clients are encouraged to identify desired behavioural goals that are not currently enacted with frequency, and are encouraged to practise these behaviours while tolerating the accompanying feelings of 'unnaturalness' and to continue doing this until the new behaviour becomes habitual. For example, one of WD's clients chose the goal of eating more slowly, which for him was a desirable, non-shameful, non-risky exercise, but one that involved monitoring of eating habits and cognitive disputing of low-frustration tolerance ideas.

Indications: Use with any clients who can see that by trying out a desired behaviour it is more likely to encourage them to adopt that behaviour, e.g. an unassertive client acts assertively on some days at work, likes the confidence it brings him and therefore incorporates the new behaviour into his response options.

Contraindications: Do not use with clients who might feel frightened, bewildered or disorientated by stepping-out-of-character and therefore seek safe behavioural exercises by staying in-character, e.g. 'I might be able to make one or two comments at the meeting instead of staying quiet.'

In vivo desensitisation

These methods require clients repeatedly to confront their fears in an implosive manner. For example, clients with elevator phobia are asked to ride in elevators 20–30 times a day at the start of treatment instead of gradually working their way up to this situation either in imagery or in actuality. Again, simultaneous cognitive disputing is urged. Neuman (1982) has written on and presented tapes of short-term group-oriented treatment of phobias. In his groups, clients are encouraged to rate their levels of anxiety. The most important goal is for clients to experience a 'level 10', which is extreme panic. Neuman continually points out to people that it is important to experience 'level 10' because only then can they learn that they can survive and live through such an experience. Similarly, if inroads to severe phobic conditions are to be made, it is important for rational emotive behavioural counsellors to work toward helping clients tolerate extreme forms of anxiety before helping them to reduce this anxiety.

There are occasions when clients refuse to undertake such assignments. When this occurs, compromises should preferably be made, as discussed in Chapter 12.

Indications: Use with clients who agree to confront their fears fully and immediately.

Contraindications: Do not use with clients who seek gradual *in vivo* exposure to their fears, with clients who are prepared to experience only imaginal exposure to their fears, or with clients who have heart complaints or other related medical conditions.

Repetition of behavioural assignments

Some clients tend to do dramatic exercises once or twice and then drop them from their repertoire. Counsellors are often so glad and so surprised that their clients will actually do these assignments that they do not show them the importance of continuing to do them. One of the reasons for continued practice has already been mentioned – namely that clients are more likely to make inferential changes than belief changes by doing these assignments infrequently. This is largely because the 'dreaded' event has a far lower probability of occurring than clients think. However, sooner or later, if clients consistently and persistently put into practice the above assignments, they may well encounter such events that will provide a context for disputing of irrational beliefs. Thus, if counsellors really want to encourage clients to make changes at B as well as at A, they are advised to encourage clients consistently to do these dramatic assignments over a long period of time.

Indications: Use with clients who are seeking elegant change and therefore need to confront and deal with expected or actual 'awful' or fearful events.

Contraindications: Do not use with clients who seek confirmation from their infrequent behavioural tasks that 'dreaded' events are probably not going to occur and therefore relief is experienced (inelegant change).

Rewards and penalties

Ellis (1979c) has consistently employed rewards and penalties to encourage clients to take responsibility for being their own primary agents of change. Here, clients are encouraged to identify and employ positive reinforcements for undertaking assignments, and penalties when they do not do so. Such penalties can involve seeking out and facing unpleasant experiences that already exist in the clients' lives, or an introduction of new unpleasant experiences into the clients' lives. While not all clients require such encouragement, difficult and resistant clients, whose resistance is due to low frustration tolerance ideas, can be encouraged to take full responsibility for not putting into practice assignments that would stimulate change. Thus, dramatic experiences like giving away a 20 pound note, throwing away an eagerly awaited meal, and cleaning a dirty room at the end of a hard day's work are experiences that are designed to be so aversive that clients would choose to do the assignment previously avoided rather than undergo the penalty. Of course clients can, and often do, refuse to do the assignment and refuse to employ operant-conditioning methods. However, many clients who have been resistant to this part of the change process have, in our experience, begun to move when the counsellor adopts this no-nonsense approach.

Indications: Use with clients who require further encouragement or an additional inducement (with the emphasis on the reward) to carry out their homework tasks.

Contraindications: Do not use with clients who would focus only on the penalty as they know they are going to fail carrying out their tasks or would enjoy the reward without doing the work. Some clients may equate penalties with punishments and therefore think they are being persecuted by the therapist or see this technique as a further sign of their problem-solving inadequacies.

Imagery techniques

Lazarus (1989) has criticised rational emotive behavioural counselling for underemphasising the imagery modality in working with clients. This criticism does have some merit in that REBC practitioners prefer, whenever possible, to encourage clients towards emotional rational insight through action rather than through imagination, believing action to be a more powerful medium than imagery for promoting such insight. Perhaps the exception to this is the technique known as rational-emotive imagery (REI), which was pioneered by Maultsby (1975) and modified by Ellis. The purpose of REI is to promote emotional rational insight while vividly imagining troublesome events at A.

REI (Ellis version)

In Ellis's version of REI, a client is asked to imagine a vivid example of the critical A about which he or she has disturbed him- or herself and to 'get in touch with' the unhealthy negative emotion at A. The client is then asked to change the unhealthy emotion to its rational alternative (e.g. from anxiety to concern) while still vividly imagining the same situation at A. When clients execute the procedure successfully, they do so by changing their irrational belief to its rational alternative. However, counsellors are recommended to check this, since clients can achieve this feeling of change by modifying inferences or by distraction. When this occurs, the counsellor encourages the client to repeat the exercise, but this time without changing inferences and without using distractions. Once the clients have learned how to execute REI in the counselling session they are instructed to practise it for 30 days (three times a day for a minimum of ten minutes on each occasion).

Indications: Use with clients who want to confront and ameliorate imaginally their emotional disturbance through philosophic restructuring.

Contraindications: Do not use with clients who are reluctant to implode or fully experience their unhealthy negative emotions or who continually alter the details of the activating event in order to reduce its disturbance-producing 'awfulness', e.g. a client says that she now imagines people laughing with her instead of at her when she makes mistakes.

REI (Maultsby version)

In Maultsby's version of REI, the client is again asked to imagine vividly the situation at A, but this time is instructed to repeat forcefully the relevant rational belief at B in order to experience a healthy negative emotion at C. Repeated practice is again recommended after the client has understood the procedure.

It is worthwhile noting that some clients experience difficulty creating images and may have to be trained in stepwise fashion to utilise this ability. Furthermore, while helpful, it is probably not necessary for clients to imagine with clarity in order to benefit from both versions of REI.

Indications: Use with clients who find Ellis's version too complicated and therefore find this one more straightforward to carry out.

Contraindications: Do not use with clients who use positive thoughts or images in order to feel better rather than reduce their emotional disturbance through rational thinking.

Imagery rehearsal

Imagery rehearsal can be used in rational emotive behavioural counselling to build a bridge between the client's intellectual insight into a rational concept and his or her attempt to act on that insight in the world. For example, one client gained intellectual insight into her shame-based philosophy and understood intellectually, but not emotionally, that she was not a fool for acting foolishly; rather she was a fallible human being who acted foolishly. In order for her to begin to act on and internalise this rational belief, she was encouraged to act foolishly in public while practising the new rational philosophy. Imagery rehearsal was used with this client, as with others, prior to the behavioural assignment because she doubted her ability to execute the assignment in the real world. Thus:

Counsellor: OK. You say that you see the sense of doing that (Here the assignment was for her to go into a confectionery shop and ask for one brand of chocolate bar, leave the shop and return to exchange the bar for another brand. She was to practise simultaneously the rational belief: 'I'm a fallible human being even though I may appear stupid to others').

Client: Yes, but I don't know whether I can do it.

Counsellor: OK, but let's see. Let's try it out in your mind's eye first. Do you think imagining yourself doing it will help you to do it?

Client: It might.

Counsellor: OK. Now close your eyes and imagine that you've begun the exercise by going into the shop and buying the first bar. Can you picture that?

Client: Yes.

Counsellor: OK, and how do you feel in this image?

Client: Fine at this point.

Counsellor: Good. Now imagine you've bought the bar and you've left the shop. Picture yourself deciding to go back to exchange the bar. How do you feel now?

Client: Anxious.

Counsellor: OK. Now see yourself using that anxiety as a cue vigorously to say to yourself your new rational belief: 'I'm a fallible human being even though I may appear stupid to the shopkeeper'. Can you imagine yourself doing that?

Client: (Pause) Yes.

Counsellor: Now keep that new belief in mind and picture yourself going into the shop and see yourself ask for a swap and imagine that the shopkeeper's attitude implies that he thinks you are stupid. Really work on keeping the new philosophy in the front of your mind even in the face of his critical attitude and even though it's a struggle. Now really work on doing that. (Pause). Can you do that?

Client: (Pause). Yes, but it's difficult.

Counsellor: Now go over that scene in your mind's eye several times a day. Keep on assuming that the shopkeeper's attitude will be critical and see yourself accept yourself in the face of his attitude. Do you think that will help you to do that in reality?

Client: Yes, I think that may well help.

It is important to offer clients a coping rather than a mastery model of themselves in imagery rehearsal. Thus, note that the counsellor stressed both that it was a struggle to keep the new belief in her mind's eye and that she could do it even though it was difficult.

Indications: Use with clients who lack the confidence or ability to execute the behavioural task straightaway, or with clients for whom the technique provides additional preparation to ensure that the task will be completed successfully.

Contraindications: Do not use with clients whose anxiety would get worse and therefore make it unlikely that they would be prepared actually to carry out the task, with clients who would take refuge in endless imagery rehearsal, or with clients who are poor imagers.

Rational role construction

We have found it helpful to draw upon Kelly's (1955) 'fixed role therapy' method to help clients construct a new attitude. Let us assume that a client has once again gained intellectual insight into the rational concept of unconditional self-acceptance as a psychologically healthy alternative to the irrational concept of conditional self-esteem. We have the client select a relevant situation in which she can practise the new rational philosophy. We then say the following:

> Now imagine someone with whom you can identify, who is like you in many ways apart from the fact that, at the moment, she is more self-accepting than you. What kind of thoughts will the person have about herself, others, and the situation she finds herself in? What will she say in this situation, what will she be feeling and what will she be doing?

After this material has been collected and modified to represent a realistic rational model, i.e. one that is not perfectly rational and thus outside the client's scope, we suggest that the client imagines in her mind's eye for a week or two that she is that person, to see how the role fits. When the client has done this, we discuss her reactions and make appropriate adjustments to the new rational role. We then suggest that the client practises in imagery the modified role for a further week. Assuming that no further adjustments are necessary, we suggest that the client tries out the new role in action as an experiment. The client's reactions to this experiment are then discussed in counselling, with the counsellor helping the client to dispute any further irrational beliefs and suggesting modifications to the role as appropriate.

A variation of this method is to use the client as her own model and to contrast her present irrational self with a perfectly rational self and a fallible, i.e. imperfect, rational self. We particularly emphasise the latter distinction with clients who demand that they must be perfectly rational.

Indications: Use with clients who appreciate that acquiring a rational outlook requires a learning phase or developmental progression.

Contraindications: Do not use with clients who demand instant or rapid change without undertaking the accompanying hard work to achieve it, who insist on equating rational with perfect, or who seek only modest behavioural change with some rational coping statements to support it.

Vivid Cues for Encouraging Clients to Initiate the Process of Promoting Emotional Rational Insight

Although some clients conscientiously do the homework assignments that they and their counsellors have negotiated, other clients do not. It is true that some clients do not follow through on these assignments because of low frustration toleration ideas; still other clients do not follow through, particularly early on in the process of promoting emotional rational insight, because they require some vivid reminders to initiate this process. With such clients, we have found it particularly helpful to ask them what they generally find memorable in everyday life experiences. For example, some people find the printed word memorable while others have visual images on which they cue. Yet others focus primarily on auditory stimuli. We find that it is profitable to capitalise on whatever channel the client finds most memorable.

Vivid visual cues

There are a number of ways clients can remind themselves to initiate the disputing process. A number of rational emotive behavioural counsellors encourage clients to carry around small cards with rational self-statements written on them to which they can refer at various times. Other counsellors have encouraged clients to write reminders to themselves either to initiate a homework assignment or to refer to a rational message. These clients are encouraged to pin up such messages at various places around the home or in their work situation.

We find it helpful to encourage those clients who find visual images powerful to associate a particular dysfunctional feeling with a visual image that would enable them to initiate the disputing process. Thus, one client found it helpful to conjure up a sign in her mind that said 'Dispute' when she began to feel anxious. Another client, who was depressed, began to associate the onset of depression with a road sign on which was written 'Act Now.'

Another strategy we have used is to ascertain from clients what, if any, in-session experiences they have found particularly memorable. We try to help them encapsulate some of these experiences as a cue either to initiate the disputing process or to remind themselves of the relevant rational principle to which this experience referred. One client, who was prone to thinking of himself as an idiot for acting idiotically, found it memorable when WD made strange faces at him to help him get the point that concluding he was an idiot for acting idiotically was an overgeneralisation. Whenever he began to make such an overgeneralisation in everyday life, he would get the image of his counsellor making faces and quickly remember to what this referred. This helped him accept himself for any idiotic act he actually made, or thought he might make in the future.

Another client who did virtually no cognitive disputing or behavioural assignments outside the sessions was helped in the following manner: first, this issue was made the focus of counselling. Instead of asking her traditional disputing questions, WD asked her to imagine what he would say to her were he to respond to her irrational beliefs. She, in fact, had understood rational principles because her answers were very good. Her problem was that she would not employ these principles. WD then asked her if there was any way she could conjure up a picture of him giving her rational messages at various emotionally vulnerable times in her everyday life. She hit on the idea of imagining that he was perched on her shoulder whispering rational messages into her ear. Additionally she began to carry around a small card that said 'Imagine that Professor Dryden is on your shoulder.' This proved a particularly effective technique where all else had failed.

Indications: Use with clients who find such striking prompts or reminders genuinely helpful in stimulating disputing or encouraging task completion.

Contraindications: Do not use with clients who are not stimulated into action by such means or who use the search for such cues as a delaying tactic to avoid tackling their problems.

Vivid language

Wexler and Butler (1976) have argued in favour of counsellors using expressive language in counselling. We have found that one of the major benefits of using vivid non-profane language is that clients remember these vivid expressions or catchphrases, and use them as shorthand ways of disputing irrational beliefs in their everyday lives. For example, several of our clients find phrases like 'just too bad', 'tough luck', 'hard cheese' as helpful vivid reminders to practise the rational philosophy of high frustration tolerance. Concerning self-worth problems, WD helped one of his clients who was ashamed of urinating in public toilets to move from intellectual to emotional insight by encouraging him to remind himself that he was a 'fallible human peeing' while he was urinating.

In a related technique, the counsellor can ask the client to give his or her own distinctive name to a faulty psychological process. Wessler and Wessler (1980) give such an example where a client came to refer to himself as 'Robert the Rule Maker' to describe his tendency to make demands on himself and other people. A knowledge of clients' subcultural values is particularly helpful here. WD used to work in a working-class area in Birmingham, England, and one word his clients frequently used, which was unfamiliar to him, was the word 'mither.' (This is pronounced 'my-the' and means to be worried or bothered.) WD helped one client who was angry with her mother to see that her mother was a fallible human being with a worrying problem, and that she could be accepted for this rather than be damned for it. The client suddenly laughed and said, 'Yes! I guess my mother is a mitherer.' She was encouraged to remember this catchy phrase whenever she began to feel angry toward her mother.

Indications: Use with any client who is able to encapsulate a rational idea or philosophy in a vivid phrase and thereby act on it.

Contraindications: Do not use with clients who use such phrases for rhetorical rather than rational effect, i.e. designed to impress others rather than be acted upon; for example, a client says he now has a 'too bad' philosophy if he gets rejected, yet avoids asking any women out, or with those clients who might feel short-changed if all therapy consists of is 'bloody catchphrases' rather than a serious analysis of their problems.

Auditory cues

As has been shown, rational emotive behavioural counsellors often make tape recordings of their sessions for clients to replay several times between sessions. This serves to remind clients of rational principles they have understood in the session but may have since forgotten. Using personal recording systems, clients can also he encouraged to develop auditory reminders to initiate either cognitive or behavioural homework assignments. In addition, they can be encouraged to put forceful and emphatic rational statements on cassettes and play these while undertaking behavioural assignments. For example, WD once saw a client who was anxious about other people looking at her for fear that they might think her strange. He suggested that she do something in her everyday life that would encourage people to look at her so that she could dispute some of her underlying irrational beliefs. She decided to wear a personal stereo system in the street, which she thought would encourage people to look at her. It was suggested that while walking she play a tape on which she had recorded the rational message, 'Just because I look strange doesn't mean that I am strange.'

The use of rational songs in counselling has already been described. Several of our clients have found that singing a particular rational song at an emotionally vulnerable time has been helpful for them. It has reminded them of a rational message they might not ordinarily have been able to focus on while being emotionally disturbed. Another client reported that her counselling sessions reminded her of a particular song, and whenever she hummed this song to herself it helped to bring to mind the fact that she could accept herself even though she did not have a man in her life. The song ironically was 'You're No-one Till Somebody Loves You.' In fact, she rewrote some of the words and changed the title to 'You're Someone Even Though Nobody Loves You.'

Indications: Use with clients who find that listening to themselves on tape or singing songs provides the necessary impetus to challenge their irrational beliefs.

Contraindications: Do not use with clients who are not too keen on the sound of their own voice and therefore might be more preoccupied with what they do not like about it rather than focus on the purpose of the auditory cue, or with clients who have some form of auditory impairment.

Olfactory cues

It is possible for clients to use various aromas as cues to remind themselves to do a homework assignment or to initiate the disputing process. One of WD's clients said that she found his pipe tobacco particularly aromatic and distinctive. Since he and the client were both seeking a memorable cue, he suggested an experiment whereby she purchased a packet of his favourite tobacco and carried this around with her to smell at various times when she was disturbed. This aroma was associated in her mind with a particular rational message. This proved helpful, and indeed the client claimed that by saying to herself the phrase 'Pipe up' she now no longer had to take the tobacco out of her handbag to smell. Just the phrase was enough to remind her of the rational message.

Indications: Use with clients who are stimulated or aroused by smells and can connect these to absorbing rational ideas or disputing irrational ideas.

Contraindications: Do not use with clients who have olfactory impairment or might associate certain smells with nausea or some other form of distress.

While we have outlined in this chapter a number of techniques that encourage clients to initiate and sustain the process of moving from intellectual to emotional insight, once again we wish to stress that it is important for counsellors to use their own creativity in devising and implementing new techniques to help their own clients to initiate the change process.

With this point in mind, in the next chapter we shall cover a compendium of other REBC techniques.

Chapter 8
A Compendium of Other REBC Techniques

Overview

So far in this book we have described common REBC techniques. In this chapter, we present those techniques that are less frequently described in the REBC literature. We have resisted labelling these techniques 'elegant' or 'inelegant' in order not to prejudge their potential and actual effectiveness. However, we do describe the aim of each technique as well as the indications for and contraindications against its use. The techniques themselves are grouped into cognitive, behavioural, imagery and emotive categories and within each category they are presented in alphabetical order. Finally, we note that creativity in REBC is not an additional feature of therapy but one of its pillars.

Introduction

The principal activity of REB counsellors is usually disputing: challenging their clients' disturbance-creating beliefs as well as teaching them the mechanics of disputing as part of their developing role as a self-therapist. In order to encourage clients to surrender their irrational ideas, REB counsellors employ a wide range of multimodal techniques (cognitive, behavioural, imaginal, emotive) as a means of chipping away at clients' ideas by exposing their illogical, unrealistic and unhelpful basis. While clients' irrational ideas (which are usually long-standing) are being attenuated, these same techniques help to strengthen their newly emerging rational ideas. Although Ellis and others have stated that REB counsellors use literally hundreds of different techniques in helping their clients towards constructive change, the actual picture as represented in much of the REBC literature is that the same limited number of techniques are repeatedly described, e.g. shame-attacking exercises, rational-emotive imagery (Ellis version), rewards and penalties, implosive desensitisation, a formal series of logical, empirical and pragmatic questions. These are important techniques to stimulate belief change and are described elsewhere in this book devoted to promoting intellectual rational insight and promoting emotional rational insight (see Chapters 6 and 7).

This chapter will concentrate on those techniques among 'the hundreds' that are less well documented in the literature. We advocate that REBC practitioners use creative persistence in determining which techniques are therapeutically productive and which need to be modified, abandoned or newly minted. Each technique used should have a therapeutic purpose in helping the client to achieve his or her goals for change and both the counsellor and client should understand and agree with this purpose. To this end, we have included indications for and contraindications against the use of each technique as we did in the previous two chapters.

REBC distinguishes between elegant change (philosophical restructuring) and inelegant change (symptom removal) and therefore it might seen appropriate to label the following techniques as 'elegant' or 'inelegant'. However, we have resisted this approach for two reasons. First, to label a technique prejudges its potential effectiveness, e.g. an REBC counsellor selecting only elegant techniques might automatically assume that he or she is helping the client to surrender his or her absolute musts and shoulds because the technique allows no other interpretation or outcome. Second, its actual effectiveness depends so much on the clinical skills of the REBC practitioner. Thus, an elegant method of change can be transformed into an inelegant one by a counsellor with poor REBC skills. What we *have* done instead is to state the purpose of each technique as a guide for practitioners.

Cognitive Techniques

These have been defined by Wessler and Wessler (1980, p.113) as 'techniques that rely solely on verbal interchange between counsellor and client (within sessions), between the client and himself (written or thinking homework), and between author and client (reading and listening to tapes as homework)'. The verbal interchange is to assess irrational beliefs, discover their self-defeating nature and replace them with self-enhancing beliefs.

Argument for adolescents

When youngsters blame their parents, peers, teachers or others for causing their problems, they can be shown their own significant contribution to maintaining these problems. For example, a 16-year-old boy claims that his parents are 'making me think I'm no good':

Counsellor: Do you agree with them?
Client: Well . . . no, but they're putting it into my head.
Counsellor: Are there other ideas that your parents try to put into your head but you resist or reject them?
Client: Oh yeah. What time I should come in, doing more homework and studying, cleaning my room, who my friends should be, not taking

drugs. All that stuff.

Counsellor: Quite a list! Now what I don't understand is this: if you don't pay any attention to what your parents say about these other things, how then can they put an idea into your head like you're 'no good' unless you let it in because you agree with them in some way?

Client: I never thought of it like that. I suppose I do agree in some way.

Counsellor: Okay. Let's explore what that 'some way' is then.

This kind of approach helps youngsters to develop emotional responsibility and control by showing them that their negative ideas and feelings are not created wholly by external forces or circumstances.

Indications: Use with youngsters whose relationships with others are fraught rather than highly disturbed.

Contraindications: Do not use with youngsters who have been sexually, physically or psychologically abused by others as they may believe they are being blamed by the therapist for their problems. REBC practitioners should focus on nurturing such youngsters and helping them to develop coping responses to past traumas.

Battling 'brainwashing'

The battle for the REBC counsellor is to show clients that their 'brainwashed beliefs' are largely self-constructed rather than implanted into their mind by others:

Client: I've been told so often by my husband that I'm a failure, so what else can I do but accept it?

Counsellor: Let's say you decided today that you will no longer agree with him. Could he still make you see yourself as a failure?

Client: I don't suppose he could if I really disagreed with him.

Counsellor: And do you really disagree with him at present?

Client: Not really. I suppose my life has not been very successful when I come to think about it.

Counsellor: Do you think it might be a case of you agreeing with him because the idea of being a failure is already in your head?

Client: Hmm . . . that's a good point. I can see what you're getting at. How do I change my ideas then?

The counsellor can show the client how to subject their beliefs to logical, empirical and pragmatic examination in order to deindoctrinate themselves and then develop self-helping beliefs, e.g. 'It's true I've had my share of failures in life, but this does not make me a failure as a person. I shall certainly analyse from now on not only what others say about me, but also what I believe about myself.' When some clients protest that the irrational idea was not already in their mind and therefore 'forced in' by others, the counsellor can still point out that they have been insufficiently critical of the idea and that is why they have absorbed it so easily.

Indications: Use with clients who claim they have been indoctrinated by an external force or agency.

Contraindications: Do not use with clients who stubbornly refuse to accept any complicity in their 'brainwashing'. REB counsellors can agree that they have been unable to withstand the brainwashing, but now they can be shown a way of fighting back to become more independently minded.

Cognitive paradox

Here the counsellor deliberately exaggerates the clients' irrational ideas rather than attempting to modify them in order to help them see their self-defeating nature, e.g. the counsellor tells clients that they have to work very much harder if they want to fulfil the demand that 'I must please everyone'. By feeding back the clients' irrational ideas in an exaggerated form, the counsellor hopes to convince them to reappraise such ideas by introducing flexibility into them, e.g. 'I would like to please everyone but I don't have to'.

Indications: Use when clients have developed some skill at and/or insight into the mechanics of cognitive disputing and are thereby more likely to understand the counsellor's paradoxical intent.

Contraindications: Do not use with literal-minded clients who might take the counsellor at his or her word or with clients for whom mottoes, parables, irony, paradox, etc. have no therapeutic resonance.

The continuum method

This method encourages clients to develop balanced and realistic thinking and thereby helps them to surrender their rigid beliefs about themselves, others or the world. The counsellor can draw a continuum on a whiteboard or flip chart to illustrate the clients' extreme thinking: 0 represents (in this example) total failure; 100 represents complete success. The clients place a cross (X) where they currently see themselves – usually on or near the 0. The counsellor can discuss with the clients the implications of being total failures: if this is the case, how did they manage to get to the counselling session on time? or get on the right train? or manage to get dressed?

Through such introspection, the clients over the course of time place successive Xs towards the centre of the continuum thereby acknowledging both their complexity (composed of many facets) and fallibility (imperfection) as human beings. It is important for the counsellor to be alert to those clients who want to place their X on or near 100 – this solution will be just as counterproductive as their self-downing belief. The continuum method can be used to chart the clients' progress as well as highlight other forms of extreme thinking, e.g. no one can be trusted . . . everyone can be trusted; the world is cruel . . . the world is caring.

Indications: Use where a visual analogue will help to deepen clients' understanding of the points being made and the problems being addressed.

Contraindications: Do not use where clients might believe that their complex problems are being trivialised by using such a device; clients with perfectionistic traits might assume that the counsellor is advocating mediocrity by suggesting moving the X away from 100. This can lead to them terminating counselling prematurely.

Countering 'Yes, but . . .' thinking

These are clients who seemingly accept their own or the counsellor's rationale for constructive change, yet express doubts or ambivalence about it:

Client: Yes, I do want to engage in public speaking, but I must have the confidence first.

Counsellor: You're putting the cart before the horse: confidence usually comes after you've undertaken some public speaking engagements.

Client: Yes, that's probably true, but what happens if I make a fool of myself? I could never do another one.

Counsellor: If you're prepared to learn through trial and error, accept yourself for making mistakes, it's more likely that your skill at public speaking will increase along with your enthusiasm to do more of it.

Client: Yes, that does sound very sensible and logical, but I still have trouble accepting it.

Counsellor: I'm not asking you to accept it. Just remain open-minded while I offer you a way to tackle this problem.

Client: Okay. Nothing ventured, nothing gained.

Here, the counsellor rebuts non-threateningly the client's 'buts' until they are exhausted. Such a method encourages clients to make a commitment to change and the hard work usually associated with it. Clients can learn to challenge their 'yes, but . . .' statements as part of their cognitive homework tasks.

Indications: Use for any client whose 'yes, but . . .' vacillations block or interfere with their progress.

Contraindications: Do not use with clients who might see this technique as abrasive, aggressive or confrontational and thereby lead to a rupture of, or impair, the therapeutic alliance.

Challenging cultural indoctrination

This dispute teaches individuals that they have the ultimate choice of whether they wish to accept cultural standards or assumptions instead of being brainwashed by them, as they claim to be. For example, a woman states that she has been 'brainwashed by women's magazines and advertising' into being on a perpetual diet because 'you have to be thin to be worthwhile in this society'. The counsellor can ask the client whether there are other cultural standards she rejects (e.g. 'I don't agree that being just a house-wife is demeaning') and then enquire why she agrees with the 'thin to be worthwhile' assumption. It is important that REBC practitioners acknowl-edge the potency of cultural propaganda in helping to shape an individual's outlook, but point out that the final determinants of that outlook are decided by the individual.

Indications: Use with clients who believe that such arguments will help to liberate them from their perceived cultural constraints.

Contraindications: Do not use with clients who believe that cultural condi-tioning is all-powerful; these clients can be encouraged to carry out a survey among their friends and colleagues to determine if such a view is widespread and, if not, what modifications they might now wish to make in their think-ing.

Disputing the 'you cannot escape the past' belief

This belief assumes that past events dictate or shape an individual's present feelings and therefore she is a prisoner of the past, e.g. 'My parents dumped me in a children's home when I was 10 years old. I was devastated. It still makes me bitter after all these years and I'll never be free of it'. The REB counsellor needs to teach the client that past grim events contribute to her present unhappiness, but do not cause it:

Counsellor: I can understand how being 'dumped' in a children's home was a thor-oughly unpleasant experience, but how do you feel today about what happened 20 years ago?

Client: It's obvious – bitter, angry and depressed. My parents made me feel worthless by what they did to me.

Counsellor: Even if that was their intention then, why do you believe you are still worthless today?

Client: As I've said, because of what happened to me when I was 10.

Counsellor: I understand how very difficult it must have been to see it any other way when you were 10, but when did you start to think for yourself?

Client: About when I was 18, I suppose.

Counsellor: So you've had 12 years to challenge this idea that you are worthless. Have you made any progress?

Client: How can I make progress? It's their idea, not mine.

Counsellor: Well, let's say you got the idea from your parents through their actions, but you have been carrying it in your head ever since (tapping his fore-head). You still choose to believe it. That is the point.

Client: Hmm. If I accepted what you say, is it really possible to change after all these years?

Counsellor: Yes it is, and it certainly won't take 20 years to do so.

While past events cannot be changed, the client's view of them can be, and this can help her to take control of her emotional destiny which she had previously believed to be in the ineluctable grip of the past.

Indications: Use with clients who are willing to concede that they have some measure of free will in determining their present responses to past events.

Contraindications: Do not use with clients who cling strongly to the belief that the past determines the present. These clients can be shown that if they try to understand past events in a less hostile or uncompromising way it may help to ameliorate their present disturbance, e.g. a client's current depression begins to moderate when he considers that his isolation as a teenager was due to long bouts of illness and not because, as he has always believed, he was unlikeable or bad in some way.

Free speech argument

The counsellor will point out to clients the contradiction between a claim that all human beings have the right to express their opinions freely and the demand that a certain individual absolutely should not be saying the things that he does. Restrictions on free speech in this instance are determined by the clients' emotional disturbance (e.g. anger) about comments, 'Of course I believe in free speech, but that bastard should keep his mouth shut!' By revealing this conflict between ideals about democracy and rigid, totalitarian beliefs, the counsellor hopes to weaken clients' disturbance-producing ideas and thereby help them to construct rational beliefs which both express a strong dislike of the counsellor's comments and support the principle and practice of free speech. The counsellor may wish to strengthen his or her point by putting clients on the receiving end by prohibiting them from saying certain things that are important to them.

Indications: Use with clients who, when undisturbed, genuinely support freedom of speech and/or see any form of totalitarianism on their part as repugnant to their self-image.

Contraindications: Do not use with clients who see free speech only as an abstract principle and not something necessarily to be implemented in their daily interactions with others.

Hedonic calculus

Clients are invited to weigh up the short- and long-term advantages and disadvantages of a particular course of action in order to arrive at a healthy and rational balance between enjoying the pleasures of the present and not jeopardising those of the future, e.g. excessive party-going coupled with a reluctance to study may result in future exam failure and diminished job prospects. The aim of this technique is to help clients embrace a longer-term perspective when tackling their problems.

Indications: Use with clients who demand instant gratification, temporary relief from, or avoidance of, their problems – this usually implies that they have a philosophy of low frustration tolerance, e.g. substance abusers, procrastinators. This technique is best used after clients have absorbed some rational principles.

Contraindications: Do not use when it would be counterproductive to introduce this technique into therapy, e.g. when the client is depressed, or still heavily dependent on drugs/alcohol.

'I'm not in control of my life' argument

Here clients are shown that though they may believe they have little or no control over their physical, workplace or interpersonal environment they can certainly learn to develop emotional control of themselves:

Counsellor: By challenging and changing the ideas that underpin your anxiety and depression you can achieve greater emotional stability.
Client: That sounds all right, but I'm still stuck in this crumbling council house.
Counsellor: Has your depression helped you to put pressure on the council to get you moved?
Client: No. I haven't really bothered. I thought the situation was hopeless.
Counsellor: If we get you over your depression, what will you do with your regained energy?
Client: I'll pester the council every day until they move me.
Counsellor: Good.

Clients often find that when they learn to control their emotional destiny, they can become more effective practical problem-solvers and positively influence adverse external factors or conditions in their lives. Even when these external conditions are slow or resistant to change, clients do not have to return to disturbing themselves about these grim realities.

Indications: Use with all clients who want to achieve greater emotional stability in their lives.

Contraindications: Do not use with clients who place the responsibility for change on to others and seek only small-scale behaviour modification in themselves, e.g. 'How can I act differently so my partner will take more notice of me?'

Invitation technique

The purpose of this technique is to dispute clients' irrational needs for approval and 'can be employed to teach clients that they do not have to accept uncritically other people's evaluations of them and that they have a choice of accepting themselves in the face of downing messages from others' (Dryden, 1993, pp. 47–8, section one). For example, clients can be presented with a formal invitation to decide whether they wish to concur with the views of others:

Invitation	Response
I, your boss, consider you to be totally weak for taking time off work because of stress. I invite you to share my opinion of you.	Thank you for your invitation to consider myself as totally useless because of my stress problems.
RSVP	I accept ☐ I decline ☑
	Comments: I can accept myself as a fallible human being for my present inability to cope at work even if obviously you don't accept me.

The important point for clients to grasp is that their disturbance is largely self-created if they put the cross next to 'I accept' because they are agreeing with the actual or inferred put-downs from others. Why they agree with these put-downs would then become the focus for therapeutic intervention.

Indications: Use with clients who might enjoy the principle of emotional responsibility being taught in a rather elaborate manner.

Contraindications: Do not use with clients who require a straightforward or very simple example to convey this principle; some clients might misinterpret the technique as poking fun at them or deliberately trying to reveal their social ignorance about the formalities of RSVPs.

Radical apathy

This teaches clients, literally, to yawn and stretch at some of their disturbance-creating ideas as a way of making them harmless (Scott, Stradling and Dryden, 1995). Clients often believe that having a particular thought means that they will act upon it immediately, e.g. 'I want to crash my car into a lorry on the motorway'. Clients may have had the same thought hundreds or thousands of times and still nothing disastrous has occurred because action has never followed the thought. Therefore, radical apathy can help clients to remove the 'horror' from their thinking, e.g. (yawning) 'Not that thought again about crashing my car. Oh, what a bore.'

Indications: Radical apathy can be used, among other techniques, in depression or anxiety disorders, including obsessive-compulsive disorder which does not include compulsive behaviours; also, as an adjunct to cognitive disput-ing, or instead of it, if the client finds disputing too difficult or not effective.

Contraindications: Do not use with clients who are passive, indifferent or apathetic about tackling their problems – this technique may well strengthen such client characteristics. Radical apathy would also be contraindicated for those clients who may believe that their problems are being belittled, e.g. 'If I could have yawned at these upsetting thoughts, then I would have done so years ago!'

'Rational barb'

This helps clients to develop both confidence and self-acceptance in dealing with the insults and hurtful or critical comments of others (Kimmel, 1976). The counsellor models for the client how to handle the barbs of others with coping self-statements and without emotional disturbance. The counsellor then engages in name-calling (uses a barb), e.g. 'No wonder they call you Marge – you spread so easily for the boys', so the client can practise her rational response, e.g. 'I do have a very active sex life, which I both enjoy and accept myself for'. It is important to stress that the client says the ration-al response out loud, not just practises it in her head, and directly to the person who has delivered the insult (in this case, the counsellor).

Indications: Use with socially anxious clients who want to include assertive-ness in their coping skills repertoire and with clients who wish to endure the barbs of others through silent self-acceptance. Responding in an assertive fashion may appear to them as descending to the same level as their detract-ors.

Contraindications: Do not use with clients who may respond to the barbs of others with name-calling (e.g. 'You stupid four-eyed bitch!') and/or phys-ical retaliation.

Rewriting the rules

Teach clients that they are the 'author' of their disturbance-inducing rigid rules of living but they can empower themselves to rewrite these rules in more flexible and goal-oriented ways (Burns, 1980). For example, a man who was unflinchingly loyal to his friends demanded reciprocation from them; however, he was frequently let down by them and retreated into hurt. Once he accepted and acted upon the principle of emotional responsibility, he was able to construct more realistic and less emotionally distressing rules of living, e.g. 'I would very much prefer my friends to exhibit the same loyalty to me as I do to them, but they don't have to because it's better if they make up their own minds on this issue.'

Indications: Use with clients who are seeking or can be persuaded to embrace a philosophical approach to emotional change.

Contraindications: Do not use with clients who are looking for a nonphilosophical outcome to their problems, such as not surrendering their absolute musts and shoulds; for example the client, in order to feel less hurt, reframes the problem as his friends lacking the superior qualities needed to guarantee unflinching loyalty.

Survey method

Burns (1989) suggests that one way to evaluate a negative attitude is to ask others if they would agree with it if they were in a similar situation to the client's; for example, a man asks his friends if they would condemn themselves as a 'complete failure' if their marriages broke up. The consensus of opinion from his friends is that they would not, and he is being too harsh on himself. This technique is useful if the client values the opinions of his friends and/or associates.

Indications: Use with clients who have friends and associates who can provide a balanced assessment of their problem, or if the people asked form a representative survey sample.

Contraindications: Do not use with clients whose friends and/or associates would help to reinforce the clients' problems; for example a friend tells the client that if he had her problems he would also be depressed and suicidal. Do not use if the survey sample is too small.

'There is really nothing to fear' dispute

Hauck (1993, p.65, section one) argues that clients suffering from repeated anxiety attacks need to be shown 'that their fears are basically unfounded'. For example, a man who fears losing control of himself during a panic attack can be asked how many times he has thought about this fear:

Client:	About five or six times every day.
Counsellor:	And how many years have you worried about this?
Client:	About ten years.
Counsellor:	(using her calculator) 6 x 365 x 10 = 21,900 times you have thought you would lose control. Have you ever lost control?
Client:	Er . . . no . . . but I thought I was going to.
Counsellor:	So is the answer 'no'?
Client:	Yes.

This can be a powerful argument against clients' fears because a veritable mountain of evidence contradicts their belief that a personal catastrophe is imminent, when it never has occurred to date. As Hauck (1993, p.66, section one) concludes: 'How can they [clients] then say that the next time they have an anxiety attack all those horrible things are still sure to happen?'

Indications: Use with clients with anxiety disorders.

Contraindications: Do not use with clients who insist that their fears might be realised 'tomorrow or the next day'. These clients need to be taught coping techniques to prepare themselves in their mind for what they see as the inevitable.

Withering away 'whingeing and whining'

This technique helps clients to see how much time they waste with their endless whingeing and whining about carrying out their goal-directed tasks, e.g. a student spends several hours incessantly complaining about the difficulty of writing his essay instead of using the time productively to do some preparatory work like reading or research. Clients can keep a 'whingeing and whining' diary to calculate how many hours they waste in a week or over a month through their self-defeating behaviour and thereby take steps to dispute the underlying low frustration tolerance beliefs, e.g. 'Things mustn't be difficult in my life and I can't stand having to work too hard to deal with them if they are'.

Indications: Use with clients who want more efficiency and effectiveness in their lives.

Contraindications: Do not use with clients who see complaining and moaning as part of their personality and/or life. The technique will need to be modified with these clients to include time-limited 'moaning periods' prior to undertaking a task.

The ultimate contract

Clients who claim that intolerable contractual conditions are the source of their workplace stress can be shown that a lot of their stress actually derives from the harsh and unforgiving self-penned contract in their head, e.g. 'I must never make any mistakes; I must be sharp and alert at all times; I must immediately and unfailingly give the right answers to any questions I'm asked'. It is highly unlikely that any business or company would devise such a contract; if it was a standard contract for all firms, then the whole working population could expect to become unemployed. It can be pointed out to the client that the company is generally more flexible and realistic than he is, and therefore he needs to adjust his mental contract accordingly.

Indications: Use for stress management programmes and/or stress counselling.

Contraindications: Do not use for clients who want help only with behavioural solutions to their workplace stress, e.g. changing jobs, moving to a less pressurised position within the company.

Behavioural techniques

These are methods that enable clients to act against their irrational beliefs and in ways that are consistent with their rational beliefs. New rational philosophies learnt in the counsellor's office will wither if not acted upon.

Acting against the 'I'm not motivated' argument

This is the frequent complaint of clients who struggle unsuccessfully to carry out their homework tasks, e.g. 'I'll be able to do them when the motivation comes.' Thus, clients wait for motivation to appear magically or occur spontaneously. As Burns (1989, p.170) observes: 'People who are extremely successful know that motivation doesn't come first – productive action does. You have to prime the pump by getting started whether you feel like it or not. Once you begin to accomplish something, it will often spur you on to do even more.' For example, a client who was reluctant to start an exercise regime until she felt motivated was urged by the counsellor 'to just get on with it'; once she started exercising, she felt motivated to do more and thereafter attended her local gym on a regular basis. This call to action can be summed up as: 'Do, don't stew!'

Indications: Use with all clients who put off any task due to lack of motivation which is not underpinned by emotional distress.

Contraindications: Do not use with clients whose lack of motivation is due to emotional disturbance, e.g. a depressed client says 'I'm worthless. There is no point in doing anything to help myself.'

Adventuring

This involves clients seeking or undertaking exciting, pleasurable, risky, etc. experiences. Adventuring can help clients to widen their opportunities, free themselves from many self-imposed restrictions and lead more fulfilling lives; for example, sexual adventuring involves experimenting with a variety of partners and practices to maximise an individual's sexual enjoyment. If a client's goal is to be more adventurous in life, the REB counsellor can help him to uncover and dispute his goal-blocking beliefs, e.g. 'I must know in advance that I will be successful as I couldn't bear making a fool of myself.'

Indications: Use with clients who have ambitious goals for change, particularly in changing their 'dull routine'.

Contraindications: Do not use with clients who are seeking only modest change in their lives and do not want to 'break free'.

Behavioural cues

These act as early warning signs (e.g. jaw tightening, pacing up and down, clenched fists) that clients might be slipping back into self-defeating patterns of behaviour and should take immediate constructive action to prevent it; e.g., a woman who wrings her hands when she hears bad news quickly remembers that this is how her panic attacks start and initiates a relaxation programme to calm herself down. Behavioural cues, along with cognitive and emotive ones, let clients know how easily they can slip back in their progress.

Indications: Use with clients who are able to monitor their behaviour for signs of backsliding.

Contraindications: Do not use with clients who have little or no sensitivity to their behavioural changes or who would be more responsive to emotive and/or cognitive cues.

Behavioural paradox

This involves asking clients to act in ways that are the opposite of their normal behaviour and seen to fly in the face of commonly accepted wisdom; e.g., a client who is worried about going insane would be encouraged to try to go insane by acting in a 'mad' way. Behavioural paradox helps to reduce such fears by teaching clients that they cannot make themselves insane no matter how hard they try and weakening their underlying irrational beliefs, e.g. 'I must be certain that I won't go mad'. Before carrying out such techniques, counsellors are advised to contact the clients' doctors for background medical and/or psychological checks.

Indications: Use with clients whose avoidance of their fears helps to perpetuate them.

Contraindications: Do not use as in the above example of the client afraid of going insane with clients with past or present psychiatric disturbances.

Courageous confrontation

Ellis (1977d, p.110) remarks that hostility and violence often stem from a lack of courage: 'you refuse to go after what you want or to confront others with their lapses; then, hating yourself for your own weakness and unassertiveness, you feel angry and combative towards those with whom you

have acted weakly'. To tackle unassertiveness and the resulting compensa-
tory anger, Ellis suggests courageously confronting those with whom an individual disagrees. This will bring open conflict – violence is to be strenuously
avoided – but may well lead to some kind of problem resolution or compromise. For example, a woman who repeatedly fails to stand up to a colleague's
overbearing behaviour simmers with barely suppressed homicidal hatred for
him; however, when she does confront him eventually about his behaviour
and says she will not tolerate it any longer, he becomes more subdued in the
following weeks in his interactions with her.

In order to undertake such direct confrontation, clients need to show
themselves that they can withstand rudeness, opposition or dislike from their
opponents without rejecting themselves in the process, e.g. 'Just because
you hate my guts doesn't mean I have to agree with you'. Clients usually find
that they have to force themselves into verbal confrontation. However, if they
avoid doing it, their underlying problems become reinforced and prolonged.

Indications: Use with clients who are unassertive, particularly if anger is
involved in their presenting problems.

Contraindications: Do not use with clients who may go beyond just verbal
confrontation and/or their opponents would resort to physical retaliation.

Cue exposure

This technique involves the deliberate exposure of a client to those situations
that act as triggers or cues for drink or drug use, e.g. internal feelings like
anxiety or anger; external events like visiting certain friends or pubs. The
client is then systematically exposed to these cues and the urges to substance
use that follow on from them. Through repeated exposure, the aim is to
extinguish these urges and develop alternative and constructive ways of
responding to these high-risk situations, e.g. 'I can stand watching other
people drink while I don't. This proves that I am in control, not the booze'.
Cue exposure is employed within the protected environment of the counsellor's office where there is no access to drink or drugs and under supervision
in the actual high-risk situation to test the client's new coping skills.

Indications: Use with substance abuse, phobias, obsessive-compulsive disorder, gambling, binge eating, other impulse control problems.

Contraindications: Do not use with clients who have not been adequately
prepared for entering high-risk situations or with clients who believe that
progress is based on cue avoidance, not exposure.

Doing v. trying exercises

These demonstrate to clients the difference between actually carrying out a
task as opposed to only attempting it. When clients agree to carry out their

homework assignments they frequently say 'I'll try to do them' rather than 'I'll do them'. The former attitude implies a good chance of failure or, at most, only half-hearted attempts; the latter attitude indicates a commitment to executing assignments and thereby the probability of making faster progress and deeper change. In-session demonstrations of this philosophical divide between trying and doing can be arranged by asking the clients to try to clap their hands or to try to stand up. For clients who still do not grasp this distinction, the counsellor can ask them to try to eat, bathe and dress in the next week. At the next session clients report that there was no trying involved – they just did these activities as they did not wish to stink, go hungry or naked. QED. The counsellor can then ask: 'Now will you apply exactly the same principle to the tasks involved in tackling your problems?'

Indications: Use with any client who says 'I'll try . . .'

Contraindications: Do not use with clients who have genuine cognitive, emotive and/or behavioural blocks in carrying out their homework tasks rather than philosophical confusion about these terms.

Five-minute plan

This is an antiprocrastination exercise that asks clients to work a minimum of five minutes on a task; when the time is up, plan another five minutes of effort and so on until the task is completed (Bernard, 1993). This gradualist approach to tackling procrastination is often the only way to generate motivation in clients, e.g. 'I think I could manage five minutes but certainly no more.'

Indications: Use with clients with chronic or abysmal LFT.

Contraindications: This is not to be used as a blanket technique as some clients with procrastination problems will want or need to be worked harder and pushed further.

In-session simulation

Attempting to reproduce in therapy the conditions or circumstances which engender the clients' problems, e.g., clients who avoid starting college essays at home can be asked to begin them in the counselling session. As Wessler and Wessler (1980) point out, in-session simulation serves a primarily diagnostic function, but it also reveals feelings and ideas that can be disputed there and then, e.g. the anxiety-inducing belief, 'I have to make sure that every sentence is perfectly constructed because I can't stand having to waste time on rewrites.'

Indications: Use as part of the assessment process if required or when clients founder in carrying out their homework tasks.

Contraindications: Do not use the technique as a substitute for clients undertaking their homework assignments outside of counselling sessions, e.g. 'If you wish, you can practise writing your essay in counselling every week rather than at home.'

'Knock-out' technique

This is a method suggested by Bernard (1993) which aims at dealing procrastination a decisive blow by carrying out immediately a previously avoided hard and distasteful activity, e.g. instead of spending more months brooding on the unpleasant task, the client clears out his or her attic in a day. This technique helps clients to develop high frustration tolerance (HFT) rapidly by challenging the discomfort disturbance-creating beliefs underlying their procrastination, e.g. 'I can't stand having to work too hard in tackling this damned task.' After the task is completed the client can reflect upon the physical and mental effort wasted in avoiding the task as opposed to the short amount of time actually required to carry out the task.

Indications: Use with clients who agree that their procrastination is reinforcing their LFT beliefs and who are willing to take bold steps to fight back.

Contraindications: Do not use with clients who insist that their procrastination can be addressed only in a gradual fashion (see five-minute plan).

Playing the probabilities

This is useful for clients who believe that they have to be inspired before they can start an activity or task, e.g. 'I can't possibly begin to write a short story until my imagination catches fire.' By waiting for that 'inspirational moment', clients help to prolong their procrastination. Ellis and Knaus (1977, p. 104) suggest clients use probability theory because 'when you *un*spontaneously force yourself to begin a project, you stand a good chance that you will *sometimes* stumble into a streak of *spontaneous* brilliance and produce a surprisingly great product' (italics in the original). Therefore, inspiration may come after or as a result of a period of forced and sustained effort rather than through inactive apprehension as the client frets that 'inspiration is still lacking and I'll never get anything done at this rate'.

Probability theory can also be used to persuade reluctant clients to force themselves to socialise regularly, as this is more likely to produce a greater sample of potential social and sexual partners to choose from than a few isolated 'evenings out'. Also, from a greater sample, clients will probably find a compatible partner rather than a less compatible one.

Indications: Use with clients who believe that success will come only when they feel inspired, motivated, 'the time has to be right', etc.

Contraindications: Do not use with clients who believe that therapy cannot truly understand the creative impulse; with clients who would undermine or sabotage this technique in order to prove that 'there is no probability of happiness, success or anything in my life'.

Relapse prevention or reduction

Relapse prevention or reduction plays an important part in REBC as it shows clients how to prepare for possible setbacks in their current progress, or how to deal with them if they actually occur; in essence, by using the ABCDE model of self-analysis and change. For example, a former alcoholic 'falls off the wagon' by having a few drinks and becomes depressed because he believes 'I'm a hopeless failure'. However, he quickly challenges his depression-inducing attitude by fully accepting himself for his lapse and takes action to stabilise the situation through stimulus control (see p.171), imposes stiff penalties upon himself for the lapse (e.g. burning his much prized opera tickets), only allows himself future pleasures contingent upon abstinence (e.g. gets more opera tickets) and engages in physical activities (e.g. swimming, going to a gym). Ellis (1984c) has written a pamphlet for clients on how to deal with their lapses or relapses, called *How to Maintain and Enhance Your Rational-Emotive Behavior Therapy Gains.* (see pp.252–258)

Indications: Use with all clients who wish to become their own counsellors for present and future emotional problem-solving.

Contraindications: Do not use with clients who might easily become discouraged from trying to overcome their problems because the counsellor wants to discuss the possibility of relapse, or clients who might terminate therapy prematurely because of the counsellor's 'pessimism'. With these clients, positive rather than realistic thinking is the order of the day.

Reminders

These can prompt clients into action and therefore make it much less likely that they will say they forgot to do their homework tasks, e.g. clients who have agreed to carry out rational-emotive imagery ten times daily leave written messages in their diaries, on mirrors at home, on the door of the kitchen fridge, ask family and friends to remind them, etc. Surrounded by such a 'barrage' of cues, clients generally conclude that they can no longer justify 'it slipped my mind' excuses and carries out the imagery exercises. Anything can be used as a reminder if it will successfully jog the memory.

Indications: Use with clients with procrastination problems or those who need specific and immediate prompts to change intention into action.

Contraindications: Do not use with clients who would find this procedure demeaning (e.g. 'I'm not a bloody idiot you know!') or do not want others to know their personal business.

Response prevention

This is one of the principal techniques for dealing with obsessive–compulsive disorder, e.g. clients who usually check many times that their front doors are locked are asked by the counsellor to test them only once and thereby prevent themselves from engaging in the anxiety-reducing ritual of repeated checking. They are also urged not to seek reassurance from others (e.g. friends, family, work colleagues, counsellor) that nothing bad will happen because they checked only once. These response prevention methods are designed to achieve habituation to anxiety and discomfort and enable the clients to evaluate realistically whether the feared consequences of not checking repeatedly will actually occur. Concomitantly, the clients can vigorously dispute their underlying dogmatic demands, e.g. 'I must check my front door 30 times before I go to work to make sure it's safe and secure. I can't stand the agony of not checking and the hardship that my life will undergo if I fail to check and my house is burgled.'

Some clients' obsessional thoughts are accompanied by covert cognitive rituals rather than overt behavioural ones, e.g. a man who thinks 'I must kill my wife' is countered by the neutralising thought 'I love my wife'. The client is exposed to the obsessional thought while the response prevention aspect to the neutralising thought can be tackled through thought-stopping or distraction techniques.

Response prevention can also be used by those with substance abuse problems to control and monitor their behaviour for a period of time so as to make it very difficult to use drink/drugs, e.g. admission to an in-patient rehabilitation centre or, if staying in the community, to be monitored by family, relatives and/or friends. Although this is response prevention performed by others, clients may be able at a later date to continue their abstinence through self-monitoring.

Indications: Use with clients with obsessive–compulsive problems, substance abusers, bulimics, and individuals with body dysmorphic disorder (intense revulsion towards one's body or an aspect of it).

Contraindications: Do not use with clients who suffer from psychosis, those with heart or other medical problems, as response prevention can trigger high levels of anxiety, or with clients who may have suicidal ideation if they cannot carry out their behavioural or cognitive rituals (Palmer and Dryden, 1995).

Riding the wave of inertia

This involves using the momentum from one task and switching it to another that is less pleasant or burdensome and usually avoided, e.g. a client who is writing a letter to his girlfriend switches his energy to starting his much postponed college essay. The fact that the writing materials are already to hand and the client is in a writing mode at that moment may indicate a greater chance of success in making some headway with the essay. As Ellis and Knaus (1977) observe, even if the client is not in the mood to tackle the essay, he may still find it easier to do than if the writing materials were not assembled and immediately to hand.

Indications: Use with clients who need to gain a positive momentum or sense of personal efficacy from one task before embarking on a more onerous one.

Contraindications: Do not use with clients who would not make the switch because of their low frustration tolerance beliefs, 'Why make work for yourself when you can avoid it?' With these clients, small-scale exercises in habituation to discomfort would be required.

Self- and body-acceptance

Brandsma (1993) suggests a three-step procedure for clients in order to achieve this dual acceptance:

1. Buy a full-length mirror, stand naked in front of it and examine the body from all angles. No matter what is seen or revealed, clients are instructed to strive for a calm acceptance of their body in all its aspects.
2. When some measure of calm acceptance has been realised, clients learn to value the body's manifold functions, i.e. movement, pleasure, sensation. This step is called functional appreciation.
3. This step involves attributing to the body and its various parts sexual and sensual potential, feelings and attractiveness.

Once this dual acceptance has been achieved, clients can from this non-disturbed perspective 'do a rational self-analysis on aspects [of their body] that would be desirable and amenable to change – for example, obesity' (Brandsma, 1993, p.64, section one).

Indications: Use with those having bulimia nervosa, anorexia nervosa or body dysmorphic disorder.

Contraindications: Do not use when this technique would actually help to increase the client's disgust with her/his body.

Skills training

REBC is a double systems therapy where, first, clients surrender their disturbance-producing beliefs about unpleasant activating events in their lives and then, second, tackle the practical aspects of these events, e.g. a woman overcomes her anxiety about public speaking and then learns a series of performance-enhancing skills. REB counsellors need to be alert to the fact that once clients are over their emotional disturbance, practical problem-solving skills will not appear automatically: clients can and do have emotional disturbance and significant skills deficits, e.g. a man who finally gets over his long-standing depression after the collapse of his marriage, has to relearn and improve upon his decayed social skills. These skills can be modelled by the counsellor and practised by the client within the counselling sessions. The client can also, more importantly, practise his skills in situations where he has opportunities to meet new partners.

Indications: Use with clients who have skills deficits and agree to stay longer in counselling for them to be addressed once their emotional problems have moderated, or with clients who are unaware of their lack of skills or who believe 'it [skills] comes naturally' even though they have not appeared to date.

Contraindications: Do not use when the clients' presenting problems are unclear, which will make teasing out any skills deficits very difficult, or where there is severe psychiatric disturbance or handicap preventing skills acquisition.

Stimulus control

This procedure helps clients to learn to reduce or avoid exposure to conditions or situations which reinforce maladaptive behaviour, e.g. a person with bulimia can be instructed to keep away from cake and sweet shops, suppress hunger with low-calorie snacks, eat slowly, throw away leftovers; an illicit drug user identifies high-risk situations where he might 'use' again (certain pubs, clubs or friends and particular areas of a town or city) and devises ways of avoiding them or quickly removing himself from such situations. Stimulus control can be a rapid way for clients to gain some control over their maladaptive behaviour. Ideally, in REBC, stimulus control is used as an important behavioural adjunct to disputing irrational beliefs – the primary source of the client's maladaptive behaviour, e.g. 'I must have food whenever I feel upset because I can't stand these uncomfortable sensations' (see cue exposure, p.165).

Indications: Use with any clients who can learn to control or reduce the stimuli that trigger their self-defeating behaviour.

Contraindications: Do not use when challenging the clients' disturbed thinking, rather than changing their behaviour, is the only realistic pathway of change.

Imagery Techniques

These are methods that use mental images or pictures to challenge clients' irrational beliefs. As McMullin (1986, p.273) points out, 'since images do not involve language, clients can often shift their perceptions more rapidly and completely using visual images rather than semantics'.

'Blow up' procedure

In this technique, clients are encouraged to exaggerate greatly their fears in order to diffuse them by seeing how unrealistic they are. For example, a client who believes that a mistake at work will have dire consequences is asked to imagine the company closing down, hundreds unemployed, whole industries disappearing and the economic life of the country grinding to a halt. The humorous intention is to place the mistake in a realistic context instead of a catastrophic one.

Indications: Use for clients who find humour a helpful way of tackling their problems and have found other imagery techniques ineffective in reducing their fears, e.g. rational-emotive imagery.

Contraindications: Do not use for clients who might become obsessively preoccupied with the catastrophic consequences of their current deeds, those who lack a sense of humour or who would interpret their genuine fears as being ridiculed by the counsellor.

Creative transformation imagery

Burns (1980) suggests that one way to reduce anger-producing images is to transform them in a creative way, often through humour, in order to make them less disturbing. For example, a woman who imagines taking a baseball bat to her rude manager fantasises instead that he is in a baby's high chair conducting a meeting. The client is encouraged to visualise the details: gurgling when someone agrees with him, throwing his rattle on the floor when others disagree; sucking his thumb and twirling his hair when he gets bored. The counsellor can gauge the effectiveness of the technique by whether the client's tense face relaxes into a smile.

Indications: Use with clients who have a sense of humour and/or see the disturbance-reducing benefits of poking fun at the object of their anger.

Contraindications: Do not use with clients who do not want to neutralise the seriousness of the situation through 'silliness'; for such clients, rational-emotive imagery (Ellis version) might be a more appropriate intervention to use.

Deathbed reflection

This technique uses irony to concentrate the client's mind on working harder or making a dramatic change in her life in order to overcome her current emotional problems. Because of the slow or negligible progress she is making, the counsellor asks her to close her eyes and imagine herself lying on her deathbed surrounded by her relatives. One of them asks her: 'If you had your life over again, what would you do differently?' The client replies: 'To have spent even more time miserable than I did'. The client usually responds that she would have said the exact opposite. The counsellor can point out that if she does not knuckle down to the hard work of change, his version of the deathbed scene will probably turn out to be more accurate than hers.

Indications: Use with clients with a sense of humour and/or irony and no aversive reactions to images of death or dying.

Contraindications: Do not use with depressed and/or suicidal clients who might agree with the counsellor's version of the deathbed scene because they see a future of relentless misery.

Fanciful imagery

Described by McMullin (1986, p.275) as 'solv[ing] problems in imagination that cannot be solved in reality', e.g. a client whose best friend died suddenly is depressed that she could not say goodbye; the counsellor encourages the client to imagine her dead friend sitting in front of her and both of them engaged in a valedictory conversation. This technique helps to ameliorate the client's depression as she now believes there has been a proper sense of closure to the relationship.

Indications: Use with clients who can accept this imaginal solution to irretrievable or unalterable events in their lives.

Contraindications: Do not use with clients who do not want 'fanciful solutions' to such events; these clients need to learn to face and accept the grim reality of what has occurred in their lives.

Imagery rescripting

This is an 'imagery-focused treatment designed to alleviate PTSD [Post Traumatic Stress Disorder] symptomatology and alter abuse-related beliefs and schemas (e.g. powerlessness, victimisation, inherent badness, unlovability) of survivors of childhood sexual abuse' (Smucker et al. 1995, p.9). The procedure combines visually recalling and re-experiencing the images, thoughts and emotions associated with the original traumatic event (imaginal exposure) and altering the survivor's abuse imagery to produce a more positive outcome (imaginal rescripting). Victimisation imagery is replaced with mastery imagery, e.g. the adult survivor of today returns to the scene of the abuse in order to protect him- or herself as a child from the abuser. Imagery rescripting can help to empower clients as they now see themselves more in control of their lives and less as helpless victims of past events.

Indications: Use with clients who cannot accept the grim reality of childhood events or that they should have acted other than they did when the abuse occurred.

Contraindications: Do not use with clients who believe that imagery rescripting is trying to 'sweeten the pill' of bitter remembrance. REBC counsellors need to teach such clients both self-acceptance and acceptance of past empirical reality.

Imagining ultimate consequences

This can be used for clients to assess the lasting consequences of their actions or of unpleasant activating events, e.g. a depressed man plans to kill himself so his family 'will be better off without me':

Counsellor: Imagine you are dead but you can still see what's going on in your family's life. Is your family better off one month from now?

Client: No. They're all still crying and shocked.

Counsellor: How about one year from now?

Client: Probably still be grieving but getting on with their lives.

Counsellor: Can you see how they're getting on – happily, miserably, or just struggling along?

Client: I expect struggling along.

Counsellor: Are they better off without you yet?

Client: I'm not sure.

Counsellor: Okay, let's jump forward 10 years. What do you see?

Client: My daughter has probably got married by now. So she'll be happy.

Counsellor: Was she happy that you were not at the wedding to give her away because you had killed yourself?

Client: I expect the day wasn't as happy for her as it could have been. That's true.

Counsellor: Has your wife remarried by now?

Client: I expect so.

Counsellor: Won't her remarriage always remind her of the circumstances in which the first one ended?

Client: I don't suppose it will ever be too far from her mind.

Counsellor: If you now imagine the rest of their lives, can you see them being happier without you, thanking you for what you did?

Client: This is not how I expected to see it. My family will carry what I did to their own graves.

Counsellor: Shall we reconsider your idea that your family will be better off without you if you kill yourself?

Client: Seems like the sensible thing to do. I never really thought that hard

about the consequences for my family – I never saw it from their viewpoint.

Indications: Use with clients who have the ability and desire to look ahead
to an outcome that may be different from the one they have foreseen.

Contraindications: Do not use with clients who think the present is bad
enough without 'looking ahead to the worst to come' or with clients who
would become very distressed with this procedure because all they see (or
are prepared to see) is unrelieved bleakness.

Inaction v. action imagery

This procedure involves asking clients to imagine, for example, remaining
anxious for the rest of their lives because they fear being disliked and are not
prepared to do anything about challenging these fears (inaction imagery).
They are encouraged to fill in specific details (e.g. letting themselves be used
continuously by others) in order to make their futures as graphic as possible.

Conversely, the clients imagine their futures without the anxiety because
they have learnt self-acceptance and assertion through hard work and struggle (action imagery). Again, the clients are encouraged to view the future in
as much detail as possible (e.g. friendships based on mutual respect) and
then contrast it with the inaction imagery.

Neenan and Palmer (in press) suggest that clients usually need to go
through this double imagery procedure frequently if it going to be a spur to
action, a commitment to change. Clinical experience suggests that the most
effective way to use this technique is the way described above. Reversing the
order and putting inaction imagery last might have a more powerful and
adverse impact on some clients' minds.

Indications: Use to reinforce verbal disputing or as an alternative to it, and
particularly with clients who find pragmatic arguments are the best way of
motivating them.

Contraindications: Do not use with depressed clients as this technique
might strengthen both their view of a bleak future and their inability to alter it.

Negating the positive

This procedure is to demonstrate to clients that something they desperately
want or see as advantageous may have unpleasant consequences they have
not considered or foreseen:

Counsellor: Now close your eyes and imagine what you've always wanted to be.
Which is . . . ?
Client: . . . to be perfect.
Counsellor: As a perfect person, will you have many friends?

Client:	Of course, my perfection will be admired.
Counsellor:	Or despised. What will you constantly be reminding people of when they are around you?
Client:	Oh, I see – their imperfection, problems, lack of success, etc. That sort of thing.
Counsellor:	As no one in the world can ever be like you, will you be pointed out as a role model or freak?
Client:	(sounding disillusioned) A freak probably.
Counsellor:	So you are now friendless and a freak. Will you be happy with that?
Client:	I'll be as miserable as sin. I never thought of perfection like that. It doesn't look so enticing any more. I'll have to have a rethink.

Such imagery can have a corrective function in encouraging clients to reconsider their goals; in the above example, the clients accept their fallibility while still striving to excel in certain areas of life.

Indications: Use with clients who see their goals in wholly positive terms and are reluctant or unable to see that, potentially, the negative consequences might be greater if their goals are realised.

Contraindications: Do not use with clients who would see the counsellor as a cynic or doom-monger. The counsellor would need to approach the issue in a less obvious way, e.g. 'It's always good to look on the positive side but are there any possible hiccups or difficulties in being perfect?'

Preventive imagery

This procedure is used to prepare clients to cope with expected or actual future life events such as rejection, redundancy, ill health, isolation, death. For example, a woman who fears losing her job in the next year and thereby will be 'on the scrap at 50' is asked by the counsellor to imagine the potential opportunities that might be available to take her off the scrap heap:

Client:	Well, if I wanted a job quickly I could apply to the supermarkets to be a shelf filler or something, as they take older people. I wouldn't be crazy about the job but it would bring in some money and fill up my time.
Counsellor:	What else can you see yourself doing besides that job?
Client:	I've always wanted to study for a degree so I would apply to the Open University or a local university as a mature student. I fancy psychology or sociology and hope I could get some job in the caring professions.
Counsellor:	Anything else you might get involved in?
Client:	I would like to do some voluntary work with the Samaritans, if they'll have me.
Counsellor:	Do you still see yourself on the scrap heap in the next year?
Client:	Not now. My image is of one door closing and another one opening – a new path lies before me.
Counsellor:	Good. Now you need to practise this preventive imagery repeatedly so you truly believe that you can cope with whatever comes your way in the future. Remember, you might not get into university, for example.

So you would have to prepare for that in your mind's eye as well.

Client: Preparation is half the battle, so these imagery exercises will help to reduce any future shocks or let-downs I might experience.

If some clients are unable to visualise themselves coping constructively with future adverse events, the counsellor can help them to brainstorm coping strategies for these events. These strategies should ideally be the ones the clients have struggled to devise rather than just appropriating the counsellor's suggestions.

Indications: Use with clients who are worried about the adverse impact of future events, who need to be encouraged to look ahead rather than just 'hope for the best', or as part of a relapse prevention programme.

Contraindications: Do not use with depressed clients who currently see their future as hopeless and themselves as helpless to change it. When the depression has ameliorated, then this exercise can be introduced to these clients.

Reality-testing the image

This technique teaches clients to treat their images like verbal automatic thoughts and to challenge them through standard Socratic questioning (Beck, 1995), e.g. a client says he has repeated images of clutching his chest and dying of a heart attack:

Counsellor: Did you actually have a heart attack?
Client: No, but it seemed so real.
Counsellor: Okay, when you're imagining this scene again, do a reality check and ask yourself: 'Am I feeling a persistent, vice-like pain in my chest which often spreads to the jaw and down the left arm? Am I about to collapse? Am I experiencing breathlessness and discomfort high in the abdomen?' These are some of the usual indicators of a heart attack.
Client: That approach sounds sensible. I can also remind myself that I have been checked by a heart specialist, and she said I was fine. There is no history of heart disease in my family and I play vigorous sports like rugby.
Counsellor: Good. Now if you had done a reality check on this frightening image, would you have felt any different?
Client: Yes, I would have been able to calm down more quickly.

Clients can use this technique to prove to themselves that imagining an unpleasant event is not synonymous with it actually occurring, and thereby 'cool down hot images'.

Indications: Clients who have many vivid, distressing images and who respond to checking their validity verbally.

Contraindications: Do not use with clients who do not respond to verbal techniques; imagery-based interventions should be used to combat upsetting images.

Step-up technique

This technique helps clients to imagine the worst outcome of a feared future situation that they had previously avoided focusing upon, e.g. the counsellor asks the client to step up to the potential consequences of giving a poor lecture to her colleagues and she concludes that 'my reputation would be shattered and my life would be over'. The client is then asked to imagine the aftermath of the poor lecture and coping with it, e.g. the client says she would learn to rebuild both her reputation and life; however, now that she has confronted the 'horror' of total failure the client decides that the actual consequences of giving a poor lecture 'may be unpleasant but hardly the end of my world'. By breaking through the client's understandable resistance to dwell on such grim consequences, she can learn to conquer her fears by appraising them in a more realistic and dispassionate way (Lazarus, 1984). Clients might need help from the counsellor to develop coping strategies when imagining that their worst fears have been realised.

Indications: Use with clients who are uncertain about the cause of their anxiety or need to be encouraged to face their fears in order to make therapeutic progress.

Contraindications: Do not use with clients who are psychologically fragile and may be overwhelmed by the technique. Also, as it can induce high levels of anxiety, its use can be inappropriate with clients who have a history of heart disease or other related medical disorders (Palmer and Dryden, 1995).

The little old man

This imagery technique is designed to increase client control of their irrational thinking (Barrish, 1993). Clients are asked to imagine a ragged, dishevelled little old man following them around and whispering frightening thoughts in their ear, e.g. 'You're always going to be miserable', 'You'll never meet anyone who wants you'. With this imagery, clients are more likely to reject the source of these depression-inducing ideas – a 'mad' old man – and thereby dispute his ideas, e.g. 'What the hell does he know about me or my life?' Barrish (1993, p.35, section one) suggests that 'using the little old man image seems to be a continual reminder to clients of how ridiculous their irrational thoughts really are'. If they will not accept the old man's crazy ideas, why accept their own?

Indications: Use with clients who can gain more objectivity about their irrational ideas by having them reflected back from a person who is as demented as the ideas.

Contraindications: Do not use with clients who would agree with the old man and thereby strengthen their own self-defeating thinking.

Traumatic incident reduction (TIR)

TIR is a guided cognitive imagery procedure developed by Gerbode (1989) for use with clients who have long-standing symptoms or recent onset of post-traumatic stress disorder (PTSD). TIR works

> 'by tracing each traumatic reaction to its original or primary trauma(ta) and by taking each primary trauma to its *full resolution or procedural end point at one sitting* (a crucial requirement) the TIR process leaves clients observably relieved, often smiling, and no longer committed to their previously errant cognitions'. (Moore, 1993, pp. 131–2, italics in original).

For example, a client who experienced almost paralysing anxiety when he went for a job interview views (imagines) this recent incident but his anxiety does not abate; this indicates there are earlier incidents to view in order to trace back the anxiety to its primary trauma – in this case being savagely punched in the face by a stranger when he was 12 years old. The primary trauma is viewed until cognitive restructuring takes place (e.g. 'It was pretty bad but I've been awfulising about it ever since. Thank God I've now shrunk that past experience to its proper size in my life') and emotional relief is experienced as the anxiety has been dissipated. The whole process has taken several hours. Moore (1993) states that TIR is the most thorough and reliable approach to the resolution of PTSD currently in use.

Indications: Use with clients with PTSD.

Contraindications: Do not use with clients who do not want, or could not cope with, the the often lengthy and highly arousing viewing process.

Visualising self-created anger

Gullo (1993) uses this technique to help clients gain emotional control over their repressed or 'bottled up' anger. Clients are instructed to close their eyes and visualise the initial situation or experience in which the anger occurred. On a scale of 0 to 10, with 10 representing the most anger and 0 no anger, the client is asked to feel angry at the level of 10 and powerfully and emotively verbalise his angry feelings to the person(s) from the initial situation as if they were now in the same room with him, e.g. 'I hope you bastards rot in hell for laughing at me just because I made some mistakes!' The client is then asked to reduce his anger to 0, and when this has been achieved to raise it to 10 again and ventilate his feelings once more (if the client finds difficulty in expressing his angry feelings, the counsellor can model how to do it). The client is then asked to reduce his anger to 0 again.

At this point the client is asked a series of questions: 'Who caused the anger to climb to 10?, 'Who caused the anger to drop to 0?' 'Who caused the anger to be there in the first place?' The client should preferably reply 'me' to all three questions but, if not, the counsellor can supply the correct answer. The client is then asked to open his eyes and is given an explanation of the ABCs of REBC in order to reinforce the principle of emotional responsibility as well as detecting the irrational ideas that have led to the client's anger (or even rational annoyance) being repressed, e.g. 'I would look like a madman if I exploded. That would be terrible.' Gullo (1993, p.79, section one) emphasises that 'it is critical to use the word 'cause' as illustrated above in this visualization exercise in order to clearly establish for the client the cause and effect relationship of his or her thoughts and feelings'.

Indications: Use with clients with repressed or barely concealed anger problems who indicate that imagery might be an effective way to explore or reveal this anger.

Contraindications: Do not use with clients who deny that they have any anger problems, repressed or explicit, who are still resisting the principle of emotional responsibility or who would hijack the imagery exercise to confirm the 'righteousness' of their anger.

Emotive Techniques

These are methods that are designed to engage fully clients' emotions by disputing forcefully and energetically their irrational beliefs as part of the process of moving from intellectual rational insight to emotional rational insight. However, it is usually difficult to influence or manipulate directly a client's emotions as can be done with his cognitions and behaviour. Therefore, REBC counsellors need to remind their clients that 'emotional change often lingers behind behavioural and cognitive change . . .' so that persisting with their cognitive-behavioural tasks may not bring clients '. . . immediate or even intermediate affective benefit' (Dryden, 1995, p. 43).

Authentic self-disclosure

This technique helps to tackle clients' shame by encouraging them to reveal to others genuine things about themselves that they would rather keep hidden, e.g. a man tells his macho colleagues that he often has great difficulty in coping with workplace stress and therefore 'I can't take it in my stride like you lot can'; a woman confesses to her feminist friends that she needs a man in her life in order to be happy. By disclosing these perceived weaknesses and failings instead of trying always to maintain a positive and coping persona, clients can learn self-acceptance, to remove the 'horror' of public exposure of their private vices and to become greater risk-takers. Authentic self-disclosure can enable clients to release themselves from their own self-imposed restraints because they no longer fear others' disapproval or rejection.

Indications: Use with clients who want to overcome their shame-inducing philosophies.

Contraindications: Do not use with clients who think that public self-disclosure would do more harm than good, and who therefore prefer to pursue constructive change at a private level.

Counsellor profanity

The counsellor's judicious use of profanity emphasises important therapeutic points, e.g. 'Why the FUCK can't you make a mistake?'; and helps to develop a working alliance by employing the intimate self-talk that the client engages in, e.g. 'Why are you a "wanker", as you call yourself, when things go wrong?' Also, profanity can be used with clients (e.g. with anti-social personality disorder) who may resent authority figures – this can present the counsellor as an unconventional figure and therefore he might be given less of a 'hard time' by the client. It is important to note that counsellor profanity is never aimed at the clients, only at their irrational ideas. Finally, the indiscriminate use of profanity can turn counselling into a 'fuckfest' i.e. swearing becomes a mindless, fun-filled end in itself and any therapeutic purpose for its use has been forgotten or obscured.

Indications: Use with clients who employ strong language as part of their interaction with the counsellor or hint at its use in times of stress.

Contraindications: Do not use with any clients who would be offended by its use, who do not employ it themselves or who do swear but would see the counsellor's profanity as condescending or ingratiating. In addition, some counselling agencies would object to the counsellor's use of profanity even if clients do not.

Emotive bibliotherapy

Grieger and Boyd (1980) suggest that highly dramatic pieces of literature can arouse some clients and then stimulate them to think about the ideas contained in the text and provide a source of inspiration for those individuals similarly afflicted (e.g. *So Desperate the Fight* (1981), Warren Johnson's account of his struggle to overcome a devastating illness by changing his attitude towards it). It is important that the counsellor ensures that the client's chosen book is consonant with rational ideas (which means that it is important for the counsellor to read the book).

Indications: Use with clients who find pleasure, insight and/or illumination from literature.

Contraindications: Do not use with clients who are illiterate (though they may enjoy an audio cassette of the nominated book), who find little if any profit in reading 'serious' literature or who are too emotionally distracted to concentrate on reading a book.

Emotive confrontation

This is described by Ellis (1985a) as a 'powerful evocative confrontation' which aims to penetrate the cognitive defences of highly resistant clients in order to show them how they are disturbing themselves about their problems:

Counsellor: Your husband is screwing your dear and trusted friend and all you can say is 'Oh well, not to worry'. You're as angry as hell, and trying to maintain that untroubled façade definitely will not help you. All you've done since you entered therapy is to pretend.

Client: These things happen. Why can't you accept what I say to you?

Counsellor: Because every time I mention his screwing your friend, you grip the arms of that chair so tightly you're in danger of pulling them off. Also your jaw tightens, your face flushes, your body goes rigid. Get the point? You're as angry as hell and nothing will be resolved in your life until you deal with your anger. It will just eat away at you.

Client: My husband has let me down, and now he's been found out it's time for me to move on and choose my friends more carefully.

Counsellor: What utter nonsense! Your life is shattered and you're not going to rebuild it successfully through self-deception. Let me hazard a guess at your real thoughts: 'That absolute bastard has kicked me in the teeth and destroyed our marriage and as for that conniving bitch if I ever get my hands on her . . .' Sounds familiar?

Client: There might be a grain of truth in what you say. However, if I was to admit to anger, which I'm not, I might worry that it could become uncontrollable and I might be frightened of the consequences.

Counsellor: We can use counselling to reveal the anger, control it and eventually defuse it by learning how to develop more personally helpful beliefs. Willing to try?

Client: Well, I suppose it will be interesting to see if I'm as angry as you think I am.

Counsellor: Does that mean you've said 'yes'?

Client: Yes!

Ellis (1985a, p. 79) cautions that by 'confronting resistant clients in this manner, you often smoke out their iBs [irrational beliefs] – though, of course, you had better be careful not to give them beliefs that they don't actually have'.

Indications: Use with clients whose recalcitrance in counselling is severe or protracted.

Contraindications: Do not use with clients who are psychologically fragile, have psychiatric difficulties or are likely to leave therapy abruptly or prematurely if so confronted.

Emotive feedback

This demonstrates to clients the adverse impact of their behaviour on significant others in their life. In this extract from group therapy the client who has dire needs for love, gets feedback from the counsellor (who is leading the group) on the likely reasons why her relationships keep on failing:

Counsellor: If I went out with you, and you kept on asking me if I loved you, I would find this most annoying. It would also show me how insecure you are, which would be another turn off. I could see you would be desperate to please me to avoid being rejected and because you had no self-respect I doubt if I would show you much. So, all in all, I would say 'stuff this' and be off looking for someone else. I'm sure that's not how you want things to be.

This kind of emotive feedback helps the clients to understand better the feelings and subsequent behaviour of significant others in their lives as well as how to change in order to elicit more positive reactions from these others. Ellis and Dryden (1997) argue that such feedback be used by the counsellor and group member educatively and correctively, not just expressively.

Indications: Use in individual, couple or group counselling with clients who need to understand forcefully the unfavourable impact they have on others.

Contraindications: Do not use with clients who could not cope with this 'assault' on their already fragile self-esteem, but who still require feedback without the emotive component.

Emotive verbalisations

This procedure encourages clients to dispute their disturbance-producing beliefs in a highly emotive manner instead of their usual tepid way, e.g. an anxious man who cannot find a sexual partner says in a hesitant voice, 'I suppose it's not the end of the world' to which the counsellor strongly replies: 'Which means that it is. Now say with power and passion "It's bad that I can't find a partner, but it's never awful!" Now keep on repeating that to me and to yourself until you truly feel it in your gut'. Persistent and forceful action on the client's part usually turns the tide against self-defeating thinking.

Indications: Use with clients who need encouragement in applying force and energy to their rational coping statements.

Contraindications: Do not use with clients who may feel intimidated by such a technique, or who see it as alien to their character to engage in such behaviour, e.g. 'I've always tackled my problems with quiet determination, not shouting and screaming'.

Encouragement

This helps to imbue clients with hope and confidence that they can overcome their problems despite the setbacks and hard work involved, e.g. through pushing, persuading and positive reinforcement, the counsellor eventually encourages a client to face her long-standing social fears. Ellis (1985a) suggests that encouragement is a particularly useful technique with difficult clients.

Indications: Use with all clients unless otherwise indicated.

Contraindications: Do not use with those clients who might interpret encouragement as counsellor glibness or insincerity, e.g. a depressed client who objects to being 'cheered up'.

Evoking laughter

This is a comic intervention to show clients the self-defeating nature of their irrational beliefs. I (MN) once saw a client who told me that she could not stand any pressure:

Counsellor: (does not speak)
Client: (after ten minutes) Aren't you going to ask me any questions?
Counsellor: I don't want to put you under any pressure.
Client: (laughing) I see what you mean.
Counsellor: (laughing) What do I mean?
Client: Well, if I don't learn how to cope with pressure then I'll just stay the way I am.
Counsellor: So can you cope with some questions?
Client: (smiling) Of course I can – and probably more besides.
Counsellor: Good. We're already making progress.

The counsellor needed to elicit from the client whether she believed the comic intervention was aimed at her or at her ideas, and did it have any therapeutic impact upon her problems.

Indications: Use when the counsellor has established a sound therapeutic alliance with the client or when the client has demonstrated that she possesses a sense of humour and has no objection to the use of humour in therapy.

Contraindications: Do not use with clients who want a formal relationship with the counsellor, see 'nothing to laugh about' when discussing their problems, or who have no sense of humour.

Expressing feelings

This procedure encourages clients to ventilate their healthy negative feelings rather than their unhealthy negative feelings, e.g. a woman expresses her annoyance to a colleague who continually interrupts her and by this assertion she hopes her colleague will stop his rude behaviour. If the client had expressed anger instead, this probably would have led to aggression rather than assertion and the colleague, along with his rudeness, would have been damned. REBC hypothesises that releasing anger can actually reinforce the client's underlying beliefs instead of weakening them. Expressing non-disturbed emotions helps clients to think, feel and act in accordance with their new rational philosophies.

Indications: Use with clients who need to be helped to feel their way into healthy negative emotions and thereby adjust to the 'strangeness' of them.

Contraindications: Do not use with clients who want dramatic expressions of disturbed feelings through techniques such as catharsis or abreaction. When they feel themselves 'purged', REBC practitioners can suggest an alternative route to emotional health.

Group counselling

This can be a powerful way of helping clients to uproot their disturbance-creating ideas through group disputation rather than by a counsellor acting on her own. Also, by seeing other group members use REBC effectively upon themselves, this can spur the client to engage in constructive change. For example, a client who withstood the counsellor's arguments against using drink and drugs as problem-solving tools found his views were considered untenable when confronted by his peers in an addictions recovery group, and thereby opted for abstinence as his treatment goal.

Indications: Use with clients who would find a group more challenging and experiential than the relative 'safety' of one-to-one counselling, e.g. shy or passive clients or those clients who might become too dependent upon the counsellor in individual counselling.

Contraindications: Do not use with clients who would try to 'hide' in the group and thereby attempt to make little if any contribution towards it, who need a closer relationship with the counsellor than a group setting would allow for, or whose problems are primarily intrapersonal rather than interpersonal.

In vivo emotional techniques

These are methods described by Ellis et al. (1989, p.65) as helping 'your clients to feel emotional during their sessions – not *merely* to get in touch with and express their feelings, but *also* to understand how they *created* them and *can change* them' (italics in original). For example, angry, disaffected partners in a couple can be encouraged in counselling to row with each other and thereby experience the unhealthy negative emotions they have for each other and themselves. When these disturbed feelings are revealed, the counsellor can show both people how they are largely creating these through their irrational beliefs, e.g. the depression-inducing belief, 'Our relationship will never get better. It's awful', and how to dispute these beliefs straightaway in order to change these feelings to healthy negative ones like sadness, the rational alternative to depression.

Indications: Use with clients who have difficulty in expressing, finding or revealing their emotions, e.g. overly intellectual clients, or with clients who have difficulty in grasping the belief–emotion link.

Contraindications: Do not use with clients who are unable or unwilling to cope with such emotional intensity and who need less dramatic ways of reducing their disturbed feelings.

Non-verbal exercises

These can be used as icebreakers to reduce inhibitions in clients, or for general 'loosening up', e.g. participants in a group have to engage in foolish activities like pulling faces to reduce their own tension as well as part of the process of drawing the group together. Non-verbal exercises are also used between couples as another source of information about their interpersonal difficulties, e.g. a woman later complains that when her partner was supposedly caressing her she felt like a cat being stroked instead of being sexually aroused by his actions. Such information can help clients to determine if their behaviour is congruent with their intentions or with the presumed wishes of others.

Indications: Use in couple or group counselling, sex therapy, with clients who need to be educated about non-verbal communication, or those who always seem to be confused by, or misinterpret, the signals sent by others.

Contraindications: Do not use with clients who are concrete thinkers and therefore need explicit and verbal instructions before they can proceed with any interaction.

Pleasurable pursuits

Clients who are anhedonic (i.e. lack pleasure in their lives or the capacity to enjoy it) and/or depressed can be encouraged to take up stimulating and rewarding activities as a way of helping themselves tackle their problems. For example, a woman who said her life was dull and boring found formal therapy unhelpful, but when the REB counsellor repeatedly urged her to commit herself to a 'larger purpose in life' she joined the Red Cross and eventually became a hard working and devoted member of her local branch.

Indications: Use with clients who find difficulty in enjoying themselves through normal interests such as romantic relationships, dinner parties, holidays or other gregarious activities.

Contraindications: Do not use with clients who may use pleasurable pursuits as a self-fulfilling prophecy to confirm their 'I feel dead inside' viewpoint.

Relationship emphasis

While REBC does not usually dwell on the nature of the relationship between the counsellor and client, Ellis (1985a) does acknowledge that with some difficult or resistant clients (e.g. troubled adolescents) developing a trusting or close relationship is important, if not essential, if therapeutic change is to occur. Therefore, the counsellor may need to understand the client in more than the usual detail and empathise strongly with his viewpoint, e.g. 'Life keeps on knocking you back every time you pick yourself up and your parents don't help one bit by always complaining about you. No wonder you think life is shit.' Even though the counsellor might eventually achieve some limited cognitive restructuring, the real breakthrough for the client will be in the quality of the relationship and not in the disputing process.

Indications: Use with clients whose emphasis is on a trusting and caring therapeutic relationship rather than on techniques and strategies for change, and with clients for whom the therapeutic alliance acts as an interpersonal laboratory in which they can learn to develop more stable relationships, e.g. clients with borderline personality disorder.

Contraindications: Do not use with clients who might become overly dependent on the counsellor and who are thereby reluctant to leave counselling, who attribute their progress to the counsellor instead of to themselves 'because I couldn't have done it without you being there for me all the time', who see therapy as friendship rather than a problem-focused collaborative endeavour, who declare their romantic feelings for the counsellor instead of their goals for change 'because you've taken such an interest in me' or with any client for whom the relationship emphasis creates more problems than it solves.

Role-playing

This procedure teaches clients how to gain more confidence in facing fearful situations through in-session rehearsal, e.g. a client who says he is unable to be assertive with a noisy neighbour is encouraged to re-enact the scene in counselling with the counsellor taking the role of the noisy neighbour. Such a re-enactment enables the counsellor to pinpoint the client's irrational beliefs largely responsible for his unassertiveness (e.g. 'I can't stand uncomfortable situations') and dispute them. As Ellis and Knaus (1977, p.116) remark: 'By this kind of role-playing, you can begin literally to act and "feel" your way into dreaded situations, to acquire more skill at them, and thereby to overcome much of your dread.'

Indications: Use with any client who requires in-session rehearsal as a prelude to entering the actual situation.

Contraindications: Do not use with any client who spurns the artifice of simulation and only wants the raw data from the real-life situation to be critiqued.

The additional multimodal techniques offered in this chapter are a reminder of the creativity of REBC in disputing clients' self-defeating thinking. To practise REBC effectively, practitioners, as noted in the introduction to this chapter, need to develop creative persistence in not only 'collecting' established REBC methods of change, but also in adapting these and devising their own. The authors of this book believe that you can never have too many techniques in your therapeutic armamentarium.

Chapter 9
The Rational Emotive Behavioural Counselling Sequence

Overview

The preceding chapters of this book have presented the essential elements involved in the theory and practice of rational emotive behavioural counselling (REBC). This chapter will provide a synthesis of these elements by describing the REB counselling sequence which illustrates the application of REBC to an actual client problem.

The REBC sequence consists of 18 important steps (Figure 9.1) that are typically part of the process of helping clients to overcome their emotional problems. In particular, it illustrates the manner in which REBC's ABC model of emotional disturbance can be used to help both counsellor and client to assess and reach an agreed understanding of the client's problems before therapeutic intervention (i.e. disputing disturbance-creating beliefs) is attempted. The counselling sequence further specifies the importance of teaching clients the relationship between their beliefs and their emotions, the central place of homework tasks within REBC, the hard work required to internalise a rational philosophy of living and the importance for clients to become their own self-therapists.

The general format of this chapter is as follows: each step of the counselling sequence is described in detail and then illustrated through the presentation of a case study that MN did with a 35-year old woman called Janet (not her real name) who presented with social avoidance. The material that follows is used to demonstrate the systematic application of the REBC sequence. However, counsellors are advised that it is not always possible or desirable to proceed in this systematic fashion – the 18 steps should never become a straitjacket for the counsellor, or 'fitted' on to the client. For example, a counsellor might insist 'I must keep to the steps at all times' or state that counselling is stalled at Step 5 until the client reveals an unhealthy negative emotion in the REBC sense. Therefore, the 18 steps should be seen only as a flexible framework for the efficient and effective practice of REBC.

Step 1:   Ask for a Problem
Step 2:   Define and Agree Upon the Target Problem
Step 3:   Agree a Goal with Respect to the Problem as Defined
Step 4:   Ask for a Specific Example of the Target Problem
Step 5:   Assess C
Step 6:   Assess A
Step 7:   Agree a Goal with Respect to the Problem as Assessed
Step 8:   Help the Client to see the Link between the Problem-as-defined Goal and the Problem-as-assessed Goal
Step 9:   Identify and Assess any Meta-emotional Problems
Step 10: Teach the B–C Connection
Step 11: Assess iB
Step 12: Connect iB and C
Step 13: Question iB and rB
Step 14: Prepare Clients to Deepen their Conviction in Rational Beliefs
Step 15: Check the Validity of A
Step 16: Negotiate a Homework Assignment
Step 17: Check the Homework Assignment
Step 18: Facilitate the Working-through Process

Figure 9.1: The rational emotive behaviour counselling sequence
A = activating event (and inferences);
B = belief:
iB = irrational belief;
rB = rational belief;
C = emotional consequence.

Finally, it is noted that the counselling sequence material presented in this chapter focuses on the treatment of only one particular client problem. It does not deal with issues pertaining to case management and the entire *process* of REBC. Such issues will be discussed in Chapter 10, The Rational Emotive Behavioural Counselling Process. The initial step of the counselling sequence is presented below.

Step 1: Ask for a Problem

Once the introductions are over, counsellors are advised to adopt a problem-solving focus immediately by asking the client what problem he or she would like first to address in counselling. Such a rapid move into discussing the client's problem conveys a number of important messages to him or her. First, counselling time is precious and therefore counsellor and client need to 'get on with it' in tackling the latter's emotional problems; idle chit-chat, extended pleasantries, etc. are avoided. Second, it demonstrates that rational emotive behavioural counselling (REBC) is efficient, usually relatively brief, and focused in its problem-solving efforts – protracted counselling prolongs the client's suffering. Third, it signals to the client that the counsellor is going to be very active during the course of therapy and directive in keeping the client (and counsellor) on track in their problem-solving progress.

However, there are times when clients are best served by being allowed a more open-ended exploration in the beginning phase of counselling flexibility, here, as elsewhere in the counselling sequence is the byword.

Two strategies: client choice vs. client's most serious problem

Two basic strategies can be used by the counsellor in attempting to elicit a target problem from the client. The first one leaves the choice to the client: 'With what problem would you like to start?' The client's selection of a problem for discussion could be a central concern or something less serious. The second strategy involves a more directive stance on the part of the counsellor: 'What are you most troubled about in your life at the moment?' Either strategy should usually provide client material for examination.

When the client fails to pinpoint a target problem quickly

If the client cannot identify a target problem to work on, the counsellor can use a number of ways with which to encourage the client to locate a problem area. First, the client can be informed that he or she does not have to 'jump in at the deep end' by starting with the most painful or difficult issue in his life. Counselling can begin with the exploration of a less threatening or demanding issue by pointing out to the client that virtually every individual has some area of his or her life where they are functioning at a suboptimal level. Such information can nudge the client into offering a problem and thereby initiating the problem-solving process.

Second, the client can be encouraged to identify feelings and behaviours to increase or decrease and attitudes to change or adopt. This approach can be particularly useful for clients who are largely naïve about the counselling process, and who may be in some confusion as to how counselling might be of help to them. With respect to this issue, the reader will recall that Chapter 5 detailed the importance of attending to induction procedures within rational emotive behavioural counselling as a means of reducing client misunderstandings and eventual disillusionment with the counselling process (see pp. 62–66).

Another, less direct, means of helping the client to identify a problem area is by asking what he or she would like to accomplish through counselling. After the client has stated a particular goal (e.g. to feel more confident with women), the counsellor can then ask him to describe the ways in which he is failing to achieve this goal at the present time (e.g. 'I always wait for women to chat me up instead of taking the initiative myself'). Such questioning can lead to fruitful discussion of self-defeating ideas, feelings and behaviours that may serve as impediments to goal attainment. The counsellor can then explore these factors with the client without necessarily labelling them as 'problems'. Some individuals (even after they have gone to the trouble of entering counselling) have difficulty owning up to the fact that they have problems; thus, they may be discouraged from becoming engaged in a problem-focused approach as rational emotive behavioural counselling. When this appears to be the case with a particular client, the counsellor can attempt to identify and employ alternative terminology that may be more acceptable to the client (e.g. challenges, concerns, difficulties, issues).

Janet

After greeting Janet and introducing myself, we discussed the referral letter from her GP which described her as suffering from social avoidance. In order to establish quickly a problem-solving focus as part of the socialisation into REBC, I asked her if she would like to begin with the GP's letter or wherever she chose:

Janet: Well, I do get very uncomfortable if I have to meet people socially. I try to avoid it if I can. This leads to rows with my husband as he likes to go out a lot. Sometimes I fear that these rows will destroy my marriage. He might meet another woman when he goes out on his own.

Michael: Why do you think you avoid social events?

Janet: I didn't tell my GP this but I was a heroin addict for a few years – only smoking it, never injecting – but I worry about people finding out. It's silly really, I've been clean for nearly 10 years. My husband says people we meet neither know about my past nor probably would care about it if I told them.

Michael: Would you agree with your husband's assessment?

Janet: No, not really. He dabbled in drugs years ago but never became addicted like me. He doesn't care if people know about his past.

Michael: Unlike you.

Janet: Exactly.

After further discussion with Janet, we compiled the following problems list so they could be dealt with one at a time:

1. Social avoidance.
2. Constant rowing with her husband.
3. Fear that her marriage will end.
4. Worried that she can never escape 'from my drug past'.

I asked Janet which problem she wanted to tackle first and she picked the social avoidance. She believed that if she could overcome this problem then the rows with her husband would probably stop or greatly reduce; this, in turn, would prevent the marriage from falling apart.

Step 2: Define and Agree Upon the Target Problem

Often, the nature of the client's problem will be clear after some initial discussion during the very first session of counselling. When this is the case, the counsellor may skip Step 2 and proceed to assess the problem as per steps 3-9 of the REBC sequence. If, however, the nature of the client's problem remains unclear, it is desirable to reach an agreed definition of it prior to implementing the assessment stage. In addition, when a client discloses a number of problems in close succession, it is important to reach agreement as to which one will receive treatment first.

Arriving at a common understanding of a target problem and agreeing to work upon it together is an important component of rational emotive behavioural counselling, as it helps to solidify the therapeutic alliance. Agreement on these issues enables counsellor and client to function as a more effective team, and also helps the client to feel understood and to have confidence in the counsellor's expertise. In our experience as supervisors of counsellors in training, we have often reviewed audiotapes of counselling sessions in which counsellor and client seemed to drift along aimlessly, largely because the novice counsellor failed to establish with the client a particular problem area on which to focus.

Distinguish between emotional and practical problems

It is useful to make a distinction with clients between *practical* problems (e.g. 'I'm £2,000 in debt to the bank') and *emotional* problems ('I'm depressed that I haven't got the money to pay off my debts to the bank') when conducting REBC. Bard (1980) has noted that REBC is an approach to counselling that is designed to assist clients in overcoming emotional rather than practical problems. However, when clients have an emotional problem about a practical issue, this emotional problem may well become the focus of therapeutic exploration. In addition, as clients make progress in removing the emotional obstacles they create for themselves, they may experience greater success in resolving their practical issues (Ellis, 1985a). If some clients fail to achieve greater practical problem-solving success, then the counsellor can teach problem-solving training through the use of an algorithm, i.e. sequential problem-solving steps (for example, see Wasik, 1984).

Target unhealthy, but not healthy, negative emotions

As noted in Chapter 2, irrational and self-defeating beliefs will tend to lead an individual to experience unhealthy negative emotional responses when faced with adverse life events. Rational and self-helping beliefs, on the other hand, will usually lead an individual to experience healthy (although still negative) emotional responses to these same events. Chapter 2 elaborated upon the distinctions between unhealthy and healthy negative emotions by presenting descriptions of the various self-defeating feelings and their self-helping alternatives. Feelings such as anxiety, hurt, unhealthy anger, guilt and depression are considered to stem from irrational beliefs and to represent unhealthy negative emotions, whereas feelings such as concern, sorrow, healthy anger and sadness are viewed as the products of rational beliefs and are regarded as healthy negative emotions.

Rational emotive behavioral counsellors do not encourage their clients to change their healthy negative emotions, as these are regarded as psychologically helpful reactions to negative events. Such emotions can motivate individuals to act on unfortunate or undesirable life circumstances in a constructive fashion, and are unlikely to impair adjustment to situations that may be largely unmodifiable. Clients are encouraged to change their unhealthy negative emotions as these are more likely to stand in the way of constructive adjustment and goal attainment. In this vein, it is wise to make sure that clients understand the distinctions between unhealthy and healthy negative emotions. Asking the question, 'How is this feeling a problem for you?' or 'How does this feeling help you deal constructively with this situation?' can often lead to a useful discussion, which will help counsellor and client to identify and define a real emotional problem in the REBC sense.

Operationalise vague problems

Clients will sometimes discuss their target problems in vague or confusing terms. When this is the case with a particular client, it is important for the counsellor to help him or her operationalise the problem. This involves defining the elements of the problem in terms that will assist the counsellor in applying REBC to it.

For example, a client might state: 'My wife drives me round the bend!' The counsellor can assist the client to specify the meaning of this statement by asking a question such as, 'What precisely does your wife do that leads you to react in this way and how do you feel when she acts in this way?' This type of question can help the counsellor to begin formulating the client's problems according to REBC's ABC model. The first part of the question may elicit descriptions of relevant activating events (As) such as his wife endlessly changing television channels, while the second part may prompt the client to report on the emotional consequences (Cs), he experiences in the face of these As (e.g. anger).

Focus on helping clients to change C, not A

Clients may often wish to focus counselling on a discussion of methods to change A rather than on their feelings (Cs) about A. Changing the A constitutes a practical solution while changing C is the emotional solution. When counsellors encounter this situation, they can use certain strategies to encourage their clients to work at changing C before attempting to change A. First, they can attempt to show clients who already possess adequate practical problem-solving skills that they may be able more effectively to deploy these skills to change A if they are not emotionally disturbed at C. Second, they can attempt to show clients who lack an adequate repertoire of problem-solving skills that they will probably experience greater success in acquiring the skills needed to modify problematic As if they remove the emotional obstacles at C rather than the A because REBC 'holds that relieving practical problems before emotional problems tends to rob clients of their motivation to solve their emotional problems, leaving them more comfortable yet still disturbed' (Grieger and Boyd, 1980, p.36).

Dealing with failure to identify a target problem

When counsellors have reached this stage of the assessment process and have not yet reached agreement with the client as to the nature of the problem to be targeted for change, they can recommend that the client keeps a *problem diary*. The client would use this to monitor and record disturbed feelings between counselling sessions, with written notes concerning the types of feelings involved and when and where they were experienced.

Aim for specificity in assessing the target problem

It is important to be as specific as possible in defining and agreeing upon the target problem with clients. Clients experience emotional problems and hold related irrational beliefs in specific contexts, so that being specific will help the counsellor to obtain reliable and valid data about A, B and C. Providing clients with a sound rationale for specificity can aid this endeavour, particularly with those clients who tend to discuss their problems in vague terms. Clients can be taught that being specific about their target problem can help them to deal with it more constructively in the situations about which they disturb themselves. A productive method for modelling specificity for clients is to ask them for a recent or typical example of the target problem, e.g. 'When was the last time A happened?'

In some cases, clients who remain unable to provide specific examples of their target problems may have secondary emotional problems (or meta-emotional problems) about their primary (or original) emotional problems (e.g. shame about feeling anxious; guilt about feeling depressed). If there is sufficient evidence to suppose that this is the case, then the counsellor should proceed to Step 9.

Janet

As stated in Step 1, Janet wanted to explore her social avoidance first, so I encouraged her to tell me more about this problem:

Janet:	As I said before, I try to avoid going out socially if I can because I feel so uncomfortable about it. Arguing with my husband only makes me feel worse.
Michael:	Can you imagine how you would feel if you didn't avoid going out?
Janet:	Terrible.
Michael:	In what specific way?
Janet:	My stomach would tighten . . . I'd be on edge all of the time . . . er . . . heart pounding and my mind would be racing. I'd be afraid that something bad was going to happen. Can you see why I avoid it now?
Michael:	I can understand why if you're feeling like that. Does feeling 'terrible' then become the justification for not going?
Janet:	Yes, but also the start of another row with my husband.
Michael:	Would you like to explore these unpleasant feelings and sensations and see how they are related to your life?
Janet:	I don't know what you nean.
Michael:	Well, if we can understand precisely why you feel so bad about attending social events, this will help us to tackle your problem more effectively.
Janet:	Oh, I see. Hmm. I too would like to know why I behave like this.

Step 3: Agree a Goal with Respect to the Problem as Defined

Once a target problem has been selected and both client and counsellor broadly agree on the nature of this problem, the next step is to choose a goal in line with the problem as defined (as we shall see later, this may not be the same goal after the problem has been assessed). Goal selection at this stage is usually provisional, as information related to the target problem is often insufficient to gain a clear picture of the determinants of the problem.

Michael:	Now, these 'terrible' feelings you experience in relation to social events, what would you like to do about them?
Janet:	Change them, of course!
Michael:	And what would happen if you could change them?
Janet:	I'd be much happier and would actually look forward to going out more with my husband.
Michael:	So can we agree that your goal at this stage is changing these 'terrible' feelings in order for you to socialise more?
Janet:	That sounds all right but why did you say 'at this stage'?
Michael:	Because goals are not set in concrete and as we uncover more information about your problem, we might find the goal shifting.
Janet:	Where to?
Michael:	I don't know yet. Shall we proceed?
Janet:	Okay.

Step 4: Ask for a Specific Example of the Target Problem

Up to this point, the client has spoken about her unpleasant feelings with regard to social situations. The next step is to anchor the target problem in a specific example so as to move counselling from the general to the concrete.

Michael: Can you give me a specific occasion when you experienced these unpleasant feelings?
Janet: Yes, about two weeks ago when I was invited to a dinner party with my husband. I didn't go of course.
Michael: You felt safer staying at home?
Janet: Absolutely.
Michael: Okay. That seems an excellent example to focus upon.

Step 5: Assess C

As stated in Chapter 5, A and C are typically assessed before B. At this stage of the counselling sequence, counsellors may assess either A or C, depending upon which element of the target problem the client discusses first. With respect to this client's problem, C will be examined first.

Check again that the target emotion is an unhealthy negative one

In assessing C, counsellors are advised to remember that the client's emotional problem will be an unhealthy negative emotion and not a healthy negative emotion. The former can be distinguished from the latter by the amount of emotional pain it inflicts upon the client, its contribution to self-defeating behaviour and its usual role as an impediment to goal attainment.

Chapter 2 contained a compendium of feeling words used in REBC theory to distinguish between unhealthy and healthy negative emotions. It is important to recognise, however, that clients probably do not use these terms in the same way as their counsellors do. Thus, a particular client may refer to depression when he really has feelings of sadness, or vice versa. Counsellors should take steps advisedly to ensure that they have identified an unhealthy negative emotion, otherwise a lot of precious counselling time will be misspent trying to convince the client to change a healthy negative emotion! Counsellor and client should use the same terminology when referring to an unhealthy negative emotion (Dryden, 1986). For example, a client of mine (MN) referred to unhealthy anger 'as going into one' and this became the term we both used throughout the course of therapy. The counsellor can teach REBC's 'emotional vocabulary' to the client or adopt the client's idiosyncratic usage. Regardless of the alternative chosen, it is helpful for counsellors to be consistent in their vocabulary during the course of treatment.

Focus on an emotional C

A client's Cs can be emotional, behavioural or cognitive. Maladaptive behaviour often serves a defensive or protective function in helping the client to avoid experiencing certain unhealthy negative emotions; for example, procrastination helps an individual to avoid feeling the intense anxiety of public speaking; excessive alcohol consumption enables a woman to dampen her angry feelings towards her husband's ill-treatment of her. When the maladaptive behaviour is stopped this usually releases the underlying feeling, and the C can now be identified. In this discussion of the counselling sequence, C, will refer only to unhealthy negative emotions.

Clarify C

Clients often refer to their Cs in vague or unclear terms. There are a number of techniques that can be used to clarify the nature of these Cs (e.g Gestalt exercises like the empty chair technique (see Passons, 1975), Gendlin's (1978) focusing technique and imagery methods, where the client is asked to imagine an example of his problem and identify any associated feelings that are experienced). When all else fails, Albert Ellis will sometimes encourage his clients to 'Take a wild guess' when they have difficulty in identifying a specific emotion. This 'shot in the dark' approach often yields surprisingly useful information about C.

Frustration is an A, not a C

Clients often talk about feeling frustrated at C. Here, it is important to note that some REB counsellors prefer to regard frustration as an activating event rather than a feeling (Trexler, 1976). As a C, frustration in REBC theory is usually regarded as a healthy negative emotion that clients experience when they are blocked from attaining their goals. When a client reports feeling frustrated, however, it is possible that he or she is referring to an unhealthy negative emotion. Counsellors can often determine whether a client's reported feeling of frustration is an unhealthy or healthy negative emotion by asking if the feeling is bearable or unbearable. If the client responds to such an enquiry by describing the feeling as unbearable, he or she may well be experiencing an unhealthy negative emotion that could be targeted for change.

Assess client motivation to change C

Clients sometimes experience unhealthy, disturbed negative emotions that they are not motivated to change. This lack of motivation can occur when clients fail to recognise the destructive, self-defeating nature of the emotion in question. This situation arises most often in the case of anger; it may also occur with feelings of guilt and depression. As such, counsellors are advised to assess clients' understanding of the maladaptive aspects of the target emotion (C). If particular clients do not understand why a disturbed emotion is unhealthy, it is beneficial to devote as much time as necessary to helping them see this point. This can be accomplished with the following steps:

1. Assist the clients to assess the consequences of the unhealthy negative emotion. What happens when they feel this way? Do they tend to act constructively or self-defeatingly?
2. Emphasise that the goal is to replace the unhealthy negative emotion with its healthy, more rational counterpart (e.g. replacing anxiety with concern). Making this point can be difficult, particularly if the clients have rigidly entrenched ideas concerning the way they are 'supposed' to feel when confronted with negative As (see DiGiuseppe, 1984, for a more extended discussion of this issue). If provided with credible models, however, the clients will usually be able to see that they can experience the healthy negative emotion in a given context. To cite an example, clients with public speaking anxiety can be helped to identify individuals they know who experience feelings of strong concern, but not anxiety, prior to giving a lecture in front of an audience.
3. Finally, work with the clients to assess the consequences that would occur if they experienced the corresponding healthy emotion when confronted with a problematic situation. As the clients probably have not thought in these terms before, help them to imagine how they would behave and how the outcome might be different if they felt the healthy negative emotion in the face of an adverse A. Then, compare the outcomes of experiencing healthy versus unhealthy negative emotions. As an example, a particular client could be encouraged to imagine how he might act (and what types of results he might get) if he felt healthily angry (instead of unhealthily angry) when his teenage son breaks his evening curfew. This may help the client better to understand the advantages of the healthy emotion, and this insight may well increase his motivation to change C.

Avoid potential pitfalls in assessing C

Counsellors may encounter a number of potential difficulties as they work to assess clients' problematic emotions at C. These difficulties may be avoided by implementing the following suggestions:

1. Avoid using questions that reinforce the notion that A causes C. Novice REB counsellors may make the error of asking clients questions such as, 'How does the situation *make you* feel?' As an alternative, counsellors might ask, 'How do you feel *about* the situation?' This question can serve to elicit descriptions of problematic Cs, and does not implicitly convey the message that A *causes* C.

2. When clients respond to enquiries concerning their feelings about A with terms such as 'bad', 'upset', 'miserable', etc., do not attempt to work with these vague descriptions of emotions. Instead, work with clients to help them clarify exactly what feelings they experience at C. Also, do not accept statements such as, 'I feel trapped' or 'I felt rejected' as descriptions of emotions occurring at C. Trapped and rejected are not emotions. These terms probably refer to combinations of A, B and C factors, and it is important to discriminate between these three factors and ensure that clients' C statements really do refer to feelings. To illustrate: if a client states, 'I felt rejected', he can be helped to see that rejection is an A and then be asked how he felt about the rejection at point C (e.g. hurt, depressed).

Janet

In Step 2, Janet spoke about the unpleasant feelings she experiences when she contemplates the prospect of socialising and therefore tries to avoid such events. In Step 3, her goal was to change these feelings so that she could enjoy social occasions with her husband. In this step, my task was to help us both to understand more fully the nature of these feelings:

Michael: You said earlier that if you didn't avoid going out socially you would feel terrible: tight stomach, on edge, heart pounding, mind racing. Which emotion do you think those feelings and sensations refer to?

Janet: I'm not sure what you mean by that.

Michael: Well, do you think you're experiencing – depression, anger, anxiety, for example?

Janet: Oh, I see what you mean. I'd feel very anxious.

Michael: And this anxiety obviously doesn't help you to achieve your goal of going out more with your husband.

Janet: It certainly doesn't.

Michael: Would it make sense to find out what lies behind your anxiety which, in turn, creates your avoidance behaviour, so that we can change or modify this anxiety in some way? Perhaps learn to feel a different way about your problem, which then could help you to achieve your goal.

Janet: Well, I'm willing to give it a try.

Janet was able to pinpoint her unpleasant feelings and sensations as anxiety – emotional specificity – and therefore agreement was reached on the use of a common emotional vocabulary. Now we would be able to explore the cognitive content of her anxiety in the next step.

Step 6: Assess A

If C is assessed first, the next step in the counselling sequence is to assess A. As noted earlier, A can refer to activating events that may be regarded as confirmable reality (i.e. neutral observers could confirm a given client's descriptions of A). In this presentation, however, A will also be used to stand for clients' personally significant inferences about the activating event.

As with assessments of C, aim for specificity when assessing A. This can be accomplished by asking the client to provide the most recent occurrence of A, a typical example of A, or the most relevant example the client can recall (Step 4 has already provided an example of A to examine).

Identify the part of A that triggers B (critical A)

In the process of assessing A, it is important to help the client identify the most relevant aspect of A (i.e. the part that generally serves to trigger irrational beliefs at B). This is known as the critical A. Identifying this trigger can sometimes be complicated by inferences the client makes about the situation. As these inferences are often linked or chained together, the technique referred to as *inference chaining* (described in Chapter 6) can be used to identify the particular inference in the chain that functions as the trigger.

By way of illustration, imagine a client who experiences anxiety at point C. Initial inquiry reveals that she is due to give a class presentation. Giving the class presentation thus represents an activating event, but the counsellor will wish to determine just what it is about the presentation that is anxiety-provoking in the client's mind. The following dialogue might then ensue:

Counsellor: What is it about giving the presentation that makes you anxious?
Client: Well, I'm afraid I may not do a very good job.
Counsellor: For the moment, let's just assume that you don't. What's anxiety-provoking in your mind about that?
Client: Well, if I don't do a good job in class, then my teacher will give me a poor grade.
Counsellor: Let's assume that as well. What would you be anxious about then?
Client: That I might flunk the course.
Counsellor: And if you did?
Client: Oh, my God. I couldn't face my father!
Counsellor: Imagine telling your father that you had failed. What then would be anxiety-provoking in your mind?
Client: I can just picture his reaction – he would be devastated!
Counsellor: And how would you feel if that happened?
Client: Oh God, that would be terrible! I really couldn't stand to see my father cry – I'd feel so very sorry for him.

The class presentation was initially identified as A by the client. Through inference chaining, however, the counsellor has discovered the client's fearful anticipation of her father's upset upon hearing of her presumed failure.

To test whether a given inference in a chain genuinely represents the most relevant aspect of A in a client's emotional problem, the counsellor might write down the inference chain, review it with the client, and ask her to identify the point she thinks is the most important. Another technique for confirming whether the newly identified aspect of A is central is to 'manipulate' A and then check the client's responses at C. Thus, for example, the counsellor could say to the client, 'Let's suppose you told your father that you flunked the course, and he wasn't devastated – in fact, he coped quite well with the news. Would that different turn of events have any impact on your anxiety about giving the class presentation?' If the client responds in the affirmative, the counsellor can be more confident that the problem has been accurately assessed. If the client indicates that she would still be anxious, this could indicate that the prospect of seeing her father cry (at A) is not the most relevant factor in her anxiety problem; therefore the clinical investigation would continue in order to locate it (for an extensive discussion of inference chaining see Neenan and Dryden, 1996b).

Once the critical A has been established, it is important to reassess any changes in the client's feelings at C since the initial analysis of the problem. Assuming that the new aspect of A revealed in the above illustration is indeed the central factor, it would be important to encourage the client to see that her anxiety is more closely associated with the overwhelming pity for her father she would feel at C than with any general fears of failure she might have. Two alternative courses then present themselves in terms of treatment: the first would involve focusing on the client's feelings of anxiety at C about the future prospect of her father's emotional devastation. The second would involve asking the client to assume that the new A (the father's upset) had already occurred, and then dealing with feelings of other-pity that would presumably occur at C.

A can refer to many things

REB counsellors generally agree that A can be a thought, an inference, an image, a sensation, or a behaviour, as well as an actual event in the client's environment that can be confirmed by neutral observers. In addition, a client's *feelings* at C may also serve as an A. For example, a client may experience guilt feelings at C. This guilt could then serve as a new A, and the client may then feel ashamed (a new C) about feeling guilty. Here, the client has a secondary emotional (or meta-emotional) problem about his or her primary (or original) emotional problem. Not all clients will present such secondary problems, but the process of determining whether or not they exist is an important part of assessment in the counselling sequence (see Step 9).

Assume (at least temporarily) that A is true

In the course of assessing A, it is sometimes becomes apparent to counsellors that the client's critical A is a clear distortion of reality. When this is the case, it can be tempting to dispute A in order to correct the client's misinterpretations.

Generally, counsellors are advised to resist this temptation and to encourage the client to assume temporarily that A is correct. In the case previously described, for example, it is not essential to determine whether or not the client's father would be truly devastated upon hearing about her failure. Rather, it is important to treat A as if it is an accurate depiction of reality in order to assist the client in identifying the irrational and self-defeating beliefs that lead to particular feelings at C.

Avoid pitfalls in assessing A

A number of potential pitfalls that counsellors may encounter in assessing A may be avoided by implementing the following suggestions:

1. Refrain from obtaining too much detail about A. Allowing clients to speak at length about A can turn counselling into an extended gripe session which will make it difficult to maintain a problem-solving approach to overcoming emotional difficulties. With clients who ramble or provide compulsive details concerning their As, counsellors can attempt to abstract the most salient theme or what appears to be the major aspect of A. At times, it is appropriate to interrupt tactfully in order to re-establish a specific focus. A counsellor might say, for instance, 'I think you may be providing me with more detail than I require. Can you tell me what it was about the situation that you were most disturbed about?'
2. Discourage clients from describing A in vague terms. Attempt to obtain as clear and specific an example of A as possible. An example of a vague A would be, 'My husband was really on my case last night'. In contrast, a specific A would be, 'My husband told me I was lazy and inept for not having dinner ready and waiting for him when he arrived from work'.
3. Discourage clients from talking about several As at one time. Some individuals will jump from event to event within a given counselling session; in REBC, it is important to work on one A at a time. Clients can be encouraged to deal with the A they consider to illustrate best the context within which they make themselves disturbed and can be assured that their other As can be dealt with later on.
4. If at this point of the counselling sequence a particular client has still not identified a clear A, encourage him to start a diary prior to the next session. This diary can be used to record examples of activating events about which he makes himself disturbed.

Janet

At this point I used inference chaining in order to identify the part of Janet's A that she was most anxious about (her critical A). The incident used below was obtained in Step 4:

Michael: What we need to do now is to try to discover what you are most anxious about in relation to social events; in this case, the invitation to a

	dinner party. Now close your eyes and try to imagine vividly actually going to the dinner party – no more avoidance. How are you feeling?
Janet:	Very anxious.
Michael:	And what are you anxious about?
Janet:	That I would let something slip out about my drug past [first inference].
Michael:	And if you did let something slip out regarding your drug past, then what?
Janet:	Then I would be judged very harshly [second inference].
Michael:	In what specific way would you be judged very harshly?
Janet:	They would think I was nothing but a dirty junkie [third inference]. In fact, I wouldn't need to let anything slip – people would know, just sense the kind of person I am as soon as I walked in the room.
Michael:	Okay, let's assume that people would know or sense that you are a 'dirty junkie', would you agree with them at that point?
Janet:	No, I don't think so.
Michael:	You seem unsure. Let's see if we can be clearer on this point. If I could totally guarantee that everyone in the room would think only positive thoughts about you, would you still be anxious?

[Counsellor manipulates the A in order to determine if others' view of her is the key factor in her anxiety.]

Janet:	(sighs) Yes, I still would be.
Michael:	Because . . . ?
Janet:	Because I believe it about myself.
Michael:	So do you bring the idea of being a 'dirty junkie' with you to the social event; it's not being foisted on you by others, so to speak?
Janet:	No, it's my own doing. I never thought about taking the idea with me.
Michael:	What kind of a person are you for being a 'dirty junkie'?
Janet:	(voice barely audible) A worthless one and not fit to mix with decent people.

[The client has revealed a derivative irrational belief about herself. This may indicate the critical A has been located.]

Michael:	So are you most anxious about attending social events because you will remind yourself or confirm in your own mind that you are a worthless person and therefore, in your words, 'not fit to mix with decent people'?

[Counsellor seeks to test that critical A has been located.]

Janet:	(tearfully): That's exactly right, but I never realised how much I believed that until just now.

Through such questioning, the counsellor has helped the client to pinpoint the specific aspect of the activating event - attending social events - that Janet was most disturbed about; namely, confirming in her own mind that she is a worthless person for her past drug use and has no right to associate with 'decent' people.

Step 7: Agree a Goal with Respect to the Problem as Assessed

In Step 3, client and counsellor negotiated a goal (emotional amelioration) based upon the problem as defined (feeling 'terrible' about the prospect of attending social events). In this step, goal selection will be based upon the information revealed about the nature of the client's anxiety (C) during the assessment of the activating event (A).

Goal consideration and agreement

It has been emphasised that it is important for counsellor and client to develop a common understanding of the client's target problem. Likewise, it is desirable to reach agreement as to the client's goals for change as this will facilitate the development of a sound therapeutic alliance between the two parties involved in the counselling process.

When to agree on goals

There are two main points at which counsellors will want to assess a client's goal's for change. The first point occurs after counsellor and client have defined and reached agreement concerning the client's target problem (Step 3). Here, it is recommended that the counsellor help the client to set a goal in line with the problem as initially defined. Thus, if a client's problem relates to being overweight, an initial goal would be for him or her to achieve and maintain a specific target weight.

Counsellors may, however, wish to reconsider and reformulate the client's goal at the assessment stage (Steps 4–9). For example, after agreeing that the client's goal is to achieve and maintain a specific weight, assessment may reveal that he or she becomes anxious and overeats when bored. At this point, the client's goal might be reformulated so that it focuses on the ability to deal more constructively with boredom, so that he or she less often resorts to the (self-defeating) coping strategy of overeating. The client can be encouraged to work at feeling concerned (rather than anxious) about being bored, and to use that feeling of concern to deal with boredom in more self-helping ways. Generally, it is helpful to encourage clients to select a healthy negative emotion as a goal, and to assist them in understanding why such an emotion represents a realistic and constructive response to a negative activating event at A.

Help clients to take a long-term perspective

When discussing goals with clients, it is useful to make them aware of the distinction between long-term and short-term goals. At times, clients may wish to settle upon a short-term goal that may in the long-term be self-defeating and therefore irrational, e.g. in the case of a shoplifting client, the desire to steal without experiencing guilt which, if this was achieved, would probably extend a shoplifting career and the probability of eventually being caught and imprisoned. Counsellors are advised to help clients adopt a broader perspective and to obtain their commitment to work towards productive long-term goals.

Avoid pitfalls when agreeing on goals

Several potential difficulties may be encountered when working with clients to establish goals. The following suggestions may prove helpful in avoiding them:

1. Do not accept clients' goal statements when they express a desire to experience less of an unhealthy negative emotion (e.g. 'I want to feel less anxious, or 'I want to feel not so guilty'). Rational emotive behavioural theory maintains that the presence of an unhealthy negative emotion (such as anxiety or guilt) indicates that the client experiencing that emotion is subscribing to an irrational belief; so a goal of less guilt, for example, would just serve to perpetuate the irrational belief albeit with less credibility. In this situation, it is advisable to help clients to distinguish between the unhealthy negative emotion in question and its healthy counterpart. Clients can be encouraged to set the latter type of emotion as their goal. They can therefore work at feeling concerned instead of anxious, or sorry rather than guilty and self-downing.
2. Do not accept client goals that express the wish to feel neutral, indifferent or calm with respect to events about which it would be rational to experience a healthy negative emotion. Emotions indicating indifference (e.g. calmness in the face of an unfortunate event) would mean that a given client did not have a rational belief about the event in question whereas, in reality, the client would probably prefer that the event did not occur. Acquiescing to the client's goal to feel calm or indifferent about a negative event may actually encourage them to deny the existence of their desires rather than to think rationally, i.e. to acknowledge and express her desire that unfortunate events did not occur.
3. For similar reasons, do not accept client goals that involve experiencing positive feelings about A. It would be unrealistic for individuals to feel happy about a negative life event they would prefer not to encounter. Accepting the goal of feeling positive about a negative event may encourage clients to believe that it is good that that a particular negative A occurred because, for example, it is character building. This is undesirable, as it fails to promote rational thinking. To repeat an earlier point, clients who become better able to experience a healthy (as opposed to an unhealthy) negative emotion in the face of a negative life event may be more psychologically prepared either to accept it or modify it.
4. Do not accept vague goals such as 'I want to be happy'. The more specific you can encourage clients to be in setting goals, the more likely it is

that they will be motivated to do the hard work of changing irrational beliefs in the service of achieving these goals.

Janet

In Step 6, Janet identified that the core of her anxiety was seeing herself as worthless, and therefore not good enough to associate with decent people – hence her avoidance, if possible, of social events. The task in this step is to negotiate a goal to target her anxiety at C along with the associated disturbance-producing ideas:

Michael: Now, the anxiety prevents you from socialising. Agreed?

Janet: Agreed.

Michael: And this anxiety stems from the idea that you see yourself as worthless when you're around 'decent' people. Now, if you want to socialise more with your husband as you said earlier [see Step 3], what kind of feeling would be more likely to help you achieve this goal?

Janet: I don't want to feel anything. I just want to be completely calm, without a care in the world.

Michael: That sounds as it you want to feel numb, just shut off from everybody.

Janet: I do in a way. I'll feel safer. If you don't feel anything then you won't get hurt.

Michael: That sounds like the things you would be saying if you were taking drugs again. So how will shutting off help you to enjoy the actual process of socialising?

Janet: It won't help at all. There's no point socialising if you're not going to try to enjoy it.

Michael: So what feeling is more likely to help you enjoy socialising?

Janet: Feeling confident, I suppose.

Michael: And what will that feeling mean to you?

Janet: That I can meet people on equal terms and not put myself down for taking drugs in the past.

Michael: And how would that feeling help if you got a crisis of nerves about attending a social event or while you were there?

Janet: It would remind me not to avoid things or run away. I'm fed up with that sort of behaviour. (slightly annoyed) But it's all right saying all these things but how the hell do I actually get to feel confident?

Michael: I can show you a way of achieving this if you're interested.

Janet: I hope so, and I am.

As sometimes happens with clients, Janet wanted to replace her feeling of anxiety with a state devoid of feeling as if to provide herself with an illusory security. This initial goal of Janet's would probably not have been successful for the following reasons: REB counsellors would not agree to help the client to achieve such an inherently self-defeating goal because feeling numb is a safety behaviour that perpetuates her problems instead of encouraging her to face them. Janet's second suggestion of 'feeling confident' appeared to be a rational and self-helping alternative to anxiety. It is important to note that, as feeling confident appeared to approximate loosely to a healthy negative emotion in the REBC sense, the counsellor did not try to 'force' the client to adopt the REBC emotional vocabulary (see Chapter 2) whereby *concern* is viewed as the rational alternative to *anxiety*. If the client was at a loss to suggest a healthy alternative, *concern* could have been used on a provisional basis until such time as the client was able to nominate a term that was personally felt or meaningful.

Step 8: Help the Client to see the Link between the Problem-as-defined Goal and the Problem-as-assessed Goal

As there have been two goal-setting stages (Steps 3 and 7), some clients can become confused as to how the goals can be so different; therefore, they can appear to be experiencing more problems than they initially realised. In addition, the problem-as-assessed goal is often based on information of which the client was not consciously aware until uncovered during the inference chaining process (Step 6).

Michael: You appear a little troubled about something.
Janet: Hmm. I'm just wondering how we got from there to here.
Michael: Could you explain what you mean by 'from there to here'?
Janet: Well, I thought the goal was to help me do something about these feelings I experience about socialising and then we end up with me seeing myself as worthless which I'm now supposed to do something about. I thought I understood what my problems were. This seems more serious.
Michael: Okay, I can understand your bewilderment and worry. I'd like to explain how we got from there to here. When we first agreed your goal it was based on a superficial understanding of your problem. When we examined in detail your problem through the use of a specific example, we discovered that at the root of your anxiety was a belief that you were a 'dirty junkie'. And when I asked you what kind of person was a 'dirty junkie', you said . . .
Janet: . . . worthless.
Michael: Right. Now, if you want to feel confident in these situations and meet people on equal terms without putting yourself down, as you said, then the goal becomes to achieve this in some way. Does that make it clearer?
Janet: Yes, it does. I do want to achieve that goal.
Michael: Good. Could you put into your own words what I've just described to you?
Janet: Well, by digging deeper into my problem, I found out I've got a very low opinion of myself which I need to change if I want to gain confidence in meeting people at parties and things like that.
Michael: Exactly.

Janet's puzzlement provided the 'way in' to explain Step 8. Even if clients do claim to see the link it is important to make it explicit through explanation and feedback so that both client and counsellor are working towards the same goal.

Step 9. Identify and Assess any Meta-emotional Problems

Meta-emotional problems are emotional problems about emotional problems, e.g. angry about feeling hurt. Another way of stating this step is: does the client have secondary emotional problems about his primary emotional problems? The counsellor can check for the presence of a meta-emotional problem by asking a question such as 'Do you have any feelings about feeling hurt, such as anger or depression?' The client might reply: 'Yes, 1 feel angry with myself for feeling hurt. Only wimps feel hurt!'

When to attend to the meta-emotional problem first

It is suggested that counsellors attend to the client's meta-emotional problem if any of the following conditions are met:

1. The client's meta-emotional problem interferes significantly with the work being or attempting to be done on their original problem (as would probably be the case in the above example).
2. From a clinical perspective, the meta-emotional problem appears to be the more important of the two.
3. The client can see the sense of working on her meta-emotional problem first.

It can be important to present clients with a plausible rationale for working on the meta-emotional problem first. If the client still wishes to work on the original problem first, even after a reasonable explanation has been provided, then it is advisable to do so. To do otherwise could jeopardise or even destroy the therapeutic alliance between client and counsellor and then no problems, original or meta-, would be tackled.

Check for an emotional problem about a healthy negative emotion

In the course of assessing a client's *stated* original problem, it may become evident that they are in fact experiencing a healthy negative emotion (e.g. sadness about an important loss). If this is the case, check to see whether the client has a problem with this healthy negative emotion. A client may, for example, feel ashamed about feeling sad (e.g. 'It's a sign of weakness to feel sad'). Work to reach an agreement that the meta-emotional problem (shame) will be the client's target problem for assessment.

Assess for the presence of shame

As noted above, clients who are reluctant to disclose an emotional problem may feel ashamed about having the problem or about admitting it to a counsellor. Counsellors can attempt to surmount this difficulty by asking such clients how they would feel if they *did* have an emotional problem about the activating event under discussion. With clients who provide indications that they would feel ashamed, the counsellor can attempt to reach agreement to work on shame as the target problem before encouraging disclosure of the original problem.

Janet

Janet's desire in Step 8 to achieve confidence in social situations by overcoming self-condemnation will now become the focus of the therapeutic process. However, before this process begins I check for the presence of a meta-emotional problem:

Michael:	Before we move on to find out how we can achieve your goal, let me just check something with you. Sometimes individuals develop problems about their problems; in other words, a person might feel angry about experiencing anxiety or feel ashamed about feeling depression. Do you follow so far?
Janet:	Hmm. I'm not sure that I do.
Michael:	Okay. Well, if a person prided himself on never getting depressed because he was always able to cope, he might feel very ashamed when he did become depressed because he now viewed himself as very inadequate. So, in this example, the shame could get in the way of dealing with his depression,
Janet:	I see what you're getting at now. I have felt ashamed and angry about my behaviour and guilty about letting my husband down, but I don't feel that way at the moment, and I don't think they'll get in the way.
Michael:	Can we monitor the situation so if they do come back, we can deal with them?
Janet:	Certainly. But wouldn't everyone feel as I do in my situation?
Michael:	Can we come back to that point a little later?
Janet:	Okay.

Janet's replies indicate that she is not troubled by meta-emotional problems at the present time. The counsellor should be on the alert for their return or the appearance of any new ones (e.g. hurt). Janet's penultimate comment reflected A–C thinking (i.e. situations directly cause our feelings) and therefore readily provided the counsellor with an example for teaching the B–C connection.

Step 10: Teach the B–C Connection

By this stage of the counselling sequence, the A and C elements of a client's original or meta-emotional problem have been assessed. The next step is for the counsellor to teach the client the *B-C connection*, that is, the concept that emotional problems are largely determined by beliefs rather than by the activating event that has been previously assessed. This step is crucial

because unless the client understands that her emotional problems are largely determined by her beliefs, she will not understand why those beliefs are
being assessed during the next step of the treatment sequence. This step also
establishes the principle of emotional responsibility for one's self-created disturbance. Using an example unrelated to the client's problem can often be
helpful in explaining the B–C connection because it allows the client to gain
greater objectivity through a dispassionate discussion of the example (see for
example, the 'teaching dialogue', Chapter 5). Alternative exercises, stories
and metaphors for teaching the B–C connection are described in a number
of other REBC texts (e.g. Ellis and Dryden, 1997; Walen, DiGiuseppe and
Dryden, 1992).

Janet

Janet's comment near the end of the dialogue in Step 9 – 'But wouldn't
everyone feel as I do in my situation?' – allowed me to use this example as a
means of teaching the B–C connection:

Michael: Can I ask what you mean by that comment?

Janet: Well, it's common sense isn't it. If people had my problems then they
would feel as anxious as I do.

Michael: Then they wouldn't be able to feel any other emotion in that situation –
just anxiety.

Janet: That's right.

Michael: So the situation makes you anxious and until the situation changes in
some way, you will have to remain anxious. Is that correct?

Janet: Well, I've always thought of it like that.

Michael: There is another way of looking at this: it's not the situation itself that
makes you anxious but the way you think (tapping his forehead) about
the situation that causes your anxiety. Another way of stating this very
important point is that you feel the way you think. Therefore, everyone
who was in the same situation as you would not necessarily feel anxious.

Janet: That's very different from the way I see things, but I'm not sure I really
understand what you're getting at.

Michael: Okay, let's look at an example then. Now imagine two men who are
attending an interview for the same job. The first man has the following belief: 'I *must* get this job at all costs and if I don't I will be a complete failure.' The second man has a different belief: 'I really want to
get this job but if I'm unsuccessful this certainly won't mean I'm a
failure as a person.' Now which man is more likely to feel anxious,
and why?

Janet: I suppose the first man because he's staking everything on getting the
job whereas the second man will take it in his stride if he doesn't get
the job. Is that right?

Michael: Well, I hope to show how powerfully our thinking affects our feelings,
but it's up to you to decide if this is right and helpful from your viewpoint.

Janet: I'm prepared to be open-minded.

Michael:	Fair enough. To return to the example: the first man has an absolute demand or *must* about getting the job which creates his anxiety. The second man obviously wants the job but isn't making any absolute demands and therefore might experience a different feeling such as . . . ?
Janet:	Er . . . probably not too bothered. More relaxed I'd say.
Michael:	He definitely wouldn't be as anxious as the first man. Does that make any kind of sense to you?
Janet:	A little. I can see what you're getting at, but I'm not sure how much I believe it yet.

Janet's comment that she is not convinced yet is hardly surprising: accepting the B–C connection often requires a paradigmatic shift in clients' understanding of emotional causation and use of language, e.g. 'He makes me anxious' (A–C thinking); 'I make myself anxious about him' (B–C thinking). Reinforcing the principle of emotional responsibility is usually a constant task for the counsellor.

Step 11: Assess Irrational Belief (iB)

In assessing a client's irrational belief, it is important for counsellors to keep in mind the distinction between irrational and rational beliefs and to help clients understand the differences between these two types of thinking.

Assess both premiss and derivative forms of irrational beliefs

Chapter 2 introduced the reader to the differences between irrational and rational beliefs, and noted that irrational beliefs are often comprised of a premiss and certain derivatives that stem from that premiss. To recapitulate, the premiss component of irrational beliefs embodies dogmatic demands on the self, on others or the world and come in the form of a must, absolute should, have to, got to, or ought. The three main irrational derivatives are awfulising, low frustration tolerance and damnation of self and/or others.

At this stage of the counselling sequence, counsellors will want to assess carefully both the premiss and derivative components of their clients' irrational beliefs. With respect to irrational derivatives, counsellors may either teach and use the REBC terms for these processes or use clients' own language. If the latter alternative is chosen, it is important to ensure that clients language accurately reflects irrational beliefs (e.g. 'My world is in pieces' is synonymous with awfulising). The choice of which alternative to pursue will be based upon clients' feedback as to which one will be the most helpful.

Distinguish between absolute and non-absolute shoulds

REB counsellors can become highly attuned to indications that clients are harbouring particular irrational beliefs in their thinking. However, it is import ant to bear in mind that every client utterance of the word 'should' does not constitute evidence for the presence of an irrational belief. In fact, most expressions of the word *should* will be unrelated to a client's emotional problems as this word has multiple meanings in the English language. These include shoulds of preference (e.g. 'I *should* tidy up my room'); empirical or probabilistic shoulds (e.g. 'When two parts of hydrogen and one part of oxygen are combined, you *should* get water'); recommendatory shoulds (e.g. 'You *should* see that film - it's so exciting'). Therefore, counsellors should help their clients to distinguish between absolute shoulds and shoulds of preference (the latter having just been used in this sentence).

REBC theory hypothesises that only *absolute shoulds* are related to emotional disturbance. When clients find the different meanings confusing, it can sometimes be useful to substitute the word *must* in cases where an irrational belief in its premiss form may be operative (compare, for instance, 'I *should* be admired by my colleagues' and 'I *must* be admired by my colleagues'). Our own clinical experience (as well as that of Albert Ellis) suggests that the word *must* conveys the meaning of absolute demandingness better than the word *should*.

Similar confusion can occur with the meaning of a *must*. In REBC, only unconditional musts (e.g. 'I *must* never show any weaknesses') are considered to be potentially pathological and therefore possible targets of challenge and change. Conditional musts (e.g. 'I must get a move on if I want to get to the cinema on time') are not usually implicated in the client's problems. However, if the individual in the last example flew into a rage if he got to the cinema late, this might require investigation to determine the presence of rigid beliefs.

Use questions to assess irrational beliefs

Counsellors are advised to use questions when assessing clients' irrational beliefs. An example of a standard question used by REB counsellors is: 'What were you telling yourself about A to make yourself disturbed at C?' This type of *open-ended question* offers both advantages and disadvantages.

One advantage of such a question is that it embodies and may convey several important elements of the REBC theory of emotional disturbance. In essence, it reinforces for the client the concept that A does not cause C; it is B that largely determines whether unhealthy or healthy negative emotions are experienced at C. An additional advantage of the above type of question is that it is unlikely to put words in the client's mouth concerning the content of her beliefs.

The main disadvantage of using this type of question is that clients (particularly those who are new to REBC) will frequently not respond to it by articulating an irrational belief. Instead, they may respond by providing further inferences about A - in some cases, these inferences may well be less relevant than the one previously selected at Step 6.

Imagine, for example, that a client is particularly anxious that other people will think he is a fool if he stammers in public. If his counsellor asks, 'What were you telling yourself about other people's criticism to make yourself anxious at C?' he might reply 'I thought they wouldn't like me'. Note that this response is actually an inference about A and that it fails to reveal the client's irrational belief. Here, the counsellor would try to help the client see that his statement does not describe an irrational belief in the REBC sense, and then educate him to look further for his anxiety-provoking irrational belief about A. This can be done by judiciously combining the use of open-ended questions with didactic explanations.

Walen, DiGiuseppe and Dryden (1992) list a number of other open-ended questions that may be used to assess clients' irrational beliefs. These include: 'What was going through your mind?'; 'Were you aware of any thoughts in your head?'; 'What was on your mind then?'; 'Are you aware of what you were thinking at that moment?' Again, clients will not necessarily disclose irrational beliefs in response to these questions; they may require help of a didactic nature.

Theory-driven questions represent an alternative to the use of open-ended questions for assessing irrational beliefs. Such questions are derived directly from REBC theory and are more specific with respect to identifying the type of response that is desired. As an example, a counsellor attempting to elicit a response concerning a client's operative must (i.e. a premiss) might ask, 'What *demand* were you making about other people's criticism to make yourself disturbed at point C?' By way of further illustration, the following question could be used to assess for a particular derivative of an irrational premiss: 'What kind of person did you think you were for stammering and incurring other people's criticism?'

Theory-driven questions are useful insofar as they orientate the client to look for his irrational beliefs. However, in using them, the counsellor runs the considerable risk of putting words in the client's mouth and encouraging him to look for irrational beliefs that he may not actually hold. This risk is minimised when careful assessment has already established that the client has an unhealthy negative emotion at point C.

Janet

Michael:	Just to recap: it's not other people, situations or events that create our feelings like anxiety but it is the beliefs that a person holds about these things that will determine how he or she feels. Okay so far?
Janet:	Yes. You're emphasising again the person's responsibility for their feelings in these situations.
Michael:	Exactly. Now, if individuals chose to stick with their wishes and wants in particular situations, how much emotional trouble might they get into?
Janet:	I expect not too much trouble because they wouldn't be closing down all their other options; if things didn't turn out all right they could try other things.

Michael:	That's right. Now if they changed those wishes and wants into rigid musts and shoulds (pounding the table), what kind of trouble might they expect now?
Janet:	Probably a lot of unhappiness. Their minds would be like a vice: it would keep them trapped in that unhappy situation.
Michael:	That's a good way of describing rigid thinking. Now, with your own problem, what's your wish?
Janet:	That I can feel confident in social situations and stop putting myself down.
Michael:	That's fine. Now what must or should are you bringing to your situation to make you feel anxious when you mix with decent people?

[Emphasises the word 'decent' to evoke her anxiety]

Janet:	I shouldn't have used drugs in the past.
Michael:	Just to be clear: is that should one of regret or a demand?
Janet:	No, it's a demand. I can hear it in my head now.
Michael:	With that should acting as a vice, how do you see yourself for doing what you absolutely shouldn't have done?
Janet:	As I said before – a worthless person.

Step 12: Connect Irrational Belief and C

After assessing clients' irrational beliefs in both premiss and derivative form, counsellors should take care to ensure that clients grasp the connection between their irrational beliefs and their disturbed emotions at point C. This step should precede any attempts at disputing these beliefs.

A simple enquiry can be used to determine whether a client understands this vital connection. Thus, a counsellor might say, 'Can you see that as long as you demand that others must not criticise you, you are bound to make yourself anxious about the possibility that this might occur?' With respect to an irrational derivative, the counsellor may ask, 'Can you see that as long as you believe that you are no good for being regarded by others as a fool, you will be anxious about being criticised?' If the client responds in the affirmative, the counsellor can then attempt to elicit from the client the B–C connection: 'So, in order to change your feeling to one of concern [or whatever self-helping term the client has chosen], what do you need to change first?' Eliciting this connection is likely to be more productive than simply telling the client that such a connection exists. If the client fails to see the connection, it is strongly advised that the counsellor spends time helping him to understand it before proceeding to dispute his irrational beliefs.

Michael:	Can you see that if you keep on firmly believing that you absolutely shouldn't have used drugs in the past, but as you did you are a worthless person, you'll keep on feeling anxious when you mix with *decent* [emphasises word] people?

Janet:	I'm beginning to see that. I take the anxiety to the party, so to speak, because of that belief.
Michael:	Right. The anxiety is not waiting to spring on you when you get to the party. So, if you want to change that feeling of anxiety to one of confidence, as you said earlier, and stop avoiding social situations, what do you need to change?
Janet:	My belief that I shouldn't have used drugs in the past.
Michael:	But as you did . . . ?
Janet:	. . . I'm a worthless person.

Step 13: Question Irrational Belief and Rational Belief

After conducting a thorough assessment of the target problem, identifying and assessing any secondary or meta-emotional problems, and teaching the B–C connection, the next step in the counselling sequence is to question or dispute concurrently clients' irrational and rational beliefs (traditionally in REBC, disputing of irrational and rational beliefs has been carried out consecutively). This procedure is known as structured disputing of clients' irrational and rational beliefs (Neenan and Dryden, 1999). We are not claiming that this is a superior form of disputing, just a different one. This step will present an overview of disputing before focusing on the concurrent form we demonstrate in the counselling excerpt.

The goals of disputing

A major goal of disputing at this stage is to help clients to understand that the irrational beliefs they subscribe to are self-defeating, i.e. they lead to unhealthy negative emotions, are illogical, and inconsistent with reality and that the rational alternatives to these beliefs lead to healthy negative emotions are logical and consistent with reality.

Even if some clients provide evidence that they have reached such an understanding, it would probably be an error for counsellors to assume that their conviction in the alternative rational belief will be strong. In this vein, it can be helpful to teach the client the distinction between *light conviction* and *deep conviction* in a rational belief. As noted in Chapters 6 and 7, the former state is considered characteristic of intellectual rational insight while the latter state is considered characteristic of emotional rational insight. Clients can be encouraged to view even a light conviction in an alternative rational belief as a sign of progress, albeit usually insufficient in itself to generate the 'gut feel' of emotional change.

With specific regard to the target problem, the goals of disputing are to help clients to understand and differentiate between the following:

1. Demands: It is very unlikely that there is any evidence to support an individual's rigid and dogmatic musts and absolute shoulds on self, others and

the world; demands frequently lead to emotional disturbance. The rational alternative to demands are flexible preferences which negate the potentially destructive effects of demands, e.g. 'I want very much to go out with her *but I don't have to*.' Ellis (quoted in Dryden, 1991b, p.15) points out 'that if humans would stick to preferences they would not get into so much emotional trouble.'

2. Awfulising: This is the denial of grim empirical reality by insisting that what has happened (or is happening) absolutely should not have, or should not be as bad as it is. In essence, clients are appealing to a non-existent reality. The rational alternative to awfulising is anti-awfulising which acknowledges grim empirical reality, or the badness of events, but does not seek refuge in a make-believe one where nothing could be worse.

3. Low frustration tolerance (LFT): This is an individual's perceived inability to put up with discomfort or frustration in his life and envisage any happiness while such conditions exist. The rational alternative to LFT is to strive for higher frustration tolerance (HFT) which enables individuals to withstand difficulty and discomfort in life without becoming emotionally disturbed about it.

4. Damnation of self/others: Individuals and/or others are given global negative ratings on the basis of particular actions or traits. Thus the complexity of human beings is nullified by a single rating, such as useless. The rational alternatives to damnation are unconditional self-acceptance (USA) and unconditional other acceptance (UOA). This means that the person is accepted but not necessarily their behaviour. These two concepts acknowledge humans as fallible (imperfect) and in a state of flux.

As treatment proceeds, counsellors can pursue the goal of helping clients to internalise a broad range of rational beliefs so that they become part of a general rational philosophy of living. This process, however, is beyond the scope of the present chapter.

Use questions during disputing

In the first stage of the disputing sequence, counsellors typically ask clients to provide evidence in support of their musts. To review material presented in Chapter 6, some standard questions used for this purpose include: 'Where is the evidence that you *must* under all conditions?'; 'Where is the proof that you *must*?'; 'Is it true that you absolutely *must*?'; 'Where is it written that you *must*?'

It is important for counsellors to ensure that clients actually answer the disputing questions asked of them. For example, in response to the question 'Why *must* you succeed?' a client might answer 'Because succeeding will bring me certain advantages.' Note that the client has really not addressed himself to the question that was asked; rather, she has actually provided a reply to the question 'Why is it *preferable* for you to succeed?'. Generally, it is good practice to expect that clients will not immediately provide correct (in the REBC sense) answers to initial disputing questions.

According to REBC theory, the only valid answer to the aforementioned question is: 'There is no reason why I absolutely must succeed, although it would be highly preferable if I did'. When clients provide any other answer, it is likely that they need to be educated as to why their answer is 1) incorrect with respect to the question asked, or 2) correct but to a different question, i.e. 'Why is it *preferable* for you to succeed?' During this process, a combination of questions and short didactic explanations may be used to help clients attain an understanding of the correct (i.e. rational) answer.

It is usually helpful at this point to assist clients in distinguishing between their rational and irrational beliefs. One means for accomplishing this is to write down two questions, such as the following:

1. Why *must* you succeed?
2. Why is it *preferable* but not an absolute necessity for you to succeed?

When clients attempt to answer these questions, it is often the case that they will give the same answer to both. When this occurs, they can be helped to see that the reasons they provided in their replies constitute evidence for their rational belief but not for their irrational belief. Here, the goal is to help clients to comprehend that the only answer to a question concerning the existence of musts is Ellis's oft-repeated statement: 'There are no musts and absolute shoulds in the universe; only desiderata - things I desire'.

DiGiuseppe (1991) stresses that helping clients to construct rational beliefs is an integral part of the disputing process and, in so doing, the same disputing questions are targeted at the rational beliefs as they were at the irrational ones.

Persistence in disputing

As noted earlier, it is important to dispute both the premiss and derivative forms of a client's irrational beliefs. If, however, the counsellor has started this process by disputing the irrational premiss, it is important to persist non-dogmatically in this endeavour until the client is able to see that there is no evidence in support of this premiss before beginning to dispute a derivative from the premiss.

Switching too quickly from premiss to derivative (and vice versa) during disputing can be confusing for the client. However, if disputing is initially aimed at an irrational premiss and it becomes clear that the client is not finding this helpful, it can make sense to redirect the clinical focus towards a derivative and monitor the client's reactions to this switch. Some clients appear to have an easier time understanding why their derivatives are irrational than why their musts are irrational. In my (MN) experience, focusing totally on the derivatives is often the only way to make some therapeutic headway with clients who have no insight into, or interest in, '*must*urbatory' thinking.

Use a variety of disputing strategies

As discussed in Chapter 6, there are three main foci for disputing irrational beliefs. It is preferable to use all three of these strategies whenever possible:

1. Focus on illogicality: The purpose here is to help clients understand why their irrational beliefs are illogical (i.e. not correctly reasoned). They are shown, for example, that because they may want something to happen, it does not logically follow that it absolutely must happen. Counsellors can show clients that their irrational beliefs often represent non sequiturs (i.e. conclusions that do not logically follow from the premises).
2. Focus on empiricism: The goal of this strategy is to demonstrate to clients that their musts and irrational derivatives are almost always inconsistent with empirical reality. To accomplish this goal, counsellors use questions that ask clients to provide evidence in support of their irrational beliefs (e.g. 'Where is the evidence that you *must* have a trouble-free life?'). Clients can be helped to see that if there was evidence to support their must, then they would have a trouble-free life because reality would be constructed that way. Because they do not have a trouble-free life, this proves that their belief is inconsistent with present reality. On the other hand, if they did have a trouble-free life this would not be evidence that reality conforms to their demands but that they have been remarkably fortunate so far!
3. Focus on pragmatism: With this strategy, counsellors focus on showing clients the pragmatic consequences of holding on to irrational beliefs. The aim is to help clients to see that as long as they invest in irrational thinking they are likely to remain emotionally disturbed. Such questions as 'Where is it going to get you if you keep on believing that you *must* have a trouble-free life?' can make explicit the self-defeating consequences of such thinking – in this example, angry and depressed.

After disputing an irrational belief, clients need to learn how to replace their irrational belief with a rational alternative. Counsellors work collaboratively with clients to construct a rational belief that appears to be most adaptive to their activating event (A). After an alternative rational belief has been formulated, the three disputing strategies described above can be applied to it in order to demonstrate to clients that their newly formed rational beliefs are, in fact, rational, i.e. logical, empirical and pragmatic. It is much better for clients to see or discover for themselves the evidence that rational beliefs are more valid, logical and helpful than for counsellors simply to tell them that this is so.

DiGiuseppe (1991) argues that counsellors need to be aware of the level of abstraction in addressing clients' beliefs, i.e. both irrational and rational beliefs can be placed along a specificity–abstractness continuum. For example, a client can have a situation-specific irrational belief: 'My boss must not give me extra work' to the very abstract: 'Life must be easy'. It follows from this that disputes should be directed at beliefs ranged along this continuum.

Counsellors can make two major errors here. First, they can direct their disputes at beliefs that are too abstract when clients' key disturbance-producing beliefs are context-bound; second, by challenging only situation-specific beliefs they may fail to deal with the source of these beliefs at the abstract level.

Use a Variety of Disputing Styles

While seasoned practitioners of REBC usually develop their own individual disputing styles, four basic disputing styles will be discussed here. These four styles are termed Socratic, didactic, humorous and self-disclosing.

Socratic style

When using the Socratic style of disputing, counsellors set themselves the task of asking clients questions concerning the usually illogical, empirically inconsistent and maladaptive aspects of irrational thinking. Such questions are intended to encourage clients to think through these aspects for themselves rather than simply accept the counsellors' viewpoint because they are perceived to be experts in emotional problem-solving. The Socratic approach is also used to help clients examine the logical, empirical and adaptive aspects of rational thinking. Although the Socratic style emphasises the use of questions, it can be supplemented with brief explanations designed to correct quickly client misconceptions that may arise during the disputing process.

Didactic style

Many REB counsellors prefer the Socratic approach but it does not always prove to be therapeutically productive. When this is the case, counsellors can shift to using direct, didactic explanations as to why irrational beliefs are self-defeating and rational beliefs are self-helping. It is quite likely that almost all counsellors find it helpful to use didactic explanations at various times in the counselling sequence.

When didactic explanations are employed, it is good practice to check, through immediate feedback, whether clients have understood the message conveyed. One way of doing this is to ask clients to put the counsellor's didactic explanation into their own words: 'I'm not sure if I made myself clear on this point. Could you use your own words to convey what you believe I've been saying to you?' It can be a mistake to accept clients' non-verbal and paraverbal signs of understanding (head nods, hmms) without questioning them. Sometimes, clients will actually show evidence of understanding when in fact they have not understood a word the counsellor has said (Dryden, 1986).

Humorous style

With some clients, the use of humour or humorous exaggeration (see Reduction to Absurdity, Chapter 6) can represent a productive vehicle for making the point that there is no evidence to support irrational beliefs. However, the use of humour as a disputing strategy is advised only when the following conditions are met: 1) the counsellor has established a good working relationship with the client; 2) the client has already provided some evidence that he or she has a good sense of humour; and 3) the humorous interventions are directed at the irrationality of the client's belief and *not* at the client as a person. In addition, Ellis (1983b) has noted that it is important for counsellors to refrain from overusing techniques that they find enjoyable at their clients' expense.

Self-disclosing style

Counsellor self-disclosure can represent another useful means of disputing clients' irrational beliefs. Generally, the coping model (as opposed to the mastery model) of self-disclosure is viewed as having features that are likely to be helpful to clients. In using the coping model, counsellors reveal that: a) they have experienced a problem that in some sense is similar to the client's problem; b) they once held an irrational belief that is similar to the one the client holds; and c) they worked at changing this belief and therefore no longer have the problem, or in only a much less disruptive form.

In contrast to the coping model of self-disclosure, the mastery model would involve telling the client that the counsellor has never experienced a problem similar to the client's because she has always thought rationally about the particular issue or, once the problem had appeared, it was rapidly and completely dealt with by the immediate adoption of rational problem-solving techniques. Although this approach can highlight the fact that rational thinking helps individuals to avoid or minimise particular emotional problems, it can be disadvantageous insofar as it accentuates the differences between counsellor and client. In our experience, the mastery model is less productive than the coping model in encouraging clients to challenge their irrationalities. We would note, however, that some clients will not find even the coping model useful. Some clients, for instance, will tend to condemn the counsellor when the latter displays any signs of 'weakness'. If it becomes apparent that attempts at self-disclosure are failing to benefit the client (and are perhaps damaging the therapeutic alliance), other disputing strategies should be used instead.

Other styles

Metaphorical disputing (DiGiuseppe, 1991) employs metaphors in order to show clients why their irrational beliefs are self-defeating and why their rational beliefs are self-helping. Feedback is used to ensure that clients understand

and agree with the message of the metaphor. Enactive disputing provides counsellors with the opportunity to challenge their clients' irrational beliefs through action. An example of this style is when a counsellor reads a book upside down in the session to demonstrate that an individual can act foolishly without condemning himself as a fool.

Creative disputing

As noted earlier, counsellors tend to develop their own individual styles as they gain experience in disputing clients' irrational beliefs. Typically, they build up a repertoire of stories, metaphors, mottoes, aphorisms and examples that are used to demonstrate why irrational beliefs are more likely to be disturbance-producing while rational beliefs are more likely to promote psychological health. As these various vehicles of change can serve to increase REBC's impact on the client, it is desirable for counsellors to work at building up their own repertoire of creative disputing strategies.

The 'Terrorist Dispute' (described in Chapter 6) can be considered as an example of a creative approach to working with clients who believe that they absolutely cannot stand the discomfort involved in changing long-standing patterns of disturbed emotions and behaviours. Another creative disputing strategy, termed the 'Friend Dispute', can be useful for pointing out the existence of rigid self-standards. If, for example, a client has failed at an important task and is engaging in self-damnation (stemming from the irrational belief 'I must do well and I'm no good if I don't'), he can be asked if he would condemn a close friend for a similar failure in the same manner that he condemns himself. When he responds in the negative, he can be shown that he has one set of standards for himself (harsh and unforgiving) and another set of quite different standards for his friend (compassionate and forgiving). He can then be helped to see that if he was as accepting of himself as he is of his friend, he would be less prone to emotional disturbance.

Additional creative strategies for disputing clients' irrational beliefs can be found in the discussion of vivid disputing methods presented in Chapter 6. Counsellors are cautioned, however, to work towards the skilful application of basic disputing skills before attempting to be too creative.

Janet

In this step, a structured disputing approach examines concurrently the premiss components of Janet's irrational and rational beliefs before moving on to their derivative components. For clarity's sake, the counsellor writes the beliefs on a whiteboard in his office:

Demand	*Preference*
I absolutely shouldn't have used drugs in the past.	I wish I'd never used drugs in the past, but regrettably I did. I was not immune from doing so.

Michael:	We are now going to take a critical look at these beliefs to see which one stands up to inspection and which one doesn't. Okay?
Janet:	Okay, I'm ready. Can I write things down?
Michael:	Of course, it will help you to remember what we've discussed. Now, looking at these beliefs, which one is sensible or logical and which one doesn't make sense or is illogical?
Janet:	Hmm. I'm not quite sure if I know about logic but that belief (pointing to the demand) doesn't make sense and that one (pointing to the preference) does.
Michael:	Why doesn't the demand make any sense?
Janet:	Well it just doesn't in the cold light of day when you write it on the board. Common sense says that the demand is ridiculous.
Michael:	So sense is not very common, then, when you express your demand, but . . .
Janet:	. . . it returns if I follow the preference. It's just making it stay that's the problem.
Michael:	Going over the preference many times in your head, as well as acting on it, is a good way to make it stay. Now, moving on, which is realistic and which one is unrealistic?
Janet:	Er . . . the demand because, realistically, I wish I hadn't taken drugs.
Michael:	Well, you've got a demand and a preference in the same sentence. They can't both be true. Let's take the demand first. Now if the universe strictly followed your demands, what wouldn't you have done in the past?
Janet:	I'm not sure I follow.
Michael:	If I said I absolutely shouldn't have made some bad mistakes in the past and the universe obeyed my demands, would I have made those mistakes?
Janet:	No.
Michael:	Why not?
Janet:	Because reality doesn't work like that – you can't order it about as if it is your servant.
Michael:	Now with your demand . . .
Janet:	I see what you're getting at – my demand bears no relation to what actually happened in the past.
Michael:	Whereas . . . (pointing to the preference)
Janet:	That belief is realistic because it doesn't run away from the truth of what I did all those years ago.
Michael:	And also allows you to express your regret for taking drugs. Your demand doesn't allow you any expression of regret because you're unrealistically demanding that you shouldn't have taken drugs in the first place. Let's move on, unless you want to go over anything so far.
Janet:	I'm okay. Let's move on.
Michael:	Which belief is likely to be more helpful in your life?
Janet:	That's easy – that one (pointing to the preference).
Michael:	In what way?
Janet:	Well, if I can really believe it then I'm going to feel a lot less anxious when I'm in social situations, I'll go out with my husband more, hold

	my head up high, stop denying my past and just have a better life in every way. I'll get the confidence that I want, which is why I'm seeing you.
Michael:	Quite a list! Is the demand unhelpful then?
Janet:	In every way.
Michael:	It must have been helpful in some ways as you've been holding on to it for a long time.
Janet:	Well, I suppose it kept me safe because I didn't have to mix with others and be exposed as a dirty junkie. But all it did was kept me isolated, miserable and rowing with my husband. Not very helpful really.
Michael:	Which of the two beliefs do you want to strengthen in your mind and act on?
Janet:	Well, obviously the demand is pretty strong but I want to get rid of that as it keeps me screwed up. I want to strengthen that one (points to preference) so I can believe it. I want to think very differently about myself and my life.
Michael:	I think you can achieve that with sufficient effort. Now we've finished for the moment part one of our examination, so let's now look at the derivative beliefs in part two. I'll just write the full beliefs on the board:

Self-deprecation belief	Self-acceptance belief
I absolutely shouldn't have used drugs in the past but because I did, I'm a worthless person.	I wish I'd never used drugs in in the past but regrettably I did. I was not immune from doing so. My drug use may not have been worthwhile but that does not mean that I'm a worthless person because of it.

Michael:	Now, if we could use the same questions again for the derivative components of your beliefs. Which belief is logical and which is illogical?
Janet:	Well I'm not sure about that word logical, as I said before, but self-acceptance sounds sensible because people shouldn't be condemned as worthless because of things that they've done.
Michael:	It's not other people doing it to you, but you condemning yourself.
Janet:	That doesn't make sense, does it. I should stop doing it to myself if I wouldn't do it to others.
Michael:	Makes good sense to me. Okay, which belief is unrealistic and which is realistic?
Janet:	Hmm. I know calling myself worthless is unrealistic but I'm not sure why.
Michael:	Well, if you were really worthless what kind of actions could you only ever carry out?
Janet:	Worthless ones.
Michael:	And is that the daily reality of your life?
Janet:	Of course it isn't.
Michael:	So does calling yourself worthless reflect reality.

Janet:	No, but why can't I think like this?
Michael:	Emotional disturbance doesn't usually produce clear thinking, so you'll need to work on becoming less disturbed and more clear-sighted. Shall we move on?
Janet:	Okay.
Michael:	Which belief is likely to be more helpful in your life?
Janet:	This is the easy part – that one (pointing to the self-acceptance belief).
Michael:	Why?
Janet:	Because if I really believed it, then I wouldn't be a dirty junkie any more and I could look people in the eye. It would be like a great weight had been lifted off my shoulders. I would feel free every day, if that doesn't sound silly to you.
Michael:	No, it doesn't. This question you find the easiest to answer.
Janet:	Because it's the most straightforward one.
Michael:	And finally, which of the two beliefs do you want to strengthen and act on?
Janet:	That one (pointing to the self-acceptance belief). And don't ask me why, it should be obvious by now.
Michael:	Okay. Obviously we need to go over again and again the arguments for your rational beliefs and the arguments against your irrational beliefs. This is definitely not a one-off exercise.
Janet:	I didn't expect it would be.

The advantage of this approach to structured disputing is that it helps the client to see more clearly that the irrational belief is false, illogical, unrealistic and unhelpful and the rational belief is true, logical, realistic and helpful because both beliefs are considered together. A disadvantage of this approach is that clients can feel overwhelmed by the simutaneous concentration on both beliefs and the accompanying questions. One question per session (for example, focused on realistic/unrealistic) might be all that some clients can manage.

In structured disputing, it is important that the client understands and agrees with the counsellor's arguments before moving on to the next line of argument. However, if the client cannot resonate with a particular argument (as she struggled to do with logical arguments in the above excerpt), then the counsellor is advised to move on to a more profitable line of enquiry (like the pragmatic question, 'Which belief is more likely to be helpful to you?' which elicited the most spontaneous response from the client).

Step 14: Prepare Clients to Deepen Their Conviction in Rational Beliefs

Once clients have acknowledged, but without wholeheartedly agreeing, that there is no logical, empirical and pragmatic evidence in favour of their irrational beliefs but there is growing evidence to support their rational beliefs, counsellors are now positioned to help their clients deepen their conviction in these newly acquired rational beliefs. Emphasise that weak conviction in a rational belief is unlikely (on its own) to promote change.

As noted in Chapter 6, intellectual rational insight is usually insufficient to bring about meaningful or deep-seated emotional and behavioural change. As such, at this stage of the counselling sequence, counsellors help their clients to see that weak conviction in rational beliefs – although important – is unlikely to help them realise their counselling goals. This understanding can be accomplished with a brief discussion of the REBC view of therapeutic change. Through the use of Socratic questioning and didactic explanations (as in the previous step), clients can be helped to understand that they will strengthen their conviction in their new rational beliefs by disputing their irrational beliefs (and replacing them with rational alternatives) within and between counselling sessions. Clients should also understand that this process will require them to *act* against their irrational beliefs as well as to dispute them cognitively. Teaching this concept now will make it easier for counsellors to encourage clients to put their new learning into practice (Steps 16–17) and to facilitate the working through process (Step 18).

Dealing with the 'head–gut' issue

As clients learn to think more rationally, they may sometimes make statements such as 'I understand that my rational belief will help me to achieve my goals, but I don't really believe it yet.' Counsellors can expect that clients will often experience some difficulty in crossing the bridge between intellectual and emotional insight and can therefore initiate a discussion on this point; this acts as a prelude to the consideration of ways to deepen conviction in rational beliefs and weaken conviction in irrational ones. For example, a counsellor might ask, 'What do you think you'll need to do in order to get your new rational belief into your gut?'

It is good practice to encourage clients to commit themselves to a process of therapeutic change that will require repeated and forceful disputing of irrational beliefs as well as considerable effort to practise rational thinking in relevant life contexts. To this end, clients are helped to design and undertake a variety of homework tasks (see Step 16).

Michael:	Let me ask you this: How often will you have to dispute your irrational beliefs in order to believe more strongly in your new rational beliefs?
Janet:	A lot. I'm not going to believe them overnight am I? I expect you're going to tell me there's a lot of work involved.
Michael:	Correct. Let's see if we can find an example to explain what's involved in changing your thinking. Do you drive?

Janet: Yes.

Michael: Now suppose, for example, a friend of yours taught you to drive but, unfortunately, she taught you very badly. So when you went for some lessons with a professional driving instructor prior to your test, he told you to give up your bad driving habits and learn the new correct ones he was going to teach you if you wanted to pass your test. Would it be as straightforward as that in dropping the old habits?

Janet: Of course not because I'd hang on to the bad habits as that's all I knew about driving.

Michael: What about the new and correct driving methods?

Janet: I'd have to practise them a lot in order to really learn them.

Michael: Would changing from the old driving habits to the new ones be easy and comfortable?

Janet: I'd like to think so, but I know in reality it would be a struggle. (laughs) Because I couldn't let go of those bad habits without a fight; they're not going to go away quietly.

Michael: So you could struggle to get rid of the bad habits while at the same time learning the new and correct driving techniques.

Janet: That's what I'd have to do if I wanted to learn to drive properly. And the moral of this story is . . .?

Michael: Well, it's the same process with your beliefs; the irrational ones still exert a powerful influence in your mind and on your feelings and probably seem natural to you. In order for those beliefs to become unnatural to you and thereby wither away . . .

Janet: Keep on disputing them.

Michael: And for your new rational beliefs to become natural to you as part of your outlook . . .

Janet: Do my best to believe that they will help me overcome my problems and that this is a better attitude to have anyway.

Michael: It is not only believing in your new rational ideas but also *acting* in accordance with them and against the old ideas. Did the example of the driving help to make my point about the change process?

Janet: Yes, because I've got to stuggle to give them up and I've got to struggle to gain new ways of looking at things.

Michael: Good. If you keep going in your mind and practising in your daily life these new beliefs, you'll find that you not only believe them up here (tapping his forehead) but also feel them down here (prodding his stomach). Once this happens, you'll probably find how spontaneously you act on them.

Janet: I hope so.

Step 15: Check the Validity of A

After clients have spent some time questioning their irrational and rational beliefs and considered the process of moving from light to deep conviction in their new rational beliefs, counsellors can revisit their clients' A (assessed at Step 6) in order to determine if it is true or if it is distorted:

Michael:	If you remember, we assessed what you were most anxious about when you imagined going to a social event you would rather avoid.
Janet:	Well, around decent people I saw myself as worthless for taking drugs in the past.
Michael:	Which you absolutely shouldn't have done.
Janet:	Well, that's what I believed at the time.
Michael:	Do you still believe it as much now? Is it still a sound basis upon which to view yourself and the situation?
Janet:	Not as much after my discussions with you. No, I don't really believe it as much and, no, it's not a sound basis – it's an unsound basis! But I've really got to convince myself of all this. And even if I succeed, some people are still going to think I'm a worthless person for taking drugs even if I don't believe that any longer myself.
Michael:	Okay, first of all, how will they know about your drug past if you or your husband haven't told them?
Janet:	(sighs) That's a good point, but I feel that somehow they'll just know.
Michael:	As I said before, your feelings are not necessarily facts or a true account of a particular situation. So your feeling something about others doesn't make it true. Now, again, how will you know they are thinking you are worthless?
Janet:	Well, I was going to say because I feel it.
Michael:	If you really knew what others were thinking, you would be a . . . ?
Janet:	A mind-reader.
Michael:	And you gained that particular skill where . . . ?
Janet:	Okay, I'm not a mind-reader.
Michael:	Isn't it the case that because you believe it about yourself then you automatically assume that others will too. Isn't that the basis for your mind-reading?
Janet:	That's exactly right. But what about if they do really believe it about me or even say it? I'm sure that will crush me.
Michael:	Well, do you have to agree with them and how can you be sure that it will crush you?
Janet:	No, I don't have to agree with them if I believe in self-acceptance, and I suppose it will only crush me if I let it.
Michael:	And I'm sure self-acceptance will come in time, along with the ability not to let yourself be crushed by the opinions of others. Once the irrational belief has weakened and the rational belief is firmly in place, you may well find that these negative assumptions you're making about the reactions of others will disappear.
Janet:	That will be a relief if it happens.

When clients check the validity of A, their thinking about it often appears less well-grounded than before. However, they may still cling to their inferential distortions about A, which, in REBC terms, stem from their irrational beliefs. Janet's cognitive distortions were discussed but linked to her irrational belief, which is the main target of disputing. Once the irrational belief has been attenuated or removed, any lingering inferential distortions can be dealt with.

Step 16: Negotiate a Homework Assignment

At this point, clients should be ready to put their rational beliefs into practice. They can be reminded that, in line with the REBC theory of therapeutic change, they will have greater success in deepening their conviction in their rational beliefs if they work at disputing irrational beliefs and strengthening rational ones in situations that are the same or similar to the activating event previously assessed. As described in Chapter 7, these assignments can be categorised according to whether they have a cognitive, emotive, behavioural or imaginal focus. In using homework (or whatever term clients wish to use) assignments with clients, counsellors should bear in mind the following important points:

1. *Ensure that homework tasks are relevant.* Counsellors are advised to develop homework activities that are relevant to the irrational belief targeted for change. Enacting the homework tasks will help the client to weaken conviction in his irrational belief and strengthen and deepen conviction in the alternative rational belief.
2. *Collaborate with clients.* It is good practice to enlist clients' active collaboration when discussing appropriate homework assignments. In order to increase the likelihood that a particular assignment will be carried out, the counsellor should ensure that the clients a) see the sense in doing the assignment; b) agree that carrying it out will help in the attainment of desired goals; c) have the requisite skills for the task at hand; and d) have some confidence in their ability to carry out the assignment (clients may have the skills but not necessarily the confidence to execute the task). The probability of clients' compliance with homework tasks can be further maximised by establishing when, where and how often the particular task will be carried out.
3. *Be prepared to compromise.* Ideally, homework tasks involve having clients actively and forcefully dispute their irrational beliefs in the most relevant life contexts possible. However, if this is not feasible, clients can be encouraged to a) dispute their irrational beliefs in situations that approximate the most relevant A, or b) use imagery to dispute irrational beliefs while vividly imagining A. Doing less-than-ideal tasks can sometimes increase the likelihood that clients will eventually take on more challenging homework activities.
4. *Assess and troubleshoot obstacles.* Counsellors can work with clients to specify in advance any obstacles that may serve as impediments to homework completion. Clients can be encouraged to find possible ways of overcoming these obstacles before carrying out the assignment.
5. *Use homework at different times during counselling.* The present discussion has focused on homework tasks that help clients to strengthen

conviction in their rational beliefs. It should be noted, however, that homework tasks can be useful at various points and for various purposes throughout the treatment sequence. Thus, homework assignments can be designed to help clients a) specify their problematic emotions at C; b) detect their irrational beliefs at B; and c) identify the most relevant aspect of A about which they are most disturbed. In addition, homework tasks can also be used as a means of educating clients about the ABCs of REBC. Clients can be encouraged to read particular books (bibliotherapy) or to listen to REBC lectures on audiotape. When suggesting such assignments, it is wise to select material that is relevant to the target problem and is readily understandable. Counsellors can consider creating their own written materials or audiotapes to use with clients when appropriate material is not available.

Michael:	Does it make sense to you to practise outside of counselling what you've learned inside of it?
Janet:	It does – it seems pointless otherwise.
Michael:	What initial task might seem beneficial to you?
Janet:	Hmm . . . well, I could go over the arguments I wrote down when we were looking at my beliefs.
Michael:	How would that help you?
Janet:	Well, it's a start to think more critically about my beliefs.
Michael:	And this might begin the process of surrendering your irrational beliefs and internalising your rational beliefs. This process takes a lot of hard work and repeated practice.
Janet:	Will it work?
Michael:	Well, this is where the great importance of the homework tasks comes in by putting the theory learnt in the counselling room into daily real-life practice. Homework acts as a kind of laboratory by testing out what helps you and what doesn't. So how often do you want to go over those arguments?
Janet:	Thirty minutes in the morning and the same in the evening.
Michael:	Good. Do you see any obstacles that might prevent you from carrying out this task?
Janet:	Only forgetting to do them, I suppose.
Michael:	How could you deal with that?
Janet:	Leaving a post-it message on the fridge door – I couldn't possibly miss that every day.
Michael:	Okay. Now if I give you a copy of the agreed homework task there shouldn't be any misunderstanding at the next session as to what you've agreed to. Good luck.
Janet:	Thanks.

Step 17: Check the Homework Assignment

It is good practice to review previously negotiated homework assignments at the start of every session. Failure to do so may inadvertently communicate to clients that the counsellor does not consider these assignments to be an integral part of the change process. This is an undesirable attitude to foster in clients, as homework assignments are central to helping them achieve their counselling goals.

Confirm that clients faced A

Unfortunately, clients can be quite creative in developing strategies to avoid problematic As. As such, it is advisable for counsellors to ascertain that clients actually faced the As they committed themselves to confronting. When clients genuinely *have* faced their As, they typically report that they first made themselves disturbed and then managed to become undisturbed (without escaping the situation) by using the disputing techniques discussed in counselling. When clients fail to carry out their homework tasks in this manner, counsellors can help them to identify and deal with the obstacles to task completion. They can then encourage clients again to confront their troublesome As and use vigorous disputing to make themselves emotionally undisturbed in that context. As necessary, appropriate disputes can be modelled and rehearsed in the session, before clients make another attempt to confront the A in question.

Verify that clients changed B

When clients report success in carrying out their homework tasks, it is good practice to determine if this success can be attributed to a) changing an irrational belief to its rational alternative; b) changing either A itself or inferences about A; or c) the use of distraction methods. If enquiry reveals that a client used the last two methods, the counsellor can acknowledge the client's efforts but then point out that these strategies may not be helping in the long term. Practical solutions (i.e. changing A) or distractions are merely palliative as they do not require clients to change the irrational beliefs that produce unhealthy negative emotions when A is faced. Many As are unavoidable and therefore the emotional problem will tend continually to reassert itself if it is not dealt with. Counsellors can attempt to convey these points to clients, encourage them again to face the situation at A, and elicit their commitment to dispute their disturbance-creating beliefs and practise acting on the basis of their new rational beliefs.

Deal with failure to complete homework assignments

When clients fail to execute agreed-upon homework, REB counsellors accept them as fallible human beings and help them to identify the reasons the task was not carried out. The ABC framework can be used to help clients identify possible irrational beliefs that interfered with task completion. In particular, counsellors will want to assess for irrational beliefs that contribute to low frustration tolerance (e.g. 'I shouldn't have to work so hard at changing – it's too damned hard!'). When clients hold such beliefs, they can be helped to challenge and change them prior to reassignment of the homework.

Janet

The following dialogue took place one week later near the beginning of the second session of counselling:

Michael:	How did you get on with your homework task? (reading from the homework form). You were going to look critically at your beliefs twice a day.
Janet:	Well, I started off all right. I was going over what we discussed in the session and my irrational belief is like a ball and chain I could do without, and my self-acceptance belief is something I really want to live by.
Michael:	Sounds good so far. Then what?
Janet:	Well, I went down to once a day and by the weekend I couldn't be bothered any more. If I've gone over the arguments a few times, why bother to keep on doing it.
Michael:	Because to keep on bothering to do it would mean . . . ?
Janet:	It was bloody boring!
Michael:	Okay, someone else might say, 'It's bloody boring, but I want to keep on reviewing these arguments to get them firmly fixed in my head.' Did you say that?
Janet:	No. I said 'I can't stand it any longer' and gave up.
Michael:	The 'it' being the boredom.
Janet:	Yes.
Michael:	Is it in your longer-term interests to keep on reviewing those arguments in order to weaken the irrational beliefs and strengthen the rational ones?
Janet:	Definitely. Do I learn to put up with the boredom then?
Michael:	If you choose to. Remember the boredom isn't the real problem, but your belief about it. You can learn to tolerate the boredom of this task or the difficulties related to future tasks by learning higher frustration tolerance – which means something like 'I can stand it even though I don't like it'.
Janet:	That sounds worth learning. These tasks are not going to be a bundle of laughs, are they.
Michael:	Probably not, but adopting rational thinking for present and future problem-solving is probably more beneficial than laugh-a-minute homework tasks. You could try to make the task more interesting in some way.
Janet:	Okay, I hear you loud and clear on both points.
Michael:	Have you agreed, then, to do the task twice a day for the next week?
Janet:	Yes, and this time I will carry it through.

The counselling session continued with further discussion of Janet's anxiogenic thinking in social situations and the development of appropriate methods to tackle this problem.

Step 18: Facilitate the Working-through Process

'Rational-emotive [behavioural] working through constitutes the heart of RE[BC]. Helping clients work through their problems – that is, systematically giving up their irrational ideas – is where most of the therapist's energy and time are directed and where longstanding change takes place. Successful working through leads to significant change, whereas unsuccessful working through leads to no gain or to superficial gain at best. It is as simple as that.' (Grieger and Boyd, 1980, p. 122).

Suggest a variety of homework tasks targeted at the same irrational belief

When clients have experienced some success in disputing particular irrational beliefs in relevant situations at A, they can be encouraged to use different types of homework tasks to erode further the degree to which they subscribe to these same beliefs. Doing so teaches clients that a variety of methods can be used to dispute their targeted irrational beliefs as well as other ones that appear during the course of counselling. In addition, introducing this sort of variety can help to sustain clients' interest in the change process.

Discuss the non-linear model of change

Counsellors can explain that change is a non-linear process in order to prepare clients for the difficulties they may encounter as they try to dispute irrational beliefs within a wide variety of contexts. Potential setbacks can be identified, and clients can be helped in advance to develop ways of dealing with them. Specifically, clients can be given assistance in identifying and challenging the irrational beliefs that might underpin their relapses.

In addition, counsellors can teach clients to evaluate change on three major dimensions:

1. *Frequency*: Are unhealthy negative emotions experienced less often than before?
2. *Intensity*: When unhealthy negative emotions are experienced, are they less intense than before?
3. *Duration*: Do unhealthy emotional episodes last for shorter periods than before?

Clients can be encouraged to keep records of their disturbed emotions at point C, using these three criteria of change. In addition, clients may find it helpful to read the booklet, *How to Maintain and Enhance Your Rational-Emotive Therapy Gains* (Ellis, 1984c). This publication (which is reproduced in Chapter 10) contains many helpful suggestions that clients may use to facilitate the working-through process.

Encourage clients to take responsibility for continued progress

At this stage, clients can be helped to develop their own homework tasks to change their target beliefs, and to change other irrational beliefs that occur in situations not initially viewed as problematic. If, for example, a client has been successful in disputing an irrational belief about approval in a work-related situation that involves criticism, he might be encouraged to dispute this belief in other situations in which criticism is encountered (e.g. with family members or friends). As clients develop competence and confidence in designing and executing their own homework tasks, they are likely to experience increasing success in acting as their own therapists. This accomplishment is most important, as the long-term goal of REBC is to encourage clients to internalise the REBC model of change and to take responsibility for further progress, sometimes lifelong, after counselling has ended.

Janet

As well as repeatedly going over in her mind why her irrational beliefs were self-defeating and her rational beliefs were self-helping, Janet also accepted more social invitations in order to test out the efficacy of her new beliefs in those situations that she had previously done her best to avoid. She reported that learning to be more self-accepting and less self-condemning helped her to feel more comfortable around 'decent' people. To speed up this process she engaged in daily imagery exercises where she, first, imploded her anxiety in social situations and then, second, felt only what she called 'confident' in the same situations. This affective shift was achieved, she reported, by changing her demands into preferences. She also gave up the idea that some people were more decent than others; instead, she viewed herself and others as equal but fallible: 'When I was able really to believe that, I could make and sustain eye contact at parties. I was always staring at the floor before.' She found some REBC self-help books useful in reinforcing the principles and practice discussed in the sessions.

By internalising a rational philosophy of living, she found considerable benefits: a more stable relationship with her husband, a wider circle of friends and a much more exciting social life. She also became a volunteer counsellor at a local community drug service. However, it was not all plain sailing. Her disturbance-producing thinking came back at various times, which made her question her progress, and she toyed with the temptation to avoid social settings again. By remembering that progress is never straight or smooth, and by using the ABCs of REBC – 'look for the must, look for the absolute should' – she was able to locate the cognitive culprit (e.g. 'I must feel confident at all times') and deal with it. By the end of counselling – a total of 12 sessions – Janet was well on her way to becoming her own counsellor. She had some lingering doubts about striking out on her own, so we agreed to three, six and twelve months' follow-up appointments to monitor her progress. If any serious problems arose that she was unable to deal with, she could contact me outside of these time periods.

Chapter 10
The Rational Emotive Behavioural Counselling Process

Overview

In Chapter 9 we presented the rational emotive behavioural counselling sequence, which provides guidelines for helping clients to deal with a specific problem area. In this chapter we review the rational emotive behavioural counselling *process*, and review treatment issues relevant to the beginning, middle and ending stages of counselling. Of particular note, we discuss issues pertaining to the formation of a sound therapeutic alliance: assisting clients in dealing with multiple problem areas, dealing with obstacles to therapeutic change, and encouraging clients to become their own counsellors. We conclude by presenting a brief account of a typical case in rational emotive behavioural counselling.

It is noted that dividing the counselling process into beginning, middle and ending phases is a somewhat artificial convention we have chosen to employ, in order to provide structure for the material presented in this chapter. Actually, it is impossible to differentiate so clearly between the various components of the counselling process. Issues pertaining to the therapeutic alliance between counsellor and client, for instance, will have importance throughout a course of treatment and, in reality, are not restricted to the beginning stage of counselling. As such, we would advise the reader to approach the material that follows with a flexible frame of mind.

The Beginning Stage

Establishing a therapeutic alliance

Within the counselling field, the quality of the therapeutic alliance between counsellor and client is generally regarded as an important determinant of treatment outcome. Bordin (1979) provides a useful framework for conceptualising the therapeutic alliance by breaking it down into three major components: bonds, goals and tasks. The *bond* between counsellor and client refers to the nature and quality of the interpersonal relationship that exists between the two individuals. *Goals* are the purposes that counsellor and client would like to see achieved through counselling. *Tasks* are the respective activities that counsellor and client take responsibility for in the service of approaching counselling goals.

Bonds

If a productive bond fails to form between counsellor and client, the likelihood of therapeutic failure may be increased. In the service of promoting a productive bond, rational emotive behavioural counsellors will attempt to identify the style of interaction most suitable for a given client. At the outset of counselling, for instance, counsellors can make enquiries concerning the client's view of what constitutes helpful versus unhelpful counsellor behaviour. Here, questions concerning the client's experiences with any previous counsellors can be particularly helpful. Some counsellors like to employ Lazarus's (1981) 'Life History Questionnaire', which contains the following questions:

1. In a few words, what do you think counselling is all about?
2. How do you think a counsellor should interact with his or her clients?
3. What personal qualities do you think the ideal counsellor should possess?

It is important to recognise that certain qualifications apply to the issue of counsellors modifying their interactional style to suit the client. Rational emotive behavioural counsellors are willing to be flexible concerning the manner in which they relate to clients, but only insofar as this does not interfere with the attainment of counselling goals.

First, as mentioned in Chapter 4, it may be wise for counsellors to take the client's own personality style into account when trying to identify an optimal style of therapeutic interaction. It may be best, for example, to avoid an overly cognitive, intellectualised style when working with clients who appear to have obsessive-compulsive personality traits. Alternatively, some variant of this sort of style may prove quite suitable with clients who tend to be excitable and histrionic. As REBC is a psychoeducational approach to counselling, a good rule of thumb is to find an interactional style that promotes an optimal learning environment for the particular client.

Second, some clients - either because of their own personality make-up or their prior experiences with counselling - may strongly prefer that their counsellor adopt a passive role within sessions. They may convey this preference directly through verbal statements, or indirectly through passive-aggressive responses to the counsellor's ministrations. It is important to bear in mind, however, that an active-directive counsellor style tends to be the preferred vehicle for implementing the problem-solving approach to counselling which is characteristic of REBC. Thus, with clients who prefer counsellor passivity, rational emotive behavioural counsellors would attempt to structure therapeutic conditions such that these clients become more receptive to a high degree of counsellor activity and directiveness. Initially, this could mean overtly presenting clients with a sound rationale for the counsellor's active–directive stance. If this fails, less direct strategies can be employed. These might include a gradual increase in the counsellor's verbal activity level over the course of the beginning stage of counselling, or the use of well-chosen, well-timed questions which promote a high degree of *client* verbal activity, while structuring sessions in a productive way. A minority of clients will remain 'allergic' to active–directive counsellor behaviour; for such individuals, a judicious referral to a practitioner who utilises a more passive approach to counselling may be in order.

It is noted that rational emotive behavioural counsellors attempt to put into practice a philosophy of unconditional acceptance in their work with clients; this can also contribute to the formation of a good bond between counsellor and client. Translated into actual behaviour, a philosophy of unconditional acceptance means that counsellors refrain from responding in a judgmental, condemning fashion when clients report acts that society would consider unethical or morally wrong, or when clients behave inconsiderately toward their counsellor. When confronted with such things, rational emotive behavioural counsellors generally attempt to respond to clients in a reasoned, matter-of-fact and objective manner. This can promote an air of trust and openness within counselling, and can indirectly convey to clients that they do not have to condemn themselves for their 'bad' acts. Counsellors will, however, sometimes opt to bring obnoxious behaviour to clients' attention, as when it appears that the clients' negative behaviour toward the counsellor is representative of a larger pattern that impairs their ability to form good relationships with others.

Goals

It is important for counsellor and client to be working mainly toward the same goals within counselling. Failure to agree upon goals can lead them to operate at cross-purposes with each other, which will probably result in eventual dissolution of the therapeutic alliance.

Assessment of client attitudes about counselling. At the start of counselling, counsellors can promote congruence in the goal domain by initiating a discussion on the clients' views as to whether and how counselling might be helpful to themselves. Just because a given client has presented him or herself at the counsellor's office, it should not be assumed that the client regards counselling as a potentially useful endeavour. Some clients, for instance, are pushed into counselling by significant others or the judicial system. Needless to say, special steps need to be taken to engage reluctant clients in the counselling process. Sociopathic individuals, for example, may not be open to counselling until the counsellor has presented strong arguments that it can help them more effectively to avoid legal problems and attain desired ends.

A number of clients willingly enter into counselling, but harbour misconceptions concerning how it might assist them. As discussed in Chapter 5, it is often advisable for counsellors to educate clients as to what counselling can and cannot provide. Clients should, for instance, understand that rational emotive behavioural counselling is focused upon helping them with their psychological problems, as opposed to their practical problems. They can be helped to see, however, that improved psychological functioning may facilitate their ability to resolve practical issues. Counsellor utilisation of induction procedures can be a worthwhile investment of session time with clients who are largely naïve about the ways in which counselling works.

Use of a problem list. Congruence in the goal domain can be further enhanced by encouraging clients to generate a 'problem list.' This is an inventory of problems for which the client is seeking help during counselling. It can be suggested to clients as an initial homework assignment to be completed prior to the next scheduled appointment, although it can be perfectly legitimate to devote session time to its production. Ideally, the list should exist in written form, with copies for both counsellor and client to keep.

When counsellor and client are ready to start focusing on a problem, the client is invited to choose an item from the problem list. This item may be the client's most pressing problem, the problem which is easiest to solve, or one which – if progress is achieved – engenders most hope for the client. The guiding principle here is that counsellor and client work together on problem selection and agree on the chosen issue, which in practice usually tends to be the client's most pressing problem.

When a client chooses an item from his or her problem list to focus upon, it will often be necessary for the counsellor to work with the client on translating that problem into an appropriate goal for rational emotive behavioural counselling. Counsellor/client collaboration in this venture also helps to ensure that both individuals are working together to achieve the same outcome in counselling.

It is noted that allowing the client to choose the problems to be dealt with in counselling can enhance the therapeutic alliance by indirectly conveying that the counsellor is sensitive to the client's concerns and priorities. In addition, encouraging client choice can serve to set the stage for the client's active involvement in the counselling process. On occasion, however, it will be evident to the counsellor that the client's choice of a problem area to focus upon is not entirely appropriate. Such a situation can arise when the counsellor obtains evidence (through enquiry and observation) that the client has a secondary (meta-emotional) problem *about* the chosen problem. In such cases, it is generally good practice for the counsellor to bring the secondary problem to the client's attention and to present a rationale for dealing with it first, if relevant. If, however, the client expresses a strong preference to work on the chosen problem rather than on the secondary problem, it may be wise for the counsellor to assent to this wish. To do otherwise could compromise the therapeutic alliance.

Use of a session agenda. When counsellors work with clients to establish a session agenda (see Beck et al. 1979) at the start of each counselling contact, they can help to promote goal congruence on a per session basis. A session agenda constitutes an agreement between counsellor and client as to what will be discussed during a particular session, and can serve as a means for structuring the proceedings. It can, for example, discourage either counsellor or client from jumping unhelpfully from problem to problem without making significant progress on any given one.

The following excerpt from *Daring to be Myself* (Dryden and Yankura, 1992) illustrates how WD introduced the concept of establishing session agendas to his client, Sarah:

Dr Dryden: What I usually like to do at the beginning of every interview is to set up an agenda with you. I'll make suggestions about any items I might want to bring up, but it's mainly for any items that you want to talk about. This way, we can actually get the sense that we're working together on the same agenda. Okay?

Today, I'd like to discuss the problem list you were going to do – did you bring it with you?

Sarah: I did it very quickly last night.

Dr Dryden: Okay. Also, did you research any places to go [for social contacts]?

Sarah: Well, I phoned up social services.

Dr Dryden: Okay – we'll go into that in a minute. But first, what would you like to spend the bulk of today's session talking about? What particular issue or problem?

Sarah: Well, to put it in a nutshell, I'd like to talk about why I'm sort of frightened to get on with people.

Dr Dryden: So, it's mainly your fear with other people?

Sarah: Mostly people I know, funnily enough.

Dr Dryden: Okay. (Writing) 'People I know . . . ' Do you think that will take up the whole of the session?

[The session proceeds with a review of the client's reactions to the last session and discussion of current agenda items.]

It is advisable for counsellors to exercise flexibility in using session agendas, and to avoid conveying the impression that an agenda *must* be thoroughly covered in any particular session. In this vein, it is usually wise to avoid agendas that contain a long list of items, especially when it seems likely that one item will require a large portion of session time.

Tasks

Counsellors can avoid a particular threat to the therapeutic alliance by taking steps to ensure that clients understand the respective tasks of counsellor and client within rational emotive behavioural counselling. Generally, rational emotive behavioural counsellors will take the role of active-directive problem-solvers, collaborate with clients to dispute their irrational beliefs and design potentially helpful homework assignments. Clients, for their part, will ideally become active participants in their counselling and accept the task of working with counsellors to identify and challenge their irrational beliefs. Hopefully, they will also take an active hand in designing homework assignments for themselves and take responsibility for enacting these homework assignments between sessions.

Counsellors can utilise both direct and indirect means to educate clients as to the respective tasks of counsellor and client. With respect to direct means, counsellors can make statements early on in counselling (and at various points later on, as appropriate) which describe the tasks for which they will take responsibility. These statements may take a form such as the following:

> Okay – as you've already noted, we've spent much of our first session together discussing your *attitudes* about your current job. As you've seen, some of these attitudes are causing you to experience feelings of anxiety and depression. As your counsellor, I propose to help you by sharpening your awareness of the attitudes that contribute to your upsets, and by showing you how you can *change* those unhelpful attitudes to more helpful ones. If you agree, we'll get down to working on that the next time we meet.

Similarly, counsellors can make direct statements that outline the tasks that clients are encouraged to take on.

Indirect means for communicating counsellor and client tasks include the following:

1. The counsellor's stance as an active-directive problem-solver throughout the course of counselling, conveyed through a high level of focused verbal activity.
2. The use of techniques such as Socratic questioning which prompt the client to engage in the task of actively examining and questioning his or her beliefs.
3. The use of prompts which encourage the client to play an active role in the design of relevant homework assignments (e.g. 'What do you think you could do during the coming week to put your new philosophy of self-acceptance into practice?').
4. Counsellors consistently devoting session time to designing and then subsequently following up on homework exercises.

The activities listed here are probably best viewed as vehicles for supplementing more direct communications concerning counsellor/client tasks. Conceivably, clients could fall into confusion and doubt if these activities are introduced into counselling sessions without direct statements describing their purpose.

It is important to note that counsellors' and clients' respective tasks will change somewhat over the course of rational emotive behavioural counselling. Counsellors attempt gradually to decrease their activity level such that clients are encouraged to take on more of the responsibility and effort involved in making progress and maintaining gains. This issue is dealt with again in the section on the middle stage of counselling.

Monitoring clients' reactions. As an additional means of promoting a sound therapeutic alliance, we have found it helpful to monitor clients' reactions to counselling throughout the course of treatment. Thus, we will routinely ask clients at the end of a given session if they found any of our statements or suggestions particularly helpful or unhelpful. At the start of the next scheduled session we inquire of clients whether they had any additional reactions to the preceding session. The feedback resulting from these enquiries allows us to identify and correct any misunderstandings or misconceptions that clients may have developed, and helps us to modify our strategies and interventions so that they are more likely to promote beneficial change for individual clients.

Some clients will be reluctant to provide their counsellor with negative feedback as they are afraid of losing the counsellor's approval and acceptance. When a given client provides only glowing responses to counsellor enquiries concerning his or her reactions to sessions, it may be appropriate to consider the hypothesis that this individual has a self-created need for the counsellor's approval. If this appears to be the case, it is generally good practice for the counsellor to broach directly (but tactfully) this issue and devote session time to exploring it with the client. In doing so, the counsellor may be able to identify and dispute any irrational beliefs (e.g. 'I *must* maintain my counsellor's approval; to lose this approval would *really* prove that I'm a worthless and unlovable person!') that could interfere with the counselling process.

Teaching the ABC model

In order for clients to make sense of their rational emotive behavioural counsellor's approach to helping them overcome emotional problems, they will require a foundation in rational emotive behavioural concepts and techniques. Thus, during the beginning stage of counselling, counsellors need to teach clients the three main insights of REBC and the means by which emotional problems can be analysed and remedied with the ABC model.

With respect to REBC's first main insight, it is important for clients to understand that their emotional problems are largely determined by their irrational beliefs, and not directly by the troublesome life events that they have experienced. This should be considered a fundamental point for counsellors to convey to clients; if clients do not attain this understanding then they will probably fail to grasp why their counsellors focus so much attention on their thinking. As a result, they may make continued efforts to focus discussions upon the details of the current negative circumstances that they face, and may be put off by the counsellor's limited interest in this material.

REBC's second major insight holds that individuals remain disturbed by continually reindoctrinating themselves in the *present* with the irrational beliefs to which they subscribe. Thus, detailed exploration of the historical antecedents of a client's irrational beliefs is eschewed within rational emotive behavioural counselling, and a focus is placed upon identifying currently held musts, shoulds and have tos. It is important for clients to understand that it is not essential for them to determine precisely where their irrational beliefs came from, as long as they see that continuing to hold these beliefs will increase their vulnerability to emotional disturbances and dysfunctional behaviour.

REBC's third main insight emphasises that clients will need to work consistently and diligently at challenging and replacing their irrational beliefs if they are to derive significant, lasting benefits from counselling. Clients who possess this understanding are in a position to be active participants within their counselling, and will be able to see the desirability of putting into practice the knowledge they gain during counselling sessions.

Clients are taught both directly and indirectly to utilise the ABC model as a means for analysing and understanding their emotional upsets. Didactic explanations represent a direct means for teaching clients about the model's components, and can be useful at various points throughout the course of counselling. The model can also be conveyed indirectly through the Socratic questioning technique, which can be used to prompt clients to identify the relevant activating events, consequent emotions and behaviours, and operative irrational beliefs involved in their emotional episodes. Brighter clients may often be able to learn how to analyse their upsets independently through the counsellor's use of Socratic questioning, and may require fewer didactic explanations. In our own practices, however, we generally employ a didactic presentation of the ABC model at some early point in the counselling process, rather than assuming that clients will pick it up indirectly.

Given that rational emotive behavioural counselling has a psychoeducational focus, it is important for counsellors to take steps to ensure that clients grasp the material they are trying to teach them. One way to accomplish this is periodically to ask clients to convey their understanding of critical points that have been covered. This can be done tactfully when counsellors use questions such as the following: 'We've been discussing how you don't have to rate yourself as either a good or a bad person, but I want to be sure I've been expressing myself clearly. Can you restate to me - in your own words - what you've understood me to be saying?'

In addition to utilising periodic checking, counsellors are advised to avoid jumping from problem to problem within any given counselling session. Remaining focused on one problem at a time (and covering the essential steps of the counselling sequence) is usually the best means for teaching clients the elements of rational emotive behavioural problem-solving.

By the end of the beginning stage of counselling, clients should have learned the three main insights of REBC. They will also have had some initial experience in identifying and disputing the irrational beliefs that underpin their emotional problems. Counsellors will also have introduced clients to the concept of homework assignments, which will serve as an important vehicle for facilitating client movement from intellectual to emotional rational insight as counselling continues. Bibliotherapy assignments (which involve suggesting that clients obtain and read some of the relevant REBC self-help texts) given at an early point in counselling can often help clients to become accustomed to the idea of devoting time and effort to working on their problem areas between sessions.

Dealing with client doubts

During the beginning stage of counselling, some clients may express doubts as to whether the rational emotive behavioural approach will be able to help them solve their own particular set of emotional problems. In responding to these expressed doubts, counsellors are advised first to assess and correct any misunderstandings about the approach that given clients may have. If the clients still appear doubtful after this intervention, counsellors can suggest that they have a brief 'trial' of counselling (consisting of five or so sessions) as a means for determining through direct experience whether they find the rational emotive behavioural approach helpful. At the end of this trial, counsellors and clients can review and discuss any remaining doubts that the clients may have. If the clients still maintain strong doubts at this point, it may be wise to make a judicious referral to another mental health professional who practises an alternative form of counselling. Such a referral would take into account the clients' views concerning the type of counselling approach most likely to promote therapeutic gains.

It should be noted that some clients may harbour doubts about counselling because they are confusing the rational emotive behavioural approach with the counsellor's interactional style. Thus, it can be important for counsellors to make enquiries that will help them to determine whether client objections are focused on issues pertaining to the counselling or the counsellor. If a given client is having a negative reaction to the counsellor's style of interaction within sessions, an appropriate modification in style may resolve this issue so that counselling may proceed.

The Middle Stage

As clients move into the middle stage of counselling, they may experience some initial success in disputing their irrational beliefs and dealing with particular episodes of emotional disturbance. At the same time, however, they may begin to see that their irrational beliefs are deeply entrenched and that they adversely affect a number of different areas of their functioning. In a related vein, they may find that it is difficult to work in a consistent and determined manner at modifying the thinking habits that contribute to their psychological problems. Thus, the middle stage of counselling presents the rational emotive behavioural practitioner with a number of significant challenges germane to promoting continued therapeutic progress. The sections that follow will provide guidelines for counsellors to follow as they attempt to facilitate client movement from intellectual to emotional rational insight.

Dealing with multiple problem areas

Typically, clients present more than one problem area during a course of counselling. In some cases these multiple problem areas will be identified and targeted for change at an early point in the counselling process. Frequently, however, new problem areas will emerge as counselling proceeds. This can occur for several reasons:

1. Clients develop a level of trust in the counsellor such that they become comfortable in disclosing problems previously considered 'too embarrassing' for discussion.
2. Clients develop an awareness of how particular irrational beliefs are adversely affecting a number of different areas of their lives.
3. Clients experience additional unfortunate activating events during the course of counselling (such as the loss of a job) that serve to trigger 'new' upsets.

Rational emotive behavioural counsellors prefer to deal with a particular problem area until the client is able to cope with it reasonably well. It will sometimes happen, however, that during the course of working on one problem area, the client wishes to change the focus to another problem area that is experienced as more pressing or important. Alternatively, circumstances may arise which lead the counsellor to wonder whether a change in tack would be desirable from a therapeutic perspective. When confronted with such situations, counsellors will find it useful to have a set of guidelines to which they can refer in deciding whether to switch to discussion of the new problem area.

First, it is important to consider the effect that persisting with treatment of the original problem area will have on the therapeutic alliance. If a client maintains a strong desire to switch to a new problem area after the counsellor has presented a rationale for staying with the original problem until it is resolved, it may be wise to accede to the client's preference and begin to work on the new problem. To do otherwise could communicate the unfortunate message that the counsellor is more interested in following his or her own agenda than in responding to the client's concerns. This, of course, could damage the working relationship between counsellor and client.

Second, clients will sometimes experience crisis situations during the course of counselling which serve as triggers for new, additional disturbances. When this occurs, efforts to resolve the original targeted problem may temporarily become irrelevant until the new upset has been dealt with. To cite an example, a given counsellor/client dyad may have been working to help the client overcome the feelings of anger and hurt he typically experiences in the face of his wife's harsh criticisms. While attending to this problem area, the client loses his job and makes himself depressed through negative self-rating and self-pity. As this depression significantly interferes with a number of areas of this client's functioning (including his ability to engage in the immediate task of job-hunting), it is appropriate for the counsellor to shift attention away from the original problem in order to focus attention to the new problem area. When the new problem area has received adequate treatment (such that the client is able to manage his depressed moods and function more effectively), counsellor and client may decide to return to their work on the original problem area.

Third, counsellors may see that it is advisable to switch attention to a 'new' emotional problem that the client is experiencing when it becomes apparent that this upset is impeding the client's ability to concentrate on the original problem area under consideration. In such a situation, it would make little sense to continue working on the original problem area as the client is not in a state to benefit from such efforts. Again, counsellor and client may decide to put aside their work on the original problem until the client is able to cope reasonably well with the new one.

Finally, there may be some circumstances in which it becomes evident to the counsellor that the client has an ongoing problem – currently, not the focus of treatment – that pervades numerous areas of his or her life. Here, the counsellor may wish to suggest to the client that they shift their attention to this other problem area. A given client may, for instance, exhibit problematic drinking behaviour that interferes with functioning at work and within interpersonal relationships. Conceivably, however, he or she might not regard drinking as being central to many of the difficulties he or she encounters and could express a preference to work on a more circumscribed area of functioning (e.g. being more assertive with co-workers). It would be wise in such a situation for the counsellor to bring to his or her attention the way in which drinking negatively affects numerous areas of life, and to present a rationale for working to modify this behaviour. In this scenario, counsellor and client could proceed to work at identifying and disputing the irrational beliefs that contribute to episodes of overdrinking, and later attend (if necessary) to other, more circumscribed problem areas of concern to the client.

Whenever counsellor and client switch from one problem area to another, it is important for the counsellor to encourage the client to maintain a focus on this new problem until a coping criterion has been attained. Frequent jumping from problem to problem is likely to interfere with the counselling process, as it will make it difficult for clients to learn the emotional problem-solving techniques that are part and parcel of REBC.

Occasionally, counsellors will encounter a client who tries to touch upon numerous problem areas during any given session, as opposed to focusing on only one or two. If a counsellor presents a rationale for dealing with one problem at a time but the client persists in this pattern, it may be appropriate for the counsellor to exercise flexibility on this issue in order to avoid endangering the therapeutic alliance. In some cases, however, the client's frequent switching can represent avoidance behaviour. Some individuals, for instance, will try to get on to a different topic when they begin to experience strong negative emotions during the course of discussing a particular problem area. If this occurs frequently, counsellors may choose to bring it to the clients' attention as another problem area to work on. Again, it is incumbent upon counsellors to exercise an appropriate degree of flexibility with respect to the issue of switching problems, and to recognise that it may be quite difficult for some clients to face and deal with their dysfunctional avoidance of disturbed feelings.

Identifying core irrational beliefs

As counsellors work with clients on the various problem areas targeted for intervention within counselling, they are advised to watch for common themes among the irrational beliefs that underpin these problems. By looking for common themes, counsellors can often identify core irrational beliefs to which clients subscribe. When core irrational beliefs are identified, it becomes possible to show clients that various problem areas (perhaps previously regarded by clients as being largely independent of one another) have similar underlying cognitive dynamics. During the middle stage of counselling, these core irrational beliefs – as opposed to specific problems – can receive more attention with respect to therapeutic exploration.

To illustrate the usefulness of identifying and dealing with core irrational beliefs, consider the case of a client who presents for counselling with complaints of non-assertiveness with friends and family, anxiety in social situations, and an unsatisfying marital relationship. As counselling proceeds with this individual, it is possible that her counsellor will identify the following irrational belief as being central to her problem areas: 'I must have the approval of others in order to consider myself a worthwhile person'. With respect to non-assertiveness with friends and family, this irrational belief may make it difficult for her to refuse unreasonable requests for favours out of fear that significant others will reject her. With regard to her social anxiety, her *must* may result in worries about saying or doing 'the wrong thing' in interpersonal situations. As concerns her unsatisfying relationship with her husband, her irrational belief may cause her to make unreasonable efforts to please him while sacrificing her own set of wants and preferences.

Once this client's counsellor has assembled a reasonable body of evidence to support the hypothesis that a particular irrational belief is at the root of many of her interpersonal difficulties, she can be shown the common theme that runs through her problem areas. This insight can help the client to have a better understanding of her own individual psychology, and can simplify the work of counselling for her to a considerable degree. Now, instead of working on the 'separate' areas of non-assertiveness, shyness and an unsatisfying marriage, she can focus her efforts on overcoming her self-created need for others' approval.

With respect to the process of identifying themes across problems, counsellors are cautioned to guard against assuming that all of a client's problems can be explained with reference to a single irrational belief. In our experience, it is more typically the case that clients will subscribe to two or three core irrational beliefs. As a potentially helpful rule of thumb, counsellors are advised to bear in mind that REBC identifies two broad categories of disturbance: ego disturbance and discomfort disturbance. Since it is relatively rare for clients to present for counselling with only one of these two categories of disturbance, counsellors can remain alert to manifestations of both forms. They can then work to identify the central irrational beliefs that underpin the manifestations of these two forms of disturbance for a particular client.

Encouraging clients to engage in relevant tasks

A primary task for counsellors during the middle stage of counselling is to assist clients in approaching emotional rational insight by encouraging them to strengthen their conviction in their rational beliefs. As noted previously, emotional rational insight – as opposed to intellectual rational insight – is likely to lead to significant emotional and behavioural changes for clients.

As described in Chapter 7, there is a variety of cognitive, behavioural and imagery techniques used within rational emotive behavioural counselling to help clients move from intellectual to emotional rational insight. Although counsellors may initiate the use of some of these techniques, it is important that by the middle stage of counselling clients see the role that *they* can play in promoting the change process. In particular, they need to see the usefulness of working hard to overcome their problems outside counselling sessions via homework assignments. Thus, by this stage of counselling, counsellors should have presented clients with a plausible rationale for homework assignments and should also have dealt with any objections or questions that clients may have had about undertaking such assignments.

Some clients will show that they understand the importance of their own efforts and homework assignments within counselling, but will harbour doubts about their ability to execute relevant tasks (i.e. those that will promote emotional rational insight) outside sessions. Counsellors can respond to these doubts in a number of different ways.

First, counsellors can work collaboratively with clients to design homework assignments that they are willing to do. Novice rational emotive behavioural counsellors will sometimes make the error of pushing behavioural 'flooding' homework assignments on clients, since they know that REBC views such assignments as representing the most efficient vehicle for promoting swift and meaningful modifications of irrational beliefs. Many clients will, however, make themselves anxious when they think about enacting flooding assignments, and will thus avoid doing them. As an example, a counsellor might insist that an agoraphobic client take on the exercise of spending an afternoon alone at a shopping mall, as a means for powerfully countering the client's self-created needs for security and comfort. The client may very well avoid implementing this assignment because the mere image of being in a crowded store (in combination with the irrational belief, 'I *must* feel emotionally comfortable at all times') leads to anxiety. Rather than suggesting assignments that clients are unlikely to implement because of the emotional obstacles they create for themselves, counsellors can work with them to design homework activities that are 'challenging, but not overwhelming'. Here, clients are encouraged to take on assignments involving behaviours not currently engaged in with frequency or complete ease (that are thus 'challenging'), but that are not regarded as too difficult or threatening (i.e. 'overwhelming'). With reference to the example described above, the counsellor could work with the client to design a homework assignment – such as going to a neighbourhood shop to complete a quick errand – that may stand a better chance of being completed. In the process of designing this assignment the counsellor can explain that tasks involving some degree of difficulty are more likely to facilitate the process of belief change.

As a second means of dealing with clients' doubts concerning their ability to execute homework assignments, counsellors can help clients to practise implementation of these assignments within counselling sessions. Certain behavioural assignments can be readily rehearsed within sessions, such as assertively requesting a rise in pay from one's employer. With other types of assignments – such as certain shame-attacking exercises – rehearsal of the behaviours involved would be more difficult. In such cases, however, the counsellor can help the client to rehearse the assignment in imagery. Whether an assignment is practised through overt behaviour or through imagery, the counsellor can use the rehearsal to assist the client in identifying emotional 'trouble spots' (i.e. points at which the client might create anxiety, or some other upset for herself) in advance of actual implementation, and can then devote time to dealing with the irrational beliefs responsible for these upsets.

A third way of increasing the likelihood of homework enactment is for counsellors to work with clients to identify when, where and how particular homework assignments will be implemented. Although this would seem to be a rather minimal standard of practice in the design of homework assignments, our experiences as counselling supervisors suggest that it is often neglected even by the more experienced REBC practitioners. A fairly large number of clients (particularly those who have difficulty in keeping themselves organised) will fail to do homework assignments because they do not plan when they will fit them into their weekly schedules. Counsellors can prompt clients to do such planning simply by asking them on what days and at what times of day they will engage in homework activities. In addition, counsellors can establish with clients the place or context within which homework assignments will be implemented, and can make sure that they are aware in advance of all the component steps that may be involved in the completion of a particular assignment.

It is also important that homework assignments be of a practical nature, meaning that clients are able to implement them without experiencing a great deal of inconvenience. Many individuals in counselling may be highly motivated to work at overcoming their disturbance; the fact remains, however, that they also have daily lives to attend to. The tasks of daily living can take up a good part of the day, and will impose limits on the amounts of time and effort that clients will be able (and willing) to devote to counselling-related activities. As such, homework assignments that require extraordinary investments of time, money, or energy will stand a much lower chance of completion.

Given the central place of homework assignments within rational emotive behavioural counselling, it is worth reiterating that it is important for counsellors to check up on clients' experiences in executing them. Failure to follow-up on homework assignments may indirectly communicate the unfortunate message that such activities are not so significant a part of the change process.

With respect to thorough-going follow-up on homework assignments, counsellors will want to keep the following suggestions in mind:

1. Make an enquiry as to what the client learned through enactment of the assignment. Is this learning beneficial in terms of countering an irrational belief that the client holds, or will it serve somehow to reinforce the client's irrational thinking?
2. Reinforce the client's success in enacting the homework assignment. If the assignment was not successfully implemented (e.g. the client did only part of it), then recognise and reinforce any efforts that *were* made to complete it.
3. Identify and deal with the client's reasons for not attempting or completing the homework assignment (see Appendix I, p.266). Help the client to identify and dispute any irrational beliefs that may have been involved here.
4. If appropriate, encourage the client to try the assignment again if he or she was not fully successful with it. Even if the criterion for success was attained, bear in mind that repetition of particular homework activities can be helpful.

As a final note, it is recommended that counsellors assess the reasons for the apparently therapeutic changes that clients may report. In some cases, clients may enact homework assignments and describe seemingly positive changes in their usual patterns of behaviour that occur for the 'wrong' (i.e. non-therapeutic) reasons. As an example, a young male client seen by JY reported at one point during his counselling that he was no longer fearful about approaching and starting conversations with women. Upon enquiry, it was learned that he had adopted the following attitude as a means for countering his approval anxiety: 'If they reject me, it doesn't mean that I'm a loser; it means that *they* are losers.' Although the first part of this statement may be logically and empirically correct, the second part is irrational as it embodies a person-rating philosophy. Conceivably, such a philosophy could lead this individual to reject other people too readily.

Dealing with obstacles to change

A number of significant obstacles to change may be encountered during the middle stage of counselling. Clients may, for instance, have had some success at this point in terms of disputing their irrational beliefs, but typically will experience recurrences of their emotional problems. This is because they are still in the process of approaching emotional rational insight. When clients bring a philosophy of low frustration tolerance (LFT) to bear upon their failure to remain free of upsets, they may block themselves from persisting with their efforts to internalise a new rational philosophy. Here, it is important for counsellors to help their clients to identify and dispute the beliefs that produce their LFT. Such beliefs may take numerous forms, including 'Change must not be difficult' and 'I absolutely should not have to work so hard in counselling'.

Also, it is important to note that change itself can be an uncomfortable experience for clients. Maultsby (1984) has described a state, which he refers to as *cognitive-emotional dissonance*, in which clients experience feelings of 'strangeness' as they work to strengthen their conviction in their irrational beliefs. Counsellors can encourage their clients to accept such feelings as being a natural part of the change process, and if necessary can dispute their irrational demands to feel natural and comfortable all of the time.

A minority of clients will develop a state of 'pseudo-rationality', which can interfere with their ability to effect meaningful emotional and behavioural changes in their lives. Such clients become avid consumers of rational emotive behavioural books and audiotapes, and make themselves extremely knowledgeable about REBC's theory and practice. They can quote extensively from the REBC literature and are able to give all the 'right' answers to counsellors' disputing questions during sessions, but fail to put their knowledge into practice between sessions. Such lack of effort may again be attributable to a philosophy of low frustration tolerance; alternatively, it may stem from the erroneous belief that intellectual insight is sufficient to bring about lasting changes. In either case, counsellors need to help clients to challenge and change the attitudes that block them from working to approach emotional rational insight.

Counsellors may sometimes encounter bright, achievement-oriented clients who are able to understand the B–C connection, but who nevertheless evince a reluctance to surrender their musts. With such clients, an enquiry may reveal that they view their musts as an important source of motivation for achieving their goals, and that they worry that giving up their musts will lead them into apathy and inertia. Counsellors can emphasise the distinction between strong desires and absolutistic demands with these clients, and can show them that their strong desires will provide sufficient motivation for working toward attainment of the goals they value. Further, they can be shown particular ways in which their musts create emotional obstacles that may function to block goal attainment.

The material presented in this section is intended to highlight some of the obstacles to client progress that are particularly germane to the middle stage of counselling. In Chapter 11 we present a broad overview of obstacles to progress, along with recommendations concerning ways of overcoming them.

Encouraging clients to maintain and enhance their gains

It is usually the case that clients will display the greatest variability in their rates of progress during the middle stage of counselling. They will at times appear to make significant gains with respect to approaching emotional rational insight; they will, however, also experience periodic backsliding. During this stage, counsellors need to help their clients to deal with setbacks, maintain the progress they have made, and explore ways to enhance their therapeutic gains. Ellis (1984c) has written an excellent pamphlet on these issues, which is reproduced below with minor modifications. It can be helpful for counsellors to provide clients with a copy of this handout when the issues it covers become salient during the course of counselling.

How to maintain your improvement (based on Ellis, 1984c)

1. When you improve and then fall back to old feelings of anxiety, depression, or self-downing, try to remind yourself and pinpoint exactly what thoughts, feelings, and behaviours you once changed to bring about your improvement. If you again feel depressed, think back to how you previously used rational emotive behavioural principles to make yourself undepressed. For example, you may remember that:
   (a) you stopped telling yourself that you were worthless and that you couldn't ever succeed in getting what you wanted
   (b) you did well in a job or in a love affair and proved to yourself that you did have some ability and that you were lovable
   (c) you forced yourself to go to interviews instead of avoiding them and thereby helped yourself overcome your anxiety about them.
   Remind yourself of thoughts, feelings and behaviours that you have changed and that you have helped yourself by changing.
2. Keep thinking, thinking and thinking rational beliefs or coping statements, such as: 'It's great to succeed but I can fully accept myself as a person and enjoy life considerably even when I fail!' Don't merely parrot

these statements but go over them carefully many times and think them through until you really begin to believe and feel that they are true.

3. Keep seeking for, discovering, and disputing and challenging your irrational beliefs with which you are once again upsetting yourself. Take each important irrational belief – such as, 'I have to succeed or else I am not a worthwhile person!' – and keep asking yourself: 'Why is this belief true?', 'Where is the evidence that my worth to myself, and my enjoyment of living, utterly depend on my succeeding at something?', 'In what way would I be totally unacceptable as a human if I failed at an important task or test?'

   Keep disputing your irrational beliefs forcefully and persistently wherever you see that you are letting them creep back again. And even when you don't actively hold them, realise that they may arise once more; so bring them to your consciousness, and preventively – and vigorously! – dispute them.

4. Keep risking and doing things that you irrationally fear – such as riding in elevators, socialising, job hunting or creative writing. Once you have partly overcome one of your irrational fears, keep acting against it on a regular basis. If you feel uncomfortable in forcing yourself to do things that you are unrealistically afraid of doing, don't allow yourself to avoid doing them – thereby preserving your discomfort forever! Often, make yourself as uncomfortable as you can be in order to eradicate your irrational fears and to become unanxious and comfortable later.

5. Try to see clearly the difference between healthy negative feelings – such as those of sadness, remorse and disappointment, when you do not get some of the important things you want – and unhealthy negative feelings – such as those of depression, unhealthy guilt and shame, when you are deprived of desirable goals and plagued with undesirable things. Whenever you feel *over*concerned (panicked) or *unduly* miserable (depressed) acknowledge that you are having a statistically normal but a psychologically unhealthy feeling and that you are bringing it on yourself with some dogmatic *should*, *ought* or *must*. Realise that you are invariably capable of changing your irrational (or *must*urbatory) feelings back into rational (or preferential) ones. Take your depressed feelings and work on them until you feel *only* sorry and regretful. Take your anxious feelings and work on them until you feel *only* concerned and vigilant. Use rational-emotive imagery to imagine unpleasant activating events vividly even before they happen: let yourself feel irrationally upset (anxious, depressed, enraged or ashamed) as you imagine them; then work on your feelings to change them to rational emotions (concern, sadness, healthy anger or disappointment) as you keep imagining some of the worst things happening. Don't give up until you actually do change your feelings.

6. Avoid self-defeating procrastination. Do unpleasant tasks fast – today! If you still procrastinate, reward yourself with certain things that you enjoy – for

example, eating, vacationing, reading and socialising – only *after* you have performed the tasks that you easily avoid. If this won't work, give yourself a severe penalty – such as talking to a person whom you find boring for two hours or giving away a £20 note to an unworthy cause – every time that you procrastinate.

7. Show yourself that it is an absorbing challenge and something of an adventure to maintain your emotional health and to keep yourself reasonably happy no matter what kind of misfortunes assail you. Make the uprooting of your misery one of the most important things in your life – something you are utterly determined to steadily work at achieving. Fully acknowledge that you almost always have some choice about how to think, feel and behave, and throw yourself actively into making that choice for yourself.

8. Remember – and use – the three main insights of rational emotive behavioural counselling:

    Insight 1: You largely *choose* to disturb yourself about the unpleasant events of your life, although you may be encouraged to do so by external happenings and by social learning. You mainly feel the way you think. When obnoxious and frustrating things happen to you at point A (activating events), you consciously or unconsciously *select* rational beliefs that lead you to feel concerned, sad and remorseful and you also *select* irrational beliefs that lead you to feel anxious, depressed and guilty.

    Insight 2: No matter how or when you acquired your irrational beliefs and your self-sabotaging habits, you now, in the present, *choose* to maintain them – and that is why you are now disturbed. Your past history and your present life conditions importantly *affect* you; but they don't *disturb* you. Your present *philosophy* is the main contributor to your *current* disturbance.

    Insight 3: There is no magical way for you to change your personality and your strong tendencies needlessly to upset yourself. Basic personality change requires persistent *work and practice* – yes, *work and practice* – to enable you to alter your irrational beliefs, your unhealthy feelings and your self-destructive behaviours.

9. Steadily – and unfrantically! – look for personal pleasures and enjoyments – such as reading, entertainment, sports, hobbies, art, science and other vitally absorbing interests. Take as your major life goal not only the achievement of emotional health but also that of real enjoyment. Try to become involved in a long-term purpose, goal, or interest in which you can remain truly absorbed. A good, happy life will give you something to live *for*; will distract you from many serious woes; and will encourage you to preserve and to improve your mental health.

10. Try to keep in touch with several other people who know something about REB counselling and who can help go over some of its aspects with you. Tell them about problems that you have difficulty coping with and let them know how you are using rational emotive behavioural prin-ciples to overcome these problems. See if they agree with your solutions and

can suggest additional and better kinds of disputing methods that you can use to work against your irrational beliefs.

11. Practise using rational emotive behavioural methods with some of your friends, relatives and associates who are willing to let you try to help them with it. The more often you use it with others, and are able to see what their irrational beliefs are and to try to talk them out of these self-defeating ideas, the more you will be able to understand the main principles of REB counselling and to use them for yourself. When you see other people act irrationally and in a disturbed manner, try to figure out – with or without talking to them about it – what their main irrational beliefs probably are and how these could be actively and vigorously disputed.

12. When you are in rational emotive behavioural counselling try to tape record many of your sessions and listen to these carefully when you are in between sessions, so that some of the rational emotive behavioural ideas that you learned in counselling sink in. After counselling has ended, keep these tape recordings and play them back to yourself from time to time, to remind you how to deal with some of your old problems, or new ones that may arise.

13. Keep going back to the rational emotive behavioural reading and audiovisual material from time to time, to keep reminding yourself of some of the main rational emotive behavioural findings and philosophies.

How to deal with backsliding

1. Accept your backsliding as normal – as something that happens to almost all people who at first improve emotionally and who then fall back. See it as part of your human fallibility. Don't feel ashamed when some of your old symptoms return, and don't think that you have to handle them entirely by yourself and that it is wrong or weak for you to seek some additional sessions of counselling and to talk to your friends about your renewed problems.

2. When you backslide, look at your self-defeating behaviour as bad and unfortunate, but work very hard at refusing to put yourself down for engaging in this behaviour. Use the highly important rational emotive behavioural principle of refraining from rating *you, yourself,* or your *being,* but of measuring your *acts, deeds* and *traits.* You are always a *person who* acts well or badly – and never a *good person* or a *bad person.* No matter how badly you fall back and bring on your old disturbances again, work at fully accepting yourself with this unfortunate or weak behaviour – and then try – and keep trying – to change your behaviour.

3. Go back to the ABCs of rational emotive behavioural counselling and see clearly what you did to fall back to your old symptoms. At A (activating event), you usually experienced some failure or rejection once again. At rB (rational belief) you probably told yourself that you didn't *like* failing

and didn't *want* to be rejected. If you had only stayed with these rational beliefs, you would merely feel sorry, remorseful, disappointed or concerned. But when you felt disturbed again, you probably then went on to some irrational beliefs (iBs) such as 'I *must* not fail! It's *horrible* when I do! 'I *have to* be accepted because, if I'm not, that makes me an *unlovable worthless person!*' Then, after convincing yourself of these iBs, you felt, at C (emotional consequence) once again depressed and self-downing.

4. When you find your irrational beliefs by which you are once again disturbing yourself, just as you originally used disputing (D) to challenge and surrender them, do so again – *immediately* and *persistently*. Thus, you can ask yourself: 'Why *must* I not fail? Is it really *horrible* if I do?' And you can answer: 'There is no reason why I *must* not fail, though I can think of several reasons why it would be highly undesirable. It's not *horrible* if I do fail – only distinctly *inconvenient*.' You can also dispute your other irrational beliefs by asking yourself, 'Where is it written that I *have* to be accepted? How do I become an *unlovable, worthless person* if I am rejected?' And you can answer: 'I never *have to be* accepted, though I would very much *prefer* to be. If I am rejected, that makes me, alas, a *person who* is rejected this time by this individual under these conditions, but it hardly makes me an *unlovable, worthless person* who will always be rejected by anyone for whom I really care.'

5. Keep looking for, finding, and actively and vigorously disputing your irrational beliefs that you have once again revived and that are now making you feel anxious or depressed once more. Keep doing this, over and over, until you build intellectual and emotional muscle (just as you would build physical muscle by learning how to exercise and then by *continuing* to exercise).

6. Don't fool yourself into believing that if you merely change your language you will always change your thinking. If you neurotically tell yourself: 'I *must* succeed and be approved' and you sanely change this self-statement to 'I *prefer* to succeed and be approved', you may still really be convinced: 'But I really *have* to do well and *have got to be* loved'. Before you stop your disputing and before you are satisfied with your answers to it (which in rational emotive behavioural counselling we call E, or an effective philosophy), keep on doing it until you are *really* convinced of your rational answers and until your feelings of disturbance truly disappear. Then do the same thing many, many times – until your new E (effective philosophy) becomes hardened and habitual – which it almost always will if you keep working at arriving at it and re-instituting it.

7. Convincing yourself lightly or 'intellectually', of your new effective philosophy or rational beliefs often won't help very much or persist very long. Do so very *strongly* and *vigorously*, and do so many times. Thus, you can *powerfully* convince yourself until you really *feel* it: 'I do not *need* what I *want*! I never *have* to succeed, no matter how greatly I wish

to do so! I *can* stand being rejected by someone I care for. It won't *kill* me – and I can *still* lead a happy life! *No* human is damnable and worthless – including and especially *me*!'

How to generalise from working on one emotional problem to working on other problems

1. Show yourself that your present emotional problem and the ways in which you bring it on are not unique and that virtually all emotional and behavioural difficulties are created by irrational beliefs. Whatever your irrational beliefs are, moreover, you can overcome them by strongly and persistently disputing and acting against these irrational beliefs.

2. Recognise that you tend to have three major kinds of irrational beliefs that lead you to disturb yourself and that the emotional and behavioural problems that you want to relieve fall into one of these three categories:

   (a) 'I *must* do well and *have* to be approved by people whom I find important.' This irrational belief leads you to feel anxious, depressed, and ashamed; and to avoid doing things at which you may fail, and avoiding relationships that may not turn out well.

   (b) 'Other people *must* treat me fairly and nicely!' This irrational belief contributes to your feeling angry, furious, violent and over-rebellious.

   (c) 'The conditions under which I live *must* be comfortable and free from major hassles!' This irrational belief tends to create your feelings of low frustration tolerance and self-pity, and sometimes those of anger and depression.

3. Recognise that when you employ one of these absolutist *musts* – or any of the innumerable variations on it that you can easily slide into – you naturally and commonly derive from them other irrational conclusions, such as:

   (a) 'Because I am not doing as well as I *must*, I am an incompetent worthless individual!' (Self-damnation.)

   (b) 'Since I am not being approved by people whom I find important, as I *have to be*, it's *awful* and *terrible*!' (Awfulising.)

   (c) 'Because others are not treating me as fairly and as nicely as they *absolutely should* treat me, they are *utterly rotten people* and deserve to be damned!' (Other-damnation.)

   (d) 'As the conditions under which I live are not that comfortable and as my life has several major hassles, as it *must* not have, I can't stand it! My existence is a horror!' (Low frustration tolerance.)

4. Work at seeing that these irrational beliefs are part of your *general* repertoire of thoughts and feelings and that you bring them to many different kinds of situations that are against your desires. Realise that in just about all cases where you feel seriously upset and act in a distinctly self-defeating manner you are consciously or unconsciously sneaking in one or more of these irrational beliefs. Consequently, if you get rid of them in one area and are still emotionally disturbed about something else, you can

always use the same rational emotive behavioural principles to discover your irrational beliefs in the new area and eliminate them there.

5. Repeatedly show yourself that it is almost impossible to disturb yourself and to remain disturbed in any way if you abandon your absolutist, dogmatic *shoulds*, *oughts* and *musts*, and consistently replace them with flexible and unrigid (though still strong) *desires* and *preferences*.

6. Continue to acknowledge that you can change your irrational beliefs by rigorously (not rigidly!) using the scientific method. With scientific thinking, you can show yourself that your irrational beliefs are only theories or hypotheses – not facts. You can logically and realistically dispute them in many ways, such as these:

   (a) You can show yourself that your irrational beliefs are self-defeating – that they interfere with your goals and your happiness. For if you firmly convince yourself: 'I *must* succeed at important tasks and *have to* be approved by all the significant people in my life', you will of course at times fail and be disapproved – and thereby inevitably make yourself anxious and depressed instead of concerned and sad.

   (b) Your irrational beliefs do not conform to reality – and especially do not conform to the facts of human fallibility. If you always *had* to succeed, if the universe commanded that you *must* do so, you obviously *would* always succeed. And of course you often don't! If you invariably *had* to be approved by others, you could never be disapproved. But obviously you frequently are! The universe is clearly not arranged so that you will always get what you demand. So although your desires are often realistic, your god-like commands definitely are not!

   (c) Your irrational beliefs are illogical, inconsistent or contradictory. No matter how much you *want* to succeed and to be approved, it never follows that therefore you *must* do well in these (or any other) respects. No matter how desirable justice or politeness is, it never *has* to exist.

   Although the scientific method is not infallible or sacred, it efficiently helps you to discover which of your beliefs are irrational and self-defeating, and how to use factual evidence and logical thinking to rid yourself of them. If you keep using scientific analysis, you will avoid dogma and set up your hypotheses about you, other people, and the world around you so that you always keep them open to change.

7. Try to set up some main goals and purposes in life – goals that you would like very much to reach but that you never tell yourself that you absolutely must attain. Keep checking to see how you are coming along with these goals; at times revise them; see how you feel about achieving them; and keep yourself goal-orientated for the rest of your days.

8. If you get bogged down and begin to lead a life that seems too miserable or dull, review the points made here and work at using them. Once again: if you fall back or fail to go forward at the pace you prefer, don't hesitate to return to counselling for some booster sessions.

Encouraging clients to become their own counsellors

During the beginning stage of counselling, the counsellor is quite active–directive with respect to helping the client to learn the ABCs of REBC. In the middle stage of counselling this material needs to be reviewed, but the client should be encouraged to take the lead in applying it to problem areas.

Counsellors are advised to be active and directive when first discussing a particular problem area with a client, but gradually to decrease their activity level as a means to promote the client's own efforts and involvement. Here, the overall goal is to help the client to internalise the rational emotive behavioural method for solving emotional problems. The counsellor thus encourages the client's attempts to identify troublesome emotions and behaviours, relate these to particular activating events, and identify operative irrational beliefs. The client would then be encouraged to dispute these irrational beliefs and to develop alternative, rational beliefs that can replace them. It is also important to prompt clients to look for links between problem areas, with the object of identifying and disputing core irrational beliefs.

Counsellors should increasingly utilise the Socratic questioning technique during the middle stage as a means of encouraging clients to do most of the work of counselling. Didactic teaching should be kept to a minimum. Short, probing questions can be used to promote independent thinking, and to decrease client dependence upon the counsellor's problem-solving skills. Thus, when a client discusses her experiences between sessions in dealing with a particular problem area, the counsellor may ask a sequence of questions, such as the following:

'How did you feel when that happened?'
'What were you telling yourself to bring on that feeling?'
'How did you dispute that?'
'How did you block yourself from disputing that?'
'What rational belief could you use to replace that must?'
'How is that rational belief more (logical, realistic, helpful) than that irrational belief?'
'If you really believed that, then how would you tend to act?' 'Could you try that during the coming week?', etc.

Some clients may not respond well to a decrease in the counsellor's level of directiveness. A number of individuals may, for instance, be prone to form dependent relationships with their counsellors because they harbour doubts about their ability to function independently as emotional problem-solvers. Counsellors can attempt to deal with these doubts (e.g. by making reference to prior instances when the client in question coped successfully with a particular upset), and can present a rationale for increased independent effort. When a given client appears genuinely stuck with respect to dealing with a particular problem area, the counsellor can temporarily revert back to a more active–directive stance. As work on this problem area proceeds, the counsellor can then gradually return the responsibility for dealing with it back to the client. When clients respond successfully to decreased counsellor directiveness over several sessions, it can be appropriate to begin taking steps to work toward termination.

The Ending Stage

The ending stage of the counselling process involves working towards the termination of regularly scheduled counselling sessions. Termination may be approached either by collaboratively decreasing the frequency of counselling sessions over time, or by setting a definite termination date. Although it is unrealistic to attempt to establish a perfect point at which termination should occur for a given client, it is possible to identify a number of general criteria that can be applied to termination decisions. These criteria are as follows:

1. The client has internalised REBC's approach to emotional problem-solving and has made significant, healthy modifications to his or her personal philosophy.
2. The client has gone beyond dealing with his or her initial presenting problems such that other significant problem areas have been tackled as well.
3. Core irrational beliefs have been identified and disputed.
4. The client has developed confidence in his or her capacity to act as his or her own counsellor.
5. Counsellor and client agree that termination is appropriate.

These criteria can be viewed as constituting an 'ideal outcome' within rational emotive behavioural counselling. In reality, however, ideal outcomes are relatively rare and clients may often want to terminate before these criteria have been fulfilled. It is thus important for counsellors to be aware of various sorts of scenario in which premature termination is a possibility, so that they can respond in an effective manner to these situations.

A number of clients will want to terminate counselling before they have made any real progress in identifying and disputing their irrational beliefs. This scenario can occur when clients' troublesome activating events fortuitously change for the better, so that they are no longer experiencing the disturbances that may have contributed to their original decision to seek counselling. When clients leave counselling under such circumstances, they will probably be vulnerable to the same sort of disturbance in the future. Counsellors can make efforts to explain to them that they have not yet dealt with the philosophical underpinnings of their emotional problems, and can encourage them to remain in counselling as a means for militating against a recurrence of their disturbance. Here, it is noted that much useful work can be accomplished within rational emotive behavioural counselling even when clients are not facing any immediate stressors. If clients are unresponsive to the provision of a rationale for continuing in counselling, counsellors can make it clear to them that they may return if their external circumstances take a turn for the worse and they once again create upsets for themselves.

A certain number of clients will state their desire to terminate counselling after having made some initial progress with respect to their original presenting problems. In this scenario, given clients may consider that they have accomplished what they set out to accomplish, and they may regard their counselling as having been very helpful. The counsellor, however, may see that these clients probably harbour particular core irrational beliefs which have not yet received formal attention within sessions. As such, it may be unlikely that clients will be able to generalise rational emotive behavioural counselling gains across problems and situations. Again, it would be appropriate for the counsellor to present a rationale for remaining in counselling, as it could still have much to offer this individual. Ellis's (1984c) handout on generalisation and maintenance, reproduced above, could be used to supplement the counsellor's rationale as it conveys the message that it is possible to make oneself generally less susceptible to emotional and behavioural difficulties. Should the clients stand by their preference to discontinue counselling, the counsellor can extend an 'open invitation' to return when they would like to enhance their treatment gains.

Scenarios also occur in which the clients have made some progress in overcoming their emotional problems as per the REBC approach, but wish to terminate formal sessions in order to pursue independent practice of self-counselling. Counsellors will generally want to be supportive of such a preference, although they may wish to engage the clients in a discussion concerning the pros and cons of continued counselling contacts. In some instances, such discussion may reveal concerns or issues related to counselling (such as time-scheduling difficulties) that may be easily resolved. If such issues are not a part of the picture and the clients maintain their desire to terminate formal contacts, the counsellor may still suggest a limited number of additional sessions that will be focused on facilitating the clients' future efforts at self-counselling. The content of these sessions can include recommendations concerning relevant self-help books and audio-tapes, reiteration of rational emotive behavioural strategies for emotional problem-solving, and attempts to help the clients anticipate (and hence be better prepared to deal with) activating events that may serve as triggers for future disturbances. Whether or not the clients agree to extra sessions, the counsellor can make it clear that it is perfectly appropriate to return for additional contacts when these are viewed as necessary.

In addition to being confronted with situations in which clients may want to terminate prematurely, counsellors will also occasionally encounter individuals who wish to continue counselling sessions beyond an appropriate point. Some clients who have made considerable progress, for instance, may still believe that they need the continued help of their counsellor in order to maintain their counselling gains. Such problems may become manifest when clients are reluctant either to set a termination date or to decrease the frequency of sessions. When this is the case, the counsellor can work to identify and dispute any irrational beliefs that are in operation (e.g. 'I *must* have the ongoing support of my counsellor; I am incapable of coping on my own'), and can suggest to the client that they attempt an experiment to assess their coping capacity. This could involve helping them to specify the aspects of their lives that they think they cannot cope with on their own, and then encouraging them to test this out as a homework assignment.

Other clients may be reluctant to terminate counselling because they do not want to lose the special sort of relationship they have developed with their counsellor. Here, it can be appropriate for the counsellor to identify and discuss any feelings of sadness that clients may have about the dissolution of the counselling relationship. It can be emphasised that, while such feelings may be negative in tone, they are an appropriate emotional response to the ending of a significant relationship. If clients believe that they must not have these somewhat painful feelings, the counsellor can encourage them to dispute this irrational belief as a means of helping them to accept this normal part of human experience.

Some counsellors may be unwilling to terminate the counselling relationship with clients who have shown considerable progress. These counsellors may believe that they need to have continued evidence of client progress in order to prove that they are competent practitioners and therefore worthwhile people. Needless to say, it would be highly desirable for such counsellors to identify and challenge their competency needs by using the methods of rational emotive behavioural counselling outlined in this book.

As a final note, counsellors may want to consider building in well spaced out follow-up sessions after regularly scheduled counselling sessions have ended. These follow-up sessions can be used as a means to help clients monitor their future progress. In one respect there is no absolute end to the rational emotive behavioural counselling process, as counsellors would want to encourage their clients to contact them for further assistance when they encounter prolonged difficulties in practising self-counselling.

A Typical Case of Rational Emotive Behavioural Counselling

The following account describes a case in which WD was the counsellor:

Mrs Haynes (pseudonym), at the time that I saw her, was a 35-year-old professional married woman who had recently discovered that her husband had been having an affair and had decided to leave her for the other woman. There were no children in this marriage. Mrs Haynes was referred to me by her general practitioner for counselling for depression and anxiety. In the initial session she made it clear to me that she did not want to involve her husband in counselling but rather she wanted an opportunity to focus on her own problems. She further did not think that joining a group would give her sufficient time or privacy to discuss her problems in as much depth as she considered to be most productive for her. We thus decided on a course of individual rational emotive behavioural counselling.

In the initial session, I asked Mrs Haynes to describe her prior experiences with counselling. She reported having had a previous spell of individual counselling with a marriage counsellor who, from her description, appeared to practise a kind of non-directive psychoanalytically oriented counselling. She considered that she had not benefited from this approach, mainly because she was confused and put off by the counsellor's passivity, and seeming lack of active involvement. I gave her a thumbnail sketch about what she might realistically expect from rational emotive behavioural counselling, and her initial reaction was favourable. We agreed to meet initially for five sessions. I like to make an initial time-limited contract to enable clients to make a more informed decision about whether or not they think that they will benefit from rational emotive behavioural counselling.

Mrs Haynes saw depression as more of a pressing problem for her than anxiety, and it was the one that she chose to make a start on. Her problem list revealed that she was particularly depressed about her own failure to make her marriage work and blamed herself for her husband's preference for another woman. I helped her to see that it was not his preference for another woman that made her depressed, but her belief about the situation which was, 'I must make my marriage work and I am a failure if I don't!' Before proceeding to help her to dispute this belief in the initial session, I worked patiently with her to enable her to see the connections between A, B and C.

I started to dispute her irrational belief only when she said that she saw clearly that it was this belief that caused her depression rather than her husband leaving her, and that in order to overcome her depression she needed to change her belief. While disputing her belief I helped her to develop a list of self-disputes that she could ask herself in the coming week whenever she felt depressed about her presumed failure in marriage. I gave her a copy of *A New Guide to Rational Living* (Ellis and Harper, 1975) and suggested that in particular she read Chapter 2 ('You feel the way you think') and Chapter 11 ('Eradicating dire fears of failure'). I also offered her an opportunity to take away a tape of our session, which she accepted gratefully. She was thus exposed to the idea of working at homework assignments between sessions.

At the beginning of the following session I asked her for her reactions to both the tape and the reading material. It transpired from this that she had a positive response to both the tape and reading material and she commented that she particularly liked the method of bibliotherapy. Her depression had lifted considerably since our first session, and she was able to use her own self-disputes to come up with plausible answers. In order to reinforce her progress I asked her if she would find it helpful to use one of the written self-help forms that exist for this purpose, and showed her three. She decided to start off with the one that I devised myself with one of my students, Maureen Millard (see Figure 6.1). We first worked on an episode of depression – even though she had progressed on that since our initial session – after we had decided that it was better to get closure on her depression before we tackled her anxiety. We spent the rest of Session 2 filling out this form, and at the end I gave her a number of these forms and suggested that she read Chapter 15 of *A New Guide to Rational Living* ('Conquering anxiety') and to use such insights to fill in a form whenever she became anxious.

At the beginning of Session 3, she reported that she benefited from reading the chapter on anxiety, but had experienced some difficulty in zeroing in on the irrational beliefs which underpinned her own anxiety. Using the inference chaining procedure, I helped her to see that she was anxious about ever finding another man again and ending up an old spinster. As is typical in rational emotive behavioural counselling, I encouraged her to assume the worst and to imagine that she was an old spinster and asked her for her feelings about that. Her reply was instructive: 'Oh God, I couldn't stand the thought of living like that.' I disputed her belief that she needed a man in her life in order to be happy and helped her to see that she could in fact gain a fair measure of happiness in her life being single even though she would prefer to he married and have a family. This led on to a discussion of her immediate anxiety, i.e. her feeling that she could not go out on her own because this would be shameful.

Often feelings of shame are related to feelings of anxiety and, assuming this to be the case with Mrs Haynes, I helped her to see that she was saying: 'If I go out on my own then other people will think that I am alone and that would prove that I am worthless.' The rest of the session was spent putting this into ABCDE format using the self-help form. I then suggested that we try rational–emotive imagery as a bridge between changing her attitude in her mind's eye and putting into practice her new belief: 'I have every right to go out on my own and if other people look down on me, then I refuse to look down on myself.' Mrs Haynes had a great deal of difficulty in using rational–emotive imagery (Ellis's version) in the session, and between Sessions 3 and 4.

At the beginning of Session 4 I went over the rational–emotive imagery, and suggested instead that she say her new rational belief quite vigorously to herself. She was able to do this, first of all out loud and then internally, and felt a mood shift which was much more profound than that she was able to achieve by using Ellis's version of rational–emotive imagery. Let me add that her feelings of depression were no longer considered by her to be a problem since Session 1.

At the end of session four we negotiated an assignment whereby she would go out socially on her own on two occasions, on one occasion to a local evening class, and second to a dance hall, while vigorously repeating the rational self-coping statements we developed. This apparently was very helpful to Mrs Haynes, for she reported that she was able to go out on both occasions without undue anxiety. This was our fifth session, the last of our therapeutic contract, and I discussed progress with Mrs Haynes and how she wished to proceed in the future. She said that she was very pleased with her progress and wanted to continue to have sessions every two weeks rather than weekly. Under the circumstances, this appeared to be a reasonable way of approaching termination.

From Sessions 5 to 10 Mrs Haynes made great progress. She had a number of dates with men and was able to resist the sexual advances of two of them, which to her was a great stride because in the past she had had great difficulty saying 'No' to men and had for a period prior to her marriage been quite promiscuous, out of desperation rather than out of choice. Between Sessions 5 and 10, I gave her *Why Do I Think I Am Nothing Without A Man* by Penelope Russianoff (1981) and *Living Alone and Liking It* by Lynn Shahan (1981) to read. She also continued to listen to the tapes of her sessions, although I suggested that she review them only once, rather than her accustomed three times, because I wished to encourage her to rely on her own resources rather than to rely on my direction, albeit secondhand through the tapes. She also continued going out on her own and used vigorous self-disputing to increasingly good effect. It seemed apparent that she was experiencing success in becoming her own counsellor.

As counselling progressed to what I thought would be termination, Mrs Haynes got quite anxious. She said that she had become quite dependent upon my help and was anxious about whether or not she could cope on her own. First of all, I disputed her belief that she needed my help and secondly, I encouraged her to view a break from counselling as an experiment and suggested a six-week gap between our tenth and eleventh sessions, stressing that she rely more on self-disputing rather than on bibliotherapy. I also suggested that she should not listen to any of the past tapes, so that we could conduct a fair experiment of her inference that she could not cope on her own.

The experiment proved to be a success, because she came in and wondered why she even thought that she could not cope on her own, since she had managed the six-week gap very well. I commented that I was pleased with her progress, to which she replied: 'That's nice to know, but even if you weren't, I am. I don't need your approval.' Having been firmly put in my place in this regard, we discussed whether she needed any future sessions and finally agreed that we would have a six-month follow-up, although I did suggest that she could contact me if she wanted to in the interim, on the condition that she used her own skills for a two-week period, and if she could not cope with any emotional problems that came up in that period then she could contact me.

At the six-month follow-up session Mrs Haynes had attained and enhanced her therapeutic gains. She was productively involved in many social and voluntary activities and had ongoing casual relationships with three men, one of which included sex out of choice and not out of desperation. Her relationship with her husband was reasonably cordial and they were proceeding towards an amicable divorce. In my keenness to encourage her to cope on her own, I made the error of moving toward termination without helping her to anticipate future problems and encourage her to see that she could use her new coping methods to deal with these problems. Although this was an error at the time, Mrs Haynes was able to do this in the intervening period. In addition, I had to do very little work in helping her set goals for increased satisfaction, since she was able to do this on her own.

Appendix I: Possible Reasons for not Completing Self-help Assignments

(To be completed by client)

The following is a list of reasons that various clients have given for not doing their self-help assignments during the course of counselling. Because the speed of improvement depends primarily on the amount of self-help assignments that you are willing to do, it is of great importance to pinpoint any reasons that you may have for not doing this work. It is important to look for these reasons at the time that you feel a reluctance to do your assignment or a desire to put off doing it. Hence, it is best to fill out this questionnaire at that time. If you have any difficulty filling out this form and returning it to the counsellor, it might be best to do it together during a counselling session. (Rate each statement by ringing 'T' (True) or 'F' (False). 'T' indicates that you agree with it; 'F' means the statement does not apply, at this time.)

1. It seems that nothing can help me so there is no point in trying.   T/F
2. It wasn't clear, I didn't understand what I had to do.   T/F
3. I thought that the particular method the counsellor had suggested would not be helpful. I didn't really see the value of it.   T/F
4. It seemed too hard.   T/F
5. I am willing to do self-help assignments, but I keep forgetting.   T/F
6. I did not have enough time. I was too busy.   T/F
7. If I do something the counsellor suggests I do, it's not as good as if I come up with my own ideas.   T/F
8. I don't really believe I can do anything to help myself.   T/F
9. I have the impression the counsellor is trying to boss me around or control me.   T/F
10. I worry about the counsellor's disapproval. I believe that what I do just won't be good enough for him/her.   T/F
11. I felt too bad, sad, nervous, upset (underline the appropriate word(s)) to do it.   T/F
12. It would have upset me to do the homework.   T/F
13. It was too much to do.   T/F
14. It's too much like going back to school again.   T/F
15. It seemed to be mainly for the counsellor's benefit.   T/F
16. Self-help assignments have no place in counselling.   T/F
17. Because of the progress I've made these assignments are likely

to be of no further benefit to me.   T/F
18. Because these assignments have not been helpful in the past, I
    couldn't see the point of doing this one.   T/F
19. I don't agree with this particular approach to counselling.   T/F
20. OTHER REASONS (please list them).   T/F

Chapter 11
Obstacles to Client Progress and How to Overcome Them

Overview

In this chapter we catalogue the major obstacles to client progress in rational emotive behavioural counselling. We deal mainly with common counsellor errors in the practice of rational emotive behavioural counselling as covered in Chapters 5–10. We also briefly discuss client factors, relationship factors and environmental factors that serve as obstacles to client progress. We conclude the chapter by considering how rational emotive behavioural counselling can be individually tailored to the unique requirements of clients.

Sources of Obstacles to Client Progress: Counsellor Factors

In this section, we discuss obstacles to client progress that can he attributed to the counsellor. We emphasise errors that are commonly made by counsellors in the beginning phase of rational emotive behavioural counselling (induction and assessment); in attempting to promote intellectual rational insight; in attempting to promote emotional rational insight; and in the general management of cases. It is, of course, desirable for REB counsellors to strive continually to improve their skills by involving themselves in ongoing supervision and training activities (Dryden, 1983; Wessler and Ellis, 1980, 1983).

Finally, we discuss the major irrational beliefs held by counsellors that appear to interfere with the practice of effective rational emotive behavioural counselling.

Beginning rational emotive behavioural counselling

Rational emotive behavioural counsellors can obstruct the progress of their clients by committing the following errors in the induction and assessment stages of beginning counselling:

1. *Failing to explore clients' expectations and preferences for counselling.* A common result of this failure is that misconceptions that clients have about the process of rational emotive behavioural counselling remain unchecked. Clients may 'resist' the counsellor's interventions when they 'expect' a different type of help from that provided. As such, it is important for counsellors to assess clients' reasons for entering counselling, the types of problems they think counselling will he able to help them deal with, and their views concerning what constitutes 'appropriate' counsellor behaviour. It is good practice to provide clarification for clients concerning the respective roles of counsellor and client within rational emotive behavioural counselling, and to convey clearly that REBC seeks to help individuals overcome their psychological problems by identifying and changing dysfunctional personal philosophies.

2. *Failing to assess clients' problems correctly.* This may mean that counsellors proceed to work on 'problems' that clients do not have. This error can be avoided by having clients prepare a problem list, as discussed in the preceding chapter. If necessary, counsellors can work with clients to translate the items on this list into problems that can be dealt with by the REBC approach.

3. *Failing to identify relevant second-order problems (i.e. meta-emotional problems).* When these problems are not identified and assessed, clients may not be helped because they may be distracted with their second-order problem when their first-order problems are being discussed. It is advisable for counsellors to be alert to indications that clients may feel ashamed, guilty, anxious or depressed about their original problems.

4. *Failing to explain why counsellor and client had better work on the meta-emotional problem first.* When this occurs, the clients often becomes puzzled when the counsellor proceeds to work on the meta-emotional problem without giving an adequate rationale for doing so. This difficulty can be circumvented by providing such a rationale, and by exploring within sessions the ways in which the meta-emotional problem may interfere with treatment of the original problem. If the clients still insist on dealing with their primary problem at this point, it may be a good idea to honour their preference. To do otherwise could damage the therapeutic alliance.

5. *Failing to identify clearly and specifically negative emotional and behavioural consequences (Cs).* Here counsellors often fail to clarify vague emotional Cs such as 'upset' or 'unhappy' and may thus assume wrongly that these emotions are unhealthy, when they may in fact be healthy. We refer readers to Chapter 3 for a discussion of how to distinguish between unhealthy and healthy negative emotions.

6. *Failing to help clients understand the dysfunctional nature of their self-defeating emotions and behaviours at C.* When this point is omitted, counsellors often assume that their clients will want to change these 'self-defeating problems' when in fact the clients do not necessarily define

them as self-defeating (a common example here is unhealthy anger). Before moving to the disputing stage of counselling it is important that clients are helped to view them as targets for change. Just because particular emotions or actions are deemed dysfunctional by rational emotive behavioural theory does not mean that clients wish to change them. As Golden (1983, p.34) has shown, clients often 'resist' working on self-defeating Cs if this means confronting a higher-order anxiety, e.g. 'an overweight client fearing that if she lost weight she would then have to deal with her social and sexual anxieties about dating'. Thus, higher-order anxieties often need to be assessed in rational emotive behavioural counselling.

7. *Spending too much time listening to irrelevant background data on activating events (As).* When counsellors make this error they unwittingly train their clients to talk about irrelevances, and thus practise inefficient counselling. As noted earlier, clients should preferably be encouraged to specify activating events as briefly as possible.

On occasion, counsellors will encounter clients who compulsively tend to provide far more detail on their activating events than is needed. When this becomes a pattern within sessions, it can be tactfully brought to clients' attention and therapeutic exploration can shift to an ABC analysis of the problem. Often, such analysis can reveal that clients harbour irrational beliefs, such as the following: 'I *must* provide my counsellor with all the details; otherwise we might miss something of importance and that would have *awful* consequences for my counselling.'

8. *Spending too much time focusing on the historical determinants of clients' problems.* Doing this may encourage clients to believe that such material is very important in understanding their current problems, whereas rational emotive behavioural theory emphasises that it is the client's current beliefs that should ideally be the focus of enquiry. Here, counsellors can convey to clients that identifying the historical determinants of their irrational beliefs will generally have little relevance with respect to the course that treatment will take.

9. *Gaining a total picture of the client's past and present problems before assessing specific problems.* While collecting such data may be helpful, in practice it does not add very much to the assessment of specific problems. Counsellors who make this error often like to place clients in relevant diagnostic categories, believing (wrongly in our opinion) that doing so will aid the treatment process.

10. *Failing to use inference chaining to identify the most relevant inference in the inference chain.* Thus, a man may be angry with his wife for forgetting to collect his suit from the cleaners – not because she is forgetful, but because her forgetfulness will get him into trouble at work, trouble which he dreads. The correct use of inference chaining often helps counsellors to identify significant problems which are not immediately apparent from clients' accounts of their problems. The reader is referred back to Chapters 5 and 9 for material on this procedure.

11. *Failing to show clients that the ideology of their problems is most frequently expressed in the form of devout, absolutist 'musts' or one of the three main derivatives of 'musturbation'.* Inexpert rational emotive behavioural counsellors tend to assume that clients' anti-empirical or inferentially distorted thinking, 'causes' their emotional and/or behavioural problems. While distorted inferences may be implicated in clients' problems, REBC theory holds that they tend to stem from irrational beliefs. Thus, from a therapeutic perspective, it makes sense to focus treatment on identifying and changing the latter.

12. *Failing to uncover clients' relevant irrational beliefs.* Here, counsellors may identify irrational beliefs that are either incorrect or too general in nature. An example of the latter occurred when a counsellor identified the general irrational belief 'I must be approved by everyone', whereas the client's actual irrational belief was more specific: 'I must be approved by significant others in my life'. Counsellors are advised first to identify the specific irrational beliefs triggered by particular activating events, and then to look for common themes across the specific beliefs. In this way clients' core irrational beliefs can be identified and dealt with as treatment proceeds.

13. *Failing to explain the B–C connection.* When this explanation is not made, clients are often puzzled when their counsellors begin to dispute their irrational beliefs. They cannot fully understand that changing their beliefs lead to their desired emotional and/or behavioural goals. Chapter 5 presented a teaching dialogue (created by Ellis) that counsellors can employ to convey the B–C connection; other vehicles for accomplishing this task appear throughout the REBC practitioners' literature (see, for example, Walen, DiGiuseppe and Dryden, 1992; Wessler and Wessler, 1980).

14. *Failing to assess clients' emotional and behavioural goals.* When counsellors fail to assess their clients' goals, they often assume that clients have goals which they do not in fact have. Here, as elsewhere, rational emotive behavioural counsellors may assume wrongly that their clients will function according to REBC theory, e.g. that they will want to he concerned rather than anxious. With respect to setting feasible emotional goals for rational emotive behavioural counselling, counsellors can teach clients the distinctions between healthy and unhealthy negative emotions (see Chapter 3). In addition, counsellors can work with clients to explore whether their behavioural goals will ultimately prove to be self-defeating.

Promoting intellectual rational insight

The following errors are often committed by inexpert rational emotive behavioural counsellors in this stage of the counselling process.

1. *Assuming that clients will automatically change their irrational beliefs once they have identified them.* Inexpert REB counsellors either fail to

dispute irrational beliefs at all or use disputing methods sparingly and with insufficient vigour. It is advisable to persist in disputing clients' irrational beliefs until they are able to acknowledge that such beliefs are illogical, anti-empirical and self-defeating. It is, however, a good idea to change tack when persistence in disputing a particular irrational belief poses a threat to the therapeutic alliance (e.g. as when a client expresses a strong preference to explore a new problem area).

2. *Disputing distorted inferences before disputing irrational beliefs.* Inexpert REB counsellors tend to eschew the preferred rational emotive behavioural strategy of assuming temporarily that distorted inferences are true so that irrational beliefs may be challenged. They tend to dispute distorted inferences because they are distorted, and fail to realise that although such inferential distortions are implicated in clients' problems, they are not central to their existence. The danger of disputing distorted inferences before irrational beliefs is that although clients may improve, this improvement is temporary and the ideological evaluative roots of their problems still need to be addressed.

3. *Failing to focus disputing interventions on clients' actual irrational beliefs.* Here, counsellors tend to stray from specific irrational beliefs that they correctly assessed earlier. The most common error here is to shift to disputing general beliefs, as noted in the previous section. It is generally good practice to dispute specific irrational beliefs first, and then later in the counselling process to work at identifying and disputing core irrational beliefs.

4. *Failing to help clients to understand the difference between rational and irrational beliefs.* Helping clients to understand this difference is important since, in response to questions asking for evidence in favour of their irrational beliefs, they will provide evidence in support of their rational beliefs. Clarifying the distinction between rational and irrational beliefs helps to refocus clients on challenging the latter.

5. *Failing to use Socratic-type disputing with clients who can benefit from this method.* As such, counsellors deprive these clients of the opportunity to think for themselves and impede them from becoming their own future counsellors. Socratic-type disputing is an important part of rational emotive behavioural counselling as it can provide an in-session model of disputing procedures. Counsellors can attempt to use the Socratic questioning technique on an experimental basis with their clients, and can make decisions on whether to continue with it based on client response.

6. *Failing to lecture didactically when it is clear that clients do not understand a concept through Socratic disputing.* Although rational emotive behavioural counsellors prefer to use Socratic disputing whenever possible, rigid adherence to this method can be counterproductive. Didactic presentations have their place in rational emotive behavioural counselling and can be fruitfully employed when clients do not benefit from Socratic disputing. When material is presented didactically it is important for

counsellors to be concise in their explanations and to check whether or not they have made themselves understood.

7. *Philosophising in an abstract manner.* Although effective rational emotive behavioural counsellors do engage in philosophical discussions with their clients, these debates are focused on clients' actual irrational beliefs, and reminders of the relevance of these discussions to the clients' problems at C are provided. Inexpert REB counsellors tend to engage their clients in abstract philosophical discussions divorced from the latter's problems. As such, both counsellor and client lose a productive therapeutic focus. When the client tries to channel discussion to abstract philosophising, the counsellor can explain that this is likely to be non-productive and can attempt to redirect the session to more relevant issues. Some clients may use abstract philosophising as a means of distancing themselves from dealing with their problems; when this appears to be the case, counsellors can raise it as an issue for therapeutic exploration.

8. *Failing to use appropriate examples, metaphors, stories etc., while disputing.* Effective disputing sequences are characterised by a variety of examples, metaphors, stories, etc., tailored to the client's own idiosyncratic situation. When these are omitted, disputing can lose its desired impact. Counsellors are again referred to the REBC literature for a variety of such devices that can be adapted for use with given clients. In addition, they are encouraged to develop their own devices, based on their knowledge of client history, occupation, hobbies, etc.

9. *Failing to remind clients of the dysfunctional consequences of adhering to irrational beliefs.* A good way of encouraging clients to work on relinquishing their irrational beliefs is to provide them with frequent reminders of the dysfunctional consequences of such beliefs. Thus, a counsellor may say 'OK, so you keep maintaining that you must achieve your certificate, but where is that belief getting you other than anxious and depressed?'

10. *Failing to counter the illogicalities that clients express during the process of disputing.* Clients often express a variety of illogicalities in defence of their irrational beliefs while responding to the disputing interventions of their counsellors (Edelstein, 1976; Guinagh, 1976). Ineffective rational emotive behavioural counsellors may not even identify these illogicalities, or when they do identify them they may not address them successfully. Commonly expressed illogical defences include:

   (a) *Statements of indifference.* Here clients think that rational alternatives to irrational beliefs are expressive of indifference, e.g. 'I don't care if . . .' rather than, 'I prefer that . . .'. We recommend that counsellors help their clients to distinguish among irrational beliefs, rational beliefs and 'indifferent' beliefs.

   (b) *'My belief is true because I feel it to be true.'* This is an example of emotional reasoning (Burns, 1980). Clients should be shown that feeling something to be true is often not a good guide to its validity.

(c) *'I can't change my belief because that's the way I am.'* Here, clients wrongly consider that their irrational belief is part of their unalterable identity. Distinctions between thinking and identity should be made, and instances of clients changing important beliefs should be sought to counter this notion.

(d) *Appeals to authority.* Here, clients point to respected authorities as the source of irrational beliefs and consider that such beliefs are true because such authorities have credibility, e.g. 'My father taught me that I must do well in life. That's why it's true.' Here, clients can be shown that such authorities probably intended to indicate relative rather than absolute values and that, even if absolute values were being taught, such respected authorities probably did not want the clients to have dysfunctional results, e.g. 'Do you think your father wanted you to be miserable? Would he prefer you to be miserable and cling to your belief, or do you think he would want you to give up the exaggerated quality of your belief if it meant you weren't miserable?' It is often not productive, however, to cast the respected authority in a negative light, since counsellors who attempt this may be viewed negatively themselves.

(e) *Evading the issues.* Clients will often evade the issue by changing the subject or by bringing up other problems. They do this to try to distract counsellors from their purpose. Effective rational emotive behavioural counsellors succeed in bringing clients back to the issue at hand while acknowledging that focusing on difficult problems is uncomfortable. In some cases, counsellors may need to dispute clients' LFT beliefs about tolerating the pain of focusing on their problems.

Promoting emotional rational insight

The following errors are often committed by inexpert rational emotive behavioural counsellors while attempting to promote emotional rational insight:

1. *Failing to show clients the differences between intellectual rational insight and emotional rational insight.* It is very important for rational emotive behavioural counsellors to help clients understand that gaining intellectual rational insight is rarely sufficient for them to solve their emotional and behavioural problems. Rather, clients should be shown that they need to challenge their irrational beliefs repeatedly and vigorously using cognitive, emotive and behavioural methods if they are to achieve lasting change.

2. *Failing to uncover and address clients' blocks to working hard to achieve emotional rational insight.* Clients refuse to work hard to achieve emotional rational insight for a number of reasons. These include:
(a) a philosophy of low frustration tolerance (LFT) where clients believe, for example, that 'It's too hard to work to achieve lasting change. Change

must not be that hard'; (b) cognitive–emotive dissonance whereby clients feel 'unnatural' as they work towards strengthening their rational beliefs, and believe that they must feel natural at all times (Maultsby, 1984). Grieger and Boyd (1980) note that this phenomenon can take a number of forms: 'I won't be me', whereby clients fear that they will lose their identities if they relinquish their irrational beliefs, and 'I'll become a robot', whereby clients believe that rationality means becoming devoid of all feeling rather than experiencing healthy negative emotions, e.g. sadness, remorse, etc. (see Chapter 3). It is important for counsellors to monitor clients' efforts to work at counselling between sessions and to be alert to beliefs that may block them from doing so.

3. *Failing to experiment with a broad range of cognitive, emotive and behavioural techniques.* Clients vary in their response to rational emotive behavioural techniques. It is recommended that counsellors adopt an experimental attitude in attempting to discover which techniques best suit which clients. Counsellors who employ only a limited range of techniques at this stage are generally less effective than counsellors who are willing to use a broad range of techniques.

4. *Insisting that clients employ implosion methods of change.* Rational emotive behavioural theory states that implosive techniques of behavioural change are more effective than gradual methods of behavioural change. Also, Ellis (1979b, 1980a) has argued that many clients perpetuate their problems and deprive themselves of learning experiences because they believe that they *must* be comfortable. Thus, rational emotive behavioural counsellors prefer to encourage their clients to confront their anxieties fully, for example, while tolerating their uncomfortable feelings. Although this is a sound strategy, it often needs to be modified for pragmatic purposes, since quite a few clients stubbornly refuse to employ such implosive methods. Rational emotive behavioural counsellors who insist that such clients use these methods are likely to damage the therapeutic alliance. For example, whereas it may be desirable for clients who are anxious about eating in public to go to an expensive restaurant and challenge their anxiety-creating cognitions in a situation where their worst fears may be realised, many clients will not do this. When we provide a rationale for homework assignments, we do so in a way that incorporates a principle that WD has termed 'challenging, but not overwhelming' and contrast it with gradual desensitisation and implosion methods (Dryden, 1985b):

> There are three ways you can overcome your fears. The first is like jumping in at the deep end; you expose yourself straightaway to the situation you are most afraid of. The advantage here is that if you can learn that nothing terrible will happen then you will overcome your problems quite quickly. However, the disadvantage is that some people just can't bring themselves to do this and get quite discouraged as a result. The second way is to go very gradually. Here, on the one hand, you only do something that you feel comfortable doing, while on

the other, you don't really get an opportunity to face putting up with discomfort, which in my opinion is a major feature of your problem. Also treatment will take much longer this way. The third way is what I call 'challenging but not over-whelming.' Here, you choose an assignment which is sufficiently challenging for you to make progress, but not one which you feel would be overwhelming for you at any given stage. Here, you are likely to make progress more quickly than with the gradual approach, but more slowly than with the 'deep end' approach.

We find that when clients are given an opportunity to choose their own rate of progress, the therapeutic alliance is strengthened. Most clients who will not employ implosive methods of change choose the 'challeng-ing but not overwhelming' approach, and only very rarely do they opt for gradual desensitisation therapy. When they do so we try to dissuade them, and frequently succeed. In the final analysis, however, we have not found it productive to insist that clients choose a particular way of tackling problems that is against their preferences.

Case management

The following errors are often committed by inexpert rational emotive behavioural counsellors in general case management:

1. *Focusing too much on the therapeutic relationship in the early stages of counselling.* Although it is important for counsellors to develop a co-opera-tive relationship with their clients, this can often be best achieved through a businesslike focus on the clients' problems, the execution of a correct assessment of these problems, and an early start on helping clients to over-come them. We have found that problem-focused counselling is more suc-cessful at consolidating the therapeutic relationship than deliberate attempts to develop this relationship in the absence of task activities.
2. *Switching from problem to problem in quick succession.* It is important for rational emotive behavioural counsellors to spend sufficient time on each of their clients' problems if clients are to benefit from counselling, otherwise clients become confused and fail to understand both the cogni-tive underpinnings of their problems and how to overcome them. A par-ticular error here occurs when counsellors switch frequently from ego to discomfort problems within a given session.
3. *Failing to identify and work with clients' priorities in counselling ses-sions.* When counsellors and clients have different priorities concerning what to discuss in sessions, it seems as if they are on parallel tracks and do not work together as a team. The result is that clients consider that their counsellors do not understand them, and as such do not benefit from counselling as much as they would if they perceived their counsel-lors as empathic (Truax and Carkhuff, 1967). Utilising a client problem list and collaborating on session agendas represent means by which this problem can be avoided.

4. *Failing to work at a pace and using language appropriate to the learning abilities of clients.* Rational emotive behavioural counselling can perhaps be best viewed as a psychoeducational approach to counselling. As such, it is important for counsellors to take into account their clients' learning abilities in executing interventions. Common errors here include working too fast or too slowly for clients and using too complicated or too simple language with the result that clients are insufficiently involved in the therapeutic process due to confusion or boredom. Here again, it is important for practitioners to utilise client reactions as the vehicle for constructing an optimal learning environment.

5. *Failing to ensure that clients understand rational concepts.* As rational emotive behavioural counselling is a psychoeducational approach to counselling, its practitioners should preferably make frequent checks that their clients understand rational concepts. It is important that counsellors do not take at face value clients' verbal assurances, e.g. 'I understand', and non-verbal assurances, e.g. head-nods, mm-hmms, that they understand and agree with rational concepts. This is particularly important when counsellors give didactic explanations of these concepts. Good questions to ask include: 'I want to make sure that I am making myself clear. Can you put into your own words what you think I said?'; 'What is your reaction to that point?'; 'Do you have any negative reactions about that?' We have found it particularly valuable to recommend that counsellors ask clients about, and deal with, their reservations concerning rational concepts, otherwise their clients may 'resist' their counsellors' interventions without the latter understanding the source of the 'resistance.'

6. *Failing to be sufficiently repetitive.* Here, counsellors believe falsely that if client change has occurred at one stage of counselling, then lasting change has taken place. Thinking that once a topic has been discussed in a counselling session the client has thoroughly learned what needs to be learned, such counsellors fail to 'go over old ground' with their clients. In practice, dealing with issues repeatedly is almost always a feature of effective rational emotive behavioural counselling, since 'one-trial' client learning hardly ever occurs.

7. *Failing to determine the basis of client change.* As has been noted in Chapter 3, client change may be inferentially based, behaviourally based or philosophically based. REB counsellors consider that long-term change is rooted in changes in clients' beliefs (i.e. philosophical change). If counsellors do not accurately establish the basis of client change they may miss opportunities of dealing with the philosophical roots of their clients' problems, since clients may terminate counselling, having made progress at the inferential or behavioural level of change. Counsellors are advised to conduct careful enquiries when clients report seemingly positive changes in their usual patterns of feeling and acting. When such enquiries reveal that these changes are not philosophically based, counsellors can present their clients with a rationale for continuing to work at modifying their irrational beliefs.

8. *Failures in the task domain of the therapeutic alliance.* Bordin (1979) has argued that counsellors and clients each have tasks to carry out during the process of counselling, and calls this the task domain of the therapeutic alliance. When obstacles to client progress occur due to problems in the task domain of the alliance the following are common counsellor errors:

(a) failing to help clients understand what their tasks are in counselling or, if they do understand these, failing to help them understand how executing them will help them achieve their goals

(b) failing to identify and deal with clients' doubts about their abilities to execute their tasks

(c) failing to help clients understand what their counsellors' tasks are and/or failing to help clients understand the link between their counsellors' tasks and their own tasks and goals

(d) encouraging clients to carry out tasks that they cannot realistically execute, e.g. some clients are not intelligent enough to engage in the tasks of Socratic disputing

(e) failing to train clients in the appropriate use of their own therapeutic tasks, e.g. clients often need to be trained in the use of rational–emotive imagery if they are to benefit from this procedure

(f) executing their own tasks in an unskilled manner

(g) employing methods which are not potent enough to promote client change, e.g. disputing irrational beliefs without exposure is unlikely to help clients with phobias.

The reader is referred back back to Chapter 10 for recommendations concerning means of avoiding problems within the task domain of counselling.

9. *Failing to negotiate homework assignments adequately.* In rational emotive behavioural counselling, clients are encouraged to put into practice what they learn in counselling sessions through the execution of a variety of homework assignments. Inexpert counsellors often fail to suggest homework assignments, and when they do suggest such tasks they make the following errors in negotiating assignments with their clients:

(a) failing to provide a persuasive rationale for the importance of homework assignments in rational emotive behavioural counselling. It is desirable to provide such a rationale early on in counselling, and to check whether clients understand it or have any objections to it.

(b) assigning the tasks unilaterally instead of involving clients in the negotiation process. This often occurs when counsellors devote insufficient time to discussion about homework. Devoting adequate time to discussion of homework allows counsellor and client to work together on its design, and provides the counsellor with an opportunity to identify and deal with any concerns the client may have about enacting the assignment.

(c) suggesting assignments that are irrelevant with respect to clients' goals

(Golden, 1983). It is important to identify homework that will help clients to approach their goals, and to make sure that clients see the relationship between homework enactment and goal attainment.

(d) suggesting assignments that do not relate to what has been discussed in the counselling session. This can be quite confusing for clients, as it obscures the relationship between homework enactment and goal attainment. As a general rule of thumb, counsellors are advised to promote the design of homework assignments that will help clients to work at disputing and replacing the irrational beliefs that were the focus of a given session. Such assignments may, of course, be cognitive, behavioural or emotive in nature.

(e) negotiating tasks that are vague rather than specific. Clients are more likely to carry out a homework task when they know what to do, when to do it, where to do it, and when they believe they are capable of doing it.

(f) failing to elicit commitment from clients that they will attempt homework assignments. A simple question (e.g. 'Do you think you'll make an effort to do that this week?') towards the session's end may be all that is required to determine a given client's commitment to doing a particular homework assignment. It is advisable, however, to allow sufficient time to deal with a negative response to this enquiry.

(g) failing to rehearse clients in homework assignments, e.g. in imagery or through role-play methods. Lazarus (1984) has argued that clients will be more likely to carry out homework assignments when they can picture themselves doing them in imagery.

(h) failing to identify and deal with potential obstacles that may prevent clients from carrying out their homework assignments. Here, it is recommended that counsellors be alert to practical as well as psychological obstacles.

(i) suggesting assignments that are too time-consuming for the client (Golden, 1983). Counsellors are advised to bear in mind that the tasks of daily living can impose significant demands on clients' time.

(j) suggesting assignments that are too threatening or anxiety provoking for clients at that stage of counselling (Golden, 1983) – see material on the 'challenging, but not overwhelming' principle discussed earlier in this chapter.

10. *Failing adequately to check clients' experiences in executing homework assignments.* When clients agree to execute homework assignments it is important that counsellors discuss with them their experiences in carrying them out. Ideally this should be done in the following session, although it is not always possible to do this. Common counsellor errors in checking on homework assignments include:

(a) failing to ask clients for a report of their experiences in carrying out assignments

(b) failing to ask clients for a report of what they learned, or did not learn, from their experiences in carrying out assignments

(c) failing to reinforce clients' attempts at executing assignments

(d) failing to correct clients' errors in written homework assignments when these have been completed

(e) failing to ask for and assess clients' reasons for not attempting, or not completing, their homework assignments

(f) failing to dispute irrational beliefs (in the domains of ego and/or discomfort disturbance) when these explain why clients did not attempt, or complete, assignments

(g) failing to reiterate the rationale for assignments when it is clear that clients did not understand them and thus did not attempt to complete them

(h) failing to obtain clients' commitment to attempt the assignments again, if appropriate.

Guidelines for conducting follow-up on clients' experiences with homework assignments are presented in Chapter 10.

Counsellors' irrational beliefs

Client progress can also be hindered because counsellors may bring their own disturbance to the therapeutic process. Ellis (1983b) has outlined five major irrational beliefs that lead to therapeutic inefficiency:

1. 'I *have* to be successful with all my clients practically all the time.'
2. 'I *must* be an outstanding counsellor, clearly better than other counsellors I know or hear about.'
3. 'I *have* to be greatly respected and loved by all my clients.'
4. 'Since I am doing my best and working so hard as a counsellor, my clients *absolutely should* be equally hard working and responsible, *should* listen to me carefully and *should* always push themselves to change.'
5. 'Because I am a person in my own right, I *must* be able to enjoy myself during counselling sessions and to use these sessions to solve my personal problems as much as to help clients with their difficulties.'

In addition, counsellors often fail to dispute clients' irrational beliefs because they share the same beliefs. Thus, one of WD's trainees did not dispute her client's belief, 'I must not die at an early age and it would be awful if I did' because she too believed that it would be awful to die prematurely. Hauck (1966) has called this the 'neurotic agreement' in counselling and psychotherapy.

In such cases, it is recommended that REB counsellors apply REBC principles and methods to search for and dispute their own self- and client-defeating beliefs which may (a) impede them from confronting their clients; (b) distract them and their clients from getting the therapeutic job done; (c) foster undue counsellor anxiety and anger; and (d) encourage inappropriate behaviour anathema to the practice of effective and ethical counselling.

Sources of Obstacles to Client Progress: Other Factors

In this section we discuss the following obstacles to client progress: client factors, relationship factors and environmental and other external factors.

Client factors

In order really to benefit from REB counselling, clients need to achieve three forms of insight, namely: (1) psychological disturbance is mainly determined by the absolutist beliefs that they hold about themselves, others, and the world; (2) even when people acquired and created their irrational beliefs in their early lives, they perpetuate their disturbance by reindoctrinating themselves in the present with these beliefs; (3) only if they consistently work and practise in the present and future to think, feel and act against these irrational beliefs are they likely to surrender their irrationalities and make themselves significantly less disturbed.

Kempel (1973) has identified a number of client attitudes and feelings which predispose them to terminate counselling prematurely:

1. *'I need to have a very close relationship with my counsellor.'* Such clients may wish to terminate counselling because their REB counsellors generally avoid developing very close therapeutic relationships with them. As outlined in Chapter 4, such relationships are deemed to be counter-therapeutic in that they reinforce clients' approval needs.
2. *'Change must be easy.'* Such clients are loath to put in the hard work that change involves and may leave REB counselling to seek a form of counselling that they perceive as less demanding.
3. *'I want changes in A (activating events) not B (beliefs).'* Such clients seek changes in significant others or troublesome events but will neither do anything themselves to try to effect such changes nor work to change their irrational beliefs about these situations. When they realise that REBC will not provide them with what they seek, they usually terminate counselling.
4. *'Shame about seeking help.'* Such clients condemn themselves for being weak and not able to solve their own problems. They are thus ambivalent about seeking help and may terminate counselling if their feelings of shame become acute.

Unless counsellors are sensitive to the existence of such client attitudes and feelings and can identify and deal with relevant irrational beliefs and misconceptions about counselling, clients will not stay in counselling long enough to achieve the three forms of insight outlined above.

Golden (1983) has noted four important client factors which impede client progress. First, some clients may have 'hidden agendas' that could interfere with rational emotive behavioural counselling, e.g. a man who comes into counselling in order to stop his wife filing for a divorce, but who has no intention of seeking personal changes for himself. It is often difficult to identify such agendas, particularly early on in the counselling process and clients are, of course, 'motivated' to keep them hidden. However, if clients are not progressing it is important for counsellors to try to answer the question: 'What has this person to gain from not improving?' and to try to help clients identify the irrational beliefs and inferential distortions that may underpin any hidden agendas that can be identified. However, it may happen that counsellors never become aware of the presence of such agendas that do in fact exist. This should be accepted as one of the occupational hazards of all forms of counselling.

The second factor discussed by Golden is poor client motivation. This occurs 'when a client does not value the desired outcome of therapy enough to devote the necessary time and effort to change' (Golden, 1983, p.35). In such cases, rational emotive behavioural counsellors would do well to renegotiate with such clients their goals for change.

Third, some clients demonstrate negative behavioural patterns such as counter-control which may take the form of negativism toward counselling or rebelliousness against the counsellor. In these instances, we have found it helpful to show clients that they have a perfect right to act in such fashion and that the logical consequence of such behaviour is that they will not improve. We then enquire whether this is the outcome from counselling that they seek. It is important for counsellors to disengage themselves from any power struggle with such clients, since the more counsellors try to 'win' such struggles, the more these clients will resist their efforts. Since these clients desperately seek to control situations, they can be calmly shown that they and not their counsellors are in control of whether they improve or not.

Finally, Golden (1983) notes that some clients do not profit from counselling because of neurological and other biological limitations. When counsellors suspect the existence of such factors, referral to and liaison with other professionals is often indicated.

In a study by Ellis (1983d) on the characteristics of clients who 'failed' in REBC, the following findings emerged:

1. Clients who did poorly in REBC failed to do consistent *cognitive* self-disputation. They were characterised among other factors by extreme disturbance, by grandiosity, by lack of organisation, and by plain refusal to do these cognitive assignments.

2. 'Failure' clients, who refused to accept responsibility for their irrational emotions and refused to change their beliefs and actions forcefully and *emotively*, were more clingy, more severely depressed and inactive, more often grandiose and more frequently stubbornly rebellious than clients who benefited from REBC.

3. 'Failure' clients who did poorly in the behavioural aspects of REBC showed 'abysmally low frustration tolerance, had serious behavioural addictions, led disorganised lives, refrained from doing their active home-

work assignments, were more frequently psychotic and generally refused to work at therapy' (Ellis, 1983d, p.165).

Thus, clients' own extreme level of disturbance is a significant obstacle to their own progress. Although a full discussion of what 'special' therapeutic methods and techniques to employ with such clients is outside the scope of this book (see Ellis, 1985a and Neenan and Dryden, 1996a), counsellors can adopt a number of strategies to enhance therapeutic effectiveness with these 'difficult' clients. Among other tactics, counsellors should first be consistently and forcefully encouraging in their therapeutic interactions with these clients, showing them that they can do better if they try. Second, counsellors would be wise to keep vigorously showing these clients that they, the counsellors, do in fact unconditionally accept them with all their psychological difficulties and that they can indeed accept themselves in the same way. Third, counsellors can often be successful with such clients by consistently showing them that their refusal to work on their problems will generally lead to bad consequences and needless suffering. Fourth, counsellors should be flexible in experimenting with a wide range of therapeutic techniques (including some unusual ones!) in their persistent efforts to help their 'difficult' clients. Above all, rational emotive behavioural counsellors should be good representatives of their therapeutic system and accept themselves and tolerate the discomfort of working with 'difficult' clients while sticking to the therapeutic task.

Relationship factors

These can be first attributed to poor counsellor–client matching, which may occur for many reasons. Thus, clients 'may have a counsellor who, according to their idiosyncratic tastes or preferences, is too young or too old, too liberal or too conservative, too active or too passive' (Ellis, 1983e, p.29). If these 'relationship match' obstacles persist, then it is preferable for that client to be transferred to a counsellor with more suitable traits. Other relationship obstacles may occur because the counsellor and client may get on 'too well' and get distracted from the more mundane tasks of counselling. In such cases, the paradox is that if the client improves, the 'life' of the satisfactory relationship is threatened. As a result, collusion may occur between counsellor and client to avoid making counselling as effective an endeavour as it might otherwise be. This problem can be largely overcome if counsellors first help themselves and then their clients to overcome the philosophy of low frustration tolerance implicit in this collusive short-range hedonism.

In previous chapters, we discussed how counsellors should preferably modify their therapeutic style with different clients. In addition, clients may not benefit from counselling when the interpersonal style of their counsellors does not maximise their opportunities for therapeutic learning. In other words, the relationship 'milieu' may promote or inhibit client learning. For example, some clients are emotionally overstimulated and hence the therapeutic task for counsellors is to create a learning environment which decreases their emotional tension to a level where they can adequately reflect on their experiences. With these clients, counsellors are advised to make use of a lot of cognitive techniques and adopt an interpersonal style which aims to decrease affect. This style may be either formal or informal in character. These strategies are particularly appropriate with clients who have a 'histrionic' style of functioning. On the other hand, other clients require a more emotionally charged learning atmosphere. Such clients often use 'intellectualisation' as a major defence and are used to denying feelings. With such clients, counsellors should preferably endeavour to inject a productive level of affect into the therapeutic session and employ emotive techniques, self-disclosure and a good deal of humour.

These 'challenging' strategies are best introduced gradually so as not to 'overwhelm' clients with an environment that they are not accustomed to utilising. However, before deciding upon which interpersonal style to emphasise with clients, counsellors should routinely gain information from them concerning how they best learn. Some clients learn best directly through experience, whereas for others vicarious experiences seem to be more productive. We personally try to develop a learning profile for each of our clients and use this information to help us plan our therapeutic strategies and choose techniques designed to implement these strategies. Care needs to be taken, however, that the counsellor does not use a mode of learning that may perpetuate the client's problems.

Environmental and other external factors

Golden has noted that the following environmental and other external factors can be obstacles to client progress in counselling:

1. Deliberate sabotage from others (for example, threats of rejection or disapproval for being more assertive or successful).
2. Inadvertent sabotage from others such as family members who become 'benevolent saboteurs.' An example is the individual who inadvertently reinforces a family member's agoraphobia by 'chauffeuring' the phobic person around, thus providing him or her with a 'secondary gain' for being phobic.
3. Other 'secondary gains', such as those from disability and welfare benefits, which provide clients with reinforcements for their 'disabilities' (Golden, 1983, p.35).

To these we would add: organisations, systems and positions that provide limited opportunities for client growth, e.g., unfulfilling jobs, unemployment, prisons, totalitarian states.

In addition to helping clients to change their irrational beliefs about these obstacles, counsellors can use the following strategies to deal with them when people who serve as willing or unwilling obstacles to client progress are members of the client's family they may be invited to attend for family or marital counselling; when such people cannot legitimately be invited to attend counselling sessions, clients may be specifically helped to deal with them – see Ellis's (1975) *How to Live with a Neurotic* – or be encouraged to distance themselves from them as far as possible; clients may be encouraged to leave situations which inhibit their growth if these situations cannot be modified; and clients may be encouraged to give up the short-term benefits of secondary gains in order to achieve the long-term benefits to their mental health of doing without such 'gains.'

It should be remembered, however, that while environmental and other external factors can limit the client's opportunities for happiness they cannot directly cause their psychological problems, since it is clients' irrational beliefs about these situations which determine their emotional and behavioural responses to these factors.

Notes on Individualising Rational Emotive Behavioural Counselling

One of the best ways of minimising obstacles to client progress is to individualise the practice of rational emotive behavioural counselling for each client. In this section we again use Bordin's (1979) concept of the therapeutic alliance as an explanatory framework. Although we cover issues that have already been introduced, we believe that Bordin's ideas provide a fresh way of looking at these issues. As described in Chapter 10, Bordin argues that there are three components of the therapeutic alliance: bonds, goals and tasks. To review: bonds refer to the interpersonal connectedness between counsellors and clients; goals are the objectives of both counsellors and clients and provide the *raison d'être* of counselling; and tasks are best viewed as the means by which counsellors and clients attempt to actualise their goals.

It is in the nature of individual REB counselling that, since counsellors are dealing with only one client, they can strive to tailor the practice of counselling with this client free from the concern that a particular style of interaction (and the use of an individually tailored treatment programme) may have an adverse effect on other clients, e.g. in couples counselling, family counselling or group counselling. Thus, as we have shown previously, the counsellor can modify his or her style of participation in individual counselling according to the personality structure of a given client, in order to maximise that client's learning and to minimise the possibility that the client's problems are being unwittingly reinforced. This refers in particular to individualising REB counselling in the bond domain of the therapeutic alliance (Bordin, 1979). Therapeutic bonds in REB counselling may change over time according to the amount of progress that the client makes and according to which bonds the client best responds.

In this latter regard, the counsellor can at the outset attempt to assess what might be a productive bond to form with a particular client, e.g. a formal or informal bond. Thus, as discussed in Chapter 10, the counsellor might ask the client (either on a biographical form or in person) what in the client's mind constitutes helpful and unhelpful counsellor behaviour. The counsellor might also ask the client about the latter's previous experiences of being helped, whether formally or informally, and during this exploration focus on what aspects of the other person's behaviour the client found most helpful and what aspects they found least helpful. It is important, however, to view such information critically because what a client has found helpful in the short term may not have been helpful in the long term. Thus, for example, counsellors can help clients feel better in the short term without helping them to get better in the long term (Ellis, 1972). Although the information that can be obtained from the client about possible helpful ways of intervening with that particular client may be useful, rational emotive behavioural counsellors would be wise to answer by experimentation the question concerning which bond is most productive with this client at this particular time. Thus, the counsellor might try particular ways of interacting with different clients, and observe how these clients respond to these different forms of therapist interaction.

Another way that REBC practitioners can individualise counselling for their clients is to ensure that there is congruence between clients' goals and the goals of counselling. Ineffective REB counselling can often occur when clients wish to achieve one goal and their counsellors are working to help them to achieve a different goal. However, we advocate that counsellors do not uncritically accept their clients' goal statements as sacred. Indeed, a good REB counsellor sometimes spends some therapeutic time trying to talk a client out of goals that the client considers to be helpful but which the counsellor considers to be harmful to the long-term welfare of the client. Good REB counselling therefore involves a fair measure of negotiation between counsellor and client concerning the client's goals. It is helpful, however, if the counsellor refrains from dogmatically insisting that a client give up his or her unrealistic or harmful goals, since such insistence may add to the client's problems.

Clients' goals can and often do change over time and counsellors should be sensitive to the changing nature of their clients' aims and attempt to track changes in their goal statements. It is particularly helpful for REB counsellors to understand (and to help their clients understand) what underlies such changes in therapeutic goals. Remember that clients' initial goals are often coloured by the nature of their disturbance and that it is advantageous for counsellors to encourage them to postpone fixing on certain goals until they have achieved a fair measure of success in overcoming their emotional and/or behavioural disturbance. Once this is accomplished, REB counsellors are noted for helping their clients to pursue the latter's own individualised goals, since they believe that a particular client does not *have to* achieve satisfaction in any given way. Thus, clients are encouraged to actualise their potential in their own individualistic way, preferably after having achieved a large measure of freedom from emotional and behavioural disturbance. In general, REB counsellors encourage clients first to work on the goals of overcoming their emotional and/or behavioural disturbance before working to pursue individualistic goals that will bring them happiness.

The third aspect of the therapeutic alliance where rational emotive behavioural counselling can be practised in an individualised way is in the task domain. Bordin (1979) has stressed that every therapeutic system favours particular counsellors' tasks *and* clients' tasks, which then become embodied in the practice of that approach to counselling. REB counselling can be practised in an individualised way if the counsellor encourages the client to carry out tasks which are best suited to that particular client and which are likely to encourage that client to achieve his or her therapeutic goals. In this way, the practice of REBC can be seen as efficient as well as effective (Ellis, 1980b).

Some clients seem to progress better by carrying out techniques that are more cognitive in nature, while other clients seem to benefit more from executing tasks that are more emotive in nature; yet a further group of clients do best by carrying out behavioural tasks. Although a particular therapeutic technique draws upon all three modalities, it is also true that a particular technique may emphasise one modality over others. There are no firm guidelines for REB counsellors to use in determining, before the event, which therapeutic techniques are most appropriate for given clients. However, it may be helpful to explore with clients their past history of effecting productive changes while paying attention to their answers concerning which modalities they used spontaneously, or were encouraged to use. In other words, it may be helpful for REB counsellors to pay attention to a client's prior learning style and modify the practice of rational emotive behavioural counselling accordingly. Once again, perhaps the best indication concerning which techniques clients will most benefit from is experimentation, which is the hallmark of individualising rational emotive behavioural counselling and the scientific method which rational emotive behavioural theory supports. This involves trying out interventions, noting clients' reactions to these, getting clients' feedback on their reactions to these interventions and modifying future interventions accordingly.

Chapter 12
The Distinctive Features of Rational Emotive Behavioural Counselling: A Review

Overview

In this final chapter, we review the distinctive features of rational emotive behavioural counselling and contrast these with other approaches to cognitive-behavioural counselling. We conclude the chapter and the book by outlining techniques that are generally avoided in rational emotive behavioural counselling.

Introduction

The major goal of rational emotive behavioural counselling is an ambitious one: *to encourage clients to make a profound philosophic change in the two main areas of ego disturbance and discomfort disturbance.* This involves helping clients, as far as is humanly possible, to give up their irrational beliefs and to replace these with rational beliefs, as discussed in Chapter 3.

In rational emotive behavioural counselling the major goals are to help clients pursue their long-range basic goals and purposes and to help them to do so as effectively as possible by fully accepting themselves and tolerating unchangeable, uncomfortable life conditions. Rational emotive behavioural practitioners further strive to help clients obtain the skills which they can use to prevent the development of future disturbance. In encouraging clients to achieve and maintain this profound philosophic change, rational emotive behavioural counsellors implement the following strategies. They help their clients see that:

1. emotional and behavioural disturbances have cognitive antecedents and that these cognitions normally take the form of absolutist devout evalu-

ations. REB counsellors train their clients to observe their own psychological disturbances and to trace these back to their ideological roots.
2. people have a distinct measure of self-determination and can thus *decide* to work at undisturbing themselves. Thus, clients are shown that they are not slaves to their biologically based irrational thinking processes.
3. people can implement their choices and maximise their freedom by actively working at changing their irrational beliefs. This is best achieved by employing cognitive, emotive and behavioural methods – often in quite a forceful and vigorous manner (Ellis, 1979d).

With the majority of clients, from the first session onward, REB counsellors are likely to use strategies designed to effect profound philosophic change. The counsellor begins the process with the hypothesis that this particular client may be able to achieve such change and thus begins to implement rational emotive behavioural methods, which he or she will abandon only after collecting sufficient data to reject this initial hypothesis. Rational emotive behavioural practitioners regularly implement this viewpoint, which is based on the notion that the client's response to counselling is the best indicator of his or her prognosis.

When it is clear that the client is not able to achieve philosophic change, either on a particular issue or in general (despite repeated and varied attempts at philosophic disputing), the counsellor may decide to effect a therapeutic 'compromise' (Dryden, 1991a) by utilising methods intended to bring about inferentially and behaviourally-based change. Inferentially-based change occurs when the client experiences some degree of improvement as a result of correcting distorted inferences such as negative predictions and overly negative interpretations of events and others' actions. Behaviourally-based change occurs when clients improve by effecting constructive changes in particular aspects of their behaviour, as with skills-training approaches. As another type of compromise, the counsellor may attempt to help the client to alter directly his or her problematic activating events in a positive fashion, so that they no longer serve to trigger his or her irrational beliefs. Such changes in tack can be appropriate when persistent efforts to conduct philosophic disputing would imperil the therapeutic alliance.

A good example of this change in strategy is one often reported by a counsellor of our acquaintance. He was working with a middle-aged married woman who reported feeling furious every time her ageing father would telephone her and enquire 'Noo, what's doing?' She inferred that this was a gross invasion of her privacy and absolutistically insisted that he had no right to do so. The counsellor initially intervened with the usual rational emotive behavioural strategy by attempting to dispute this client's dogmatic belief, and tried to help her see that there was no law in the universe which stated that he must not do such a thing. Meeting initial resistance, the counsellor persisted with different variations of this theme, all to no avail. Changing tack, he began to implement a different strategy designed to help the client question her inference that her father was actually invading her privacy. Given her father's age, the counsellor inquired, was it not more likely that his question represented his usual manner of beginning telephone conversations rather than an intense desire to pry into her affairs? This enquiry proved successful in that the client's rage subsided because she began to reinterpret her father's motives. Interestingly enough, although he returned to disputing her irrational belief later, the counsellor never succeeded in helping this client to give up this irrational belief!

However, some clients are more amenable to re-evaluating their irrational beliefs *after* they have been helped to correct distorted inferences. We should do research on this topic if we are to answer the question: 'Which strategy is most appropriate for which clients at which stage in counselling?' Meanwhile, it is important to note that REB counsellors, if they follow this lead, are unique in that they are more likely to challenge their client's irrational beliefs and to dispute them much earlier in the therapeutic process than are other cognitive-behavioural counsellors. Further differences between rational emotive behavioural counselling and other approaches to cognitive-behavioural counselling are listed below. Although it should be noted that rational emotive behavioural counsellors do use strategies derived from other cognitive-behavioural approaches, we wish to reiterate that the focus in the previous chapters has been on strategies and techniques that are mainly associated with rational emotive behavioural counselling.

Differences between rational emotive behavioural counselling and other forms of cognitive–behavioural counselling

As opposed to other approaches to cognitive-behavioural counselling, rational emotive behavioural counselling:

1. has a distinct philosophic emphasis, which is one of its central features and which other forms of cognitive-behavioural counselling appear to omit. Thus, it stresses that humans appraise themselves, others and the world in terms of: (a) rational, preferential, flexible and tolerant philosophies, and (b) irrational, *must*urbatory, rigid, intolerant and absolutist philosophies.
2. has an existential-humanistic outlook which is intrinsic to it and which is omitted by most other approaches to cognitive-behavioural counselling. Thus, it sees people 'as holistic, goal-directed individuals who have importance in the world just because they are human and alive; it unconditionally focuses upon their experiences and values, including their self-actualising potentialities' (Ellis, 1980c, p.327). It also shares the views of ethical humanism by encouraging people to emphasise human interest (self and social) over the interests of deities, material objects and lower animals.
3. favours striving for pervasive and long-lasting, philosophically based change, rather than symptomatic change.
4. attempts to help humans eliminate all self-ratings and views self-esteem as

a self-defeating concept which encourages them to make conditional evaluations of self. Instead, it teaches people *un*conditional self-acceptance (Ellis, 1972).

5. considers psychological disturbance to reflect an attitude of taking life 'too' seriously and thus advocates the appropriate use of various humorous therapeutic methods (Ellis, 1977a, 1977b, 1981c).

6. stresses the use of anti*must*urbatory rather than anti-empirical disputing methods. As it considers that inferential distortions often stem from dogmatic musts, shoulds, etc., rational emotive behavioural counselling favours going to the philosophic core of emotional disturbance and disputing the irrational beliefs at this core rather than merely disputing anti-empirical inferences, which are more peripheral. Also, rational emotive behavioural counselling favours the use of forceful logico-empirical disputing of irrational beliefs whenever possible, rather than the employment of rationally oriented, coping self-statements. When feasible, rational emotive behavioural counselling teaches clients how to become their own scientists instead of parroting counsellor-inculcated rational beliefs.

7. employs, but only mildly encourages, the use of palliative cognitive methods that serve to distract people from their disturbed philosophies, e.g. relaxation methods. Rational emotive behavioural counselling holds that such techniques may help clients in the short term, but do not encourage them to identify, challenge and change in the long term the devout philosophies that underpin their psychological problems. Indeed, these palliative methods may make it harder for people to engage in philosophic disputing, since they may be less likely to do this when they are calm and relaxed than when they are motivated by their emotional distress. For these reasons, rational emotive behavioural counselling also employs problem-solving and skill-training methods, along with, but not instead of, teaching people to work at understanding and changing their irrational beliefs.

8. gives a more central explanatory role to the concept of discomfort anxiety in psychological disturbance than do other cognitive-behavioural approaches to counselling. Discomfort anxiety is defined as 'emotional hypertension that arises when people feel that their life or comfort is threatened; that they *must* not feel uncomfortable and *have to* feel at ease; and that it is awful or catastrophic (rather than merely inconvenient or disadvantageous) when they don't get what they supposedly must' (Ellis, 1980c, p.331). While other cognitive–behavioural approaches to counselling recognise specific instances of discomfort anxieties, e.g. 'fear of fear' (Mackay, 1984) they tend not to regard discomfort disturbance to be as centrally implicated in psychological problems as does rational emotive behavioural counselling.

9. emphasises, more than other approaches to cognitive–behavioural counselling, that humans frequently make themselves disturbed about their original disturbances. Thus, rational emotive behavioural counsellors

actively look for meta-emotional problems and encourage clients to work on overcoming these before addressing themselves to the primary disturbance.

10. has clear-cut theories of disturbance and its treatment, but is eclectic or multi-modal in its techniques. However, it favours some techniques, e.g. active disputing, over others such as cognitive distraction, and strives for profound or elegant philosophic change where feasible.

11. discriminates between healthy and unhealthy negative emotions. Rational emotive behavioural theory considers such negative emotions as sadness, healthy anger, concern, remorse and disappointment as healthy affective responses to thwarted desires based on a non-devout philosophy of desire. Further, it views them as healthy when they do not needlessly interfere with people's goals and purposes. However, it sees depression, unhealthy anger, anxiety, guilt and shame usually as unhealthy negative emotions based on absolutist demands about thwarted desires. Rational emotive behavioural counselling considers these latter feelings as symptoms of disturbance because they very frequently, but not always, sabotage people from pursuing constructively their goals and purposes. Other approaches to cognitive–behavioural counselling do not make such fine discriminations between healthy and unhealthy negative emotions.

12. advocates counsellors giving unconditional acceptance rather than giving warmth or approval to clients. Other cognitive–behavioural approaches to counselling tend not to make this distinction. Rational emotive behavioural counselling holds that counsellor warmth and approval have their distinct dangers in that they may unwittingly encourage clients to strengthen their dire needs for love and approval. When REB counsellors unconditionally accept their clients they also serve as good role models, in that they also help clients to accept themselves unconditionally.

13. stresses the importance of the use of vigour and force in counteracting irrational philosophies and behaviours (Ellis, 1979d; Dryden, 1984c). Rational emotive behavioural counselling is alone among cognitive–behavioural approaches to counselling in stressing that humans are, for the most part, biologically predisposed to originate and perpetuate their disturbances and often experience great difficulty in changing the ideological roots of these problems. Since it holds this view, it urges both counsellors and clients to use considerable force and vigour in interrupting clients' irrationalities.

14. is more selective than most other cognitive–behavioural approaches to counselling in choosing behavioural change methods. Thus, it favours the use of penalisation in encouraging resistant clients to change. Often, these clients will not change to obtain positive reinforcements, but may be encouraged to change to avoid stiff penalties. Furthermore, rational emotive behavioural practitioners have reservations concerning the use of social reinforcement in counselling. They consider that humans are too reinforceable and that they often do the right thing for the wrong reason

Thus, they may change to please their socially reinforcing counsellors, but in doing so they have not been encouraged to think and act for their own sake. REB counsellors aim to help clients become maximally non-conformist, non-dependent and individualistic and would thus use social reinforcement techniques sparingly. Finally, rational emotive behavioural counselling favours the use of in vivo desensitisation techniques, since it argues that the former procedures best help clients to raise their level of frustration tolerance (Ellis, 1983c).

Whilst REB counsellors prefer to use these distinctive features of rational emotive behavioural counselling wherever feasible, they do not dogmatically insist that they be employed. When, on pragmatic grounds, they employ other cognitive-behavioural methods, their therapeutic practice is frequently indistinguishable from that of other cognitive-behavioural counsellors.

Sources of other cognitive–behavioural methods

We have mentioned that rational emotive behavioural counsellors use other cognitive–behavioural methods when rational emotive behavioural methods are insufficient to help the client. Since this book focuses on the distinctive features of rational emotive behavioural counselling, we have not discussed these other methods here. However, we recommend the following as resource material on these methods: disputing distorted inferences (Beck et al., 1979; Beck and Emery, 1985); decision therapy (Greenwald, 1973; Wessler and Hankin-Wessler, 1986); self-instructional training (Meichenbaum, 1977, 1985); problem-solving therapy (D'Zurilla and Goldfried, 1971; Spivack, Platt and Shure, 1976); imagery methods (Lazarus, 1984); skills training (Lange and Jakubowski, 1976; Trower, Bryant and Argyle, 1978). Finally, a good general text on cognitive–behavioural counselling has been written by Cormier and Cormier (1985).

Techniques that are avoided in rational emotive behavioural counselling

By now it will be clear that rational emotive behavioural counselling is a multi-modal form of counselling and advocates the employment of techniques in the cognitive, emotive and behavioural modalities. However, because the choice of therapeutic techniques is inspired by rational emotive behavioural theory, the following available therapeutic techniques are avoided, or used sparingly in the practice of rational emotive behavioural counselling (Ellis, 1979c, 1983c, 1984b):

1. techniques that help people become more dependent, e.g. undue counsellor warmth as a strong reinforcement and the creation and analysis of a transference neurosis.

2. techniques that encourage people to become more gullible and suggestible, e.g. pollyannaish positive thinking.
3. techniques that are long-winded and inefficient, e.g. psychoanalytic methods in general and free association in particular; encouraging clients to give lengthy descriptions of activating experiences at A.
4. methods that help people feel better in the short term rather than get better in the long term (Ellis, 1972), e.g. some experiental techniques like fully expressing one's feelings in a dramatic, cathartic and abreactive manner, i.e. some gestalt methods and primal techniques. The danger here is that such methods may encourage people to practise irrational philosophies underlying such emotions as anger.
5. techniques that distract clients from working on their irrational philosophies, e.g. relaxation methods, yoga and other cognitive distraction methods. These methods may be employed, however, *along with* cognitive disputing designed to yield some philosophic change.
6. methods that may unwittingly reinforce clients' philosophy of low frustration tolerance, e.g. gradual desensitisation.
7. techniques that include an antiscientific philosophy, e.g. faith healing and mysticism.
8. techniques that attempt to change activating events (A) before or without showing clients how to change their irrational beliefs (B), e.g. some strategic family systems techniques.
9. techniques that have dubious validity, e.g. neurolinguistic programming.

Finally, to reiterate, REB counsellors do not avoid using the above methods in any absolute sense. They may, on certain restricted occasions with certain clients, utilise such techniques, particularly for pragmatic purposes. For example, if faith healing is the only method that will prevent some clients from harming themselves, then REB counsellors might either employ it themselves or, more probably, refer such clients to a faith healer (Ellis, 1985a).

We have now reached the end of this book and hope that you have enjoyed it. We would value any feedback that you may wish to give to improve future editions.

References

Adler, A. (1927). Understanding Human Nature. New York: Garden City.

Adler, A. (1964). Social Interest: A Cballenge to Mankind. New York: Capricorn.

Anchin, J.C. and Kiesler, D. J. (1982). Handbook of Interpersonal Psychotherapy. New York: Pergamon.

Bandura, A. (1969). Principles of Behavior Modification. New York: Holt, Rinehart & Winston.

Bandura, A. (1977). Social Learning Theory. Englewood Cliffs, NJ: Prentice-Hall.

Bandura, A. (1986). Social Foundations of Thought and Action: A Social Cognitive Theory. Englewood Cliffs, NJ: Prentice-Hall.

Bard, J. A. (1973). Rational proselytizing. Rational Living, 12(1), 2-6.

Bard, J. A. (1980). Rational-Emotive Therapy in Practice. Champaign, IL: Research Press.

Barrish, I. J. (1993). The little old man. In: Bernard, M. E. and Wolfe, J. L. (eds) The RET Resource Book for Practitioners. New York: Albert Ellis Institute for Rational Emotive Behavior Therapy.

Beck, A. T. (1976). Cognitive Therapy and the Emotional Disorders. New York: International Universities Press.

Beck, A. T. and Emery, G. (1985). Anxiety Disorders and Phobias: A Cognitive Perspective. New York: Basic Books.

Beck, A. T., Rush, A. J., Shaw, B. F. and Emery, G. (1979). Cognitive Therapy of Depression. New York: Guilford.

Beck, J. S. (1995). Cognitive Therapy: Basics and Beyond. New York: Guilford Press

Bernard, M. E. (1993). Common techniques for overcoming procrastination. In: Bernard, M. E. and Wolfe, J. L. (eds) The RET Resource Book for Practitioners. New York: Albert Ellis Institute for Rational Emotive Behavior Therapy.

Beutler, L. E. (1983). Eclectic Psychotherapy: A Systematic Approach. New York: Pergamon.

Bordin, E. S. (1979). The generalizability of the psychoanalytic concept of the working alliance. Psychotherapy: Theory, Research and Practice, 16, 252-260.

Brandsma, J. M. (1993) Self- and body-acceptance. In: Bernard, M. E. and Wolfe, J. L. (eds) The RET Resource Book for Practitioners. New York: Albert Ellis Institute for Rational Emotive Behavior Therapy.

Burns, D. D. (1980). Feeling Good: The New Mood Therapy. New York: Morrow.

Burns, D. D. (1989). The Feeling Good Handbook. New York: William Morrow.

Cormier, W. H. and Cormier, L. S. (1985). Interviewing Strategies for Helpers: Fundamental Skills and Cognitive-Behavioral Interventions, 2nd ed. Monterey, CA: Brooks/Cole.

Dies, R. R. (1973). Group counsellor self-disclosure: An evaluation by clients. Journal of Counseling Psychology, 20, 344-348.

DiGiuseppe, R. (1984). Thinking what to feel. British Journal of Cognitive Psychotherapy, 2(1), 27-33.

DiGiuseppe, R. (1991). Comprehensive cognitive disputing in rational-emotive therapy. In: M. Bernard (Ed.), Using Rational-Emotive Therapy Effectively. New York: Plenum.

Dryden, W. (1983). Audiotape supervision by mail: a rational-emotive approach. British Journal of Cognitive Psychotherapy, 1(1), 57-64.

Dryden, W. (1984a). Rational-emotive therapy. In: W. Dryden (Ed.), Individual Therapy in Britain. London: Harper & Row.

Dryden, W. (1984b). Therapeutic arenas. In: W. Dryden (Ed.), Individual Therapy in Britain. London: Harper & Row.

Dryden, W. (1984c). Rational-Emotive Therapy: Fundamentals and Innovations. Beckenham, Kent: Croom-Helm.

Dryden, W. (1985b). Challenging but not overwhelming: A compromise in negotiating homework assignments. British Journal of Cognitive Psychotherapy. 3(1), 77-80.

Dryden, W. (1986). Language and meaning in rational-emotive therapy. In: W. Dryden and P. Trower (Eds.), Rational-Emotive Therapy: Recent Developments in Theory and Practice. Bristol: Institute for RET (UK).

Dryden, W. (1987). Theoretically consistent eclecticism: Humanizing a computer 'addict.' In: J. C. Norcross (Ed.), Casebook of Eclectic Psychotherapy. New York: Brunner/Mazel.

Dryden, W. (1991a). Reason and Therapeutic Change. London: Whurr.

Dryden, W. (1991b). A Dialogue with Albert Ellis: Against Dogma. Buckingham: Open University Press.

Dryden, W. (1993). Invitation technique. In: Bernard, M. E. and Wolfe, J. L. (eds) The RET Resource Book for Practitioners. New York: Albert Ellis Institute for Rational Emotive Behavior Therapy.

Dryden, W. (1995). Facilitating Client Change in Rational Emotive Behaviour Therapy. London: Whurr.

Dryden, W. (1996). Rational emotive behaviour therapy. In: Dryden, W. Individual Therapy in Britain, 3rd edn. London: Sage.

Dryden, W., Ferguson, J. and Clark, T. (1989). Beliefs and inferences - a test of a rational-emotive hypothesis: Performing in an academic seminar. Journal of Rational-Emotive and Cognitive-Behavior Therapy, 7(3), 119-129.

Dryden, W., Ferguson, J. and Hylton, B. (1989). Beliefs and inferences - a test of a rational-emotive hypothesis: 3. On expectations about enjoying a party. British Journal of Guidance and Counselling, 17(1), 68-75.

Dryden, W., Ferguson, J. and McTeague, S. (1989). Beliefs and inferences - a test of a rational-emotive hypothesis: 2. On the prospect of seeing a spider. Psychological Reports, 64, 115-123.

Dryden, W. and Golden, W. L. (Eds.) (1986). Cognitive-Behavioural Approaches to Psychotherapy. London: Harper & Row.

Dryden, W. and Gordon, J. (1990). Think Your Way to Happiness. London: Sheldon Press.

Dryden, W. and Yankura, J. (1992). Daring to be Myself: A Case Study in Rational-Emotive Therapy. Buckingham: Open University Press.

Duckro, P., Beal, D. and George, C. (1979). Research on the effects of disconfirmed client role expectations in psychotherapy: A critical review. Psychological Bulletin, 86, 260-275.

Dunlap, K. (1932). Habits: Their Making and Unmaking. New York: Liveright.

D'Zurilla, T. J. and Goldfried, M. R. (1971). Problem-solving and behavior modification. Journal of Abnormal Psychology, 78, 101-126.

Edelstein, M. R. (1976). The ABCs of rational-emotive therapy: Pitfalls of going from D to E. Rational Living, 11(1), 12-13.

Ellis, A. (1958). Rational psychotherapy. Journal of General Psychology, 59, 35-49.

Ellis, A. (1962). Reason and Emotion in Psychotherapy. Secaucus, NJ: Lyle Stuart.

Ellis, A. (1968a). Is Objectivism a Religion?. New York: Lyle Stuart.

Ellis, A. (1968b). Personality Data Form. New York: Albert Ellis Institute for REBT.

Ellis, A. (1972). Helping people get better: Rather than merely feel better. Rational Living, 7(2), 2-9.

Ellis, A. (1973). Humanistic Psychotherapy: The Rational-Emotive Approach. New York: McGraw-Hill.

Ellis, A. (1975). How to Live with a Neurotic At Home and at Work, Rev. ed. New York: Crown.

Ellis, A. (1976). The biological basis of human irrationality Journal of Individual Psychology. 32, 145-168.

Ellis, A. (1977a). Fun as psychotherapy. Rational Living, 12(1), 2-6.

Ellis, A. (Speaker, cassette recording). (1977b). A Garland of Rational Humorous Songs. New York: Albert Ellis Institute for REBT.

Ellis, A. (1977c). Intimacy in psychotherapy. Rational Living, 12(2), 13-19.

Ellis, A. (1977d). Anger: How to Live With and Without It. Secaucus, NJ: Citadel Press.

Ellis, A. (1978). Personality characteristics of rational-emotive therapists and other kinds of therapists. Psychotherapy: Theory, Research and Practice, 15, 329-332.

Ellis, A. (1979a). The theory of rational-emotive therapy. In: A. Ellis and J. M. Whiteley. (Eds.), Theoretical and Empirical Foundations of Rational-Emotive Therapy. Monterey, CA: Brooks/Cole.

Ellis, A. (1979b). Discomfort anxiety: A new cognitive behavioral construct. Part I Rational Living, 14(2), 3-8.

Ellis, A. (1979c). The practice of rational-emotive therapy. In. A. Ellis and J. M. Whiteley, (Eds.), Theoretical and Empirical Foundations of Rational-Emotive Therapy. Monterey, CA: Brooks/Cole.

Ellis, A. (1979d). The issue of force and energy in behavioral change. Journal of Contemporary Psychotherapy, 10(2), 83-97

Ellis, A. (1980a). Discomfort anxiety: A new cognitive behavioral construct. Part 2. Rational Living, 15(1), 25-30.

Ellis, A. (1980b). The value of efficiency in psychotherapy: Psychotherapy: Theory, Research and Practice, 17, 414-418.

Ellis, A. (1980c). Rational-emotive therapy and cognitive behavior therapy: Similarities and differences. Cognitive Therapy and Research, 4, 325-340.

Ellis, A. (1981a). The place of Immanuel Kant in cognitive psychotherapy. Rational Living, 16(2), 13-16.

Ellis, A. (1981b, Sept.). New Developments in Rational-Emotive Therapy. Address given at the First European Conference on the Cognitive-Behavioral Therapies, Lisbon, Portugal.

Ellis, A. (1981c). The use of rational humorous songs in psychotherapy. Voices, 16(4), 29-36.

Ellis, A. (1982a). The treatment of alcohol and drug abuse: The rational-emotive approach. Rational Living, 17(2), 13-16.

Ellis, A. (1982b). Intimacy in rational-emotive therapy. In: M. Fisher and G. Striker (Eds), Intimacy. New York: Plenum.

Ellis, A. (1982c). Must most psychotherapists remain as incompetent as they now are? Journal of Contemporary Psychotherapy, 13(1), 17-28.

Ellis, A. (1983a). The Case against Religiosity. New York: Albert Ellis Institute for REBT.

Ellis, A. (1983b). How to deal with your most difficult client: You. Journal of Rational-Emotive Therapy, 1(1), 3-8.

Ellis, A. (1983c). The philosophic implications and dangers of some popular behavior therapy techniques. In: M. Rosenbaum, C. M. Franks and Y. Jaffe (Eds), Perspectives in Behavior Therapy in the Eighties. New York: Springer.

Ellis, A. (1983d). Failures in rational-emotive therapy. In: E. B. Foa and P. M. G. Emmelkamp (Eds.). Failures in Behavior Therapy. New York: Wiley.

Ellis, A. (1983e). Rational-emotive therapy, (RET) approaches to overcoming resistance. 1: Common forms of resistance. British Journal of Cognitive Psychotherapy, 1(1), 28-38.

Ellis, A. (1984a). The essence of RET - 1984. Journal of Rational-Emotive Therapy, 2(1), 19-25.

Ellis, A. (1984b). Rational-emotive therapy. In: R. J. Corsini (Ed.), Current Psychotherapies. (2nd ed.). Itasca, IL: Peacock.

Ellis, A. (1984c). How to Maintain and Enhance your Rational-Emotive Therapy Gains. New York: Albert Ellis Institute for REBT.

Ellis, A. (1985a). Overcoming Resistance: Rational-Emotive Therapy with Difficult Clients. New York: Springer.

Ellis, A. (1985b). Expanding the ABCs of rational-emotive therapy. In: M. J. Mahoney and A. Freeman (Eds.), Cognition and Psychotherapy. New York: Plenum.

Ellis, A. (1985c). Dilemmas in giving warmth or love to clients: An interview with Windy Dryden. In: W. Dryden, Therapists' Dilemmas. London: Harper & Row.

Ellis, A. (1987). The use of rational humorous songs in psychotherapy. In: W. F. Fry, Jr and W. A. Salameh (Eds), Handbook of Humor in Psychotherapy: Advances in the Clinical Use of Humor. Sarasota, FL: Professional Resource Exchange, Inc.

Ellis, A. (1990). Treating the widowed client with rational-emotive therapy (RET). Psychotherapy Patient, 6(3), 105-111.

Ellis, A. (1994) Reason and Emotion in Psychotherapy. Revised and updated edition. New York: Birch Lane Press.

Ellis, A. and Becker, I. (1982). A Guide to Personal Happiness. No. Hollywood, CA: Wilshire.

Ellis, A. and Bernard, M. E. (1985). Clinical Applications of Rational-Emotive Therapy. New York: Plenum.

Ellis, A. and Dryden, W. (1997). The Practice of Rational Emotive Behavior Therapy, 2nd edn. New York: Springer

Ellis, A. and Harper, R. A. (1975). A New Guide to Rational Living. No. Hollywood, CA: Wilshire.

Ellis, A. and Knaus, W. J. (1977). Overcoming Procrastination. New York: Albert Ellis Institute for Rational Emotive Behavior Therapy.

Ellis, A., McInerney, J. F., DiGiuseppe, R. and Yeager, R. J. (1988). Rational-Emotive Therapy with Alcoholics and Substance Abusers. New York: Pergamon Press.

Ellis, A., Sichel, J. L., Yeager, R. J., DiMattia, D. J. and DiGiuseppe, R. (1989). Rational--Emotive Couples Therapy. New York: Pergamon Press.

Eschenroeder, C. (1979). Different therapeutic styles in rational-emotive therapy. Rational Living, 14(1), 3-7.

Festinger, L. (1957). A Theory of Cognitive Dissonance. Evanston, IL: Row, Peterson.

Fransella, F. (1985). Resistance. British Journal of Cognitive Psychotherapy, 3(1), 1–11.

Freud, A. (1937). The Ego and the Mechanisms of Defense. London: Hogarth.

Freeman, A. (1981). Dreams and imagery in cognitive therapy. In: G. Emery, S. D. Hollon and R. C. Bedrosian (Eds.), New Directions in Cognitive Therapy. New York: Guilford.

Garcia, E. J. (1977). Working on the E in RET. In: J. L. Wolfe and E. Brand (Eds.), Twenty Years of Rational Therapy. New York: Albert Ellis Institute for REBT.

Gendlin, E. T. (1978). Focusing. New York: Everest House.

Gerbode, F. A. (1989). Beyond Psychology: An Introduction to Metapsychology. Palo Alto, CA: IRM.

Golden, W. L. (1983). Resistance in cognitive–behaviour therapy. British Journal of Cognitive Psychotherapy, 1(2), 33–42.

Goldfried, M. and Davison, G. (1976). Clinical Behavior Therapy. New York: Holt, Rinehart & Wilson.

Greenwald, H. (1973). Direct Decision Therapy. San Diego: Edits.

Gregory, R. L. (1966). Eye and Brain. London: Weidenfeld & Nicholson.

Grieger, R. M. (1985). The process of rational–emotive therapy. Journal of Rational–Emotive Therapy 3(2), 138–148.

Grieger, R. M. and Boyd, J. (1980). Rational-Emotive Therapy: A Skills-based Approach. New York: Van Nostrand Reinhold.

Guidano, V. F. (1988). A systems, process-oriented approach to cognitive therapy. In: K. S. Dobson (Ed.), Handbook of the Cognitive-Behavioral Therapies, pp. 307–356. New York: Guilford.

Guinagh, B. (1976). Disputing clients' logical fallacies. Rational Living, 11(2), 15–18.

Gullo, J. M. (1993). Visualizing self-created anger. In: Bernard, M. E. and Wolfe, J. L. (eds) The RET Resource Book for Practitioners. New York: Albert Ellis Institute for Rational Emotive Behavior Therapy.

Gurman, A. S. and Kniskern, D. P. (1978). Research in marital and family therapy. In: S. L. Garfield and A. E. Bergin (Eds.), Handbook of Psychotherapy and Behavior Change, 2nd edn. New York: Wiley.

Hauck, P. A. (1966). The neurotic agreement in psychotherapy. Rational Living, 1(1), 31–34.

Hauck, P. A. (1972). Reason in Pastoral Counseling. Philadelphia: Westminster.

Hauck, P. (1993). There is really nothing to fear. In: Bernard, M. E. and Wolfe, J. L. (eds) The RET Resource Book for Practitioners. New York: Albert Ellis Institute for Rational Emotive Behavior Therapy.

Heidegger, M. (1949). Existence and Being. Chicago: Henry Regnery.

Horney, K. (1950). Neurosis and Human Growth. New York: Norton.

Janis, I. L. (1983). Short-Term Counseling. New Haven, CT: Yale University Press.

Johnson, W. R. (1981). So Desperate the Fight. New York: Albert Ellis Institute for Rational Emotive Behavior Therapy.

Jones, M. C. (1924). A laboratory study of fear: The case of Peter. Journal of Genetic Psychology, 31, 308–315.

Jones, R. A. (1977). Self-Fulfilling Prophecies: Social, Psychological and Physiological Effects of Expectancies. Hillside, NJ: LEA.

Kassinove, H. and DiGiuseppe, R. (1975). Rational role reversal. Rational Living, 10(1), 44–45.

Kelly, G. A. (1955). The Psychology of Personal Constructs. New York: Norton.

Kempel, L. T. (1973). Identifying and confronting ways of prematurely terminating therapy. Rational Living, 8(1), 6–9.

Kimmel, J. (1976). The rational barb in the treatment of social rejection. Rational Living, 11, 23-25.

Knaus, W. and Wessler, R. L. (1976). Rational-emotive problem simulation. Rational Living, 11(2), 8-11.

Korzybski, A. (1933). Science and Society. San Francisco: ISGS.

Kranzler, G. D. (1974) You Can Change How You Feel: A Rational Emotive Approach. Eugene, OR: RETC Press.

Kuhn, T. (1970). The Structure of Scientific Revolutions, 2nd edn. Chicago: University of Chicago Press.

Lange, A. J. and Jakubowski, P. (1976). Responsible Assertive Behavior: Cognitive-Behavioral Procedures for Trainers. Champaign, IL: Research Press.

Lazarus, A. A. (1977). Toward an egoless state of being. In: A. Ellis and R. Grieger (Eds.), Handbook of Rational-Emotive Therapy. New York: Springer.

Lazarus, A. A. (1981). The Practice of Multimodal Therapy. New York: McGraw-Hill.

Lazarus, A. A. (1984). In the Mind's Eye. New York: Guilford.

Lazarus, A. A. (1989). The practice of rational-emotive therapy. In: M. E. Bernard and R. DiGiuseppe (Eds.), Inside Rational-Emotive Therapy: A Critical Appraisal of the Theory and Therapy of Albert Ellis. New York: Academic Press.

Macaskill, N. D. and Macaskill, A. (1983). Preparing patients for psychotherapy. British Journal of Clinical and Social Psychiatry, 2, 80-84.

Mackay, D. (1984). Behavioural psychotherapy. In: W. Dryden (Ed.), Individual Therapy in Britain. London: Harper & Row.

Mahoney, M. (1977). Personal science: A cognitive learning theory: In: A. Ellis and R. Grieger (Eds.), Handbook of Rational-Emotive Therapy. New York: Springer.

Mahoney, M. J. (1988). The cognitive sciences and psychotherapy: Patterns in a developing relationship. In: K. S. Dobson (Ed.), Handbook of the Cognitive-Behavioral Therapies, pp. 357-386. New York: Guilford.

Maultsby, M. C. Jr (1975). Help Yourself to Happiness: Through Rational Self-counseling. New York: Albert Ellis Institute for REBT.

Maultsby, M. C. Jr (1984). Rational Behavior Therapy. Englewood Cliffs, NJ: Prentice-Hall.

McMullin, R. E. (1986). Handbook of Cognitive Therapy Techniques. New York: W. W. Norton & Co.

Meichenbaum, D. (1977). Cognitive-Behavior Modification. New York: Plenum.

Meichenbaum, D. (1985). Stress Inoculation Training. New York: Pergamon.

Moore, R. H. (1983). Inference as "A" in RET. British Journal of Cognitive Psychotherapy. 1(2), 17-23.

Moore, R. H. (1993). Traumatic incident reduction: a cognitive-emotive treatment of post-traumatic stress disorder. In: Dryden, W. and Hill, L. K. (eds.) Innovations in Rational-Emotive Therapy. London: Sage.

Muran, E. M. and DiGiuseppe, R. (1994). Rape. In: Dattilio, F. M. and Freeman, A. (eds.), Cognitive-Behavioral Strategies in Crisis Intervention. New York: Guilford.

Neenan, M. and Dryden, W. (1996a). Dealing with Difficulties in Rational Emotive Behaviour Therapy. London: Whurr.

Neenan, M. and Dryden, W. (1996b). The intricacies of inference chaining. Journal of Rational-Emotive and Cognitive-Behavior Therapy, 14(4), 231-43.

Neenan, M. and Dryden, W. (1998). Rational Emotive Behaviour Therapy: Advances in Theory and Practice. London: Whurr.

Neenan, M. and Palmer, S. (in press). Problem-solving counselling and training. In: Palmer, S. (ed.) Introduction to Counselling and Psychotherapy. London: Sage.

Neuman, F. (Leader). (1982). An Eight-week Treatment Group for Phobics. (Series of eight cassette recordings). White Plains, NY: F. Neuman.

Norcross, J. C., Dryden, W. and Brust, A. M. (1992). British clinical psychologists: 1. A national survey of the BPS Clinical Division. Clinical Psychology, Forum, 40, 19–24.

Norcross, J. C. and Prochaska, J. O. (1982). A national survey of clinical psychologists: Characteristics and activities. The Clinical Psychologist, 35, 1–8.

Palmer, S. and Dryden, W. (1995). Counselling for Stress Problems. London: Sage.

Passons, W. R. (1975). Gestalt Approaches in Counseling. New York: Holt Rinehart and Winston.

Persons, J. B., Burns, D. D. and Perloff, J. M. (1988). Predictors of dropout and outcome in cognitive therapy for depression in a private practice setting. Cognitive Therapy and Research, 12, 557–575.

Phadke, K. M. (1982). Some innovations in RET theory and practice. Rational Living, 17(2), 25–30.

Platt, J. J., Prout, M. F. and Metzger, D. (1986). Interpersonal cognitive problem-solving (ICPS). In: W. Dryden and W. L. Golden (Eds.), Cognitive-Behavioural Approaches to Psychotherapy, London: Harper & Row.

Popper, K. R. (1959). The Logic of Scientific Discovery. New York: Harper & Bros.

Popper, K. R. (1963). Conjectures and Refutations. New York: Harper & Bros.

Powell, J. (1976). Fully Human, Fully Alive. Niles, IL: Argus.

Prochaska, J. O. and Norcross, J. C. (1983). Contemporary, psychotherapists: A national survey, of characteristics, practices, orientations, and attitudes. Psychotherapy: Theory, Research and Practice, 20, 161–173.

Ravid, R. (1969). Effect of group therapy, on long-term individual therapy. Dissertation Abstracts International, 30, 2427B.

Reichenbach, H. S. (1953). The Rise of Scientific Philosophy. Berkeley, CA: University of California Press.

Rogers, C. R. (1957). The necessary and sufficient conditions of therapeutic personality change. Journal of Consulting Psychology, 21, 95–103.

Russell, B. S. (1930). The Conquest of Happiness. New York: New American Library.

Russell, B. (1965). The Basic Writings of Bertrand Russell. New York: Simon & Schuster.

Russianoff, P. (1981). Why Do I Think I Am Nothing Without a Man? New York: Bantam.

Sacco, W. P. (1981). Cognitive therapy in vivo. In: G. Emery, S. D. Hollon and R. C. Bedrosian (Eds.), New Directions in Cognitive Therapy. New York: Guilford.

Scott, M. J., Stradling, S. G. and Dryden, W. (1995). Developing Cognitive-Behavioural Counselling. London: Sage.

Shahan, L. (1981). Living Alone and Liking It. New York: Warner.

Sichel, J. and Ellis, A. (1984). RET Self-Help Form. New York: Albert Ellis Institute for REBT.

Smucker, M. R., Dancu, C., Foa, E. B. and Niederee, J. L. (1995). Imagery rescripting: A new treatment for survivors of childhood sexual abuse suffering from post-traumatic stress. Journal of Cognitive Psychotherapy, 9(1): 3–17.

Snyder, C. R. and Smith, T. W. (1982). Symptoms as self-handicapping strategies: The virtues of old wine in a new bottle. In: G. Weary and H. L. Mirels (Eds.), Integration of Clinical and Social Psychology. New York: Oxford University Press.

Spivack, G., Platt, J. J. and Shure, M. B. (1976). The Problem-solving Approach to Adjustment. San Francisco: Jossey-Bass.

Tillich, P. (1977). The Courage to Be. New York: Fountain.

Trexler, L. D. (1976). Frustration is a fact, not a feeling. Rational Living, 11(2), 19–22.

Trower, P., Bryant, B. and Argyle, M. (1978). Social Skills and Mental Health. London: Methuen.

Truax, C. B. and Carkhuff, R. R. (1967). Toward Effective Counseling and Psychotherapy: Training and practice. Chicago: Aldine.

Wachtel, P. L. (1977). Psychoanalysis and Behavior Therapy: Toward an Integration. New York: Basic Books.

Walen, S. R., DiGiuseppe, R. and Dryden, W. (1982). A Practitioner's Guide to Rational-Emotive Therapy, 2nd edn. New York: Oxford University Press.

Wasik, B. (1984). Teaching parents effective problem-solving: A handbook for professionals. Unpublished manuscript. Chapel Hill, NC: University of North Carolina.

Watson, J. B. and Rayner, R. (1920). Conditioned emotional reactions. Journal of Experimental Psychology, 3, 1-14.

Werner, E. E. and Smith, R. S. (1982). Vulnerable but Invincible: A Study of Resilient Children. New York: McGraw-Hill.

Wessler, R. A. and Wessler, R. L. (1980). The Principles and Practice of Rational-Emotive Therapy. San Francisco: Jossey-Bass.

Wessler, R. A. (1981). So you are angry: Now what's your problem? Rational Living, 16(1), 29-31.

Wessler, R. L. (1984). Alternative conceptions of rational–emotive therapy.: Toward a philosophically neutral psychotherapy. In: M. A. Reda and M. J. Mahoney (Eds.), Cognitive Psychotherapies: Recent Developments in Theory, Research and Practice. Cambridge, MA: Ballinger.

Wessler, R. L. and Ellis, A. (1980). Supervision in rational–emotive therapy. In: A. K. Hess (Ed.), Psychotherapy Supervision. New York: Wiley.

Wessler, R. L. and Ellis, A. (1983). Supervision in counseling: rational–emotive therapy. The Counseling Psychologist, 11, 43-49.

Wessler, R. L. and Hankin-Wessler, S. W. R. (1986). Cognitive appraisal therapy. (CAT). In: W. Dryden and W. L. Golden (Eds.), Cognitive–Behavioural Approaches to Psychotherapy, London: Harper & Row.

Wexler, D. A. and Butler, J. M. (1976). Therapist modification of client expressiveness in client-centred therapy: Journal of Consulting and Clinical Psychology, 44, 261-265.

Yankura, J. and Dryden, W. (1990). Doing RET: Albert Ellis in Action. New York: Springer.

Young, H. S. (1974). A Rational Counseling Primer. New York: Albert Ellis Institute for REBT.

Young, H. S. (1977). Counseling strategies with working class adolescents. In: J. L. Wolfe and E. Brand (Eds.), Twenty Years of Rational Therapy. New York: Institute for RET.

Young, H. S. (1984a). Practising RET with lower-class clients. British Journal of Cognitive Psychotherapy, 2(2), 33-59.

Young, H. S. (1984b). Teaching rational self-value concepts to tough customers. British Journal of Cognitive Psychotherapy, 2(2), 77-97.

Index